PATHWAYS TO TRANSFORMATION

THE BAHÁ'Í JOURNEY

Selections from the Bahá'í Writings
Compiled by John Davidson PhD

© Bahá'í Publications Australia 2001

First edition 2001

ISBN 1 876322 01 2

Bahá'í Publications Australia

173 Mona Vale Road

Ingleside NSW 2101

Australia

Telephone + 61 2 9913 1554

Fax + 61 2 9970 7275

Email bpa@bahai.org.au

Website: www.bahaibooks.com

Designed by Faizi Designs, Brisbane

Printed in Australia

PATHWAYS TO TRANSFORMATION
THE BAHÁ'Í JOURNEY

SELECTIONS FROM THE BAHÁ'Í WRITINGS

O wayfarer in the path of God!
Take thou thy portion of
the ocean of His grace,
and deprive not thyself of the things
that lie hidden in its depths.

Bahá'u'lláh, Gleanings from the Writings of Bahá'u'lláh, CXXIX, p. 279.

*A*nd yet, is not the object
of every Revelation to effect a
transformation in the
whole character of mankind,
a transformation that shall
manifest itself both outwardly
and inwardly, that shall affect
both its inner life and
external conditions?

Bahá'u'lláh, The Kitáb-i-Íqán, p. 240.

Contents

INTRODUCTION	15
ACKNOWLEDGEMENTS	21
PART 1 - THE BAHÁ'Í REVELATION AND THE PROCESS OF TRANSFORMATION	23
CHAPTER 1 THE AIMS OF BAHÁ'U'LLÁH	24
The Renewal of Religion	25
Restatement of Spiritual Truths	25
Adaptation to the Needs of the Time	25
Fulfilment of Past Religions	26
The Spiritualization of Human Beings	27
Building a Global Community	27
Seven Lights of Unity	28
The Uniting of Nations	29
The Advancement of Civilization	30
CHAPTER 2 THE ORIGINS AND GROWTH OF THE BAHÁ'Í FAITH	31
The Ministry of the Báb	31
The Childhood and Early Life of the Báb	32
The Birth of the Bábí Revelation	33
The Imprisonment of the Báb and His Declaration at Tabríz	35
The Relationship of the Báb to Bahá'u'lláh	37
The Conference of Badasht	38
Upheavals in Mázindarán, Nayríz and Zanján	39
The Martyrdom of the Báb	40
The Martyrdom of Ṭáhirih	42
The Influence of the Báb's Ministry Throughout the World	42
The Ministry of Bahá'u'lláh	43
The Childhood and Early Life of Bahá'u'lláh	43
The Role of Bahá'u'lláh in the Ministry of the Báb	44
The Birth of the Bahá'í Revelation	45
The Exile of Bahá'u'lláh to 'Iráq	47
The Withdrawal of Bahá'u'lláh to Kurdistán	48
Return to Baghdád	50
The Declaration of Bahá'u'lláh	52
The Exile to Constantinople	53
The Exile of Bahá'u'lláh to Adrianople	54
The Rebellion of Mírzá Yaḥyá	55
The Proclamation of Bahá'u'lláh	57
Bahá'u'lláh's Incarceration in 'Akká	57

The Death of Mírzá Mihdí	59
Release from Prison	60
The Passing of Bahá'u'lláh	61
The Covenant of Bahá'u'lláh	62

The Ministry of 'Abdu'l-Bahá — 63
The Role of 'Abdu'l-Bahá in the Ministry of Bahá'u'lláh	63
The Rebellion of Mírzá Muḥammad-'Alí	64
The Rise of the Faith in the West	64
Renewal of 'Abdu'l-Bahá's Incarceration	65
Entombment of the Báb's Remains on Mt. Carmel	67
'Abdu'l-Bahá's Travels in Europe and America	68
The Passing of 'Abdu'l-Bahá	71
The Will and Testament of 'Abdu'l-Bahá	72

The Formative Age — 72
The Ministry of Shoghi Effendi	73
Successive Epochs of the Formative Age	74
The First Epoch of the Formative Age: 1921–1944/46	75
The Second Epoch of the Formative Age: 1946–1963	75
The Third Epoch of the Formative Age: 1963–1986	76
The Fourth Epoch of the Formative Age: 1986–	76
Future Epochs	76

The Growth of The Bahá'í Faith — 77
The Inevitability of Opposition	78

CHAPTER 3 FUNDAMENTAL BAHÁ'Í BELIEFS — 80

The Dispensation of Bahá'u'lláh — 80
The Station of Bahá'u'lláh	80
The Station of the Báb	81
The Station of 'Abdu'l-Bahá	82
The Bahá'í Revelation	82

The Covenant of God with Humanity to Accept Bahá'u'lláh and Follow His Teachings — 83

The Covenant of Bahá'u'lláh with His Followers Concerning the Next Manifestation — 84

The Covenant of Bahá'u'lláh with His Followers Concerning the Succession — 85
Excerpts from the Kitáb-i-'Ahd (Book of the Covenant)	86
Excerpts from the Will and Testament of 'Abdu'l-Bahá	87
The Significance of the Covenant	88
Firmness in the Covenant	89
Freedom of Thought and Expression in the Bahá'í Faith	89
Covenant Breaking	91
The Station to which Bahá'ís are Called	91

Basic Truths of the Faith	92
God's Transcendence and Loving Providence	92
Progressive Revelation	92
The Purpose Underlying Creation	93
Spiritual Development: God's Grace and Human Striving	94
The Immortality of the Soul	95
The Next Life	95

PART 2 - GROWING AS A BAHÁ'Í   97

CHAPTER 4 THE PROCESS OF SPIRITUAL DEVELOPMENT   98

The Spiritual Reality of Human Beings	98
Relating to God and Developing Our Spiritual Powers	99
Faith and Steadfastness	101
Love and Sacrifice	102
Knowledge and Insight	105
Choice and Action	107
The Divine Education Programme	109
Bestowals and Blessings	109
Tests and Difficulties	111
Guidance and Confirmations	112

CHAPTER 5   TURNING TOWARDS GOD   114

Requisites for Spiritual Growth	114
Prayer	114
How to Pray	115
The Obligatory Prayers	116
The Dynamics of Prayer	118
Meditation and Reading of the Sacred Scriptures	119
Systematic Study of the Teachings	120
Meditation	121
Meditation on the Greatest Name	123
Fasting	124
The Ordinance of Fasting	124
The Spiritual Significance of the Fast	124
Right Speech and Action	125
Striving to Bring Our Behaviour into Accordance with the Teachings	125
Teaching the Cause of God	127
Selfless Service in the Work of the Cause and One's Trade or Profession	128
Voluntary Sharing of Wealth	129
Ḥuqúqu'lláh	130
Pilgrimage	132
The Spiritual Meaning of Pilgrimage	134

Chapter 6 Developing Character and Spiritual Relationships — 135

Happiness — 136
- Gratitude — 137
- Inner Peace and Certitude — 138

Purity and Detachment — 139
- Purity of Motive — 140
- Physical Cleanliness — 140
- Chastity — 140
- Avoidance of Alcohol and Habit Forming Drugs — 142
- Moderation — 142

Love and Unity — 143
- Friendship — 144
- Kindness — 145
- Courtesy — 146

Justice — 147
- Not Causing Harm — 147
- Prohibitions — 148
- Truthfulness — 148
- Not Backbiting — 149
- Honesty — 149
- Fairness — 150
- Trustworthiness — 151

Chapter 7 Teaching the Bahá'í Faith: Learning about Growth — 152

Orientation to Teaching — 152
- Valuing Teaching — 152
- Teaching for the Sake of God — 153
- Sustaining Expectancies of Success — 153

Preparing for Teaching — 155
- Memorizing Points from the Writings — 155
- Planning Ways to Contact People — 155
- Preparing Oneself for Teaching Opportunities — 156
- Learning from Experience — 156

The Practice of Personal Teaching — 157
- Setting an Example of Bahá'í Life — 157
- Showing Sincere Friendship to All — 158
- Interesting People in the Faith — 159
- Attracting Seekers to the Spiritual World — 161
- Setting Forth Reasons for Accepting the Faith — 162
  - The Life of Bahá'u'lláh — 162
  - The Teachings of Bahá'u'lláh — 163
  - The Influence of Bahá'u'lláh — 163
  - The Prophecies of Bahá'u'lláh — 163
  - Prophecies in Previous Scripture — 163
- Accepting the Response of the Hearer — 163

Using Various Teaching Methods	164
Firesides	164
Travelling	165
Pioneering	165
Arts and Music	166
Writing	166
Supporting New Believers	167
Receiving Declarations of Belief	167
Nurturing New Believers	169
Maintaining Love and Unity in the Community	169
Teaching the Masses	169
The Process of Entry by Troops	169
The Principle of Universality: Reaching all Strata of Society	170
Reaching People of Capacity	171
Flexible Teaching Plans	172
Relating the Faith to Contemporary Social and Humanitarian Issues	172
Expansion and Consolidation Go Hand in Hand	173
Summary	177

PART 3 - COMMUNITY BUILDING

CHAPTER 8 BAHÁ'Í MARRIAGE AND FAMILY LIFE: SHAPING SPIRITUAL IDENTITY   178

Bahá'í Marriage	179
The Nature of Bahá'í Marriage	179
Laws of Bahá'í Marriage	179
The Marriage Relationship	180
Love	180
Equality and Mutual Respect	181
Chastity and Fidelity	181
The Bahá'í Family	182
Children and Family Planning	182
Family Roles, Relationships and Responsibilities	183
Prayers for Family Members	184
Rearing and Educating Children	185
Developing Spirituality	185
Moral Education	186
Fostering Learning	187
Creating and Maintaining Harmony	188
Consultation	189
Seeking Outside Help Before Problems Become Too Great	132
Divorce	192
The Year of Patience	192
Sexual Relationships	194
The Bahá'í Attitude to Same Sex Relationships	194
Death, Burial and Inheritance	196
Wills	196
Bahá'í Burial	197

Chapter 9 The Bahá'í Administrative Order: The Primary Agency for Spiritual and Social Change — 199

The Nature of the Bahá'í Administrative Order — 199
- Its Animating Purpose — 200
- Abolition of a Professional Clergy and Leadership — 200
- The Distinctive Character of the Bahá'í Administrative Order — 201
- Its Source and Foundation — 202

The Guardianship and the Universal House of Justice — 203
- Authority and Divine Guidance — 203
- Appointment of Shoghi Effendi as Guardian — 204
- Events Following the Passing of Shoghi Effendi — 205
- The Universal House Of Justice — 206
- Election of The Universal House of Justice — 207
- Signature of The Universal House of Justice — 208
- Bahá'í International Community — 208

The Hands of the Cause of God, Boards of Counsellors and Auxiliary Boards — 209
- The Hands of the Cause of God — 210
- The International Teaching Centre — 210
- The Continental Boards of Counsellors — 211
- The Auxiliary Boards — 212

National Institutions of the Faith — 213
- The National Spiritual Assembly — 213
  - Role in Expansion and Consolidation — 214
  - Maintenance of Harmony and Bahá'í Standards — 216
  - Avoidance of Over-Administration — 218
- National and Unit Conventions — 218
- National Committees and Institutes — 221
  - National Teaching Committee — 221
  - Institutes — 222

Regional Agencies — 223
- Regional Bahá'í Councils — 224

The Local Spiritual Assembly — 225

The Bahá'í Funds — 228
- The Spirit of Giving — 229
- Only Bahá'ís May Contribute — 230
- Ḥuqúqu'lláh — 230

Bahá'í Elections — 233

Bahá'í Consultation and Decision Making — 235
- How to Consult — 236
- Making Decisions — 237
- Carrying out Decisions — 237
- Appeals and Criticism — 239

Re-visioning Relationships: The Administrative Institutions and the Community — 241

CHAPTER 10 THE BAHÁ'Í COMMUNITY: THE MATRIX OF TRANSFORMATION	245
Fostering Universal Participation	246
Individual Enterprise	247
Recognizing the Capacity of Women	249
Providing Spiritual Education for Children	250
Drawing upon the Vitality of the Youth	252
Youth Year of Service	254
Encouraging Minorities	255
Protection of Minorities	255
Valuing Indigenous Believers	256
Preserving Spiritual Relationships	257
When Differences Arise	258
The Bahá'í Calendar	259
Bahá'í Holy Days	260
The Bahá'í Feasts, Anniversaries and Days of Fasting	260
Bahá'í Holy Days on which Work should be Suspended	260
Suspension of Work	261
Remembrance	261
The Nineteen-Day Feast	262
Programme	263
Attaining the Spiritual Reality of the Bahá'í Feast	264
The Nineteen-Day Feast Calendar:	265
Devotional Meetings and the Institution of the Ma<u>sh</u>riqu'l-A<u>dh</u>kár	266
National and Local Bahá'í Centres: Ḥaẓíratu'l-Quds	268
PART 4 - THE ADVANCEMENT OF CIVILIZATION	
CHAPTER 11 THE ESTABLISHMENT AND MAINTENANCE OF THE LESSER PEACE	270
Requisites for World Peace	270
The Principle of Collective Security	270
Global Reconstruction and Demilitarization	271
The Collaborative Role of the Bahá'í Community	275
Collaboration for Social and Economic Development	277
Areas of Collaboration	279
Human Rights	279
Moral Education	280
Equality of Women and Men	281
Racial Unity	282
Harmony Between Religions	284
Global Prosperity	285
Protection of the Environment	287

Global Governance	289
Loyalty and Obedience to Government	289
Non-involvement in Politics	290
The United Nations and Global Institutions Necessary for the Lesser Peace	292
Bahá'í Attitude to Military Service	294
CHAPTER 12 THE MOST GREAT PEACE: CREATING A SPIRITUAL CIVILIZATION	295
Spiritual Civilization	295
Cultural Diversity	297
The Special Contribution of Music	299
The Development of Arts and Crafts	301
The Advancement of Science	302
The Development of Health and Healing	304
The Role of Bahá'í Scholarship	305
The Process of Bahá'í Review	309
The Internet	310
The Special Role of the Bahá'í Faith	311
Into the Future	313
BIBLIOGRAPHY	316
Authoritative Bahá'í Sources	316
Writings of Bahá'u'lláh	316
Writings of the Báb	316
Writings and Talks of 'Abdu'l-Bahá	316
Writings of or on behalf of Shoghi Effendi	317
Writings of or on behalf of the Universal House of Justice	318
Compilations	318
Journals, Newsletters and Yearbooks	319
Sacred Writings of Other Faiths	319
Other Sources	319
INDEX	321

Introduction

The arduous struggles and remarkable achievements of the last century have enabled humanity to rupture, but not yet to cast off the chrysalis of its early cultural, scientific, ideological and religious beliefs, and the limiting forms of identity that derive from class, gender, race, nation and ethnicity. It has reached the threshold of its maturity as a planetary being, able to preserve, develop, cultivate and enjoy a global homeland throughout a vista of countless centuries to come, but it cannot yet imagine its own mature form. It peers into the half-light of the dawn; its hope for the future constrained by words and images that reflect past experiences and fears. Will it emerge as an Emperor butterfly fluttering between the blossoms of an earthly paradise, or as a trapdoor spider zealously guarding a tiny dark abode, or as a kind of biological black hole consuming and destroying whatever it touches? Or does humanity hold a spiritual potential that is far beyond the ability of our best minds of the present day to conceive?

Part 1 of this book begins by sketching the challenging dimensions of this transforming process from the perspective of the Bahá'í Faith. It considers the necessity for the spiritualization of human beings through a recognition of their inherent capacities for love and knowledge and a sense of the nearness of God; the achievement of a peaceful and harmonious social order, which involves no less than the reconstruction and demilitarization of the whole civilized world, thereby freeing humanity from the misery of war and exploitation; the advancement of civilization through a renewed appreciation of the contributions of science and religion; and the renewal and re-evaluation of religious faith following the recognition of the divine origin of the great religions of the world and of the latest revelations through the Báb and the Founder of the Bahá'í Faith, Bahá'u'lláh.

The remainder of Part 1 outlines the origins and development of the Bahá'í Faith—the lives, personalities and achievements of its Central Figures, their initial impact on the societies around them and in other countries, leading to the emergence of an extremely diverse but united global community of more than five million people representing all of the nations and races of the planet. A summary of the central beliefs of the Bahá'í Faith is given to assist the reader in understanding this background to the Faith.

Part 2 focuses on the spiritual development of the individual through the quickening of the innate capacities of every human being for faith, love, insight and service, persevering through tests and difficulties and responding to divine blessings, guidance and confirmations. Spiritual life is fostered by the cultivation of daily prayer and meditation, by the reading of the Sacred Writings, by annual fasting, by striving to bring one's daily actions into accord with the teachings, by the voluntary sharing of wealth, and, where possible, by pilgrimage to the Spiritual Centre of the Faith. The interior qualities of the spiritual life are not confined to the individual, but are necessarily expressed in each person's character and relationships with others, through such qualities as happiness, purity, love and justice. Beyond this is the spiritual obligation to share the Faith with all who wish to learn of it.

Part 3 explores relationships within the Bahá'í community. The bonds of friendship and collaboration are the beginning of community life, but its basic unit, from a Bahá'í view, is the family. Since Bahá'í marriage is an ongoing spiritual relationship, which will endure in the life to come, it involves a commitment to foster a harmonious and mutually supportive family life, including the rearing and education of children. A community develops through the mutual interactions and co-operative activities of individuals, families and organizations, which share common values and strive to achieve common goals. No community, however, can operate effectively without some administrative structure to co-ordinate its activities, represent its members, serve their needs and foster their development. As there are no clergy in the Bahá'í Faith, these responsibilities in the Bahá'í Community devolve upon elected or appointed institutions at the global, continental, national and local levels, as envisaged by Bahá'u'lláh and invested with His guidance and authority. The emergence of dynamic and united communities interacting with these representative agencies is a unique feature of the Bahá'í approach to community life.

Part 4 extends the discussion to the wider community. Bahá'u'lláh has described the process of transformation as evolving through at least two stages. The first He has termed the "Lesser Peace", a peace which is to be established by the nations of the earth, acting independently of the Bahá'í institutions, to achieve a new level of inter-governmental collaboration and some form of supranational organization, such as the United Nations, which will be empowered to keep the peace. An essential part of this development is a massive grass-roots change in social values involving the fostering of moral education, the recognition of human rights, the equality of women and men, respect for all races, harmony between religions, the protection and preservation of the environment and the achievement of an acceptable level of global prosperity. Bahá'u'lláh has termed the second stage of the transformative process "the Most Great Peace". It involves spiritual and social transformation in the development of culture and civilization as expressed in music, in the arts and crafts, in the development of science and technology, in health and healing, education, knowledge and communication as well as in religion. The spirit that animates all these developments is unity in diversity—respecting and appreciating the differences that add interest and vitality to the life of the community.

A critical aspect of transformation is the inseparability of the spiritual and the social. This is well illustrated in a charming anecdote about 'Abdu'l-Bahá, recounted in *The Diary of Juliet Thompson*. Juliet gave 'Abdu'l-Bahá a message from an American believer, Mrs Parsons, that she longed to establish a spiritual city on the Potomac, "the inhabitants of which would live for the good of the whole rather than the one." Juliet writes that 'Abdu'l-Bahá became reflective and commented: *"That city I hope will be a spiritual city and that the people of such a city will be perfectly united. In a physical city, of course, it is impossible to have everyone united. But in a spiritual city it is possible that all be united and in every way cemented. That spiritual city is like the sea, and the inhabitants of this city are like the waves of the sea. In every way they are connected and united."*[1] The point has been further emphasized by Shoghi Effendi, in extending the vision of the Bahá'í community through his remarkable letters on world order, in which he describes the principle of the oneness of mankind as "the pivot round which all the teachings of Bahá'u'lláh revolve".[2] Similarly, the Universal House of Justice, while enunciating a number of principles relating to the process of reconciliation of the differences among members of the Bahá'í community, has identified the first principle as unity: "The importance of unity as both the goal of Bahá'u'lláh's Message and the means for its establishment."[3]

Every transformative process, be it individual, social or cultural, is bound to encounter many significant blocks and challenges. Psychologist Carl Jung saw in the language of the alchemists a model for the transformation of the base metal of human nature into the gold of spiritual illumination, and made the following comment in his introduction to the Chinese text, *The Secret of the Golden Flower*:

"... the greatest and most important problems of life are all in a certain sense insoluble. They must be so because they express the necessary polarity inherent in every self-regulating system. They can never be solved, but only outgrown ....

"This 'outgrowing' ... on further experience was seen to consist in a new level of consciousness. Some higher or wider interest arose on the person's horizon, and through this widening of his view the insoluble problem lost its urgency. It was not solved logically in its own terms, but faded out when confronted with a new and stronger life-tendency. It was not repressed and made unconscious, but merely appeared in a different light, and so did indeed become different."[4]

A number of such polarities will be found in the following pages. For example, there is the recognition that a human being is unable to transcend the experience of his or her own reality to envisage the nature of God as the Source of all existence, while at the same time affirming the necessity of recognizing such a Divine Origin, and of the sense of a deeper meaning in life, of profounder relationships, and of a more intimate nearness to God enjoyed by those who follow the path of faith with love and sincerity. There is, to cite just one of innumerable other examples, the challenge of respecting and reconciling the conscientious beliefs of the individual with the process of group decision-making in the light of the guidance of the Bahá'í Writings and the advice of the Bahá'í Institutions.

---

1 Juliet Thompson, *The Diary of Juliet Thompson*, p. 28.
2 Shoghi Effendi, *The World Order of Bahá'u'lláh*, p. 42.
3 Universal House of Justice, *Issues Related to the Study of the Bahá'í Faith*, p. 26.
4 Carl Jung, Introduction to *The Secret of the Golden Flower*, pp. 91-92.

Richard Tarnas, in his epic survey of Western thought, has pointed out that our present differences in acceptance of the concept of God and the methods of acquiring knowledge were already well developed in the thoughts of the ancient Greeks. Plato regarded the celestial realm as the realm of perfection, and held as blasphemous the suggestion that the planets might be termed "wanderers" because their trajectories were not yet accommodated in a theory of perfect circular orbits.[5] With the same conviction, modern day physicists seek a "theory of everything" with complete assurance that when it is truly found the equations which define it will reflect the same beauty of perfection, or to use an expression favoured by Albert Einstein, "a pre-established harmony".[6] The great religious systems of the past, though diminished in their influence by their differences, contradictions, and deficiencies in practising their own teachings, continue to exert a significant sway over the minds and consciousness of the masses. The number of people who sense a significant degree of unity underlying these Faiths is growing. Likewise Martin Luther's triumphant affirmation of the primacy of the individual conscience has undergone elaboration by generations of philosophers and social theorists, leading inexorably to the post-modern conviction of the centrality of subjective interpretation, as incommensurable paradigms of knowledge are placed side by side. If a spiritual as opposed simply to a material civilization is to become possible, these three separate strands of knowledge, the body of scientific research, the sacred tradition of the world's Faiths, and the intellectual understandings and spiritual intuitions of individuals, though never interchangeable, must some day converge and intertwine.

The path to spiritual understanding is strewn with truths and part-truths in polarity or opposition. It is not the task of the present text, but that of individual insight and the consultative processes of many generations to achieve that higher standpoint of vision to which Jung refers, and in which such reconciliations can be part of the culture of a new civilization. When Moses lead the children of Israel into the desert, they had the benefit of scriptural guidance, but lacked the preparedness to enter the Promised Land. Today the majority of the people of the world journey unprepared across a wasteland more hazardous and unforgiving than any Egyptian sands. For the Bahá'í community, the Writings of their Faith provide an understanding of the path before them, of the challenges they are experiencing, of the goals they seek, and of the means to achieve them.

The quotations that follow are selected primarily from authoritative Bahá'í sources. These consist of the authenticated translations of the Writings of Bahá'u'lláh and the Báb, expositions of them by 'Abdu'l-Bahá and Shoghi Effendi as authorized exponents and interpreters of the Bahá'í Revelation, and the statements and elucidations of the Universal House of Justice, the governing body of the Bahá'í Faith. Also included are excerpts from published talks of 'Abdu'l-Bahá that were given during his travels in Europe and America (but the texts of which have not yet been confirmed as

---

5   Richard Tarnas, *The Passion of the Western Mind*, p. 52.
6   Albert Einstein, *Ideas and Opinions*, p. 226.

fully authenticated), a few key statements from various Bahá'í agencies such as the Hands of the Cause and the Bahá'í International Community, and some selections from histories of the Faith, which, though not in the category of authoritative Bahá'í Writings, are included to give further background to the history and the personalities of the Central Figures.

As is customary in Bahá'í compilations, within each sub-section, precedence is accorded to the Sacred Writings of Bahá'u'lláh and the Báb. These are followed by quotations from the works of 'Abdu'l-Bahá, which are also drawn upon by Bahá'ís in the Nineteen Day Feast for worship and for instruction. Then follow the writings of Shoghi Effendi, of the Universal House of Justice, and those of any other sources. In a few instances an exception to this order has been made when the quotations describe events or issues that have a clear historical or logical sequence.

A fundamental distinction is made in the Bahá'í Faith between written texts, which are binding, and oral traditions or pilgrims' notes, which, although not suppressed, have no authority. 'Abdu'l-Bahá clearly states: *"For the people of Bahá, the Text, and only the Text, is authentic."*[7] In relation to the text of *Some Answered Questions* and the public talks of 'Abdu'l-Bahá in the West, the Universal House of Justice has provided the following guidance:

> The original of *Some Answered Questions* in Persian is preserved in the Holy Land; its text was read in full and corrected by 'Abdu'l-Bahá Himself. Unfortunately, 'Abdu'l-Bahá did not read and authenticate all transcripts of His other talks, some of which have been translated into various languages and published. For many of His addresses included in *The Promulgation of Universal Peace* and *Paris Talks*, for example, no original authenticated text has yet been found. However, the Guardian allowed such compilations to continue to be used by the friends. In the future each talk will have to be identified and those which are unauthenticated will have to be clearly distinguished from those which form a part of Bahá'í Scripture. This does not mean that the unauthenticated talks will have to cease to be used—merely that the degree of authenticity of every document will have to be known and understood.[8]

In the following compilation the use of a quotation from an oral talk will be signalled by adding the expression "Words of" or "Public Talk of", as appropriate, at the beginning of the reference citation, e.g. Public Talk of 'Abdu'l-Bahá, *Paris Talks*.

The original Writings of the Báb and Bahá'u'lláh are in Persian and Arabic. One of the most important works of Shoghi Effendi in his thirty-six years of Guardianship (1921-1957) was to translate the major Writings into English. To perform this task with the greatest possible fidelity he chose a style reminiscent of the King James Version of the Bible, which conveys a unique blend of intimacy and reverence. For instance,

---

7 Helen Hornby, *Lights of Guidance*, no. 1431, p. 438.
8 Letter written on behalf of the Universal House of Justice to an individual believer, 23 March 1987.

the noonday prayer begins: *"I bear witness, O my God, that Thou hast created me to know Thee and to worship Thee."* In this style, words such as "mankind", which today are sometimes regarded as having masculine connotations, have been used with their primary and inclusive meaning of the human species. Subsequent translators have also followed the same style.

The present publication is based on an earlier work entitled *Bahá'í Life* which was first published in 1969. The changes since this first edition reflect the growth and transformation of the Bahá'í Community over this period. There has been a great expansion in the body of material on the functioning of communities, education, social and economic development, and collaboration with the wider community in the fulfilment of the ancient promise cherished in all the world religions of the achievement of a peaceful and progressive world society.

This selection from the Writings of the Bahá'í Faith is warmly and respectfully offered to all who would like a deeper understanding of its aims and teachings. A sense of its scope may be readily obtained from the Table of Contents, or those who wish to have a first taste of the teachings may like to skim some of the quotations inside. To obtain a real feel for the Bahá'í Revelation, however, there is no substitute for total immersion. This book, like any other, can only hold a cupful—but within that cup is the shoreless sea ...

# Acknowledgements

The preparation and publication of this selection from the Bahá'í Writings has proceeded for more than a decade. It has been a major undertaking that would not have reached completion without a great deal of help from many sources. I acknowledge with warm appreciation the guidance of the Universal House of Justice on several points, and thank them in particular for permission to publish a number of previously unpublished letters by or on behalf of the Universal House of Justice. I also acknowledge the guidance of the Research Department at the Bahá'í World Centre on various issues related to the identification of Bahá'í Scripture, and thank them for the provision of several newer translations of previously published writings, as well as texts of some letters written on behalf of the Guardian. (Texts that vary from previously published versions are identified in the reference citation). Mr Douglas Martin has also kindly given permission for the reproduction of his summary of the life and achievements of Shoghi Effendi from his introduction to "Poems of the Passing".

Thanks also to Counsellor Sirus Naraqi for advice on the contents, to Martin and Alexandra Roberts for research assistance, typing, editing, computer and internet support, (especially for help in bringing the first draft to completion, and for Martin's work in preparing the index), to Counsellor David Chittleborough and Dr Marjorie Tidman who commented on the first draft, to Dawn and Geoff Dibdin for assistance with proof-reading, and Nigel Davidson for preparation of the reference list. Barry Anderson at Bahá'í Publications Australia provided the encouragement and stimulation that kept the project alive over many years when it could easily have lapsed through many other commitments. Dr Graham Hassall undertook the final review and Michael W. Thomas the final editing and proof-reading. Zohreh and Naysan Faizi provided the professional skills for the cover design and layout, and Angie Tan at Bahá'í Publications Australia co-ordinated the publication.

I would also like to thank all my family and especially Erica who not only assisted as needed with proof-reading, but managed to maintain a supportive family environment despite the demands of yet another of her husband's projects.

John Davidson
20 October 2000

Erica and I would like to dedicate

this work to our parents,

Annie and Alex Davidson and

Lorna and Joseph Salter,

and beyond them to all whose lives have

been touched by the Bahá'í Writings

drawing them into the

process of transformation.

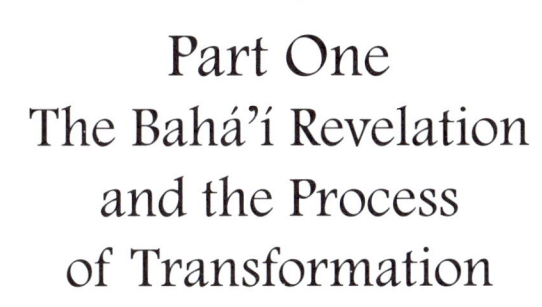

Part One
The Bahá'í Revelation and the Process of Transformation

Chapter One
The Aims of Bahá'u'lláh

*T*hink not that We have revealed unto you a mere code of laws. Nay, rather, We have unsealed the choice Wine with the fingers of might and power. To this beareth witness that which the Pen of Revelation hath revealed. Meditate upon this, O men of insight!

Bahá'u'lláh, The Kitáb-i-Aqdas (The Most Holy Book), para. 5, p. 21.

*T*he Blessed Perfection was a prisoner twenty-five years. During all this time He was subjected to the indignities and revilement of the people. He was persecuted, mocked and put in chains. In Persia His properties were pillaged and His possessions confiscated. First, there was banishment from Persia to Baghdád, then to Constantinople, then Adrianople, finally from Roumelia to the prison fortress of 'Akká.

During His lifetime He was intensely active. His energy was unlimited. Scarcely one night was passed in restful sleep. He bore these ordeals, suffered these calamities and difficulties in order that a manifestation of selflessness and service might become apparent in the world of humanity; that the Most Great Peace should become a reality; that human souls might appear as the angels of heaven; that heavenly miracles would be wrought among men; that human faith should be strengthened and perfected; that the precious, priceless bestowal of God—the human mind—might be developed to its fullest capacity in the temple of the body; and that man might become the reflection and likeness of God, even as it hath been revealed in the Bible, "Let us make man in our image".

Public talk of 'Abdu'l-Bahá, The Promulgation of Universal Peace, p. 28.

*D*early loved friends, this is the theme we must pursue in our efforts to deepen in the Cause. What is Bahá'u'lláh's purpose for the human race? For what ends did He submit to the appalling cruelties and indignities heaped upon Him? What does He mean by "a new race of men"? What are the profound changes which He will bring about? The answers are to be found in the Sacred Writings of our Faith and in their interpretation by 'Abdu'l-Bahá and our beloved Guardian. Let the friends immerse themselves in this ocean, let them organize regular study classes for its constant consideration, and as reinforcement to their effort, let them remember conscientiously the requirements of daily prayer and reading of the Word of God enjoined upon all Bahá'ís by Bahá'u'lláh.

Messages from the Universal House of Justice 1963-1986, para. 42.24, pp. 107-108. (Riḍván 1967)

The Renewal of Religion

O King! I was but a man like others, asleep upon My couch, when lo, the breezes of the All-Glorious were wafted over Me and taught Me the knowledge of all that hath been. This thing is not from Me, but from One Who is Almighty and All-Knowing.

Bahá'u'lláh, Tablet to Náṣiri'd-Dín <u>Sh</u>áh, Epistle to the Son of the Wolf, p. 11.[9]

Restatement of Spiritual Truths

*T*his is that which hath descended from the realm of glory, uttered by the tongue of power and might, and revealed unto the Prophets of old. We have taken the inner essence thereof and clothed it in the garment of brevity, as a token of grace unto the righteous, that they may stand faithful unto the Covenant of God, may fulfil in their lives His trust, and in the realm of spirit obtain the gem of Divine virtue.

Bahá'u'lláh, The Hidden Words, preface.

*E*very true Prophet hath regarded His Message as fundamentally the same as the Revelation of every other Prophet gone before Him.

Bahá'u'lláh, Gleanings from the Writings of Bahá'u'lláh, section XXXIV, pp. 78-79.

Adaptation to the Needs of the Time

*E*very Divine Revelation hath been sent down in a manner that befitted the circumstances of the age in which it hath appeared.

Bahá'u'lláh, Gleanings from the Writings of Bahá'u'lláh, section XXXIV, p. 81.

*T*he distinguishing feature that marketh the pre-eminent character of this Supreme Revelation consisteth in that We have, on the one hand, blotted out from the pages of God's holy Book whatsoever hath been the cause of strife, of malice and mischief amongst the children of men, and have, on the other, laid down the essential prerequisites of concord, of understanding, of complete and enduring unity.

Bahá'u'lláh, Gleanings from the Writings of Bahá'u'lláh, section XLIII, p. 97.[10]

*T*he Purpose of the one true God, exalted be His glory, in revealing Himself unto men is to lay bare those gems that lie hidden within the mine of their true and inmost selves. That the divers communions of the earth, and the manifold systems of religious belief, should never be allowed to foster the feelings of animosity among men, is, in this Day, of the essence of the Faith of God and His Religion. These principles and laws, these firmly-established and mighty systems, have proceeded from one Source, and are the

---

9   Also *The Proclamation of Bahá'u'lláh*, p. 57.
10   Also *Tablets of Bahá'u'lláh*, p. 94.

rays of one Light. That they differ one from another is to be attributed to the varying requirements of the ages in which they were promulgated.

... Religious fanaticism and hatred are a world-devouring fire, whose violence none can quench. ...

... Deal ye one with another with the utmost love and harmony, with friendliness and fellowship.

Bahá'u'lláh, Gleanings from the Writings of Bahá'u'lláh, section CXXXII, pp. 287-288.

Fulfilment of Past Religions

The Revelation which, from time immemorial, hath been acclaimed as the Purpose and Promise of all the Prophets of God, and the most cherished Desire of His Messengers, hath now, by virtue of the pervasive Will of the Almighty and at His irresistible bidding, been revealed unto men. The advent of such a Revelation hath been heralded in all the sacred Scriptures.

Bahá'u'lláh, Gleanings from the Writings of Bahá'u'lláh, section III, p. 5.

In this most mighty Revelation all the Dispensations of the past have attained their highest and final consummation.

Bahá'u'lláh, Gleanings from the Writings of Bahá'u'lláh, section CXV, p. 244.

How vast is the tabernacle of the Cause of God! It hath overshadowed all the peoples and kindreds of the earth, and will, erelong, gather together the whole of mankind beneath its shelter.

Bahá'u'lláh, Gleanings from the Writings of Bahá'u'lláh, section XLIII, p. 92.[11]

In the *Bayán* the Báb says that every religion of the past was fit to become universal. The only reason why they failed to attain that mark was the incompetence of their followers. He then proceeds to give a definite promise that this would not be the fate of the revelation of "Him Whom God would make manifest", that it will become universal and include all the people of the world.

Shoghi Effendi, The Compilation of Compilations, Vol. II (Living the Life), no. 1275, p. 4.

A race of men, incomparable in character, shall be raised up which, with the feet of detachment, will tread under all who are in heaven and on earth, and will cast the sleeve of holiness over all that hath been created from water and clay.

Bahá'u'lláh, cited in The Advent of Divine Justice, p. 31.

---

[11] Also *Tablets of Bahá'u'lláh*, p. 84

The Spiritualization of Human Beings

I swear by Thy glory! I have accepted to be tried by manifold adversities for no purpose except to regenerate all that are in Thy heaven and on Thy earth.

Bahá'u'lláh, Prayers and Meditations, section CXVI, p. 198.

O Son of Being!
Thy heart is My home; sanctify it for My descent. Thy spirit is My place of revelation; cleanse it for My manifestation.

Bahá'u'lláh, The Hidden Words, Arabic No. 59.

*T*he secret of the Day that is to come is now concealed. It can neither be divulged nor estimated. The newly born babe of that Day excels the wisest and most venerable men of this time, and the lowliest and most unlearned of that period shall surpass in understanding the most erudite and accomplished divines of this age.

Words of the Báb, The Dawn-Breakers, p. 94.

*T*hese children are neither Oriental nor Occidental, neither Asiatic nor American, neither European nor African, but they are of the Kingdom; their native home is heaven and their resort is the Kingdom of Abhá.

'Abdu'l-Bahá, Tablets of Abdul-Baha Abbas, Vol. III, p. 648.

*P*ray that God may assist in this heavenly undertaking, that the world of mankind shall be saved from the ordeals of ignorance, blindness and spiritual death. Then will you behold light upon light, joy upon joy, absolute happiness reigning everywhere, the people of the religions consorting together in fragrance and felicity, this world in its maturity becoming the reflection of the eternal Kingdom and this terrestrial abode of man the very paradise of God. Pray for this! Pray for this!

Public talk of 'Abdu'l-Bahá, The Promulgation of Universal Peace, p. 441.

Building a Global Community

*Y*e are the fruits of one tree, and the leaves of one branch. Deal ye one with another with the utmost love and harmony, with friendliness and fellowship. He Who is the Day-Star of Truth beareth Me witness! So powerful is the light of unity that it can illuminate the whole earth. ...

... At one time We spoke in the language of the lawgiver; at another in that of the truth-seeker and the mystic, and yet Our supreme purpose and highest wish hath always been to disclose the glory and sublimity of this station.

Bahá'u'lláh, Epistle to the Son of the Wolf, p. 15.

... it is Our purpose, through the loving providence of God—exalted be His glory—and His surpassing mercy, to abolish, through the force of Our utterance, all disputes, war, and bloodshed, from the face of the earth.

Bahá'u'lláh, Epistle to the Son of the Wolf, p. 34.

Seven Lights of Unity

For none is self-sufficiency any longer possible, inasmuch as political ties unite all peoples and nations, and the bonds of trade and industry, of agriculture and education, are being strengthened every day. Hence the unity of all mankind can in this day be achieved. Verily this is none other but one of the wonders of this wondrous age, this glorious century. Of this past ages have been deprived, for this century—the century of light—hath been endowed with unique and unprecedented glory, power and illumination. Hence the miraculous unfolding of a fresh marvel every day. Eventually it will be seen how bright its candles will burn in the assemblage of man.

Behold how its light is now dawning upon the world's darkened horizon.

- The first candle is unity in the political realm, the early glimmerings of which can now be discerned.
- The second candle is unity of thought in world undertakings, the consummation of which will ere long be witnessed.
- The third candle is unity in freedom which will surely come to pass.
- The fourth candle is unity in religion which is the corner-stone of the foundation itself, and which, by the power of God, will be revealed in all its splendour.
- The fifth candle is the unity of nations—a unity which in this century will be securely established, causing all the peoples of the earth to regard themselves as citizens of one common fatherland.
- The sixth candle is unity of races, making of all that dwell on earth peoples and kindreds of one race.
- The seventh candle is unity of language, i.e., the choice of a universal tongue in which all peoples will be instructed and converse.

Each and every one of these will inevitably come to pass, inasmuch as the power of the kingdom of God will aid and assist in their realization.

'Abdu'l-Bahá, Selections from the Writings of 'Abdu'l-Bahá, no. 15, p. 32.[12]

---

[12] Also cited in The Goal of A New World Order, The World Order of Bahá'u'lláh, p. 39.

The Uniting of Nations

*T*he well-being of mankind, its peace and security, are unattainable unless and until its unity is firmly established.

> Bahá'u'lláh, *Gleanings from the Writings of Bahá'u'lláh*, section CXXXI, p. 286.

*T*he rulers and kings of the earth ... must consider such ways and means as will lay the foundations of the world's Great Peace amongst men. Such a peace demandeth that the Great Powers should resolve, for the sake of the tranquillity of the peoples of the earth, to be fully reconciled among themselves. Should any king take up arms against another, all should unitedly arise and prevent him. If this be done, the nations of the world will no longer require any armaments, except for the purpose of preserving the security of their realms and of maintaining internal order within their territories. ...

... The day is approaching when all the peoples of the world will have adopted one universal language and one common script. When this is achieved, to whatsoever city a man may journey, it shall be as if he were entering his own home. These things are obligatory and absolutely essential.

> Bahá'u'lláh, *Gleanings from the Writings of Bahá'u'lláh*, section CXVII, pp. 249-250.

O ye the elected representatives of the people in every land! Take ye counsel together, and let your concern be only for that which profiteth mankind, and bettereth the condition thereof ...

> Bahá'u'lláh, Tablet to The Elected Representatives, *Gleanings from the Writings of Bahá'u'lláh*, section CXX, p. 254.[13]

*I*t is not for him to pride himself who loveth his own country, but rather for him who loveth the whole world. The earth is but one country, and mankind its citizens.

> Bahá'u'lláh, *Gleanings from the Writings of Bahá'u'lláh*, section CXVII, p. 250.[14]

*L*et there be no mistake. The principle of the Oneness of Mankind—the pivot round which all the teachings of Bahá'u'lláh revolve—is no mere outburst of ignorant emotionalism or an expression of vague and pious hope. Its appeal is not to be merely identified with a reawakening of the spirit of brotherhood and good-will among men, nor does it aim solely at the fostering of harmonious co-operation among individual peoples and nations. ... It calls for no less than the reconstruction and demilitarization of the whole civilized world—a world organically unified in all the essential aspects of its life, its political machinery, its spiritual aspiration, its trade and finance, its script and language, and yet infinite in the diversity of the national characteristics of its federated units.

> Shoghi Effendi, The Goal of A New World Order, *The World Order of Bahá'u'lláh*, pp. 42-43.

---

13   Also *The Proclamation of Bahá'u'lláh*, p. 67.
14   Also *Tablets of Bahá'u'lláh*, p. 167, and *The Proclamation of Bahá'u'lláh*, p. 116.

The Advancement of Civilization

*A*ll men have been created to carry forward an ever-advancing civilization.

Bahá'u'lláh, *Gleanings from the Writings of Bahá'u'lláh*, section CIX, p. 215.

*T*he third Tajallí is concerning arts, crafts and sciences. Knowledge is as wings to man's life, and a ladder for his ascent. Its acquisition is incumbent upon everyone. The knowledge of such sciences, however, should be acquired as can profit the peoples of the earth, and not those which begin with words and end with words. Great indeed is the claim of scientists and craftsmen on the peoples of the world. ... In truth, knowledge is a veritable treasure for man, and a source of glory, of bounty, of joy, of exaltation, of cheer and gladness unto him. Thus hath the Tongue of Grandeur spoken in this Most Great Prison.

Bahá'u'lláh, Tajallíyát (Effulgences), *Tablets of Bahá'u'lláh*, pp. 51-52.

*E*very word that proceedeth out of the mouth of God is endowed with such potency as can instil new life into every human frame ... Through the mere revelation of the word "Fashioner," issuing forth from His lips and proclaiming His attribute to mankind, such power is released as can generate, through successive ages, all the manifold arts that the hands of man can produce. ... In the days to come, ye will, verily, behold things of which ye have never heard before. ... In like manner, the moment the word expressing My attribute "The Omniscient" issueth forth from My mouth, every created thing will, according to its capacity and limitations, be invested with the power to unfold the knowledge of the most marvellous sciences, and will be empowered to manifest them in the course of time ...

Bahá'u'lláh, *Gleanings from the Writings of Bahá'u'lláh*, section LXXIV, pp. 141-142.

hapter Two
The Origins and Growth of the Bahá'í Faith

*I*n its broadest outline the first century of the Bahá'í Era may be said to comprise the Heroic, the Primitive, the Apostolic Age of the Faith of Bahá'u'lláh, and also the initial stages of the Formative, the Transitional, the Iron Age which is to witness the crystallization and shaping of the creative energies released by His Revelation. The first eighty years of this century may roughly be said to have covered the entire period of the first age, while the last two decades may be regarded as having witnessed the beginnings of the second. The former commences with the Declaration of the Báb, includes the mission of Bahá'u'lláh, and terminates with the passing of 'Abdu'l-Bahá. The latter is ushered in by His Will and Testament, which defines its character and establishes its foundation.

The century under our review may therefore be considered as falling into four distinct periods, of unequal duration, each of specific import and of tremendous and indeed unappraisable significance. These four periods are closely interrelated, and constitute successive acts of one, indivisible, stupendous and sublime drama, whose mystery no intellect can fathom, whose climax no eye can even dimly perceive, whose conclusion no mind can adequately foreshadow. Each of these acts revolves around its own theme, boasts of its own heroes, registers its own tragedies, records its own triumphs, and contributes its own share to the execution of one common, immutable Purpose. To isolate any one of them from the others, to dissociate the later manifestations of one universal, all-embracing Revelation from the pristine purpose that animated it in its earliest days, would be tantamount to a mutilation of the structure on which it rests, and to a lamentable perversion of its truth and of its history.

Shoghi Effendi, God Passes By, pp. xiii–xiv.

The Ministry of the Báb

*T*he first period (1844-1853), centres around the gentle, the youthful and irresistible person of the Báb, matchless in His meekness, imperturbable in His serenity, magnetic in His utterance, unrivalled in the dramatic episodes of His swift and tragic ministry. It begins with the Declaration of His Mission, culminates in His martyrdom, and ends in a veritable orgy of religious massacre revolting in its hideousness. It is characterized by nine years of fierce and relentless contest, whose theatre was the whole of Persia, in which above ten thousand heroes laid down their lives, in which two sovereigns of the Qájár dynasty and their wicked ministers participated, and which was supported by the entire Shí'ah ecclesiastical hierarchy, by the military resources of the state, and by the implacable hostility of the masses.

Shoghi Effendi, *God Passes By*, p. xiv.

The Childhood and Early Life of the Báb

*T*he Báb, whose name was Siyyid 'Alí-Muḥammad, was born in the city of Shíráz, on the first day of Muḥarram, in the year AH 1235 [20 October AD 1819]. He belonged to a house which was renowned for its nobility and which traced its origin to Muḥammad Himself. ... In His early childhood He lost His father, Siyyid Muḥammad-Riḍá, a man who was known throughout the province of Fárs for his piety and virtue, and was held in high esteem and honour. Both His father and His mother were descendants of the Prophet, both were loved and respected by the people. He was reared by His maternal uncle, Ḥájí Mírzá Siyyid 'Alí, a martyr to the Faith, who placed Him, while still a child, under the care of a tutor named Shaykh 'Ábid. ...

Shaykh 'Ábid, known by his pupils as Shaykhuná, was a man of piety and learning. He had been a disciple of both Shaykh Aḥmad and Siyyid Kázim."One day," he related, "I asked the Báb to recite the opening words of the Qur'án: 'Bismi'lláhi'r-Raḥmáni'r-Raḥím.' He hesitated, pleading that unless He were told what these words signified, He would in no wise attempt to pronounce them. I pretended not to know their meaning. 'I know what these words signify,' observed my pupil; 'by your leave, I will explain them.' He spoke with such knowledge and fluency that I was struck with amazement. He expounded the meaning of 'Alláh' of 'Raḥmán', and 'Raḥím', in terms such as I had neither read nor heard. The sweetness of His utterance still lingers in my memory. I felt impelled to take Him back to His uncle and to deliver into his hands the Trust he had committed to my care. I determined to tell him how unworthy I felt to teach so remarkable a child. I found His uncle alone in his office. 'I have brought Him back to you,' I said, 'and commit Him to your vigilant protection. He is not to be treated as a mere child, for in Him I can already discern evidences of that mysterious power which the Revelation of the Sáḥibu'z-Zamán[15] alone can reveal. It is incumbent upon you to surround Him with your most loving care. Keep Him in your house, for He, verily, stands in no need of teachers such as I.'

Nabíl-i-A'ẓam, *The Dawn-Breakers*, pp. 72, 75.

*H*e left Shíráz for Búshihr at the age of 17, and remained there for five years engaged in commercial pursuits. During this time he won the esteem of all the merchants with whom he was brought in contact, by his integrity and piety. He was extremely attentive to his religious duties, and gave away large sums to charity.

Nabíl-i-A'ẓam, *The Dawn-Breakers*, Footnote 1, p. 77.

---

15   "The Lord of the Age", one of the titles of the promised Qá'im.

*A*s I was already acquainted with Ḥájí Mírzá Siyyid 'Alí, I was enabled to meet the Báb on several occasions. Every time I met Him, I found Him in such a state of humility and lowliness as words fail me to describe. His downcast eyes, His extreme courtesy, and the serene expression of His face made an indelible impression upon my soul. I often heard those who were closely associated with Him testify to the purity of His character, to the charm of His manners, to His self-effacement, to His high integrity, and to His extreme devotion to God.

Words of Ḥájí Siyyid Javád-i-Karbilá'í, in Nabíl-i-A'ẓam, *The Dawn-Breakers*, p. 79.

... the Báb was united in wedlock with the sister of Mírzá Siyyid Ḥasan and Mírzá Abu'l-Qásim. The child which resulted from this union, He named Aḥmad. He died in the year AH 1259, the year preceding the declaration of the Faith by the Báb.

Nabíl-i-A'ẓam, *The Dawn-Breakers*, p. 76.

The Birth of the Bábí Revelation

*H*e Who communicated the original impulse to so incalculable a Movement was none other than the promised Qá'im (He who ariseth), the Sáḥibu'z-Zamán (the Lord of the Age), Who assumed the exclusive right of annulling the whole Qur'ánic Dispensation, Who styled Himself *"the Primal Point from which have been generated all created things ... the Countenance of God Whose splendour can never be obscured, the Light of God Whose radiance can never fade."* The people among whom He appeared were the most decadent race in the civilized world, grossly ignorant, savage, cruel, steeped in prejudice, servile in their submission to an almost deified hierarchy ... Fiercely fanatic, unspeakably corrupt, enjoying unlimited ascendancy over the masses, jealous of their position, and irreconcilably opposed to all liberal ideas, the members of this caste had for one thousand years invoked the name of the Hidden Imám, their breasts had glowed with the expectation of His advent ...

Shoghi Effendi, *God Passes By*, p. 4.

O thou who art the first to believe in Me! Verily I say, I am the Báb, the Gate of God, and thou art the Bábu'l-Báb, the gate of that Gate. Eighteen souls must, in the beginning, spontaneously and of their own accord, accept Me and recognize the truth of My Revelation. ... We shall instruct them to teach the Word of God and to quicken the souls of men.

Words of the Báb to Mullá Ḥusayn, Nabíl-i-A'ẓam, *The Dawn-Breakers*, p. 63.

*H*e took up His pen and with incredible rapidity revealed the entire Súrih of Mulk, the first chapter of His commentary on the Súrih of Joseph. The overpowering effect of the manner in which He wrote was heightened by the gentle intonation of His voice which accompanied His writing. Not for one moment did He interrupt the flow of the verses which streamed from His pen. Not once did He pause till the Súrih of Mulk was finished.

Nabíl-i-A'ẓam, *The Dawn-Breakers*, p. 61.

I sat spellbound by His utterance, oblivious of time and those who awaited me. Suddenly the call of the muadhdhin, summoning the faithful to their morning prayer, awakened me from the state of ecstasy into which I seemed to have fallen. All the delights, all the ineffable glories, which the Almighty has recounted in His Book as the priceless possessions of the people of Paradise—these I seemed to be experiencing that night. Methinks I was in a place of which it could be truly said: "Therein no toil shall reach us, and therein no weariness shall touch us"; "No vain discourse shall they hear therein, nor any falsehood, but only the cry, 'Peace! Peace!'

Words of Mullá Ḥusayn, Nabíl-i-A'ẓam, The Dawn-Breakers, p. 62.

*S*ay to Him, from me, "The effulgence of Thy face flashed forth, and the rays of Thy visage arose on high. Then speak the word, 'Am I not your Lord?' and 'Thou art, Thou art!' we will all reply."

Message of Ṭáhirih to the Báb, Nabíl-i-A'ẓam, The Dawn-Breakers, pp. 81-82.

O My beloved friends! You are the bearers of the name of God in this Day. You have been chosen as the repositories of His mystery. It behoves each one of you to manifest the attributes of God, and to exemplify by your deeds and words the signs of His righteousness, His power and glory. The very members of your body must bear witness to the loftiness of your purpose, the integrity of your life, the reality of your faith, and the exalted character of your devotion. For verily I say, this is the Day spoken of by God in His book:[16] 'On that Day will We set a seal upon their mouths; yet shall their hands speak unto Us, and their feet shall bear witness to that which they shall have done.' ... O My Letters! Verily I say, immensely exalted is this Day above the days of the Apostles of old. Nay, immeasurable is the difference! You are the witnesses of the Dawn of the promised Day of God. You are the partakers of the mystic chalice of His Revelation. Gird up the loins of endeavour, and be mindful of the words of God as revealed in His Book:[17] 'Lo, the Lord thy God is come, and with Him is the company of His angels arrayed before Him!' ... I am preparing you for the advent of a mighty Day. Exert your utmost endeavour that, in the world to come, I, who am now instructing you, may, before the mercy-seat of God, rejoice in your deeds and glory in your achievements. ... Heed not your weaknesses and frailty; fix your gaze upon the invincible power of the Lord, your God, the Almighty. ... Arise in His name, put your trust wholly in Him, and be assured of ultimate victory.

Instructions of the Báb to the Letters of the Living, Nabíl-i-A'ẓam, The Dawn-Breakers, pp. 92-94.

*T*o the care of Mullá Ḥusayn He committed a mission, more specific in character and mightier in import. He affirmed that His covenant with him had been established, cautioned him to be forbearing with the divines he would encounter, directed him to proceed to Ṭihrán, and alluded, in the most glowing terms, to the as yet unrevealed Mystery enshrined in that city—a Mystery that would, He affirmed, transcend the light shed by both Ḥijáz and Shíráz.

Galvanized into action by the mandate conferred upon them, launched on their peril-

---

16 The Qur'án
17 The Qur'án

ous and revolutionizing mission, these lesser luminaries who, together with the Báb, constitute the First Váhid (Unity) of the Dispensation of the Bayán, scattered far and wide through the provinces of their native land, where, with matchless heroism, they resisted the savage and concerted onslaught of the forces arrayed against them, and immortalized their Faith by their own exploits and those of their co-religionists, raising thereby a tumult that convulsed their country and sent its echoes reverberating as far as the capitals of Western Europe.

It was not until, however, the Báb had received the eagerly anticipated letter of Mullá Husayn, His trusted and beloved lieutenant, communicating the joyful tidings of his interview with Bahá'u'lláh, that He decided to undertake His long and arduous pilgrimage to the Tombs of His ancestors. In the month of Sha'bán, of the year AH 1260 (September, 1844) He Who, both on His father's and mother's side, was of the seed of the illustrious Fáṭimih, and Who was a descendant of the Imám Husayn, the most eminent among the lawful successors of the Prophet of Islám, proceeded, in fulfilment of Islámic traditions, to visit the Kaaba.

Shoghi Effendi, God Passes By, pp. 8-9.

The Imprisonment of the Báb and His Declaration at Tabríz

The period of the Báb's banishment to the mountains of Ádhirbáyján, lasting no less than three years, constitutes the saddest, the most dramatic, and in a sense the most pregnant phase of His six year ministry. It comprises His nine months' unbroken confinement in the fortress of Máh-Ku, and His subsequent incarceration in the fortress of Chihríq, which was interrupted only by a brief yet memorable visit to Tabríz.

Shoghi Effendi, God Passes By, p. 17.

Upon His arrival in Máh-Kú, surnamed by Him Jabal-i-Básit (the Open Mountain) no one was allowed to see Him for the first two weeks except His amanuensis, Siyyid Husayn, and his brother. So grievous was His plight while in that fortress that, in the *Persian Bayán*, He Himself has stated that at night-time He did not even have a lighted lamp, and that His solitary chamber, constructed of sun-baked bricks, lacked even a door ...

Secluded on the heights of a remote and dangerously situated mountain on the frontiers of the Ottoman and Russian empires; imprisoned within the solid walls of a four-towered fortress; cut off from His family, His kindred and His disciples; living in the vicinity of a bigoted and turbulent community who, by race, tradition, language and creed, differed from the vast majority of the inhabitants of Persia; guarded by the people of a district which, as the birthplace of the Grand Vizir, had been made the recipient of the special favours of his administration, the Prisoner of Máh-Kú seemed in the eyes of His adversary to be doomed to languish away the flower of His youth, and witness, at no distant date, the complete annihilation of His hopes. That adversary was soon to realize, however, how gravely he had misjudged both his Prisoner and those on whom he had lavished his favours. An unruly, a proud and unreasoning people were gradually subdued by the gentleness of the Báb, were chastened by His modesty, were edified by His counsels, and instructed by His wisdom. They were so carried away by their love for Him that their first act every morning, notwithstanding the remonstrations of the domineering 'Alí Khán, and the repeated threats of disciplinary measures received from Ṭihrán, was to seek a place where they could catch a glimpse of His face, and beseech from afar His benediction upon their daily work.

Shoghi Effendi, God Passes By, pp. 18-19.

Secret agents, however, charged to watch 'Alí Khán, informed Ḥájí Mírzá Áqásí of the turn events were taking, whereupon he immediately decided to transfer the Báb to the fortress of Chihríq (about 10 April 1848), surnamed by Him the Jabal-i-Shadíd (the Grievous Mountain). There He was consigned to the keeping of Yaḥyá Khán, a brother-in-law of Muḥammad Sháh. Though at the outset he acted with the utmost severity, he was eventually compelled to yield to the fascination of his Prisoner. Nor were the Kurds, who lived in the village of Chihríq, and whose hatred of the Shí'ahs exceeded even that of the inhabitants of Máh-Kú, able to resist the pervasive power of the Prisoner's influence. They too were to be seen every morning, ere they started for their daily work, to approach the fortress and prostrate themselves in adoration before its holy Inmate. "So great was the confluence of the people," is the testimony of a European eye-witness, writing in his memoirs of the Báb, "that the courtyard, not being large enough to contain His hearers, the majority remained in the street and listened with rapt attention to the verses of the new Qur'án."

Shoghi Effendi, God Passes By, pp. 19-20.

To allay the rising excitement the Báb was summoned to Tabríz. ... The circumstances attending the examination of the Báb, as a result of so precipitate an act, may well rank as one of the chief landmarks of His dramatic career. The avowed purpose of that convocation was to arraign the Prisoner, and deliberate on the steps to be taken for the extirpation of His so-called heresy. It instead afforded Him the supreme opportunity of His mission to assert in public, formally and without any reservation, the claims inherent in His Revelation.

Shoghi Effendi, God Passes By, pp. 20-21.

Upon His arrival, the Báb observed that every seat in the hall was occupied except one which had been reserved for the Valí-'Ahd[18]. He greeted the assembly and, without the slightest hesitation, proceeded to occupy that vacant seat. The majesty of His gait, the expression of overpowering confidence which sat upon His brow—above all, the spirit of power which shone from His whole being, appeared to have for a moment crushed the soul out of the body of those whom he had greeted. A deep, a mysterious silence, suddenly fell upon them. Not one soul in that distinguished assembly dared to breathe a single word. At last the stillness which brooded over them was broken by the Niẓámu'l-

---

18   The heir to the throne.
19   The Prince's tutor.

'Ulamá[19]. 'Who do you claim to be,' he asked the Báb, 'and what is the message you have brought?' 'I am,' thrice exclaimed the Báb, 'I am, I am, the promised One! I am the One whose name you have for a thousand years invoked, at whose mention you have risen, whose advent you have longed to witness, and the hour of whose Revelation you have prayed God to hasten. Verily I say, it is incumbent upon the peoples of both the East and the West to obey my word and pledge allegiance to My person.'

Nabíl-i-A'ẓam, The Dawn-Breakers, pp. 315-316.

I am the Mystic Fane which the Hand of Omnipotence hath reared. I am the Lamp which the Finger of God hath lit within its niche and caused to shine with deathless splendour. I am the Flame of that supernal Light that glowed upon Sinai in the gladsome Spot, and lay concealed in the midst of the Burning Bush.

The Báb, Selections from the Writings of the Báb, p. 74.

The Relationship of the Báb to Bahá'u'lláh

*T*o this period of incarceration in the fortresses of Máh-Ku and Chihríq—a period of unsurpassed fecundity, yet bitter in its humiliations and ever-deepening sorrows—belong almost all the written references, whether in the form of warnings, appeals or exhortations, which the Báb, in anticipation of the approaching hour of His supreme affliction, felt it necessary to make to the Author of a Revelation that was soon to supersede His own. Conscious from the very beginning of His twofold mission, as the Bearer of a wholly independent Revelation and the Herald of One still greater than His own, He could not content Himself with the vast number of commentaries, of prayers, of laws and ordinances, of dissertations and epistles, of homilies and orations that had incessantly streamed from His pen. The Greater Covenant into which, as affirmed in His writings, God had, from time immemorial, entered, through the Prophets of all ages, with the whole of mankind, regarding the new-born Revelation, had already been fulfilled. It had now to be supplemented by a Lesser Covenant which He felt bound to make with the entire body of His followers concerning the One Whose advent He characterized as the fruit and ultimate purpose of His Dispensation. Such a Covenant had invariably been the feature of every previous religion. It had existed, under various forms, with varying degrees of emphasis, had always been couched in veiled language, and had been alluded to in cryptic prophecies, in abstruse allegories, in unauthenticated traditions, and in the fragmentary and obscure passages of the sacred Scriptures. In the Bábí Dispensation, however, it was destined to be established in clear and unequivocal language, though not embodied in a separate document. Unlike the Prophets gone before Him, Whose Covenants were shrouded in mystery, unlike Bahá'u'lláh, Whose clearly defined Covenant was incorporated in a specially written Testament, and designated by Him as *"the Book of My Covenant,"* the Báb chose to intersperse His Book of Laws, the *Persian Bayán*, with unnumbered passages, some designedly obscure, mostly indubitably clear and conclusive, in which He fixes the date of the promised Revelation, extols its virtues, asserts

PATHWAYS TO TRANSFORMATION

its pre-eminent character, assigns to it unlimited powers and prerogatives, and tears down every barrier that might be an obstacle to its recognition. *"He, verily,"* Bahá'u'lláh, referring to the Báb in His *Kitáb-i-Badí'*, has stated, *"hath not fallen short of His duty to exhort the people of the Bayán and to deliver unto them His Message. In no age or dispensation hath any Manifestation made mention, in such detail and in such explicit language, of the Manifestation destined to succeed Him."*

Shoghi Effendi, *God Passes By*, pp. 27-28.

A successor or vicegerent the Báb never named, an interpreter of His teachings He refrained from appointing. So transparently clear were His references to the Promised One, so brief was to be the duration of His own Dispensation, that neither the one nor the other was deemed necessary. All He did was, according to the testimony of 'Abdu'l-Bahá in *A Traveller's Narrative*, to nominate on the advice of Bahá'u'lláh and of another disciple, Mírzá Yaḥyá, who would act solely as a figure-head pending the manifestation of the Promised One, thus enabling Bahá'u'lláh to promote, in relative security, the Cause so dear to His heart.

Shoghi Effendi, *God Passes By*, pp. 28-29.

*T*he first confinement that the Báb suffered at the hands of His enemies was in the house of 'Abdu'l-Ḥamíd Khán, the chief constable of Shíráz; the first confinement of Bahá'u'lláh was in the home of the kad-khudás of Ṭihrán. The Báb's second imprisonment was in the castle of Máh-Kú; that of Bahá'u'lláh was in the private residence of the governor of Ámul. The Báb was scourged in the namáz-khanih of the Shaykhu'l-Islám of Tabríz; the same indignity was inflicted on Bahá'u'lláh in the namáz-khánih of the mujtahid of Ámul. The Báb's third confinement was in the castle of Chihríq; Bahá'u'lláh's was in the Síyáh-Chál of Ṭihrán. The Báb, whose trials and sufferings had preceded, in almost every case, those of Bahá'u'lláh, had offered Himself to ransom His beloved from the perils that beset that precious Life; whilst Bahá'u'lláh, on His part, unwilling that He who so greatly loved Him should be the sole Sufferer, shared at every turn the cup that touched His lips. Such love no eye has ever beheld, nor has mortal heart conceived such mutual devotion.

Nabíl-i-A'ẓam, *The Dawn-Breakers*, pp. 372-373.

The Conference of Badasht

*T*he last three and most eventful years of the Báb's ministry had, as we have observed in the preceding pages, witnessed not only the formal and public declaration of His mission, but also an unprecedented effusion of His inspired writings, including both the revelation of the fundamental laws of His Dispensation and also the establishment of that Lesser Covenant which was to safeguard the unity of His followers and pave the way for the advent of an incomparably mightier Revelation. It was during this same period, in the early days of His incarceration in the fortress of Chihríq, that the independence of the new-born Faith was openly recognized and asserted by His disciples. The laws underlying the new Dispensation had been revealed by its Author in a prison-fortress in the mountains of Ádhirbáyján, while the Dispensation itself was now to be inaugurated in a plain on the border of Mázindarán, at a conference of His assembled followers.

Shoghi Effendi, *God Passes By*, p. 31.

... Suddenly the figure of Ṭáhirih, adorned and unveiled, appeared before the eyes of the assembled companions. Consternation immediately seized the entire gathering. All stood aghast before this sudden and most unexpected apparition. To behold her face unveiled was to them inconceivable. Even to gaze at her shadow was a thing which they deemed improper, inasmuch as they regarded her as the very incarnation of Fáṭimih, the noblest emblem of chastity in their eyes.

Quietly, silently, and with the utmost dignity Ṭáhirih stepped forward and, advancing towards Quddús, seated herself on his right-hand side. Her unruffled serenity sharply contrasted with the affrighted countenances of those who were gazing on her face. Fear, anger, and bewilderment stirred the depths of their souls. That sudden revelation seemed to have stunned their faculties. 'Abdu'l-Kháliq-i-Iṣfáhání was so gravely shaken that he cut his throat with his own hands. Covered with blood and shrieking with excitement, he fled away from the face of Ṭáhirih. ...

... She rose from her seat and, undeterred by the tumult she had raised in the hearts of her companions, began to address the remnant of that assembly. Without the least premeditation, and in a language that bore a striking resemblance to that of the Qur'án, she delivered her appeal with matchless eloquence and profound fervour. ...

... Ṭáhirih invited those who were present to celebrate befittingly this great occasion. 'This day is the day of festivity and universal rejoicing,' she added, 'the day on which the fetters of the past are burst asunder. Let those who have shared in this great achievement arise and embrace each other.'

That memorable day and those which immediately followed it witnessed the most revolutionary changes in the life and habits of the assembled followers of the Báb.

Nabíl-i-A'ẓam, *The Dawn-Breakers*, pp. 294-296.

Upheavals in Mázindarán, Nayríz and Zanján

The Báb's captivity in a remote corner of Ádhirbáyján, immortalized by the proceedings of the Conference of Badasht, and distinguished by such notable developments as the public declaration of His mission, the formulation of the laws of His Dispensation and the establishment of His Covenant, was to acquire added significance through the dire convulsions that sprang from the acts of both His adversaries and His disciples. The commotions that ensued, as the years of that captivity drew to a close, and that culminated in His own martyrdom, called forth a degree of heroism on the part of His followers and a fierceness of hostility on the part of His enemies which had never been witnessed during the first three years of His ministry. Indeed, this brief but most turbulent period may be rightly regarded as the bloodiest and most dramatic of the Heroic Age of the Bahá'í Era.

Shoghi Effendi, *God Passes By*, p. 35.

*I*n remote and isolated Centres the scattered disciples of a persecuted community were pitilessly struck down by the sword of their foes, while in Centres where large numbers had congregated measures were taken in self-defence, which, misconstrued by a cunning and deceitful adversary, served in their turn to inflame still further the hostility of the authorities, and multiply the outrages perpetrated by the oppressor. In the East at Shaykh Ṭabarsí, in the south in Nayríz, in the west in Zanján, and in the capital itself, massacres, upheavals, demonstrations, engagements, sieges, acts of treachery proclaimed, in rapid succession, the violence of the storm which had broken out, and exposed the bankruptcy, and blackened the annals, of a proud yet degenerate people.

Shoghi Effendi, *God Passes By*, pp. 37–38.

*A*rise, and with complete detachment proceed, in the guise of a traveller, to Mázindarán, and there visit, on My behalf, the spot which enshrines the bodies of those immortals who, with their blood, have sealed their faith in My Cause. As you approach the precincts of that hallowed ground, put off your shoes and, bowing your head in reverence to their memory, invoke their names and prayerfully make the circuit of their shrine. Bring back to Me, as a remembrance of your visit, a handful of that holy earth that covers the remains of My beloved ones, Quddús and Mullá Ḥusayn. Strive to be back here ere the day of Naw-Rúz, that you may celebrate with Me that festival, the only one I probably shall ever see again.

Words of the Báb, Nabíl-i-A'ẓam, *The Dawn-Breakers*, pp. 431–432.

The Martyrdom of the Báb

*T*he farrásh-báshí had abruptly interrupted the last conversation which the Báb was confidentially having in one of the rooms of the barracks with His amanuensis Siyyid Ḥusayn, and was drawing the latter aside, and severely rebuking him, when he was thus addressed by his Prisoner: *"Not until I have said to him all those things that I wish to say can any earthly power silence Me. Though all the world be armed against Me, yet shall it be powerless to deter Me from fulfilling, to the last word, My intention."* To the Christian Sam Khán—the colonel of the Armenian regiment ordered to carry out the execution—who, seized with fear lest his act should provoke the wrath of God, had begged to be released from the duty imposed upon him, the Báb gave the following assurance: *"Follow your instructions, and if your intention be sincere, the Almighty is surely able to relieve you of your perplexity."*

... The firing squad ranged itself in three files, each of two hundred and fifty men. Each file in turn opened fire until the whole detachment had discharged its bullets. So dense was the smoke from the seven hundred and fifty rifles that the sky was darkened. As soon as the smoke had cleared away the astounded multitude of about ten thousand souls, who had crowded onto the roof of the barracks, as well as the tops of the adjoining houses, beheld a scene which their eyes could scarcely believe.

The Báb had vanished from their sight! Only his companion remained, alive and unscathed, standing beside the wall on which they had been suspended. The ropes by which they had been hung alone were severed. "The Siyyid-i-Báb has gone from our sight!" cried out the bewildered spectators. A frenzied search immediately ensued. He was found, unhurt and unruffled, in the very room He had occupied the night before, engaged in completing His interrupted conversation with His amanuensis. *"I have finished My conversation with Siyyid Ḥusayn"* were the words with which the Prisoner, so providentially preserved, greeted the appearance of the farrásh-báshí, *"Now you may proceed to fulfil your intention."* Recalling the bold assertion his Prisoner had previously made, and shaken by so stunning a revelation, the farrásh-báshí quitted instantly the scene, and resigned his post.

Sam Khán, likewise, remembering, with feelings of awe and wonder, the reassuring words addressed to him by the Báb, ordered his men to leave the barracks immediately, and swore, as he left the courtyard, never again, even at the cost of his life, to repeat that act. Áqá Ján-i-Khamsih, colonel of the body-guard, volunteered to replace him. On the same wall and in the same manner the Báb and His companion were again suspended, while the new regiment formed in line and opened fire upon them. This time, however, their breasts were riddled with bullets, and their bodies completely dissected, with the exception of their faces which were but little marred. *"O wayward generation!"* were the last words of the Báb to the gazing multitude, as the regiment prepared to fire its volley, *"Had you believed in Me every one of you would have followed the example of this youth, who stood in rank above most of you, and would have willingly sacrificed himself in My path. The day will come when you will have recognized Me; that day I shall have ceased to be with you."*

Shoghi Effendi, God Passes By, pp. 52-53.

On the evening of the very day of the Báb's execution, which fell on the ninth of July 1850 (28th of Sha'bán AH 1266), during the thirty-first year of His age and the seventh of His ministry, the mangled bodies were transferred from the courtyard of the barracks to the edge of the moat outside the gate of the city. Four companies, each consisting of ten sentinels, were ordered to keep watch in turn over them. On the following morning the Russian Consul in Tabríz visited the spot, and ordered the artist who had accompanied him to make a drawing of the remains as they lay beside the moat. In the middle of the following night a follower of the Báb, Ḥájí Sulaymán Khán, succeeded, through the instrumentality of a certain Ḥájí Alláh-Yár, in removing the bodies to the silk factory owned by one of the believers of Mílán, and laid them, the next day, in a specially made wooden casket, which he later transferred to a place of safety. Meanwhile the mullás were boastfully proclaiming from the pulpits that, whereas the holy body of the Immaculate Imám would be preserved from beasts of prey and from all creeping things, this man's body had been devoured by wild animals. No sooner had the news of the transfer of the remains of the Báb and of His fellow-sufferer been communicated to Bahá'u'lláh than He ordered that same Sulaymán Khán to bring them to Ṭihrán, where they were taken to the Imám-Zádih-Ḥasan, from whence they were removed to different places, until the time when, in pursuance of 'Abdu'l-Bahá's instructions, they were transferred to the Holy

Land, and were permanently and ceremoniously laid to rest by Him in a specially erected mausoleum on the slopes of Mt. Carmel.

Shoghi Effendi, *God Passes By*, p. 54.

The Martyrdom of Ṭáhirih

One night, aware that the hour of her death was at hand, she put on the attire of a bride, and anointed herself with perfume, and, sending for the wife of the Kalantar, she communicated to her the secret of her impending martyrdom, and confided to her last wishes. Then, closeting herself in her chambers, she awaited, in prayer and meditation, the hour which was to witness her reunion with her Beloved. She was pacing the floor of her room, chanting a litany expressive of both grief and triumph, when the farráshes of 'Azíz Khán-i-Sardár arrived, in the dead of night, to conduct her to the Ílkhání garden, which lay beyond the city gates, and which was to be the site of her martyrdom. When she arrived the Sardár was in the midst of a drunken debauch with his lieutenants, and was roaring with laughter; he ordered offhand that she be strangled at once and thrown into a pit. With that same silken kerchief which she had intuitively reserved for that purpose, and delivered in her last moments to the son of Kalantar who accompanied her, the death of this immortal heroine was accomplished. Her body was lowered into a well, which was then filled with earth and stones, in the manner she herself had desired.

Thus ended the life of this great Bábí heroine, the first woman suffrage martyr, who, at her death, turning to the one in whose custody she had been placed, had boldly declared: "You can kill me as soon as you like, but you cannot stop the emancipation of women." Her career was as dazzling as it was brief, as tragic as it was eventful. Unlike her fellow-disciples, whose exploits remained, for the most part unknown, and unsung by their contemporaries in foreign lands, the fame of this immortal woman was noised abroad, and travelling with remarkable swiftness as far as the capitals of Western Europe, aroused the enthusiastic admiration and evoked the ardent praise of men and women of divers nationalities, callings and cultures. Little wonder that 'Abdu'l-Bahá should have joined her name to those of Sarah, of Ásíyih, of the Virgin Mary and of Fáṭimih, who, in the course of successive Dispensations, have towered, by reason of their intrinsic merits and unique position, above the rank and file of their sex.

Shoghi Effendi, *God Passes By*, p. 75.

The Influence of the Báb's Ministry Throughout the World

"Many persons from all parts of the world," is 'Abdu'l-Bahá's written assertion, "set out for Persia and began to investigate wholeheartedly the matter." The Czar of Russia, a contemporary chronicler has written, had even, shortly before the Báb's martyrdom, instructed the Russian Consul in Tabríz to fully inquire into, and report the circumstances of so startling a Movement, a commission that could not be carried out in view of the Báb's execution. In countries as remote as those of Western Europe an interest no less profound was kindled, and spread with great rapidity to literary, artistic, diplomatic and intellectual circles. "All Europe," attests the above-mentioned French publicist, "was stirred to pity and indignation ... Among the littérateurs of my generation, in the Paris of 1890, the martyrdom of the Báb was still as fresh a topic as had been the first news of His death. We wrote poems about Him. Sarah Bernhardt entreated Catulle Mendès for a play on the theme of this historic tragedy." A Russian poetess, member of the Philosophic, Oriental and Bibliological Societies of St Petersburg, published in 1903 a drama entitled "The Báb," which a year later was played in one of the principal theatres of that city, was subsequently given publicity in London, was translated into French in Paris, and into German by the poet Fiedler, was presented again, soon after the Russian Revolution, in the Folk Theatre in Leningrad, and succeeded in arousing the genuine sympathy and interest of the renowned Tolstoy, whose eulogy of the poem was later published in the Russian press.

It would indeed be no exaggeration to say that nowhere in the whole compass of the world's religious literature, except in the Gospels, do we find any record relating to the death of any of the religion-founders of the past comparable to the martyrdom suffered by the Prophet of Shíráz.

Shoghi Effendi, God Passes By, pp. 55-56.

The Ministry of Bahá'u'lláh

The second period (1853–1892) derives its inspiration from the august figure of Bahá'u'lláh, pre-eminent in holiness, awesome in the majesty of His strength and power, unapproachable in the transcendent brightness of His glory. It opens with the first stirrings, in the soul of Bahá'u'lláh while in the Síyáh-Chál of Ṭihrán, of the Revelation anticipated by the Báb, attains its plenitude in the proclamation of that Revelation to the kings and ecclesiastical leaders of the earth, and terminates in the ascension of its Author in the vicinity of the prison-town of 'Akká. It extends over thirty-nine years of continuous, of unprecedented and overpowering Revelation, is marked by the propagation of the Faith to the neighbouring territories of Turkey, of Russia, of 'Iráq, of Syria, of Egypt and of India, and is distinguished by a corresponding aggravation of hostility, represented by the united attacks launched by the Sháh of Persia and the Ṣulṭán of Turkey, the two admittedly most powerful potentates of the East, as well as by the opposition of the twin sacerdotal orders of Shí'ah and Sunní Islám.

Shoghi Effendi, God Passes By, pp. xiv-xv.

The Childhood and Early Life of Bahá'u'lláh

When Bahá'u'lláh was still a child, the Vazír, His father, dreamed a dream. Bahá'u'lláh appeared to him swimming in a vast, limitless ocean. His body shone upon the waters with a radiance that illumined the sea. Around His head, which could distinctly be seen above the waters, there radiated, in all directions, His long, jet-black locks, floating in great profusion above the waves. As he dreamed, a multitude of fishes gathered round Him, each holding fast to the extremity of one hair. Fascinated by the effulgence of His face, they followed Him in whatever direction He swam. Great as was their number, and however firmly they clung to His locks, not one single hair seemed to have been detached from His head, nor did the least injury affect His person. Free and unrestrained, He moved above the waters and they all followed Him.

The Vazír, greatly impressed by this dream, summoned a soothsayer, who had achieved fame in that region, and asked him to interpret it for him. This man, as if inspired by a premonition of the future glory of Bahá'u'lláh, declared: "The limitless ocean that you have seen in your dream, O Vazír, is none other than the world of being. Single-handed and alone, your son will achieve supreme ascendancy over it. Wherever He may please, He will proceed unhindered. No one will resist His march, no one will hinder His progress. The multitude of fishes signifies the turmoil which He will arouse amidst the peoples and kindreds of the earth. Around Him will they gather, and to Him will they cling. Assured of the unfailing protection of the Almighty, this tumult will never harm His person, nor will His loneliness upon the sea of life endanger His safety.

Nabíl-i-A'ẓam, The Dawn-Breakers, pp. 119-120.

When Bahá'u'lláh was nearly fifteen years old, His elder sister Sárih Khánum and Mírzá Mahmúd, the son of Mírzá Ismá'íl-i-Vazír of Yálrúd, were married. This Mírzá Mahmúd, who never espoused the new Faith, had a younger sister, Ásíyih Khánum: winsome, vivacious and exceedingly beautiful. As soon as she came of age, and Bahá'u'lláh was nearly eighteen, Sárih Khánum requested her father, Mírzá Buzurg, to ask the hand of this sister-in-law for her Brother, Mírzá Ḥusayn-'Alí. Their marriage took place in Jamádíyu'l-Ukhrá (Jamádíyu'th-Thání) AH 1251 (about October 1835). Ásíyih Khánum was the mother of 'Abdu'l-Bahá.

H. M. Balyuzi, Bahá'u'lláh: The King of Glory, p. 23.

The Role of Bahá'u'lláh in the Ministry of the Báb

He[20] it was Who, scarce three months after the Faith was born, received, through the envoy of the Báb, Mullá Ḥusayn, the scroll which bore to Him the first tidings of a newly announced Revelation, Who instantly acclaimed its truth, and arose to champion its cause. ... It was He Who, through His correspondence with the Author of the newly founded Faith, and His intimate association with the most distinguished amongst its disciples, such as Váhid, Ḥujjat, Quddús, Mullá Ḥusayn and Ṭáhirih, was able to foster its growth, elucidate its principles, reinforce its ethical foundations, fulfil its urgent requirements, avert some of the immediate dangers threatening it and participate effectually in its rise and consolidation. ... He it was Who, in the hey-day of His life, flinging aside every consideration of earthly fame, wealth and position, careless of danger, and risking the obloquy of His caste, arose to identify Himself, first in Ṭihrán and later in His native province of Mázindarán, with the cause of an obscure and proscribed sect; won to its support a large number of the officials and notables of Núr, not excluding His own associates and relatives ... He it was Who unobtrusively and unerringly directed the proceedings of the Conference of Bada<u>sh</u>t; Who entertained as His guests Quddús, Ṭáhirih and the eighty-one disciples who had gathered on that occasion; Who revealed every day a Tablet and bestowed on each of the participants a new name; Who faced unaided the assault of a mob of more than five hundred villagers in Níyálá ... It was exclusively to His care that the documents of the Báb, His pen-case, His seals, and agate rings, together with a scroll on which He had penned, in the form of a pentacle, no less than three hundred and sixty derivatives of the word Bahá, were delivered, in conformity with instructions He Himself had issued prior to His departure from <u>Ch</u>ihríq. It was solely due to His initiative, and in strict accordance with His instructions, that the precious remains of the Báb were safely transferred from Tabríz to the capital, and were concealed and safeguarded with the utmost secrecy and care throughout the turbulent years following His martyrdom.

Shoghi Effendi, God Passes By, pp. 66–69.

The Birth of the Bahá'í Revelation

*O*ne day I remember well, though I was only six years old at the time. It seemed that an attempt had been made on the life of the <u>Sh</u>áh by a half-crazy young Bábí.

My father was away at his country house in the village of Níyávarán, which was his property, the villagers of which were all and individually cared for by him.

Suddenly and hurriedly a servant came rushing in great distress to my mother.

The master, the master, he is arrested—I have seen him! He has walked many miles! Oh, they have beaten him! They say he has suffered the torture of the bastinado! His feet are bleeding! He has no shoes on! His turban has gone! His clothes are torn! There are chains upon his neck!

Words of Bahíyyih <u>Kh</u>ánum, Lady Blomfield, The Chosen Highway, pp. 40–41.

*E*very day Our gaolers, entering Our cell, would call the name of one of Our companions, bidding him arise and follow them to the foot of the gallows. With what eagerness would the owner of that name respond to that solemn call! Relieved of his chains, he would spring to his feet and, in a state of uncontrollable delight, would approach and embrace Us. We would seek to comfort him with the assurance of an everlasting life in the world beyond, and filling his heart with hope and joy, would send him forth to win the crown of glory. He would embrace, in turn, the rest of his fellow-prisoners and then proceed to die as dauntlessly as he had lived.

Words of Bahá'u'lláh, Nabíl-i-A'ẓam, The Dawn-Breakers, pp. 632–633.

*A*s to the subterranean dungeon into which He was thrown, and which originally had served as a reservoir of water for one of the public baths of the capital, let His own words, recorded in His *Epistle to the Son of the Wolf*, bear testimony to the ordeal which He endured in that pestilential hole. *"We were consigned for four months to a place* foul beyond comparison .... Upon Our arrival We were first conducted along a pitch-black corridor, from whence We descended three steep flights of stairs to the place of confinement assigned to Us. The dungeon was wrapped in thick darkness, and Our fellow-prisoners numbered nearly one hundred and fifty souls: thieves, assassins and highwaymen. Though crowded, it had no other outlet than the passage by which We entered. No pen can depict that place, nor any tongue describe its loathsome smell. Most of those men had neither clothes nor bedding to lie on. God alone knoweth what befell Us in that most foul-smelling and gloomy place!" Bahá'u'lláh's feet were placed in stocks, and around His neck were fastened the Qará-Guhar chains of such galling weight that their mark remained imprinted upon His body all the days of His life. ... The place was chill and damp, filthy, fever-stricken, infested with vermin, and filled with a noisome stench. Animated by a relentless hatred His enemies went even so far as to intercept and poison His food, in the hope of obtaining the favour of the mother of their sovereign, His most implacable foe—an attempt which, though it impaired His health for years to come, failed to achieve its purpose.

Shoghi Effendi, *God Passes By*, pp. 71-72.

... *A*t so critical an hour and under such appalling circumstances the *"Most Great Spirit,"* as designated by Himself, and symbolized in the Zoroastrian, the Mosaic, the Christian, and Muḥammadan Dispensations by the Sacred Fire, the Burning Bush, the Dove and the Angel Gabriel respectively, descended upon, and revealed itself, personated by a *"Maiden,"* to the agonized soul of Bahá'u'lláh.

"*One night in a dream,*" He Himself, calling to mind, in the evening of His life, the first stirrings of God's Revelation within His soul, has written, "*these exalted words were heard on every side: 'Verily, We shall render Thee victorious by Thyself and by Thy pen. Grieve Thou not for that which hath befallen Thee, neither be Thou afraid, for Thou art in safety. Ere long will God raise up the treasures of the earth—men who will aid Thee through Thyself and through Thy Name, wherewith God hath revived the hearts of such as have recognized Him.'*"

Shoghi Effendi, *God Passes By*, p. 101.

*I*n His Súratu'l-Haykal (the Súrih of the Temple) He thus describes those breathless moments when the Maiden, symbolizing the *"Most Great Spirit"* proclaimed His mission to the entire creation: "*While engulfed in tribulations I heard a most wondrous, a most sweet voice, calling above My head. Turning My face, I beheld a Maiden—the embodiment of the remembrance of the name of My Lord—suspended in the air before Me. So rejoiced was she in her very soul that her countenance shone with the ornament of the good-pleasure of God, and her cheeks glowed with the brightness of the All-Merciful. Betwixt earth and heaven she was raising a call which captivated the hearts and minds of men. She was imparting to both My inward and outer being tidings which rejoiced My soul, and the souls of God's honoured servants. Pointing with her finger unto My head, she addressed all who are in heaven and all who are on earth, saying: 'By God! This is the Best-Beloved of the worlds, and yet ye comprehend not. This is the Beauty of God* amongst you, and the power of His sovereignty within you, could ye but understand. This is the Mystery of God and His Treasure, the Cause of God and His glory unto all who are in the kingdoms of Revelation and of creation, if ye be of them that perceive.'"

Shoghi Effendi, God Passes By, pp. 101-102.

The Exile of Bahá'u'lláh to 'Iráq

On the first day of the month of Rabí'u'th-Thání, of the year AH 1269, (12 January 1853), nine months after His return from Kárbilá, Bahá'u'lláh, together with some of the members of His family, and escorted by an officer of the Imperial body-guard and an official representing the Russian Legation, set out on His three months' journey to Baghdád. Among those who shared His exile was His wife, the saintly Navváb, entitled by Him the "Most Exalted Leaf," who, during almost forty years, continued to evince a fortitude, a piety, a devotion and a nobility of soul which earned her from the pen of her Lord the posthumous and unrivalled tribute of having been made His *"perpetual consort in all the worlds of God."* His nine-year-old son, later surnamed the "Most Great Branch," destined to become the Centre of His Covenant and authorized Interpreter of His teachings, together with His seven-year-old sister, known in later years by the same title as that of her illustrious mother, and whose services until the ripe old age of four score years and six, no less than her exalted parentage, entitle her to the distinction of ranking as the outstanding heroine of the Bahá'í Dispensation, were also included among the exiles who were now bidding their last farewell to their native country. Of the two brothers who accompanied Him on that journey the first was Mírzá Músá, commonly called Áqáy-i-Kalím, His staunch and valued supporter, the ablest and most distinguished among His brothers and sisters, and one of the *"only two persons who,"* according to Bahá'u'lláh's testimony, *"were adequately informed of the origins"* of His Faith. The other was Mírzá Muhammad-Qulí, a half-brother, who, in spite of the defection of some of his relatives, remained to the end loyal to the Cause he had espoused.

Shoghi Effendi, God Passes By, p. 108.

This journey was filled with indescribable difficulties. My mother had no experience, no servants, no provisions and very little money left. My father was extremely ill, not having recovered from the ordeals of the torture and the prison. No one of all our friends and relations dared to come to our help, or even to say good-bye, but one old lady, the grandmother of Ásíyih Khánum.

... At length we started on that fearful journey, which lasted about four weeks; the weather was bitterly cold, snow was upon the ground.

On the way to Baghdád we sometimes encamped in wilderness places, but in that month of December, the cold was intense and we were not well prepared!

Words of Bahíyyih Khánum, Lady Blomfield, The Chosen Highway, pp. 45-46.

The Withdrawal of Bahá'u'lláh to Kurdistán

*O*ne such crisis which, as it deepened, threatened to jeopardize His new-born Faith and to subvert its earliest foundations, overshadowed the first years of His sojourn in 'Iráq, the initial stage in His life-long exile, and imparted to them a special significance. Unlike those which preceded it, this crisis was purely internal in character, and was occasioned solely by the acts, the ambitions and follies of those who were numbered among His recognized fellow-disciples.

Shoghi Effendi, God Passes By, p. 111.

*A*s the character of the professed adherents of the Báb declined and as proofs of the deepening confusion that afflicted them multiplied, the mischief-makers, who were lying in wait, and whose sole aim was to exploit the progressive deterioration in the situation for their own benefit, grew ever more and more audacious. The conduct of Mírzá Yaḥyá, who claimed to be the successor of the Báb, and who prided himself on his high sounding titles of Mir'atu'l-Azalíyyih (Everlasting Mirror), of Ṣubḥ-i-Azal (Morning of Eternity), and of Ismu'l-Azal (Name of Eternity), and particularly the machinations of Siyyid Muḥammad, exalted by him to the rank of the first among the "Witnesses" of the *Bayán*, were by now assuming such a character that the prestige of the Faith was becoming directly involved, and its future security seriously imperilled.

Shoghi Effendi, God Passes By, p. 114.

A clandestine opposition, whose aim was to nullify every effort exerted, and frustrate every design conceived, by Bahá'u'lláh for the rehabilitation of a distracted community, could now be clearly discerned. Insinuations, whose purpose was to sow the seeds of doubt and suspicion and to represent Him as a usurper, as the subverter of the laws instituted by the Báb, and the wrecker of His Cause, were being incessantly circulated.

Shoghi Effendi, God Passes By, p. 117.

*A*ttired in the garb of a traveller, coarsely clad, taking with Him nothing but his kashkúl (alms-bowl) and a change of clothes, and assuming the name of Darvísh Muḥammad, Bahá'u'lláh retired to the wilderness, and lived for a time on a mountain named Sar-Galú, so far removed from human habitations that only twice a year, at seed sowing and harvest time, it was visited by the peasants of that region. Alone and undisturbed, He passed a considerable part of His retirement on the top of that mountain in a rude structure, made of stone, which served those peasants as a shelter against the extremities of the weather.

Shoghi Effendi, God Passes By, p. 120.

*W*hen Bahá'u'lláh arrived in Sulaymáníyyih none at first, owing to the strict silence and reserve He maintained, suspected Him of being possessed of any learning or wisdom. It was only accidentally, through seeing a specimen of His exquisite penmanship shown to them by one of the students who waited upon Him, that the curiosity of the learned instructors and students of that seminary was aroused, and they were impelled to approach Him and test the degree of His knowledge and the extent of His familiarity with the arts and sciences current amongst them. That seat of learning had been renowned for its vast endowments, its numerous takyihs, and its association with Saláhí'd-Dín-i-Ayyúbí and his descendants; from it some of the most illustrious exponents of Sunní Islám had gone forth to teach its precepts, and now a delegation, headed by Shaykh Ismá'íl himself, and consisting of its most eminent doctors and most distinguished students, called upon Bahá'u'lláh, and, finding Him willing to reply to any questions they might wish to address Him, they requested Him to elucidate for them, in the course of several interviews, the abstruse passages contained in the Futúḥát-i-Makkíyyih, the celebrated work of the famous Shaykh Muḥyi'd-Dín-i-'Arabí. *"God is My witness,"* was Bahá'u'lláh's instant reply to the learned delegation, *"that I have never seen the book you refer to. I regard, however, through the power of God, ... whatever you wish me to do as easy of accomplishment."* ...

Amazed by the profundity of His insight and the compass of His understanding, they were impelled to seek from Him what they considered to be a conclusive and final evidence of the unique power and knowledge which He now appeared in their eyes to possess. "No one among the mystics, the wise, and the learned," they claimed, while requesting this further favour from Him, "has hitherto proved himself capable of writing a poem in a rhyme and meter identical with that of the longer of the two odes, entitled Qaṣídiy-i-Tá'iyyih composed by Ibn-i-Faríd. We beg you to write for us a poem in that same meter and rhyme." This request was complied with, and no less than two thousand verses, in exactly the manner they had specified, were dictated by Him, out of which He selected one hundred and twenty-seven, which He permitted them to keep, deeming the subject matter of the rest premature and unsuitable to the needs of the times. It is these same one hundred and twenty-seven verses that constitute the Qaṣídiy-i-Varqá'íyyih, so familiar to, and widely circulated amongst, His Arabic speaking followers.

Such was their reaction to this marvellous demonstration of the sagacity and genius of Bahá'u'lláh that they unanimously acknowledged every single verse of that poem to be endowed with a force, beauty and power far surpassing anything contained in either the major or minor odes composed by that celebrated poet.

This episode, by far the most outstanding among the events that transpired during the two years of Bahá'u'lláh's absence from Baghdád, immensely stimulated the interest with which an increasing number of the 'ulamás, the scholars, the Shaykhs, the doctors, the holy men and princes who had congregated in the seminaries of Sulaymáníyyih and Kárkúk, were now following His daily activities. Through His numerous discourses and epistles He disclosed new vistas to their eyes, resolved the perplexities that agitated their minds, unfolded the inner meaning of many hitherto obscure passages in the writings of various commentators, poets and theologians, of which they had remained unaware, and reconciled the seemingly contradictory assertions which abounded in these dissertations, poems and treatises.

Shoghi Effendi, *God Passes By*, pp. 122-124.

Return to Baghdád

*W*ithin a few years after Bahá'u'lláh's return from Sulaymáníyyih the situation had been completely reversed. The house of Sulaymán-i-Ghannam, on which the official designation of the Bayt-i-A'ẓam (the Most Great House) was later conferred, known, at that time, as the house of Mírzá Músá, the Bábí, an extremely modest residence, situated in the Karkh quarter, in the neighbourhood of the western bank of the river, to which Bahá'u'lláh's family had moved prior to His return from Kurdistán, had now become the focal centre of a great number of seekers, visitors and pilgrims, including Kurds, Persians, Arabs and Turks, and derived from the Muslim, the Jewish and Christian Faiths. It had, moreover, become a veritable sanctuary to which the victims of the injustice of the official representative of the Persian government were wont to flee, in the hope of securing redress for the wrongs they had suffered.

Shoghi Effendi, *God Passes By*, pp. 129–130.

*F*oremost among the priceless treasures cast forth from the billowing ocean of Bahá'u'lláh's Revelation ranks the Kitáb-i-Íqán (Book of Certitude), revealed within the space of two days and two nights, in the closing years of that period (AH 1278—AD 1862). It was written in fulfilment of the prophecy of the Báb, Who had specifically stated that the Promised One would complete the text of the unfinished *Persian Bayán*, and in reply to the questions addressed to Bahá'u'lláh by the as yet unconverted maternal uncle of the Báb, Ḥájí Mírzá Siyyid Muḥammad, while on a visit, with his brother, Ḥájí Mírzá Ḥasan-'Alí, to Karbilá. A model of Persian prose, of a style at once original, chaste and vigorous, and remarkably lucid, both cogent in argument and matchless in its irresistible eloquence, this Book, setting forth in outline the Grand Redemptive Scheme of God, occupies a position unequalled by any work in the entire range of Bahá'í literature, except the *Kitáb-i-Aqdas*, Bahá'u'lláh's Most Holy Book.

... Well may it be claimed that of all the books revealed by the Author of the Bahá'í Revelation, this Book alone, by sweeping away the age-long barriers that have so insurmountably separated the great religions of the world, has laid down a broad and unassailable foundation for the complete and permanent reconciliation of their followers.

Next to this unique repository of inestimable treasures must rank that marvellous collection of gem-like utterances, the *Hidden Words* with which Bahá'u'lláh was inspired, as He paced, wrapped in His meditations, the banks of the Tigris. ...

To these two outstanding contributions to the world's religious literature, occupying respectively, positions of unsurpassed pre-eminence among the doctrinal and ethical writings of the Author of the Bahá'í Dispensation, was added, during that same period, a treatise that may well be regarded as His greatest mystical composition, designated as the *Seven Valleys*, which He wrote in answer to the questions of Shaykh Muḥyi'd-Dín, the Qáḍí of Khániqayn, in which He describes the seven stages which the soul of the seeker must needs traverse ere it can attain the object of its existence.

Shoghi Effendi, *God Passes By*, pp. 138–140.

*M*any learned and interesting people gathered round Bahá'u'lláh ... As he spoke to them of the 'Most Great Peace' which will come to the world, and showed his kindness to all who were in trouble and in want, and became known to the poor as 'Our Father of Compassion', they understood how it was that for the teaching of true peace and brotherhood and loving-kindness he was driven into exile, and all his vast possessions taken from him.

Words of Bahíyyih Khánum, Lady Blomfield, *The Chosen Highway*, pp. 56–57.

I know not how to explain it, were all the sorrows of the world to be crowded into my heart they would, I feel, all vanish, when in the presence of Bahá'u'lláh. It is as if I had entered Paradise itself.

Words of Prince Zaynu'l-'Abidín Khán, Shoghi Effendi, *God Passes By*, p. 135.

*T*he undeniable evidences of the range and magnificence of Bahá'u'lláh's rising power; His rapidly waxing prestige; the miraculous transformation which, by precept and example, He had effected in the outlook and character of His companions from Baghdád to the remotest towns and hamlets in Persia; the consuming love for Him that glowed in their bosoms; the prodigious volume of writings that streamed day and night from His pen, could not fail to fan into flame the animosity which smouldered in the breasts of His Shí'ah and Sunní enemies.

Shoghi Effendi, *God Passes By*, p. 141.

*B*alked in his repeated attempts to achieve his malevolent purpose, Shaykh 'Abdu'l-Ḥusayn now diverted his energies into a new channel. He promised his accomplice he would raise him to the rank of a minister of the crown, if he succeeded in inducing the government to recall Bahá'u'lláh to Ṭihrán, and cast Him again into prison. He despatched lengthy and almost daily reports to the immediate entourage of the Sháh. He painted extravagant pictures of the ascendancy enjoyed by Bahá'u'lláh by representing Him as having won the allegiance of the nomadic tribes of 'Iráq. He claimed that He was in a position to muster, in a day, fully one hundred thousand men ready to take up arms at His bidding. He accused Him of meditating, in conjunction with various leaders in Persia, an insurrection against the sovereign. By such means as these he succeeded in bringing sufficient pressure on the authorities in Ṭihrán to induce the Sháh to grant him a mandate, bestowing on him full powers, and enjoining the Persian 'ulamás and functionaries to render him every assistance. This mandate the Shaykh instantly forwarded to the ecclesiastics of Najaf and Kárbilá, asking them to convene a gathering in Káẓimayn, the place of his residence. A concourse of shaykhs, mullás and mujtahids, eager to curry favour with the sovereign, promptly responded. Upon being informed of the purpose for which they had been summoned, they determined to declare a holy war against the colony of exiles, and by launching a sudden and general assault on it to destroy the Faith at its heart. To their amazement and disappointment, however, they found that the leading mujtahid amongst them, the celebrated Shaykh Murtaḍáy-i-Anṣárí, a man renowned for his tolerance, his wisdom, his undeviating justice, his piety and nobility of character, refused, when apprized of their designs, to pronounce the necessary sentence against the Bábís. ...

Frustrated in their designs, but unrelenting in their hostility, the assembled divines delegated the learned and devout Ḥájí Mullá Ḥasan-i-'Ammú, recognized for his integrity and wisdom, to submit various questions to Bahá'u'lláh for elucidation. When these were submitted, and answers completely satisfactory to the messenger were given, Ḥájí Mullá Ḥasan, affirming the recognition by the 'ulamás of the vastness of the knowledge of Bahá'u'lláh, asked, as an evidence of the truth of His mission, for a miracle that would satisfy completely all concerned. *"Although you have no right to ask this,"* Bahá'u'lláh replied, *"for God should test His creatures, and they should not test God, still I allow and accept this request .... The 'ulamás must assemble, and, with one accord, choose one miracle, and write that, after the performance of this miracle they will no longer entertain doubts about Me, and that all will acknowledge and confess the truth of My Cause. Let them seal this paper, and bring it to Me. This must be the accepted criterion: if the miracle is performed, no doubt will remain for them; and if not, We shall be convicted of imposture."* This clear, challenging and courageous reply, unexampled in the annals of any religion, and addressed to the most illustrious Shí'ah divines, assembled in their time-honoured stronghold, was so satisfactory to their envoy that he instantly arose, kissed the knee of Bahá'u'lláh, and departed to deliver His message. Three days later he sent word that that august assemblage had failed to arrive at a decision, and had chosen to drop the matter, a decision to which he himself later gave wide publicity, in the course of his visit to Persia, and even communicated it in person to the then Minister of Foreign Affairs, Mírzá Sa'íd Khán.

Shoghi Effendi, God Passes By, pp. 143-144.

The nine months of unremitting endeavour exerted by His enemies, and particularly by Shaykh 'Abdu'l-Ḥusayn and his confederate Mírzá Buzurg Khán, were about to yield their fruit. Náṣiri'd-Dín Sháh and his ministers, on the one hand, and the Persian Ambassador in Constantinople, on the other, were incessantly urged to take immediate action to insure Bahá'u'lláh's removal from Baghdád.

Shoghi Effendi, God Passes By, p. 146.

The Declaration of Bahá'u'lláh

The arrival of Bahá'u'lláh in the Najíbíyyih Garden, subsequently designated by His followers the Garden of Riḍván, signalizes the commencement of what has come to be recognized as the holiest and most significant of all Bahá'í festivals, the festival commemorating the Declaration of His Mission to His companions. So momentous a Declaration may well be regarded both as the logical consummation of that revolutionizing process which was initiated by Himself upon His return from Sulaymáníyyih, and as a prelude to the final proclamation of that same Mission to the world and its rulers from Adrianople.

Shoghi Effendi, God Passes By, p. 151.

Undaunted by the prospect of the appalling adversities which, as predicted by Himself, were soon to overtake Him; on the eve of a second banishment which would be fraught with many hazards and perils, and would bring Him still farther from His native land, the cradle of His Faith, to a country alien in race, in language and in culture; acutely conscious of the extension of the circle of His adversaries, among whom were soon to be numbered a monarch more despotic than Náṣiri'd-Dín Sháh, and ministers no less unyielding in their hostility than either Ḥájí Mírzá Áqásí or the Amir-Niẓám; undeterred by the perpetual interruptions occasioned by the influx of a host of visitors who thronged His tent, Bahá'u'lláh chose in that critical and seemingly unpropitious hour to advance so challenging a claim, to lay bare the mystery surrounding His person, and to assume, in their plenitude, the power and the authority which were the exclusive privileges of the One Whose advent the Báb had prophesied.

Shoghi Effendi, God Passes By, p. 152.

*A*s to the significance of that Declaration let Bahá'u'lláh Himself reveal to us its import. Acclaiming that historic occasion as the *"Most Great Festival,"* the *"King of Festivals,"* the *"Festival of God,"* He has, in His *Kitáb-i-Aqdas*, characterized it as the Day whereon *"all created things were immersed in the sea of purification,"* whilst in one of His specific Tablets, He has referred to it as the Day whereon *"the breezes of forgiveness were wafted over the entire creation." "Rejoice, with exceeding gladness, O people of Bahá!"*, He, in another Tablet, has written, *"as ye call to remembrance the Day of supreme felicity, the Day whereon the Tongue of the Ancient of Days hath spoken, as He departed from His House proceeding to the Spot from which He shed upon the whole of creation the splendours of His Name, the All-Merciful ..."*

Shoghi Effendi, God Passes By, pp. 153-154.

*I*n the Rose Garden of changeless splendour a Flower hath begun to bloom, compared to which every other flower is but a thorn, and before the brightness of Whose glory the very essence of beauty must pale and wither. Arise, therefore, and, with the whole enthusiasm of your hearts, with all the eagerness of your souls, the full fervour of your will, and the concentrated efforts of your entire being, strive to attain the paradise of His presence, and endeavour to inhale the fragrance of the incorruptible Flower, to breathe the sweet savours of holiness, and to obtain a portion of this perfume of celestial glory

Bahá'u'lláh, Gleanings from the Writings of Bahá'u'lláh, section CLI, pp. 320-321.

The Exile to Constantinople

*M*ounted on his steed, a red roan stallion of the finest breed, the best His lovers could purchase for Him, and leaving behind Him a bowing multitude of fervent admirers, He rode forth on the first stage of a journey that was to carry Him to the city of Constantinople. "Numerous were the heads," Nabíl himself a witness ... "which, on every side, bowed to the dust at the feet of His horse, and kissed its hoofs, and countless were those who pressed forward to embrace His stirrups." "How great the number of those embodiments of fidelity, testifies a fellow-traveller, "who, casting themselves before that charger, preferred death to separation from their Beloved!"

Eyewitness accounts of Bahá'u'lláh leaving The Garden of Riḍván in Baghdád. Shoghi Effendi,
God Passes By, p. 155.

*T*he same tokens of devotion shown to Bahá'u'lláh at the time of His departure from His House, and later from the Garden of Riḍván, were repeated when, on the 20th of Dhi'l-Qa'dih (9 May 1863), accompanied by members of His family and twenty-six of His disciples, He left Firayját, His first stopping-place in the course of that journey. A caravan, consisting of fifty mules, a mounted guard of ten soldiers with their officer, and seven pairs of howdahs, each pair surmounted by four parasols, was formed, and wended its way, by easy stages, and in the space of no less than a hundred and ten days, across the uplands, and through the defiles, the woods, valleys and pastures, comprising the picturesque scenery of eastern Anatolia, to the port of Sámsún, on the Black Sea.

Shoghi Effendi, *God Passes By*, pp. 155-156.

*W*ith the arrival of Bahá'u'lláh at Constantinople, the capital of the Ottoman Empire and seat of the Caliphate (acclaimed by the Muḥammadans as "the Dome of Islám," but stigmatized by Him as the spot whereon the *"throne of tyranny"* had been established) the grimmest and most calamitous and yet the most glorious chapter in the history of the first Bahá'í century may be said to have opened. A period in which untold privations and unprecedented trials were mingled with the noblest spiritual triumphs was now commencing. The day-star of Bahá'u'lláh's ministry was about to reach its zenith. The most momentous years of the Heroic Age of His Dispensation were at hand. The catastrophic process, foreshadowed as far back as the year sixty by His Forerunner in the Qayyúmu'l-Asmá', was beginning to be set in motion.

Shoghi Effendi, *God Passes By*, p. 157.

The Exile of Bahá'u'lláh to Adrianople

... *I*n the Garden of Riḍván, on the eve of His banishment to Constantinople, the ten-year delay, ordained by an inscrutable Providence, had been terminated through the Declaration of His Mission and the visible emergence of what was to become the nucleus of a world-embracing Fellowship. What now remained to be achieved was the proclamation, in the city of Adrianople, of that same Mission to the world's secular and ecclesiastical leaders ....

Shoghi Effendi, *God Passes By*, p. 158.

*T*he initial phase of that Proclamation may be said to have opened in Constantinople with the communication (the text of which we, alas, do not possess) addressed by Bahá'u'lláh to Sulṭán 'Abdu'l-'Azíz himself, the self-styled vicar of the Prophet of Islám and the absolute ruler of a mighty empire. So potent, so august a personage was the first among the sovereigns of the world to receive the Divine Summons, and the first among Oriental monarchs to sustain the impact of God's retributive justice. The occasion for this communication was provided by the infamous edict the Sulṭán had promulgated, less than four months after the arrival of the exiles in his capital, banishing them, suddenly and without any justification whatsoever, in the depth of winter, and in the most humiliating circumstances, to Adrianople, situated on the extremities of his empire.

Shoghi Effendi, *God Passes By*, pp. 158-159.

No less a personage than the highly-respected brother-in-law of the Ṣadr-i-A'ẓam was commissioned to apprize the Captive of the edict pronounced against Him—an edict which evinced a virtual coalition of the Turkish and Persian imperial governments against a common adversary, and which in the end brought such tragic consequences upon the Ṣulṭánate, the Caliphate and the Qájár dynasty.

Shoghi Effendi, *God Passes By*, pp. 159-160.

The Rebellion of Mírzá Yaḥyá

... The monstrous behaviour of Mírzá Yaḥyá, one of the half-brothers of Bahá'u'lláh, the nominee of the Báb, and recognized chief of the Bábí community, brought in its wake a period of travail which left its mark on the fortunes of the Faith for no less than half a century. ... It perplexed and confused the friends and supporters of Bahá'u'lláh, and seriously damaged the prestige of the Faith in the eyes of its western admirers. ... It brought incalculable sorrow to Bahá'u'lláh, visibly aged Him, and inflicted, through its repercussions, the heaviest blow ever sustained by Him in His lifetime.

Shoghi Effendi, *God Passes By*, pp. 163-164.

A constant witness of the ever deepening attachment of the exiles to Bahá'u'lláh and of their amazing veneration for Him ... allowing himself[21] to be duped by the enticing prospects of unfettered leadership held out to him by Siyyid Muḥammad, the Antichrist of the Bahá'í Revelation, ... this arch-breaker of the Covenant of the Báb, spurred on by his mounting jealousy and impelled by his passionate love of leadership, was driven to perpetrate such acts as defied either concealment or toleration.

Shoghi Effendi, *God Passes By*, pp. 164-165.

Desperate designs to poison Bahá'u'lláh and His companions, and thereby reanimate his own defunct leadership, began, approximately a year after their arrival in Adrianople, to agitate his mind. Well aware of the erudition of his half-brother, Áqáy-i-Kalím, in matters pertaining to medicine, he, under various pretexts, sought enlightenment from him regarding the effects of certain herbs and poisons, and then began, contrary to his wont, to invite Bahá'u'lláh to his home, where, one day, having smeared His tea-cup with a substance he had concocted, he succeeded in poisoning Him sufficiently to produce a serious illness which lasted no less than a month, and which was accompanied by severe pains and high fever, the aftermath of which left Bahá'u'lláh with a shaking hand till the end of His life.

Shoghi Effendi, *God Passes By*, p. 165.

The moment had now arrived for Him Who had so recently, both verbally and in numerous Tablets, revealed the implications of the claims He had advanced, to acquaint formally the one who was the nominee of the Báb with the character of His Mission. Mírzá

Áqá Ján was accordingly commissioned to bear to Mírzá Yaḥyá the newly revealed Súriy-i-Amr, which unmistakably affirmed those claims, to read aloud to him its contents, and demand an unequivocal and conclusive reply. Mírzá Yaḥyá's request for a one day respite, during which he could meditate his answer, was granted. The only reply, however, that was forthcoming was a counter-declaration, specifying the hour and the minute in which he had been made the recipient of an independent Revelation, necessitating the unqualified submission to him of the peoples of the earth in both the East and the West.

So presumptuous an assertion, made by so perfidious an adversary to the envoy of the Bearer of so momentous a Revelation was the signal for the open and final rupture between Bahá'u'lláh and Mírzá Yaḥyá—a rupture that marks one of the darkest dates in Bahá'í history. Wishing to allay the fierce animosity that blazed in the bosom of His enemies, and to assure to each one of the exiles a complete freedom to choose between Him and them, Bahá'u'lláh withdrew with His family to the house of Riḍá Big (Shavval 22, AH 1282), which was rented by His order, and refused, for two months, to associate with either friend or stranger, including His own companions. He instructed Áqáy-i-Kalím to divide all the furniture, bedding, clothing and utensils that were to be found in His home, and send half to the house of Mírzá Yaḥyá; to deliver to him certain relics he had long coveted, such as the seals, rings, and manuscripts in the handwriting of the Báb; and to insure that he received his full share of the allowance fixed by the government for the maintenance of the exiles and their families. He, moreover, directed Áqáy-i-Kalím to order to attend to Mírzá Yaḥyá's shopping, for several hours a day, any one of the companions whom he himself might select, and to assure him that whatever would henceforth be received in his name from Persia would be delivered into his own hands.

Shoghi Effendi, God Passes By, pp. 166-167.

Bahá'u'lláh's reaction to this most distressful episode in His ministry was, as already observed, characterized by acute anguish. *"He who for months and years,"* He laments, *"I reared with the hand of loving-kindness hath risen to take My life."* *"The cruelties inflicted by My oppressors,"* He wrote, in allusion to these perfidious enemies, *"have bowed Me down, and turned My hair white. Shouldst thou present thyself before My throne, thou wouldst fail to recognize the Ancient Beauty for the freshness of His countenance is altered, and its brightness hath faded, by reason of the oppression of the infidels."*

Shoghi Effendi, God Passes By, p. 169.

Nor can this subject be dismissed without special reference being made to the Arch-Breaker of the Covenant of the Báb, Mírzá Yaḥyá, who lived long enough to witness, while eking out a miserable existence in Cyprus, termed by the Turks "the Island of Satan," every hope he had so maliciously conceived reduced to naught. ... Eleven of the eighteen "Witnesses" he had appointed forsook him and turned in repentance to Bahá'u'lláh. He himself became involved in a scandal which besmirched his reputation and that of his eldest son, ... It was this same eldest son who, through the workings of a strange destiny, sought years after, together with his nephew and niece, the presence of 'Abdu'l-Bahá, the appointed Successor of Bahá'u'lláh and Centre of His Covenant, expressed repentance, prayed for forgiveness, was graciously accepted by Him, and remained, till the hour of his death, a loyal follower of the Faith which his father had so foolishly, so shamelessly and so pitifully striven to extinguish.

Shoghi Effendi, *God Passes By*, p. 233.

The Proclamation of Bahá'u'lláh

*A*lmost immediately after the "Most Great Separation" had been effected, the weightiest Tablets associated with His sojourn in Adrianople were revealed. The Súriy-i-Múlúk, the most momentous Tablet revealed by Bahá'u'lláh (Súrih of Kings) in which He, for the first time, directs His words collectively to the entire company of the monarchs of East and West, and in which the Sultán of Turkey, and his ministers, the kings of Christendom, the French and Persian Ambassadors accredited to the Sublime Porte, the Muslim ecclesiastical leaders in Constantinople, its wise men and inhabitants, the people of Persia and the philosophers of the world are separately addressed; the *Kitáb-i-Badí'*, His apologia, written to refute the accusations levelled against Him by Mírzá Mihdíy-i-Rashtí, corresponding to the *Kitáb-i-Íqán*, revealed in defence of the Bábí Revelation; the Munájátháy-i-Şíyám (Prayers for Fasting), written in anticipation of the Book of His Laws; the first Tablet to Napoleon III, in which the Emperor of the French is addressed and the sincerity of his professions put to the test; the *Lawḥ-i-Sultán*, His detailed epistle to Náṣiri'd-Dín Sháh, in which the aims, purposes and principles of His Faith are expounded and the validity of His Mission demonstrated; the Súriy-i-Ra'ís, begun in the village of Káshánih on His way to Gallipoli, and completed shortly after at Gyáwur-Kyuy—these may be regarded not only as the most outstanding among the innumerable Tablets revealed in Adrianople, but as occupying a foremost position among all the writings of the Author of the Bahá'í Revelation.

Shoghi Effendi, *God Passes By*, pp. 171-172.

Bahá'u'lláh's Incarceration in 'Akká

*T*he fateful decision was eventually arrived at to banish Bahá'u'lláh to the penal colony of 'Akká, and Mírzá Yaḥyá to Famagusta in Cyprus. This decision was embodied in a strongly worded Farmán, issued by Sulṭán 'Abdu'l-'Azíz.

Shoghi Effendi, *God Passes By*, p. 179.

*S*o grievous were the dangers and trials confronting Bahá'u'lláh at the hour of His departure from Gallipoli that He warned His companions that "*this journey will be unlike any of the previous journeys*" and that whoever did not feel himself "*man enough to face the future*" had best "*depart to whatever place he pleaseth, and be preserved from tests, for hereafter he will find himself unable to leave*"—a warning which His companions unanimously chose to disregard.

Shoghi Effendi, *God Passes By*, p. 182.

*A*ll the townspeople had assembled to see the arrival of the prisoners ... Their yelling of curses and execrations filled us with fresh misery.

We were taken to the old fortress of 'Akká, where we were crowded together. There was no air; a small quantity of very bad coarse bread was provided; we were unable to get fresh water to drink; our sufferings were not diminished. Then an epidemic of typhoid broke out. Nearly all became ill.

Words of Bahíyyih Khánum, Lady Blomfield, *The Chosen Highway*, p. 66.

*B*ahá'u'lláh and His family were imprisoned in three little rooms, up many steps, for two years.

Words of Bahíyyih Khánum, Lady Blomfield, *The Chosen Highway*, p. 67.

*E*xplicit orders had been issued by the Sultán and his ministers to subject the exiles, who were accused of having grievously erred and led others far astray, to the strictest confinement. Hopes were confidently expressed that the sentence of life-long imprisonment pronounced against them would lead to their eventual extermination. The farmán of Sultán 'Abdu'l-'Azíz, dated the fifth of Rabí'u'th-Thání AH 1285 (26 July 1868), not only condemned them to perpetual banishment, but stipulated their strict incarceration, and forbade them to associate either with each other or with the local inhabitants. The text of the farmán itself was read publicly, soon after the arrival of the exiles, in the principal mosque of the city as a warning to the population.

Shoghi Effendi, *God Passes By*, p. 186.

*T*he writings of Bahá'u'lláh during this period, as we survey the vast field which they embrace, seem to fall into three distinct categories. The first comprises those writings which constitute the sequel to the proclamation of His Mission in Adrianople. The second includes the laws and ordinances of His Dispensation, which, for the most part, have been recorded in the *Kitáb-i-Aqdas*, His Most Holy Book. To the third must be assigned those Tablets which partly enunciate and partly reaffirm the fundamental tenets and principles underlying that Dispensation.

Shoghi Effendi, *God Passes By*, pp. 205-206.

O Queen in London! Incline thine ear unto the voice of thy Lord, the Lord of all mankind, calling from the Divine Lote-Tree: Verily, no God is there but Me, the Almighty, the All-Wise! ... He in truth, hath come unto the world in His most great glory, and all that hath been mentioned in the Gospel hath been fulfilled.

Bahá'u'lláh, Tablet to Queen Victoria, *Epistle to the Son of the Wolf*, pp. 59-60.[22]

O Kings of the earth! ...

Now that ye have refused the Most Great Peace, hold ye fast unto this, the Lesser Peace, that haply ye may in some degree better your own condition and that of your dependents.

Bahá'u'lláh, Tablet to Queen Victoria, *Gleanings from the Writings of Bahá'u'lláh*, section CXIX, pp. 253-254.[23]

---

22   Also *The Proclamation of Bahá'u'lláh*, p. 33.
23   Also *The Proclamation of Bahá'u'lláh*, p. 12

O Ye the elected representatives of the people in every land! ...

... That which the Lord hath ordained as the sovereign remedy and mightiest instrument for the healing of all the world is the union of all its peoples in one universal Cause, one common Faith. This can in no wise be achieved except through the power of a skilled, an all-powerful and inspired Physician.

Bahá'u'lláh, Tablet to Queen Victoria, *Gleanings from the Writings of Bahá'u'lláh*, section CXX, p. 254.[24]

*U*nique and stupendous as was this Proclamation, it proved to be but a prelude to a still mightier revelation of the creative power of its Author, and to what may well rank as the most signal act of His ministry—the promulgation of the *Kitáb-i-Aqdas*. ...

Revealed soon after Bahá'u'lláh had been transferred to the house of Údí Khammár (circa 1873), at a time when He was still encompassed by the tribulations that had afflicted Him, through the acts committed by His enemies and the professed adherents of His Faith, this Book, this treasury enshrining the priceless gems of His Revelation, stands out, by virtue of the principles it inculcates, the administrative institutions it ordains and the function with which it invests the appointed Successor of its Author, unique and incomparable among the world's sacred Scriptures.

Shoghi Effendi, *God Passes By*, p. 213.

The Death of Mírzá Mihdí

To the galling weight of these tribulations was now added the bitter grief of a sudden tragedy—the premature loss of the noble, the pious Mírzá Mihdí, the Purest Branch, 'Abdu'l-Bahá's twenty-two year old brother, an amanuensis of Bahá'u'lláh and a companion of His exile from the days when, as a child, he was brought from Ṭihrán to Baghdád to join his Father after His return from Sulaymáníyyih. He was pacing the roof of the barracks in the twilight, one evening, wrapped in his customary devotions, when he fell through the unguarded skylight onto a wooden crate, standing on the floor beneath, which pierced his ribs, and caused, twenty-two hours later, his death, on the 23rd of Rabí'u'l-Avval AH 1287 (23 June 1870). His dying supplication to a grieving Father was that his life might be accepted as a ransom for those who were prevented from attaining the presence of their Beloved.

In a highly significant prayer, revealed by Bahá'u'lláh in memory of His son—a prayer that exalts his death to the rank of those great acts of atonement associated with Abraham's intended sacrifice of His son, with the crucifixion of Jesus Christ and the martyrdom of the Imám Ḥusayn—we read the following: *"I have, O my Lord, offered up that which Thou hast given Me, that Thy servants may be quickened, and all that dwell on earth be united."* And, likewise, these prophetic words, addressed to His martyred son: *"Thou art the Trust of God and His Treasure in this Land. Erelong will God reveal through thee that which He hath desired."*

Shoghi Effendi, *God Passes By*, p. 188.

---

24   Also *The Proclamation of Bahá'u'lláh*, pp. 67–68

Release from Prison

*T*he gradual recognition by all elements of the population of Bahá'u'lláh's complete innocence; the slow penetration of the true spirit of His teachings through the hard crust of their indifference and bigotry; the substitution of the sagacious and humane governor, Aḥmad Big Tawfíq, for one whose mind had been hopelessly poisoned against the Faith and its followers; the unremitting labours of 'Abdu'l-Bahá, now in the full flower of His manhood, Who, through His contacts with the rank and file of the population, was increasingly demonstrating His capacity to act as the shield of His Father; the providential dismissal of the officials who had been instrumental in prolonging the confinement of the innocent companions—all paved the way for the reaction that was now setting in, a reaction with which the period of Bahá'u'lláh's banishment to 'Akká will ever remain indissolubly associated.

Such was the devotion gradually kindled in the heart of that governor, through his association with 'Abdu'l-Bahá, and later through his perusal of the literature of the Faith, which mischief-makers, in the hope of angering him, had submitted for his consideration, that he invariably refused to enter His presence without first removing his shoes, as a token of his respect for Him. It was even bruited about that his favoured counsellors were those very exiles who were the followers of the Prisoner in his custody. His own son he was wont to send to 'Abdu'l-Bahá for instruction and enlightenment. It was on the occasion of a long-sought audience with Bahá'u'lláh that, in response to a request for permission to render Him some service, the suggestion was made to him to restore the aqueduct which for thirty years had been allowed to fall into disuse—a suggestion which he immediately arose to carry out.

Shoghi Effendi, *God Passes By*, pp. 191-192.

*T*hough Bahá'u'lláh Himself practically never granted personal interviews, as He had been used to do in Baghdád, yet such was the influence He now wielded that the inhabitants openly asserted that the noticeable improvement in the climate and water of their city was directly attributable to His continued presence in their midst. The very designations by which they chose to refer to him, such as the "august leader," and "his highness" bespoke the reverence with which He inspired them. On one occasion, a European general who, together with the governor, was granted an audience by Him, was so impressed that he "remained kneeling on the ground near the door." Shaykh 'Alíy-i-Mírí, the Muftí of 'Akká, had even, at the suggestion of 'Abdu'l-Bahá, to plead insistently that He might permit the termination of His nine-year confinement within the walls of the prison-city, before He would consent to leave its gates. The garden of Na'mayn, a small island, situated in the middle of a river to the east of the city, honoured with the appellation of Riḍván, and designated by Him the *"New Jerusalem"* and *"Our Verdant Isle,"* had, together with the residence of 'Abdu'lláh Páshá,—rented and prepared for Him by 'Abdu'l-Bahá, and situated a few miles north of 'Akká—become by now the favourite retreats of One Who, for almost a decade, had not set foot beyond the city walls, and Whose sole exercise had been to pace, in monotonous repetition, the floor of His bed-chamber.

Two years later the palace of 'Údí Khammár, on the construction of which so much wealth had been lavished, while Bahá'u'lláh lay imprisoned in the barracks, and which its owner had precipitately abandoned with his family owing to the outbreak of an epidemic disease, was rented and later purchased for Him—a dwelling-place which He characterized as the *"lofty mansion,"* the spot which *"God hath ordained as the most sublime vision of mankind."*

Shoghi Effendi, God Passes By, pp. 192-193.

*T*he drastic farmán of Sulṭán 'Abdu'l-'Azíz, though officially unrepealed, had by now become a dead letter. Though Bahá'u'lláh was still nominally a prisoner, *"the doors of majesty and true sovereignty were,"* in the words of 'Abdu'l-Bahá, *"flung wide open." "The rulers of Palestine,"* He moreover has written, *"envied His influence and power. Governors and Mutisarrifs, generals and local officials, would humbly request the honour of attaining His presence—a request to which He seldom acceded."*

Shoghi Effendi, God Passes By, p. 193.

*I*t was in that same mansion that the distinguished Orientalist, Prof. E. G. Browne of Cambridge, was granted his four successive interviews with Bahá'u'lláh, during the five days he was His guest at Bahjí (15-20 April 1890), interviews immortalized by the Exile's historic declaration that *"these fruitless strifes, these ruinous wars shall pass away and the 'Most Great Peace' shall come."* "The face of Him on Whom I gazed," is the interviewer's memorable testimony for posterity, "I can never forget, though I cannot describe it. Those piercing eyes seemed to read one's very soul; power and authority sat on that ample brow .... No need to ask in whose presence I stood, as I bowed myself before one who is the object of a devotion and love which kings might envy and emperors sigh for in vain."

Shoghi Effendi, God Passes By, p. 194.

The Passing of Bahá'u'lláh

*A*lready nine months before His ascension Bahá'u'lláh, as attested by 'Abdu'l-Bahá, had voiced His desire to depart from this world. From that time onward it became increasingly evident, from the tone of His remarks to those who attained His presence, that the close of His earthly life was approaching, though He refrained from mentioning it openly to any one. On the night preceding the eleventh of Shavval AH 1309 (8 May 1892) He contracted a slight fever which, though it mounted the following day, soon after subsided. He continued to grant interviews to certain of the friends and pilgrims, but it soon became evident that He was not well. His fever returned in a more acute form than before, His general condition grew steadily worse, complications ensued which at last culminated in His ascension, at the hour of dawn, on the 2nd of Dhi'l-Qa'dih AH 1309 (29 May 1892), eight hours after sunset, in the 75th year of His age. His spirit, at long last released from the toils of a life crowded with tribulations, had winged its flight to His *"other dominions,"* dominions *"whereon the eyes of the people of names have never* *fallen,"* and to which the *"Luminous Maid," "clad in white,"* had bidden Him hasten, as described by Himself in the *Lawḥ-i-Ru'ya* (Tablet of the Vision), revealed nineteen years previously, on the anniversary of the birth of His Forerunner.

Shoghi Effendi, God Passes By, p. 221.

*T*he news of His ascension was instantly communicated to Ṣultán 'Abdu'l-Ḥamíd in a telegram which began with the words "the Sun of Bahá has set" and in which the monarch was advised of the intention of interring the sacred remains within the precincts of the Mansion, an arrangement to which he readily assented. ...

Shoghi Effendi, God Passes By, p. 222.

*F*or a full week a vast number of mourners, rich and poor alike, tarried to grieve with the bereaved family ... Notables, among whom were numbered Shí'ahs, Sunnís, Christians, Jews and Druzes, as well as poets, 'ulamás and government officials, all joined in lamenting the loss, and in magnifying the virtues and greatness of Bahá'u'lláh, many of them paying to Him their written tributes, in verse and in prose, in both Arabic and Turkish. From cities as far afield as Damascus, Aleppo, Beirut and Cairo similar tributes were received. These glowing testimonials were, without exception, submitted to 'Abdu'l-Bahá, Who now represented the Cause of the departed Leader, and Whose praises were often mingled in those eulogies with the homage paid to His Father.

Shoghi Effendi, God Passes By, pp. 222-223.

The Covenant of Bahá'u'lláh

*T*o direct and canalize these forces let loose by this Heaven-sent process, and to insure their harmonious and continuous operation after His ascension, an instrument divinely ordained, invested with indisputable authority, organically linked with the Author of the Revelation Himself, was clearly indispensable. That instrument Bahá'u'lláh had expressly provided through the institution of the Covenant, an institution which He had firmly established prior to His ascension. This same Covenant He had anticipated in His *Kitáb-i-Aqdas*, had alluded to it as He bade His last farewell to the members of His family, who had been summoned to His bed-side, in the days immediately preceding His ascension, and had incorporated it in a special document which He designated as *the Book of My Covenant*, and which He entrusted, during His last illness, to His eldest son 'Abdu'l-Bahá.

Written entirely in His own hand; unsealed, on the ninth day after His ascension in the presence of nine witnesses chosen from amongst His companions and members of His Family; read subsequently, on the afternoon of that same day, before a large company assembled in His Most Holy Tomb, including His sons, some of the Báb's kinsmen, pilgrims and resident believers, this unique and epoch-making Document, designated by Bahá'u'lláh as His "Most Great Tablet," and alluded to by Him as the "Crimson Book" in His *Epistle to the Son of the Wolf*, can find no parallel in the Scriptures of any previous Dispensation, not excluding that of the Báb Himself. For nowhere in the books pertaining to any of the world's religious systems, not even among the writings of the Author of the Bábí Revelation, do we find any single document establishing a Covenant endowed with an authority comparable to the Covenant which Bahá'u'lláh had Himself instituted.

"*So firm and mighty is this Covenant,*" He Who is its appointed Centre has affirmed, "*that from the beginning of time until the present day no religious Dispensation hath produced its like.*"

Shoghi Effendi, God Passes By, pp. 237-238.

The Ministry of 'Abdu'l-Bahá

The third period (1892-1921) revolves around the vibrant personality of 'Abdu'l-Bahá, mysterious in His essence, unique in His station, astoundingly potent in both the charm and strength of His character. It commences with the announcement of the Covenant of Bahá'u'lláh, a document without parallel in the history of any earlier Dispensation, attains its climax in the emphatic assertion by the Centre of that Covenant, in the City of the Covenant, of the unique character and far-reaching implications of that Document, and closes with His passing and the interment of His remains on Mt. Carmel. It will go down in history as a period of almost thirty years' duration, in which tragedies and triumphs have been so intertwined as to eclipse at one time the Orb of the Covenant, and at another time to pour forth its light over the continent of Europe, and as far as Australasia, the Far East and the North American continent.

Shoghi Effendi, God Passes By, p. xv.

The Role of 'Abdu'l-Bahá in the Ministry of Bahá'u'lláh

That such a unique and sublime station should have been conferred upon 'Abdu'l-Bahá did not, and indeed could not, surprise those exiled companions who had for so long been privileged to observe His life and conduct, nor the pilgrims who had been brought, however fleetingly, into personal contact with Him, nor indeed the vast concourse of the faithful who, in distant lands, had grown to revere His name and to appreciate His labours, nor even the wide circle of His friends and acquaintances who, in the Holy Land and the adjoining countries, were already well familiar with the position He had occupied during the lifetime of His Father.

Shoghi Effendi, God Passes By, p. 240.

On Him Bahá'u'lláh, as the scope and influence of His Mission extended, had been led to place an ever greater degree of reliance, by appointing Him, on numerous occasions, as His deputy, by enabling Him to plead His Cause before the public, by assigning Him the task of transcribing His Tablets, by allowing Him to assume the responsibility of shielding Him from His enemies, and by investing Him with the function of watching over and promoting the interests of His fellow-exiles and companions. He it was Who had been commissioned to undertake, as soon as circumstances might permit, the delicate and all-important task of purchasing the site that was to serve as the permanent resting-place of the Báb, of insuring the safe transfer of His remains to the Holy Land, and of erecting for Him a befitting sepulchre on Mt. Carmel. He it was Who had been chiefly instrumental in providing the necessary means for Bahá'u'lláh's release from His nine-year confinement within the city walls of 'Akká, and in enabling Him to enjoy, in the evening of His life, a measure of that peace and security from which He had so long been debarred.

Shoghi Effendi, God Passes By, p. 241.

*P*raise be to Him Who hath honoured the Land of Bá (Beirut) through the presence of Him round Whom all names revolve ... the Most Mighty Branch of God—His ancient and immutable Mystery—proceeding on its way to another land. Sorrow, thereby, hath enveloped this Prison-city, whilst another land rejoiceth.

Bahá'u'lláh, Tablets of Bahá'u'lláh, p. 227.

The Rebellion of Mírzá Muhammad-'Alí

*F*ar from being allayed by the provisions of a Will which had elevated him to the second-highest position within the ranks of the faithful, the fire of unquenchable animosity that glowed in the breast of Mírzá Muhammad-'Alí burned even more fiercely as soon as he came to realize the full implications of that Document. All that 'Abdu'l-Bahá could do, during a period of four distressful years, His incessant exhortations, His earnest pleadings, the favours and kindnesses He showered upon him, the admonitions and warnings He uttered, even His voluntary withdrawal in the hope of averting the threatening storm, proved to be of no avail. Gradually and with unyielding persistence, through lies, half-truths, calumnies and gross exaggerations, this "Prime Mover of sedition" succeeded in ranging on his side almost the entire family of Bahá'u'lláh, as well as a considerable number of those who had formed his immediate entourage.

Shoghi Effendi, God Passes By, pp. 246-247.

'*A*bdu'l-Bahá's grief over so tragic a development, following so swiftly upon His Father's ascension, was such that, despite the triumphs witnessed in the course of His ministry, it left its traces upon Him till the end of His days. The intensity of the emotions which this sombre episode aroused within Him were reminiscent of the effect produced upon Bahá'u'lláh by the dire happenings precipitated by the rebellion of Mírzá Yahyá.

Shoghi Effendi, God Passes By, pp. 249-250.

The Rise of the Faith in the West

*T*he stout-hearted Thornton Chase, surnamed Thábit (Steadfast) by 'Abdu'l-Bahá and designated by Him *"the first American believer,"* who became a convert to the Faith in 1894, the immortal Louisa A. Moore, the mother teacher of the West, surnamed Livá (Banner) by 'Abdu'l-Bahá, Dr. Edward Getsinger, to whom she was later married, Howard MacNutt, Arthur P. Dodge, Isabella D. Brittingham, Lillian F. Kappes, Paul K. Dealy,

Chester I. Thacher and Helen S. Goodall, whose names will ever remain associated with the first stirrings of the Faith of Bahá'u'lláh in the North American continent, stand out as the most prominent among those who, in those early years, awakened to the call of the New Day, and consecrated their lives to the service of the newly proclaimed Covenant.

Shoghi Effendi, God Passes By, p. 257.

The arrival of fifteen pilgrims, in three successive parties, the first of which, including Dr and Mrs Getsinger, reached the prison-city of 'Akká on 10 December 1898; the intimate personal contact established between the Centre of Bahá'u'lláh's Covenant and the newly arisen heralds of His Revelation in the West; the moving circumstances attending their visit to His Tomb and the great honour bestowed upon them of being conducted by 'Abdu'l-Bahá Himself into its innermost chamber; the spirit which, through precept and example, despite the briefness of their stay, a loving and bountiful Host so powerfully infused into them; and the passionate zeal and unyielding resolve which His inspiring exhortations, His illuminating instructions and the multiple evidences of His divine love kindled in their hearts—all these marked the opening of a new epoch in the development of the Faith in the West, an epoch whose significance the acts subsequently performed by some of these same pilgrims and their fellow-disciples have amply demonstrated.

"Of that first meeting," one of these pilgrims, recording her impressions, has written, "I can remember neither joy nor pain, nor anything that I can name. I had been carried suddenly to too great a height, my soul had come in contact with the Divine Spirit, and this force, so pure, so holy, so mighty, had overwhelmed me ... We could not remove our eyes from His glorious face; we heard all that He said; we drank tea with Him at His bidding; but existence seemed suspended; and when He arose and suddenly left us, we came back with a start to life; but never again, oh! never again, thank God, the same life on this earth."

Shoghi Effendi, God Passes By, pp. 257-258.

Renewal of 'Abdu'l-Bahá's Incarceration

Embittered by his abject failure to create a schism on which he had fondly pinned his hopes; stung by the conspicuous success which the standard-bearers of the Covenant had, despite his machinations, achieved in the North American continent; encouraged by the existence of a régime that throve in an atmosphere of intrigue and suspicion, and which was presided over by a cunning and cruel potentate; determined to exploit to the full the opportunities for mischief afforded him by the arrival of Western pilgrims at the prison-fortress of 'Akká, as well as by the commencement of the construction of the Báb's sepulchre on Mt. Carmel, Mírzá Muḥammad-'Alí, seconded by his brother, Mírzá Badí'u'lláh, and aided by his brother-in-law, Mírzá Majdi'd-Dín, succeeded through strenuous and persistent endeavours in exciting the suspicion of the Turkish government and its officials, and in inducing them to reimpose on 'Abdu'l-Bahá the confinement from which, in the days of Bahá'u'lláh, He had so grievously suffered.

Shoghi Effendi, God Passes By, pp. 263-264.

*S*uch grave accusations, embodied in numerous reports, could not fail to perturb profoundly the mind of a despot already obsessed by the fear of impending rebellion among his subjects. A commission was accordingly appointed to inquire into the matter, and report the result of its investigations.

Shoghi Effendi, God Passes By, p. 266.

*I*n the early part of the winter of 1907 another Commission of four officers, headed by 'Árif Bey, and invested with plenary powers, was suddenly dispatched to 'Akká by order of the Sulṭán. A few days before its arrival 'Abdu'l-Bahá had a dream, which He recounted to the believers, in which He saw a ship cast anchor off 'Akká, from which flew a few birds, resembling sticks of dynamite, and which, circling about His head, as He stood in the midst of a multitude of the frightened inhabitants of the city, returned without exploding to the ship.

No sooner had the members of the Commission landed than they placed under their direct and exclusive control both the Telegraph and Postal services in 'Akká; arbitrarily dismissed officials suspected of being friendly to 'Abdu'l-Bahá, including the governor of the city ...

Shoghi Effendi, God Passes By, pp. 269-270.

... *N*ews was received that a bomb had exploded in the path of the Sulṭán while he was returning to his palace from the mosque where he had been offering his Friday prayers.

A few days after this attempt on his life the Commission submitted its report to him; but he and his government were too pre-occupied to consider the matter. The case was laid aside, and when, some months later, it was again brought forward it was abruptly closed forever by an event which, once and for all, placed the Prisoner of 'Akká beyond the power of His royal enemy. The "Young Turk" Revolution, breaking out swiftly and decisively in 1908, forced a reluctant despot to promulgate the constitution which he had suspended, and to release all religious and political prisoners held under the old régime. Even then a telegram had to be sent to Constantinople to inquire specifically whether 'Abdu'l-Bahá was included in the category of these prisoners, to which an affirmative reply was promptly received.

Shoghi Effendi, God Passes By, pp. 271-272.

*W*hen we said 'We are glad, oh! so full of gladness that you are free,' He said: 'Freedom is not a matter of place, but of condition. I was happy in that prison, for those days were passed in the path of service.'

'To me prison was freedom.'

'Troubles are a rest to me.'

'Death is life.'

'To be despised is honour.'

'Therefore was I full of happiness all through that prison time.'

'When one is released from the prison of self, that is indeed freedom! For self is the greatest prison.'

When this release takes place, one can never be imprisoned. Unless one accepts dire vicissitudes, not with dull resignation, but with radiant acquiescence, one cannot attain this freedom.'

Lady Blomfield, *The Chosen Highway*, p. 166.

Entombment of the Báb's Remains on Mt. Carmel

*W*ithin a few months of the historic decree which set Him free, in the very year that witnessed the downfall of Sulṭán 'Abdu'l-Ḥamíd, that same power from on high which had enabled 'Abdu'l-Bahá to preserve inviolate the rights divinely conferred on Him, to establish His Father's Faith in the North American continent, and to triumph over His royal oppressor, enabled Him to achieve one of the most signal acts of His ministry: the removal of the Báb's remains from their place of concealment in Ṭihrán to Mt. Carmel. He Himself testified, on more than one occasion, that the safe transfer of these remains, the construction of a befitting mausoleum to receive them, and their final interment with His own hands in their permanent resting-place constituted one of the three principal objectives which, ever since the inception of His mission, He had conceived it His paramount duty to achieve. This act indeed deserves to rank as one of the outstanding events in the first Bahá'í century.

Shoghi Effendi, *God Passes By*, p. 273.

*N*o need to dwell on the manifold problems and pre-occupations which, for almost a decade, continued to beset 'Abdu'l-Bahá until the victorious hour when He was able to bring to a final consummation the historic task entrusted to Him by His Father.

Shoghi Effendi, *God Passes By*, p. 275.

"*E*very stone of that building, every stone of the road leading to it," He, many a time was heard to remark, "I have with infinite tears and at tremendous cost, raised and placed in position." "One night," He, according to an eye-witness, once observed, "I was so hemmed in by My anxieties that I had no other recourse than to recite and repeat over and over again a prayer of the Báb which I had in My possession, the recital of which greatly calmed Me. The next morning the owner of the plot himself came to Me, apologized and begged Me to purchase his property."

Shoghi Effendi, *God Passes By*, pp. 275-276.

... *T*he day of the first Naw-Rúz (1909), which He celebrated after His release from His confinement, 'Abdu'l-Bahá had the marble sarcophagus transported with great labour to the vault prepared for it, and in the evening, by the light of a single lamp, He laid within it, with His own hands—in the presence of believers from the East and from the West and in circumstances at once solemn and moving—the wooden casket containing the sacred remains of the Báb and His companion.

When all was finished, and the earthly remains of the Martyr-Prophet of <u>Sh</u>íráz were, at long last, safely deposited for their everlasting rest in the bosom of God's holy mountain, 'Abdu'l-Bahá, Who had cast aside his turban, removed His shoes and thrown off His cloak, bent low over the still open sarcophagus, His silver hair waving about His head and His face transfigured and luminous, rested His forehead on the border of the wooden casket, and, sobbing aloud, wept with such a weeping that all those who were present wept with Him. That night He could not sleep, so overwhelmed was He with emotion.

Shoghi Effendi, God Passes By, p. 276.

'Abdu'l-Bahá's Travels in Europe and America

'Abdu'l-Bahá was at this time broken in health. He suffered from several maladies brought on by the strains and stresses of a tragic life spent almost wholly in exile and imprisonment. He was on the threshold of three-score years and ten. Yet as soon as He was released from His forty-year long captivity, as soon as He had laid the Báb's body in a safe and permanent resting-place, and His mind was free of grievous anxieties connected with the execution of that priceless Trust, He arose with sublime courage, confidence and resolution to consecrate what little strength remained to Him, in the evening of His life, to a service of such heroic proportions that no parallel to it is to be found in the annals of the first Bahá'í century.

Shoghi Effendi, God Passes By, p. 279.

It was in the course of these epoch-making journeys and before large and representative audiences, at times exceeding a thousand people, that 'Abdu'l-Bahá expounded, with brilliant simplicity, with persuasiveness and force, and for the first time in His ministry, those basic and distinguishing principles of His Father's Faith, which together with the laws and ordinances revealed in the *Kitáb-i-Aqdas* constitute the bed-rock of God's latest Revelation to mankind.

Shoghi Effendi, God Passes By, p. 281.

Whilst He sojourned in England the house placed at His disposal in Cadogan Gardens became a veritable mecca to all sorts and conditions of men, thronging to visit the Prisoner of 'Akká Who had chosen their great city as the first scene of His labours in the West. ... Every day, all day long, a constant stream, an interminable procession! Ministers and missionaries, oriental scholars and occult students, practical men of affairs and mystics, Anglicans, Catholics, and Non-conformists, Theosophists and Hindus, Christian Scientists and doctors of medicine, Muslims, Buddhists and Zoroastrians. There also called: politicians, Salvation Army soldiers and other workers for human good, women suffragists, journalists, writers, poets and healers, dressmakers and great ladies, artists and artisans, poor workless people and prosperous merchants, members of the dramatic and musical world, these all came; and none were too lowly, nor too great, to receive the sympathetic consideration of this holy Messenger, Who was ever giving His life for others' good.

Shoghi Effendi, God Passes By, p. 283.

A reception was given by Sir Richard and Lady Stapley in honour of 'Abdu'l-Bahá ... Who spoke earnestly to us of the duty of each one of those assembled to work, body and soul and spirit, for the Most Great Peace.

'When a thought of war enters your mind, suppress it, and plant in its stead a positive thought of peace. These thoughts, vital and dynamic, will affect the minds of all with whom you come into contact, and like doves of peace, will grow and increase till they spread over all the land'

Lady Blomfield, *The Chosen Highway*, p. 167.

"*W*hen 'Abdu'l-Bahá visited this country for the first time in 1912," a commentator on His American travels has written, "He found a large and sympathetic audience waiting to greet Him personally and to receive from His own lips His loving and spiritual message ... Beyond the words spoken there was something indescribable in His personality that impressed profoundly all who came into His presence. The dome-like head, the patriarchal beard, the eyes that seemed to have looked beyond the reach of time and sense, the soft yet clearly penetrating voice, the translucent humility, the never failing love—but above all, the sense of power mingled with gentleness that invested His whole being with a rare majesty of spiritual exaltation that both set Him apart, and yet that brought Him near to the lowliest soul,—it was all this, and much more that can never be defined, that have left with His many ... friends, memories that are ineffaceable and unspeakably precious."

Shoghi Effendi, *God Passes By*, p. 290.

*A*t the [Bowery] Mission, in April 1912, He spoke most lovingly to the several hundred men who were present: "You must be thankful to God that you are poor, for His Holiness Jesus Christ has said 'Blessed are the poor'; He never said Blessed are the rich. He said too that the kingdom is for the poor and that it is easier for a camel to enter a needle's eye than for a rich man to enter God's kingdom." And then He told them, "when Jesus Christ appeared it was the poor who first accepted Him, not the rich." ...[25]

He closed with characteristic humbleness, asking the men to accept Him as their servant. After the talk, He stood at the Mission Hall entrance. He took each hand and placed in each a number of coins—the price of a bed for the night. However, at least one man kept his money, explaining. "That was a heavenly man, and his quarter was not like other quarters, it will bring me luck!"

Annamarie Honnold, *Vignettes from the Life of 'Abdu'l-Bahá*, pp. 67-68.

*U*pstairs in 'Abdu'l-Bahá's room the Master was seen at the door greeting each boy with a handclasp or an arm around the shoulder, with warm smiles and boyish laughter. His happiest welcome seemed to be directed to the thirteen-year-old boy near the end of the line. He was quite dark-skinned and didn't seem too sure he would be welcome. The Master's face lighted up and in a loud voice that all could hear exclaimed with delight that 'here was a black rose'. The boy's face shone with happiness and love. Silence fell across the room as the boys looked at their companion with a new awareness.

Annamarie Honnold, *Vignettes from the Life of 'Abdu'l-Bahá*, p. 89.

---

25   Refer also to 'Abdu'l-Bahá, The Promulgation of Universal Peace, pp. 32-33.

... He picked from it a long chocolate nougat; it was very black. He looked at it a moment and then around at the group of boys who were watching Him intently and expectantly. Without a word, He walked across the room to where the coloured boy was sitting, and, still without speaking, but with a humorously piercing glance that swept the group, laid the chocolate against the black cheek. His face was radiant as He laid His arm around the shoulder of the boy and that radiance seemed to fill the room. No words were necessary to convey His meaning ...

... as for the boy himself, upon whom all eyes were now fixed, he seemed perfectly unconscious of all but 'Abdu'l-Bahá. Upon Him his eyes were fastened with an adoring, blissful look such as I had never seen upon any face.

Howard Colby Ives, *Portals to Freedom*, pp. 66-67.

On Wednesday, 1 May, the day 'Abdu'l-Bahá was to lay the foundation stone for the first Bahá'í House of Worship in the Western Hemisphere, weather forecasters in the *Chicago Daily News* predicted unsettled conditions "and probably occasional showers tonight." A marquee tent had been set up on the Temple site, with three hundred chairs arranged in nine sections separated by aisles leading to a central open area. A special entryway had been prepared for 'Abdu'l-Bahá's carriage in the middle of the eastern side of the tract. He arrived, instead, by taxi and entered on the northern side. Pacing back and forth before the filled chairs and two hundred additional persons who were standing, He spoke of the importance of the Mashriqu'l-Adhkár.

They moved outside the tent and spadefuls of earth were turned by persons from Persia, Syria, Egypt, India, Japan, South Africa, England, France, Germany, Holland, Norway, Sweden and Denmark and by North American Indians; 'Abdu'l-Bahá finished the effort and placed the stone.

Allan Ward, *239 Days: 'Abdu'l-Bahá's Journey in America*, pp. 51-52.

It was a wonderful experience in the midst of the chaos of war conditions to visit the Master at His Mount Carmel home, which even at that time was a haven of peace and refreshment. I can remember Him, majestic yet gentle, pacing up and down His garden whilst He spoke to me about eternal realities, at a time when the whole material world was rocking on its foundations. The divine power of the spirit shone through His presence, giving one the feeling that a great prophet from Old Testament days had risen up in a war-stricken world, as an inspirer and spiritual guide for the human race.

Lady Blomfield, *The Chosen Highway*, p. 224.

Preparation for war conditions had been made by 'Abdu'l-Bahá even before His return to Palestine, after His world tour. The people of the villages of Nughayb, Samrih and 'Adasíyyih were instructed by the Master how to grow corn, so as to produce prolific harvests, in the period before and during the lean years of the war.

A vast quantity of this corn was stored in pits, some of which had been made by the Romans, and were now utilized for this purpose. So it came about that 'Abdu'l-Bahá was able to feed numberless poor of the people of Haifa, 'Akká, and the neighbourhood in the famine years of 1914-1918.

We learned that when the British marched into Haifa there was some difficulty about

the commissariat. The office in command went to consult the Master.
"I have corn," was the reply.
"But for the army?" said the astonished soldier.
"I have corn for the British Army," said 'Abdu'l-Bahá.
He truly walked the Mystic way with practical feet.

Lady Blomfield, The Chosen Highway, p. 210.

*T*he British Government, with its usual gesture of appreciating a heroic act, conferred a knighthood upon 'Abdu'l-Bahá 'Abbás, Who accepted this honour as a courteous gift "from a just king".

The dignitaries of the British crown from Jerusalem were gathered in Haifa, eager to do honour to the Master, Whom every one had come to love and reverence for His life of unselfish service. An imposing motor car had been sent to bring 'Abdu'l-Bahá to the ceremony. The Master, however, could not be found. People were sent in every direction to look for Him, when suddenly from an unexpected side He appeared, alone, walking His kingly walk, with that simplicity of greatness which always enfolded Him.

Lady Blomfield, The Chosen Highway, p. 214.

The Passing of 'Abdu'l-Bahá

*A*bdu'l-Bahá's great work was now ended. The historic Mission with which His Father had, twenty-nine years previously, invested Him had been gloriously consummated. A memorable chapter in the history of the first Bahá'í century had been written. The Heroic Age of the Bahá'í Dispensation, in which He had participated since its inception, and played so unique a rôle, had drawn to a close. He had suffered as no disciple of the Faith, who had drained the cup of martyrdom, had suffered, He had laboured as none of its greatest heroes had laboured. He had witnessed triumphs such as neither the Herald of the Faith nor its Author had ever witnessed.

*A*t the close of His strenuous Western tours, which had called forth the last ounce of His ebbing strength, He had written: *"Friends, the time is coming when I shall be no longer with you. I have done all that could be done. I have served the Cause of Bahá'u'lláh to the utmost of My ability. I have laboured night and day all the years of My life. O how I long to see the believers shouldering the responsibilities of the Cause! ... My days are numbered, and save this there remains none other joy for me."*

Shoghi Effendi, God Passes By, p. 309.

*T*ill the very last day of His earthly life 'Abdu'l-Bahá continued to shower that same love upon high and low alike, to extend that same assistance to the poor and the downtrodden, and to carry out those same duties in the service of His Father's Faith, as had been His wont from the days of His boyhood.

Shoghi Effendi, God Passes By, p. 311.

The news of His passing, so sudden, so unexpected, spread like wildfire throughout the town, and was flashed instantly over the wires to distant parts of the globe, stunning with grief the community of the followers of Bahá'u'lláh of the East and West. Messages from far and near, from high and low alike, through cablegrams and letters, poured in conveying to the members of a sorrow-stricken and disconsolate family expressions of praise, of devotion, of anguish and of sympathy.

Shoghi Effendi, God Passes By, p. 311.

The Will and Testament of 'Abdu'l-Bahá

The Covenant of Bahá'u'lláh had been instituted solely through the direct operation of His Will and purpose. The Will and Testament of 'Abdu'l-Bahá, on the other hand, may be regarded as the offspring resulting from that mystic intercourse between Him Who had generated the forces of a God-given Faith and the One Who had been made its sole Interpreter and was recognized as its perfect Exemplar.

Shoghi Effendi, God Passes By, p. 325.

The Document establishing that Order, the Charter of a future world civilization, which may be regarded in some of its features as supplementary to no less weighty a Book than the *Kitáb-i-Aqdas*; signed and sealed by 'Abdu'l-Bahá; entirely written with His own hand; its first section composed during one of the darkest periods of His incarceration in the prison-fortress of 'Akká, proclaims, categorically and unequivocally, the fundamental beliefs of the followers of the Faith of Bahá'u'lláh; reveals, in unmistakable language, the twofold character of the Mission of the Báb; discloses the full station of the Author of the Bahá'í Revelation; asserts that "all others are servants unto Him and do His bidding"; stresses the importance of the *Kitáb-i-Aqdas*; establishes the institution of the Guardianship as a hereditary office and outlines its essential functions; provides the measures for the election of the International House of Justice, defines its scope and sets forth its relationship to that Institution; prescribes the obligations, and emphasizes the responsibilities, of the Hands of the Cause of God; and extols the virtues of the indestructible Covenant established by Bahá'u'lláh.

Shoghi Effendi, God Passes By, p. 328.

The Formative Age

The fourth period (1921–1944) is motivated by the forces radiating from the *Will and Testament* of 'Abdu'l-Bahá, that Charter of Bahá'u'lláh's New World Order, the offspring resulting from the mystic intercourse between Him Who is the Source of the Law of God and the mind of the One Who is the vehicle and interpreter of that Law. The inception of this fourth, this last period of the first Bahá'í century synchronizes with the birth of the Formative Age of the Bahá'í Era, with the founding of the Administrative Order of the Faith of Bahá'u'lláh—a system which is at once the harbinger, the nucleus and pattern of

His World Order. This period, covering the first twenty-three years of this Formative Age, has already been distinguished by an outburst of further hostility, of a different character, accelerating on the one hand the diffusion of the Faith over a still wider area in each of the five continents of the globe, and resulting on the other in the emancipation and the recognition of the independent status of several communities within its pale.

Shoghi Effendi *God Passes By*, p. xv.

The Ministry of Shoghi Effendi

*T*his Most Great Jubilee is the crowning victory of the lifework of Shoghi Effendi, Guardian of the Cause of God. He it was, and he alone, who unfolded the potentialities of the widely scattered, numerically small, and largely unorganized Bahá'í community which had been called into being during the Heroic Age of the Faith. He it was who unfolded the grand design of God's Holy Cause, set in motion the great plans of teaching already outlined by 'Abdu'l-Bahá, established the institutions and greatly extended the endowments at the World Centre, and raised the Temples of America, Africa, Australasia and Europe, developed the Administrative Order of the Cause throughout the world, and set the Ark of the Cause true on its course. He appointed the Hands of the Cause of God.

The Universal House of Justice, *Messages from the Universal House of Justice 1963-1886*, para. 1.2, pp. 5-6. (30 April 1963.)

*A*s head for thirty-six years (1921-1957) of the Bahá'í movement, Shoghi Effendi devoted himself to giving practical expression to Bahá'u'lláh's ideals.

In this effort he was brilliantly successful. Today, embracing people from more than 2,100 ethnic, racial and tribal groups, and established in the most remote corners of the earth, the community he inspired and shaped represents the most diverse organized body of people on the planet. Its unity and achievements pose searching challenges for materialistic theories of human nature.

Neither the scale nor the diversity of the expansion, however, adequately conveys the creative genius that achieved it. Faced with the need to inspire in the small, widely-scattered and heterogeneous body of Bahá'u'lláh's followers in various countries the passion and sense of common purpose needed for this enormous task, Shoghi Effendi found in himself a range of talents and resources whose rapid cultivation is breathtaking to contemplate. His life offers an instance of that phenomenon—rare indeed in the twentieth century—for which an earlier age coined the term "uomo universale". Any one of the major pursuits that occupied his thirty-six years at the helm of Bahá'í activities would have distinguished the lifetime achievement of most professional careers. Driven by the historic imperative he found in Bahá'u'lláh's perception that contemporary civilization is breaking apart, Shoghi Effendi made of himself variously an author, an administrator, a historian, an inspired translator (from Arabic and Persian to English and the reverse), a daring patron of architecture, a trenchant analyst of world trends, and a master planner able to conceive in his mind the components of undertakings whose scope of operations was the entire planet.

Somehow, this awesome array of occupations left time for unhurried hours of informal conversations over the dinner table with a constant stream of collaborators and admirers drawn from all over the world to the international centre of his work in Haifa. Hundreds of written accounts speak of the impact of a personality that made the evenings spent at his table among the most memorable experiences of his guests' lives ...

Douglas Martin, Introduction to *Poems of the Passing*.

Successive Epochs of the Formative Age

*I*n disclosing the panoramic vision of the unfoldment of the Dispensation of Bahá'u'lláh, Shoghi Effendi refers to three major evolutionary stages through which the Faith must pass—the Apostolic or Heroic Age (1844-1921) associated with the Central Figures of the Faith; the Formative or Transitional Age (1921-), the "hallmark" of which is the rise and establishment of the Administrative Order, based on the execution of the provisions of 'Abdu'l-Bahá's Will and Testament, and, the Golden Age which will represent the "consummation of this glorious dispensation."

Messages from the Universal House of Justice 1963-1986, para. 451.3, p. 711. (5 February 1986)

*T*he Formative Age, in which we now live and serve, was ushered in with the passing of 'Abdu'l-Bahá. Its major thrust is the shaping, development and consolidation of the local, national and international institutions of the Faith. It is clear from the enumeration of the tasks associated with the Formative Age that their achievement will require increasingly mature levels of functioning of the Bahá'í community:

During this Formative Age of the Faith, and in the course of present and succeeding epochs, the last and crowning stage in the erection of the framework of the Administrative Order of the Faith of Bahá'u'lláh—the election of the Universal House of Justice—will have been completed, the *Kitáb-i-Aqdas*, the Mother Book of His Revelation, will have been codified and its laws promulgated, the Lesser Peace will have been established, the unity of mankind will have been achieved and its maturity attained, the Plan conceived by 'Abdu'l-Bahá will have been executed, the emancipation of the Faith from the fetters of religious orthodoxy will have been effected, and its independent religious status will have been universally recognized, ...[26]

---

26 Shoghi Effendi, *The Citadel of Faith*, p. 6. Letter dated 5 June 1947 to the American Bahá'ís.

The Epochs of the Formative Age mark progressive stages in the evolution of the organic Bahá'í community and signal the maturation of its institutions, thus enabling the Faith to operate at new levels and to initiate new functions.

> *Messages from the Universal House of Justice 1963-1986*, paras 451.5-451.6, pp. 711-712.
> (5 February 1986)

The First Epoch of the Formative Age: 1921-1944/46

The first epoch of this Age witnessed the "birth and primary stages in the erection of the framework of the Administrative Order of the Faith."[27] The epoch was characterized by concentration on the formation of local and national institutions in all five continents ...

> *Messages from the Universal House of Justice 1963-1986*, para. 451.9, p. 713. (5 February 1986)

The Second Epoch of the Formative Age: 1946-1963

This epoch extended the developments of the first epoch by calling for the "consummation of a laboriously constructed Administrative Order,"[28] and was to witness the formulation of a succession of teaching plans designed to facilitate the development of the Faith beyond the confines of the Western Hemisphere and the continent of Europe.

> *Messages from the Universal House of Justice 1963-1986*, para. 451.10, p. 713. (5 February 1986)

The internal consolidation and the administrative experience gained by the National Assemblies was utilized and mobilized by the Guardian with the launching of the Ten Year World Crusade—a crusade involving the simultaneous prosecution of the twelve national plans.

> *Messages from the Universal House of Justice 1963-1986*, para. 451.10, p. 714. (5 February 1986)

The second epoch thus clearly demonstrated the further maturation of the institutions of the Administrative Order. It witnessed the appointment of the Hands of the Cause, the introduction of the Auxiliary Boards, and the establishment of the International Bahá'í Council. The culminating event of the epoch was the election of the Universal House of Justice in 1963. It further demonstrated the more effective and co-ordinated use of the administrative machinery to prosecute the goals of the first global spiritual crusade, and the emergence in ever sharper relief of the World Centre of the Faith.

> *Messages from the Universal House of Justice 1963-1986*, para. 451.11, p. 714. (5 February 1986)

---

27 Shoghi Effendi, *The Citadel of Faith*, p. 6. Letter dated 5 June 1947 to the American Bahá'ís.
28 Shoghi Effendi, *The Citadel of Faith*, p. 6. Letter dated 5 June 1947 to the American Bahá'ís.

The Third Epoch of the Formative Age 1963-1986

The period of the third epoch encompassed three world plans, involving all National Spiritual Assemblies, under the direction of the Universal House of Justice, namely the Nine Year Plan (1964-1973), the Five Year Plan (1974-1979), and the Seven Year Plan (1979-1986). This third epoch witnessed the emergence of the Faith from obscurity and the initiation of activities designed to foster the social and economic development of communities. The institution of the Continental Boards of Counsellors was brought into existence leading to the establishment of the International Teaching Centre. Assistants to the Auxiliary Boards were also introduced. At the World Centre of the Faith, the historic construction and occupation of the Seat of the Universal House of Justice was a crowning event.

Messages from the Universal House of Justice 1963-1986, para. 451.12b, p. 715. (5 February 1986)

The Fourth Epoch of the Formative Age 1986-

Whereas national plans had previously derived largely from the World Centre, in this new epoch the specific goals for each national community will be formulated, within the framework of the overall objectives of the Plan, by means of consultation between the particular National Spiritual Assembly and the Continental Board of Counsellors.

Messages from the Universal House of Justice 1963-1986, para. 451.13, pp. 715-716. (5 February 1986)

Future Epochs

The last twenty-three years of the same century coincided with the first epoch of the second, the Iron and Formative, Age of the Dispensation of Bahá'u'lláh—the first of a series of epochs which must precede the inception of the last and Golden Age of that Dispensation—a Dispensation which, as the Author of the Faith has Himself categorically asserted, must extend over a period of no less than one thousand years, and which will constitute the first stage in a series of Dispensations, to be established by future Manifestations, all deriving their inspiration from the Author of the Bahá'í Revelation, and destined to last, in their aggregate, no less than five thousand centuries.

Shoghi Effendi, *Citadel of Faith*, p. 5.

The tasks that remain to be accomplished during the course of the Formative Age are many and challenging. Additional epochs can be anticipated, each marking significant stages in the evolution of the Administrative Order and culminating in the Golden Age of the Faith. The Golden Age, itself, will involve "successive epochs" leading ultimately to the establishment of the Most Great Peace, the World Bahá'í Commonwealth and to the "birth and efflorescence of a world civilization."

Messages from the Universal House of Justice 1963-1986, para. 451.14, p. 716. (5 February 1986)

The Growth of The Bahá'í Faith

*T*he work that the members of your small family are doing in spreading the Cause and infusing its divine spirit among the people you meet, is a fact that no one familiar with your life can deny ... In time you will see how abundant the fruit of your services will be. It is not sufficient to number the souls that embrace the Cause to know the progress that it is making. The more important consequences of your activities are the spirit that is diffused into the life of the community, and the extent to which the teachings we proclaim become part of the consciousness and belief of the people that hear them. For it is only when the spirit has thoroughly permeated the world that the people will begin to enter the Faith in large numbers. At the beginning of spring only the few, exceptionally favoured seeds will sprout, but when the season gets in its full sway, and the atmosphere gets permeated with the warmth of true springtime, then masses of flowers will begin to appear, and a whole hillside suddenly blooms. We are still in the state when only isolated souls are awakened, but soon we shall have the full swing of the season and the quickening of whole groups and nations into the spiritual life breathed by Bahá'u'lláh.

Letter dated 18 February 1932 written on behalf of Shoghi Effendi, *Promoting Entry by Troops*, Letter no. 2, pp. 23-24.

*D*ear Mr and Mrs ... have a great ability for kindling in the hearts the love of God. It is for this wholesome, warming, spiritualizing love that the world is thirsting today. The Bahá'ís will never succeed in attracting large numbers to the Faith until they see in our individual and community life acts, and the atmosphere, that bespeaks the love of God.

Letter dated 17 February 1945 written on behalf of Shoghi Effendi, *Promoting Entry By Troops*, Letter no. 11, p. 26.

*T*here are two things which will contribute greatly to bringing more people into the Cause more swiftly: one is the maturity of the Bahá'ís within their Communities, functioning according to Bahá'í laws and in the proper spirit of unity, and the other is the disintegration of society and the suffering it will bring in its wake. When the old forms are seen to be hopelessly useless, the people will stir from their materialism and spiritual lethargy, and embrace the Faith.

Letter dated 3 July 1948 written on behalf of Shoghi Effendi, *Promoting Entry By Troops*, Letter no. 13, pp. 27-28.

*T*his [is] the ebb of the tide. The Bahá'ís know that the tide will turn and come in, after mankind has suffered, with mighty waves of faith and devotion. Then people will enter the Cause of God in troops, and the whole condition will change. The Bahá'ís see ... the first glimpse of the dawn, before others are aware of it; and it is toward this that the Bahá'ís must work.

Letter dated 5 October 1953 written on behalf of Shoghi Effendi, *Japan Will Turn Ablaze*, p. 102.[29]

---

29 Also *Promoting Entry By Troops*, Letter no. 19, p. 30.

*T*he Faith advances, not at a uniform rate of growth, but in vast surges, precipitated by the alternation of crisis and victory. In a passage written on 18 July 1953, in the early months of the Ten Year Crusade, Shoghi Effendi, referring to the vital need to ensure through the teaching work a "steady flow" of "fresh recruits to the slowly yet steadily advancing army of the Lord of Hosts", stated that this flow would "presage and hasten the advent of the day which, as prophesied by 'Abdu'l-Bahá, will witness the entry by troops of peoples of divers nations and races into the Bahá'í world". This day the Bahá'í world has already seen in Africa, the Pacific, in Asia and in Latin America, and this process of entry by troops must, in the present plan, be augmented and spread to other countries for, as the Guardian stated in this same letter, it "will be the prelude to that long-awaited hour when a mass conversion on the part of these same nations and races, and as a direct result of a chain of events, momentous and possibly catastrophic in nature, and which cannot as yet be even dimly visualized, will suddenly revolutionize the fortunes of the Faith, derange the equilibrium of the world, and reinforce a thousand-fold the numerical strength as well as the material power and the spiritual authority of the Faith of Bahá'u'lláh". This is the time for which we must now prepare ourselves; this is the hour whose coming it is our task to hasten.
The Universal House of Justice, *Promoting Entry By Troops*, Letter no. 39, p. 40.
Letter dated 31 August 1987.

The Inevitability of Opposition

*I*n the beginning of every Revelation adversities have prevailed, which later on have been turned into great prosperity.
Bahá'u'lláh cited by *The Compilation of Compilations*, Vol. I (Crisis and Victory), p. 132.[30]

*K*now ye that trials and tribulations have, from time immemorial, been the lot of the chosen Ones of God and His beloved, and such of His servants as are detached from all else but Him, they whom neither merchandise nor traffic beguile from the remembrance of the Almighty, they that speak not till He hath spoken, and act according to His commandments.
Bahá'u'lláh, *Gleanings from the Writings of Bahá'u'lláh*, section LXVI, p. 129.

*N*ow ye, as well, must certainly become my partners to some slight degree, and accept your share of tests and sorrows. But these episodes shall pass away, while that abiding glory and eternal life shall remain unchanged forever. Moreover, these afflictions shall be the cause of great advancement.
'Abdu'l-Bahá, *Selections from the Writings of 'Abdu'l-Bahá*, no. 196, pp. 238-239.

*T*his day the powers of all the leaders of religion are directed towards the dispersion of the congregation of the All-Merciful, and the shattering of the Divine Edifice. The hosts of the world, whether material, cultural or political are from every side launching their assault, for the Cause is great, very great. Its greatness is, in this day, clear and manifest to men's eyes.
'Abdu'l-Bahá, cited in *The Advent of Divine Justice*, p. 6.

---

30   Also Shoghi Effendi, *The Advent of Divine Justice*, p. 82.

*B*ut after I leave, some people may arise in opposition, heaping persecutions upon you in their bitterness, and in the newspapers there may be articles published against the Cause. Rest ye in the assurance of firmness. Be well poised and serene, remembering that this is only as the harmless twittering of sparrows and that it will soon pass away. ...

... Therefore, my purpose is to warn and strengthen you against accusations, criticisms, revilings and derision in newspaper articles or other publications. Be not disturbed by them. They are the very confirmation of the Cause, the very source of upbuilding to the Movement.

Public Talk of 'Abdu'l-Bahá, *The Promulgation of Universal Peace*, pp. 428-429.

*H*ow can the beginnings of a world upheaval, unleashing forces that are so gravely deranging the social, the religious, the political, and the economic equilibrium of organized society, throwing into chaos and confusion political systems, racial doctrines, social conceptions, cultural standards, religious associations, and trade relationships—how can such agitations, on a scale so vast, so unprecedented, fail to produce any repercussions on the institutions of a Faith of such tender age whose teachings have a direct and vital bearing on each of these spheres of human life and conduct?

Little wonder, therefore, if they who are holding aloft the banner of so pervasive a Faith, so challenging a Cause, find themselves affected by the impact of these world-shaking forces. Little wonder if they find that in the midst of this whirlpool of contending passions their freedom has been curtailed, their tenets condemned, their institutions assaulted, their motives maligned, their authority jeopardized, their claim rejected.

Shoghi Effendi, *The Advent of Divine Justice*, pp. 2-3.[31]

... undeterred by the clamour which the exponents of religious orthodoxy are sure to raise, or by the restrictive measures which political leaders may impose; undismayed by the smallness of their numbers and the multitude of their potential adversaries; armed with the efficacious weapons their own hands have slowly and laboriously forged in anticipation of this glorious and inevitable encounter with organized forces of superstition, of corruption and of unbelief; placing their whole trust in the matchless potency of Bahá'u'lláh's teachings, in the all-conquering power of His might and infallibility of His glorious and oft-repeated promises, let them press forward ...

Shoghi Effendi, *Citadel of Faith*, p. 120.

*W*ho knows but that triumphs, unsurpassed in splendour, are not in store for the mass of Bahá'u'lláh's toiling followers? Surely, we stand too near the colossal edifice His hand has reared to be able, at the present stage of the evolution of His Revelation, to claim to be able even to conceive the full measure of its promised glory. Its past history, stained by the blood of countless martyrs, may well inspire us with the thought that, whatever may yet befall this Cause, however formidable the forces that may still assail it, however numerous the reverses it will inevitably suffer, its onward march can never be stayed, and that it will continue to advance until the very last promise, enshrined within the words of Bahá'u'lláh, shall have been completely redeemed.

Shoghi Effendi in Nabíl-i-A'ẓam, *The Dawn-Breakers*, pp. 667-668.

---

31   Also *Messages to The Bahá'í World 1950-1957*, pp. 38-39.

Chapter Three
Fundamental Bahá'í Beliefs

The Dispensation of Bahá'u'lláh

Dearly-beloved friends! I feel it incumbent upon me by virtue of the obligations and responsibilities which as Guardian of the Faith of Bahá'u'lláh I am called upon to discharge, to lay special stress, at a time when the light of publicity is being increasingly focused upon us, upon certain truths which lie at the basis of our Faith and the integrity of which it is our first duty to safeguard. These verities, if valiantly upheld and properly assimilated, will, I am convinced, powerfully reinforce the vigour of our spiritual life ....

Shoghi Effendi, The Dispensation of Bahá'u'lláh, *The World Order of Bahá'u'lláh*, p. 99.

Dominating the entire range of this fascinating spectacle towers the incomparable figure of Bahá'u'lláh, transcendental in His majesty, serene, awe-inspiring, unapproachably glorious. Allied, though subordinate in rank, and invested with the authority of presiding with Him over the destinies of this supreme Dispensation, there shines upon this mental picture the youthful glory of the Báb, infinite in His tenderness, irresistible in His charm, unsurpassed in His heroism, matchless in the dramatic circumstances of His short yet eventful life. And finally there emerges, though on a plane of its own and in a category entirely apart from the one occupied by the twin Figures that preceded Him, the vibrant, the magnetic personality of 'Abdu'l-Bahá, reflecting to a degree that no man, however exalted his station, can hope to rival, the glory and power with which They who are the Manifestations of God are alone endowed.

Shoghi Effendi, The Dispensation of Bahá'u'lláh, *The World Order of Bahá'u'lláh*, pp. 97-98.

The Station of Bahá'u'lláh

Naught is seen in My temple but the Temple of God, and in My beauty but His Beauty, and in My being but His Being, and in My self but His Self, and in My movement but His Movement, and in My acquiescence but His Acquiescence, and in My pen but His Pen, the Mighty, the All-Praised. There hath not been in My soul but the Truth, and in Myself naught could be seen but God.

Bahá'u'lláh, The Dispensation of Bahá'u'lláh, cited in *The World Order of Bahá'u'lláh*, p. 109.

Verily I say, this is the Day in which mankind can behold the Face, and hear the Voice, of the Promised One. The Call of God hath been raised, and the light of His countenance hath been lifted up upon men. It behoveth every man to blot out the trace of every idle word from the tablet of his heart, and to gaze, with an open and unbiased mind, on the signs of His Revelation, the proofs of His Mission, and the tokens of His glory.

Bahá'u'lláh, The Great Announcement to Mankind, *Gleanings from the Writings of Bahá'u'lláh*, section VII, pp. 10-11.[32]

*S*ay, O high priests! Ye are held in reverence because of My Name, and yet ye flee Me! Ye are the high priests of the Temple. Had ye been the high priests of the Omnipotent One, ye would have been united with Him, and would have recognized Him ...

Bahá'u'lláh, Tablets to the Clergy and People of Various Faiths.[33]

O people hearken unto that which is revealed to you .... If ye obey Me you will see that which We have promised you, and I will make you the friends of My Soul in the realm of My Greatness and the Companions of My Perfection in the heaven of My Might forever.

Bahá'u'lláh, Tablet to Pope Pius IX, *Bahá'í Scriptures*, p. 103.

"*T*he foundation of the belief of the people of Bahá is this," thus proclaims one of the weightiest passages of that last document left to voice in perpetuity the directions and wishes of a departed Master, "His Holiness the Exalted One (the Báb) is the Manifestation of the unity and oneness of God and the Forerunner of the Ancient Beauty. His Holiness the Abhá Beauty (Bahá'u'lláh) (may my life be a sacrifice for His steadfast friends) is the supreme Manifestation of God and the Day-Spring of His most divine Essence. All others are servants unto Him and do His bidding."

Shoghi Effendi, The Dispensation of Bahá'u'lláh, *The World Order of Bahá'u'lláh*, p. 133.

*T*hat Bahá'u'lláh should, notwithstanding the overwhelming intensity of His Revelation, be regarded as essentially one of these Manifestations of God, never to be identified with that invisible Reality, the Essence of Divinity itself, is one of the major beliefs of our Faith ...'

Shoghi Effendi, The Dispensation of Bahá'u'lláh, *The World Order of Bahá'u'lláh*, p. 114.

The Station of the Báb

*T*he substance wherewith God hath created Me is not the clay out of which others have been formed. He hath conferred upon Me that which the worldly-wise can never comprehend, nor the faithful discover ... I am one of the sustaining pillars of the Primal Word of God. Whosoever hath recognized Me, hath known all that is true and right, and hath attained all that is good and seemly; ...

Extracts from an Epistle to Muḥammad S͟háh, The Báb, *Selections from the Báb*, p. 11.

---

32   Also *The Proclamation of Bahá'u'lláh*, p. 111.
33   Also *The Proclamation of Bahá'u'lláh*, pp. 106-107.

*A*ll the keys of heaven God hath chosen to place on My right hand, and all the keys of hell on My left ...

I am the Primal Point from which have been generated all created things. I am the Countenance of God Whose splendour can never be obscured, the Light of God Whose radiance can never fade.

Extracts from an Epistle to Muḥammad Sh͟áh, The Báb, *Selections from the Báb*, p. 11.

*T*hat the Báb, notwithstanding the duration of His Dispensation, should be regarded primarily, not as the chosen Precursor of the Bahá'í Faith, but as One invested with the undivided authority assumed by each of the independent Prophets of the past, seemed to me yet another basic principle ...

Shoghi Effendi, The Dispensation of Bahá'u'lláh, *The World Order of Bahá'u'lláh*, p. 131.

The Station of 'Abdu'l-Bahá

*T*hat 'Abdu'l-Bahá is not a Manifestation of God, that, though the successor of His Father, He does not occupy a cognate station, that no one else except the Báb and Bahá'u'lláh can ever lay claim to such a station before the expiration of a full thousand years—are verities which lie embedded in the specific utterances of both the Founder of our Faith and the Interpreter of His teachings."

Shoghi Effendi, The Dispensation of Bahá'u'lláh, *The World Order of Bahá'u'lláh*, p. 132.

*H*e is, and should for all time be regarded, first and foremost, as the Centre and Pivot of Bahá'u'lláh's peerless and all-enfolding Covenant, His most exalted handiwork, the stainless Mirror of His light, the perfect Exemplar of His teachings, the unerring Interpreter of His Word, the embodiment of every Bahá'í ideal, the incarnation of every Bahá'í virtue ...

Shoghi Effendi, The Dispensation of Bahá'u'lláh, *The World Order of Bahá'u'lláh*, p. 134.

The Bahá'í Revelation

*T*he Faith of Bahá'u'lláh should indeed be regarded, if we wish to be faithful to the tremendous implications of its message, as the culmination of a cycle, the final stage in a series of successive, of preliminary and progressive revelations. These, beginning with Adam and ending with the Báb, have paved the way and anticipated with an ever-increasing emphasis the advent of that Day of Days in which He Who is the Promise of All Ages should be made manifest.

Shoghi Effendi, The Dispensation of Bahá'u'lláh, *The World Order of Bahá'u'lláh*, p. 103.

*N*or does the Bahá'í Revelation, claiming as it does to be the culmination of a prophetic cycle and the fulfilment of the promise of all ages, attempt, under any circumstances, to invalidate those first and everlasting principles that animate and underlie the religions that have preceded it.

Shoghi Effendi, The Dispensation of Bahá'u'lláh, *The World Order of Bahá'u'lláh*, p. 114.

*I*t should also be borne in mind that, great as is the power manifested by this Revelation and however vast the range of the Dispensation its Author has inaugurated, it emphatically repudiates the claim to be regarded as the final revelation of God's will and purpose for mankind.

Shoghi Effendi, The Dispensation of Bahá'u'lláh, *The World Order of Bahá'u'lláh*, p. 115.

The Covenant of God with Humanity to Accept Bahá'u'lláh and Follow His Teachings

*T*he first duty prescribed by God for His servants is the recognition of Him Who is the Dayspring of His Revelation and the Fountain of His laws, Who representeth the Godhead in both the Kingdom of His Cause and the world of creation. Whoso achieveth this duty hath attained unto all good; and whoso is deprived thereof hath gone astray, though he be the author of every righteous deed. It behoveth every one who reacheth this most sublime station, this summit of transcendent glory, to observe every ordinance of Him Who is the Desire of the world. These twin duties are inseparable. Neither is acceptable without the other. Thus hath it been decreed by Him Who is the Source of Divine inspiration.

They whom God hath endued with insight will readily recognize that the precepts laid down by God constitute the highest means for the maintenance of order in the world and the security of its peoples. ... They that have violated the Covenant of God by breaking His commandments, and have turned back on their heels, these have erred grievously in the sight of God, the All-Possessing, the Most High.

Bahá'u'lláh, *The Kitáb-i-Aqdas* (The Most Holy Book), paras 1-2, pp. 19-20.

*I*f it be your wish, O people, to know God and to discover the greatness of His might, look, then, upon Me with Mine own eyes, and not with the eyes of any one besides Me. Ye will, otherwise, be never capable of recognizing Me, though ye ponder My Cause as long as My Kingdom endureth, and meditate upon all created things throughout the eternity of God, the Sovereign Lord of all, the Omnipotent, the Ever-Abiding, the All-Wise. Thus have We manifested the truth of Our Revelation, that haply the people may be roused from their heedlessness, and be of them that understand.

Bahá'u'lláh, *Gleanings from the Writings of Bahá'u'lláh*, section CXXVII, pp. 272-273.

*I*n His Name who shines forth from the Horizon of Might! Verily the Tongue of the Ancient gives glad tidings to those who are in the world concerning the appearance of the Greatest Name, and who takes His Covenant among the nations. Verily, He is Myself; the Shining-Place of My Identity; the East of My Cause; the Heaven of My Bounty; the Sea of My Will; the Lamp of My Guidance; the Path of My Justice; the Standard of My Love. The one who hath turned to Him hath turned to My Face and is illumined through the lights of My Beauty; hath acknowledged My Oneness and confessed My Singleness. The one who hath denied Him hath been deprived of the Salsabíl of My Love, of the Kawthar of My Grace, the cup of My Mercy and of the Wine by which the sincere ones have been attracted and the monotheists have taken flight in the air of My Compassion, which no one hath known except him whom I have taught the matter revealed in My Hidden Tablet.

Bahá'u'lláh, *Bahá'í Scriptures*, no. 527, p. 255.

*I*t should be made clear to every one reading those extracts that by the phrase "the Tongue of the Ancient" no one else is meant but God, and that the term "the Greatest Name" is an obvious reference to Bahá'u'lláh, and that "the Covenant" referred to is not the specific Covenant of which Bahá'u'lláh is the immediate Author and 'Abdu'l-Bahá the Centre but that general Covenant which, as inculcated by the Bahá'í teaching, God Himself invariably establishes with mankind when He inaugurates a new Dispensation. "The Tongue" that "gives," as stated in those extracts, the "glad-tidings" is none other than the Voice of God referring to Bahá'u'lláh, and not Bahá'u'lláh referring to 'Abdu'l-Bahá.

Shoghi Effendi, The Dispensation of Bahá'u'lláh, *The World Order of Bahá'u'lláh*, p. 137.

The Covenant of Bahá'u'lláh with His Followers Concerning the Next Manifestation

*G*od hath sent down His Messengers to succeed to Moses and Jesus, and He will continue to do so till 'the end that hath no end'; so that His grace may, from the heaven of Divine bounty, be continually vouchsafed to mankind.

Bahá'u'lláh, cited in The Dispensation of Bahá'u'lláh, *The World Order of Bahá'u'lláh*, p. 116.

*W*hoso layeth claim to a Revelation direct from God, ere the expiration of a full thousand years, such a man is assuredly a lying impostor. We pray God that He may graciously assist him to retract and repudiate such claim. Should he repent, God will, no doubt, forgive him. If, however, he persisteth in his error, God will, assuredly, send down one who will deal mercilessly with him. Terrible, indeed, is God in punishing! Whosoever interpreteth this verse otherwise than its obvious meaning is deprived of the Spirit of God and of His mercy which encompasseth all created things.

Bahá'u'lláh, *The Kitáb-i-Aqdas* (The Most Holy Book), para. 37, p. 32.

*A*s regards the meaning of the Bahá'í Covenant: The Guardian considers the existence of two forms of Covenant both of which are explicitly mentioned in the literature of the Cause. First is the covenant that every prophet makes with humanity or more definitely with His people that they will accept and follow the coming Manifestation Who will be the reappearance of His reality. The second form of covenant is such as the one Bahá'u'lláh made with His people that they should accept the Master. This is merely to establish and strengthen the succession of the series of Lights that appear after every Manifestation. Under the same category falls the covenant the Master has made with the Bahá'ís that they should accept His administration after Him.

Letter dated 21 October 1932 written on behalf of Shoghi Effendi, *Directives from the Guardian*, no. 43, p. 15 (revised).

A Covenant in the religious sense is a binding agreement between God and man, whereby God requires of man certain behaviour in return for which He guarantees certain blessings, or whereby He gives man certain bounties in return for which He takes from those who accept them an undertaking to behave in a certain way. There is, for example, the Greater Covenant which every Manifestation of God makes with His followers, promising that in the fullness of time a new Manifestation will be sent, and taking from them the undertaking to accept Him when this occurs. There is also the Lesser Covenant that a Manifestation of God makes with His followers that they will accept His appointed successor after Him. If they do so, the Faith can remain united and pure. If not, the Faith becomes divided and its force spent. It is a Covenant of this kind that Bahá'u'lláh made with His followers regarding 'Abdu'l-Bahá, and that 'Abdu'l-Bahá perpetuated through the Administrative Order ...

The Universal House of Justice, *The Compilation of Compilations*, Vol. I (Covenant), p. 111. (23 March 1975 to an individual believer.)

The Covenant of Bahá'u'lláh with His Followers Concerning the Succession

*T*o direct and canalize these forces let loose by this Heaven-sent process, and to insure their harmonious and continuous operation after His ascension, an instrument divinely ordained, invested with indisputable authority, organically linked with the Author of the Revelation Himself, was clearly indispensable. That instrument Bahá'u'lláh had expressly provided through the institution of the Covenant, an institution which He had firmly established prior to His ascension. This same Covenant He had anticipated in His *Kitáb-i-Aqdas* ... and had incorporated it in a special document which He designated as "the Book of My Covenant," ...

Shoghi Effendi, *God Passes By*, pp. 237-238.

... *T*his Covenant has been bequeathed to posterity in a Will and Testament which, together with the *Kitáb-i-Aqdas* and several Tablets, in which the rank and station of

'Abdu'l-Bahá are unequivocally disclosed, constitute the chief buttresses designed by the Lord of the Covenant Himself to shield and support, after His ascension, the appointed Centre of His Faith and the Delineator of its future institutions.

Shoghi Effendi, *God Passes By*, p. 239.

*A*bove all the Covenant that was to perpetuate the influence of that Faith, insure its integrity, safeguard it from schism, and stimulate its world-wide expansion, had been fixed on an inviolable basis.

Shoghi Effendi, *God Passes By*, pp. 244-245.

Excerpts from the *Kitáb-i-'Ahd* (Book of the Covenant)

*T*he aim of this Wronged One in sustaining woes and tribulations, in revealing the Holy Verses and in demonstrating proofs hath been naught but to quench the flame of hate and enmity, that the horizon of the hearts of men may be illumined with the light of concord and attain real peace and tranquillity. ... We exhort you, O peoples of the world, to observe that which will elevate your station. Hold fast to the fear of God and firmly adhere to what is right. Verily I say, the tongue is for mentioning what is good, defile it not with unseemly talk. God hath forgiven what is past. Henceforward everyone should utter that which is meet and seemly, and should refrain from slander, abuse and whatever causeth sadness in men. ... Great and blessed is this Day—the Day in which all that lay latent in man hath been and will be made manifest. Lofty is the station of man, were he to hold fast to righteousness and truth and to remain firm and steadfast in the Cause. In the eyes of the All-Merciful a true man appeareth even as a firmament; its sun and moon are his sight and hearing, and his shining and resplendent character its stars. His is the loftiest station, and his influence educateth the world of being.

Bahá'u'lláh, *Kitáb-i-'Ahd* (Book of the Covenant) in *Tablets of Bahá'u'lláh*, pp. 219-220.

O ye that dwell on earth! The religion of God is for love and unity; make it not the cause of enmity or dissension. In the eyes of men of insight and the beholders of the Most Sublime Vision, whatsoever are the effective means for safeguarding and promoting the happiness and welfare of the children of men have already been revealed by the Pen of Glory. ...

O ye the loved ones and the trustees of God! Kings are the manifestations of the power, and the daysprings of the might and riches, of God. Pray ye on their behalf. He hath invested them with the rulership of the earth and hath singled out the hearts of men as His Own domain.

Conflict and contention are categorically forbidden in His Book. This is a decree of God in this Most Great Revelation. It is divinely preserved from annulment and is invested by Him with the splendour of His confirmation.

Bahá'u'lláh, *Kitáb-i-'Ahd* (Book of the Covenant) in *Tablets of Bahá'u'lláh*, pp. 220-221.

In the *Kitáb-i-'Ahd*, moreover, Bahá'u'lláh solemnly and explicitly declares: "It is incumbent upon the Aghsán, the Afnán and My kindred to turn, one and all, their faces towards the Most Mighty Branch. Consider that which We have revealed in Our Most Holy Book: 'When the ocean of My presence hath ebbed and the Book of My Revelation is ended, turn your faces toward Him Whom God hath purposed, Who hath branched from this Ancient Root.' The object of this sacred verse is none other except the Most Mighty Branch ('Abdu'l-Bahá). Thus have we graciously revealed unto you our potent Will, and I am verily the Gracious, the All-Powerful."

Shoghi Effendi, The Dispensation of Bahá'u'lláh, *The World Order of Bahá'u'lláh*, p. 134.

Excerpts from the Will and Testament of 'Abdu'l-Bahá

The sacred and youthful branch, the Guardian of the Cause of God, as well as the Universal House of Justice to be universally elected and established, are both under the care and protection of the Abhá Beauty, under the shelter and unerring guidance of the Exalted One (may my life be offered up for them both). Whatsoever they decide is of God. Whoso obeyeth him not, neither obeyeth them, hath not obeyed God ...

'Abdu'l-Bahá, *The Will and Testament of 'Abdu'l-Bahá*, p. 11.

O ye the faithful loved ones of 'Abdu'l-Bahá! It is incumbent upon you to take the greatest care of Shoghi Effendi ...

For he is, after 'Abdu'l-Bahá, the Guardian of the Cause of God, the Afnán, the Hands (pillars) of the Cause and the beloved of the Lord must obey him and turn unto him. ... All must seek guidance and turn unto the Centre of the Cause and the House of Justice. And he that turneth unto whatsoever else is indeed in grievous error.

The Glory of Glories rest upon you!

'Abdu'l-Bahá, *The Will and Testament of 'Abdu'l-Bahá*, pp. 25-26.

... The Hands of the Cause of God must be ever watchful and so soon as they find anyone beginning to oppose and protest against the Guardian of the Cause of God, cast him out from the congregation of the people of Bahá and in no wise accept any excuse from him. How often hath grievous error been disguised in the garb of truth, that it might sow the seeds of doubt in the hearts of men!

'Abdu'l-Bahá, *The Will and Testament of 'Abdu'l-Bahá*, p. 12.

And now, one of the greatest and most fundamental principles of the Cause of God is to shun and avoid entirely the Covenant-breakers, for they will utterly destroy the Cause of God, exterminate His Law and render of no account all efforts exerted in the past.

'Abdu'l-Bahá, *The Will and Testament of 'Abdu'l-Bahá*, p. 20.

In these days, the most important of all things is the guidance of the nations and peoples of the world. Teaching the Cause is of utmost importance for it is the head corner-stone of the foundation itself. This wronged servant has spent his days and nights in promoting the Cause and urging the peoples to service. He rested not a moment, till the fame of the Cause of God was noised abroad in the world and the celestial strains from the Abhá Kingdom roused the East and the West. The beloved of God must also follow the same example. This is the secret of faithfulness, this is the requirement of servitude to the Threshold of Bahá!

'Abdu'l-Bahá, *The Will and Testament of 'Abdu'l-Bahá*, p. 10.

The Significance of the Covenant

... *A* Covenant so firm and mighty that from the beginning of time until the present day no religious Dispensation hath produced its like.

'Abdu'l-Bahá, cited in The Dispensation of Bahá'u'lláh, Shoghi Effendi, *The World Order of Bahá'u'lláh*, p. 136.

*T*oday no power can conserve the oneness of the Bahá'í world save the Covenant of God; otherwise differences like unto a most great tempest will encompass the Bahá'í world. It is evident that the axis of the oneness of the world of humanity is the power of the Covenant and nothing else.

'Abdu'l-Bahá, *Tablets of the Divine Plan*, p. 51.

*T*he confirmation of the Kingdom of Abhá shall descend uninterruptedly upon those souls who are firm in the COVENANT. Thou hast well observed that every firm one is assisted and aided and every violator is degraded, humiliated, and lost. It is very astonishing that people are not admonished. They have observed how Mírzá Muḥammad-'Alí, on account of violation of the Covenant, descended to the lowest degree of humiliation and yet they do not become mindful. They have seen how others through disobedience to the Testament, have fallen into a well of degradation, and yet they are not awakened.

This Covenant is the Covenant of His Holiness Bahá'u'lláh. Now, its importance is not known befittingly, but in the future it shall attain to such a degree of importance that if a king violates to the extent of one atom, he shall be cut off immediately.

'Abdu'l-Bahá, *Star of the West*, Vol. IV:14, 23 November 1913, p. 241.

*T*o accept the Prophet of God in His time and to abide by His bidding are the two essential, inseparable duties which each soul was created to fulfil. One exercises these twin duties by one's own choice, an act constituting the highest expression of the free will with which every human being has been endowed by an all-loving Creator.

The vehicle in this resplendent Age for the practical fulfilment of these duties is the Covenant of Bahá'u'lláh; it is, indeed, the potent instrument by which individual belief in Him is translated into constructive deeds. The Covenant comprises divinely conceived arrangements necessary to preserve the organic unity of the Cause. It therefore engenders a motivating power which, as the beloved Master tells us, "like unto the artery, beats and pulsates in the body of the world." "It is indubitably clear," He asserts, "that the pivot of the oneness of mankind is nothing else but the power of the Covenant." Through it the meaning of the Word, both in theory and practice, is made evident in the life and work of 'Abdu'l-Bahá, the appointed Interpreter, the perfect Exemplar, the Centre of the Covenant. Through it the processes of the Administrative Order—"this unique, this wondrous System"—are made to operate.

The Universal House of Justice, Rights and Responsibilities, p. 5. (29 December 1988.)

Firmness in the Covenant

Although in the body of the universe there are innumerable nerves, yet the main artery, which pulsates, energizes, and invigorates all beings, is the power of the Covenant. All else is secondary to this. Nobody is assisted and confirmed save that soul who is firm. Consider it well that every soul who is firm in the Covenant is luminous, like unto a candle which emanates its light on those around it. While every wavering soul is an utter failure, frozen, lifeless, dead yet moving. This one proof is sufficient.

'Abdu'l-Bahá, Star of the West, Vol. XI:18, 7 February 1921, p. 308.

Freedom of Thought and Expression in the Bahá'í Faith

... The Bahá'í Faith upholds the freedom of conscience which permits a person to follow his chosen religion; no one may be compelled to become a Bahá'í, or to remain a Bahá'í if he conscientiously wishes to leave the Faith. As to the thoughts of the Bahá'ís themselves—that is, those who have chosen to follow the religion of Bahá'u'lláh—the institutions do not busy themselves with what individual believers think unless those thoughts become expressed in actions which are inimical to the basic principles and vital interests of the Faith.

Letter dated 8 February 1998 written on behalf of the Universal House of Justice, Issues Related to the Study of the Bahá'í Faith, p. 42.

As you well understand, not only the right but also the responsibility of each believer to explore truth for himself or herself are fundamental to the Bahá'í teachings. This principle is an integral feature of the coming of age of humankind, inseparable from the social transformation to which Bahá'u'lláh is calling the peoples of the world. It is as relevant to specifically scholarly activity as it is to the rest of spiritual and intellectual life. Every human being is ultimately responsible to God for the use which he or she makes of these possibilities; conscience is never to be coerced, whether by other individuals or institutions.

Letter dated 8 February 1998 written on behalf of the Universal House of Justice, Issues Related to the Study of the Bahá'í Faith, p. 39.

In many of His utterances, 'Abdu'l-Bahá extols governments which uphold freedom of conscience for their citizens. As can be seen from the context, these statements refer to the freedom to follow the religion of one's choice. In the original of a passage to which you refer in your email of ..., He gives the following analysis of freedom:

> There are three types of freedom. The first is divine freedom, which is one of the inherent attributes of the Creator for He is unconstrained in His will, and no one can force Him to change His decree in any matter whatsoever ....
>
> The second is the political freedom of Europeans, which leaves the individual free to do whatsoever he desires as long as his action does not harm his neighbour. This is natural freedom, and its greatest expression is seen in the animal world. Observe these birds and notice with what freedom they live. However much man may try, he can never be as free as an animal, because the existence of order acts as an impediment to freedom.
>
> The third freedom is that which is born of obedience to the laws and ordinances of the Almighty. This is the freedom of the human world, where man severs his affections from all things. When he does so, he becomes immune to all hardship and sorrow. Wealth or material power will not deflect him from moderation and fairness, neither will poverty or need inhibit him from showing forth happiness and tranquillity. The more the conscience of man develops, the more will his heart be free and his soul attain unto happiness. In the religion of God, there is freedom of thought because God, alone, controls the human conscience, but this freedom should not go beyond courtesy. In the religion of God, there is no freedom of action outside the law of God. Man may not transgress this law, even though no harm is inflicted on one's neighbour. This is because the purpose of Divine law is the education of all—others as well as oneself—and, in the sight of God, the harm done to one individual or to his neighbour is the same and is reprehensible in both cases. Hearts must possess the fear of God. Man should endeavour to avoid that which is abhorrent unto God. Therefore, the freedom that the laws of Europe offer to the individual does not exist in the law of God. Freedom of thought should not transgress the bounds of courtesy, and actions, likewise, should be governed by the fear of God and the desire to seek His good pleasure.
>
> Letter dated 8 February 1998 written on behalf of the Universal House of Justice, *Issues Related to the Study of the Bahá'í Faith*, pp. 41-42.

*I*t is not surprising that individual Bahá'ís hold and express different and sometimes defective understandings of the Teachings; this is but an evidence of the magnitude of the change that this Revelation is to effect in human consciousness. As believers with various insights into the Teachings converse—with patience, tolerance and open and unbiased minds—a deepening of comprehension should take place. The strident insistence on individual views, however, can lead to contention, which is detrimental not only to the spirit of Bahá'í association and collaboration but to the search for truth itself.

Beyond contention, moreover, is the condition in which a person is so immovably attached to one erroneous viewpoint that his insistence upon it amounts to an effort to change the essential character of the Faith. This kind of behaviour, if permitted to continue unchecked, could produce disruption in the Bahá'í community, giving birth to countless sects as it has done in previous Dispensations. The Covenant of Bahá'u'lláh prevents this. The Faith defines elements of a code of conduct, and it is ultimately the responsibility of the Universal House of Justice, in watching over the security of the Cause and upholding the integrity of its Teachings, to require the friends to adhere to standards thus defined.

Letter dated 8 February 1998 written on behalf of the Universal House of Justice, Issues Related to the Study of the Bahá'í Faith, p. 38.

Covenant Breaking

... Bahá'u'lláh and the Master in many places and very emphatically have told us to shun entirely all Covenant-breakers as they are afflicted with what we might try and define as a contagious spiritual disease; They have also told us, however, to pray for them. These souls are not lost forever. In the *Aqdas* Bahá'u'lláh says that God will forgive Mírzá Yahyá if he repents. It follows therefore that God will forgive any soul *if he repents*. Most of them don't want to repent, unfortunately. If the leaders can be forgiven it goes without saying that their followers can also be forgiven.

Letter dated 30 November 1944 written on behalf of Shoghi Effendi, Directives from the Guardian, no. 45, pp. 16-17 (revised).

The institution of the Hands of the Cause of God, charged in the sacred Texts with the specific duties of protecting and propagating the Faith, has a particularly vital responsibility to discharge. In their capacity as protectors of the Faith, the Hands will continue to take action to expel Covenant-breakers and to reinstate those who sincerely repent, subject in each instance to the approval of the Universal House of Justice.

Messages from the Universal House of Justice 1963-1986, para. 6.4, pp. 15-16. (October 1963.)

The Station to which Bahá'ís are Called

O people of Bahá! Ye are the breezes of spring that are wafted over the world. Through you We have adorned the world of being with the ornament of the knowledge of the Most Merciful. Through you the countenance of the world hath been wreathed in smiles, and the brightness of His light shone forth. Cling ye to the Cord of steadfastness, in such wise that all vain imaginings may utterly vanish.

Bahá'u'lláh, cited by Shoghi Effendi, The Advent of Divine Justice, pp. 75-76.

Blessed are the people of Bahá! God beareth Me witness! They are the solace of the eye of creation. Through them the universes have been adorned, and the Preserved Tablet embellished. They are the ones who have sailed on the ark of complete independence, with their faces set towards the Dayspring of Beauty. How great is their blessedness that they have attained unto what their Lord, the Omniscient, the All-Wise, hath willed. Through their light the heavens have been adorned, and the faces of those that have drawn nigh unto Him made to shine.

Bahá'u'lláh, cited by Shoghi Effendi, The Advent of Divine Justice, p. 76.

*S*uch is the station ordained for the true believer that if to an extent smaller than a needle's eye the glory of that station were to be unveiled to mankind, every beholder would be consumed away in his longing to attain it. For this reason it hath been decreed that in this earthly life the full measure of the glory of his own station should remain concealed from the eyes of such a believer.

Bahá'u'lláh, cited by Shoghi Effendi, *The Advent of Divine Justice*, pp. 76-77.

Basic Truths of the Faith

God's Transcendence and Loving Providence

O Children of the Divine and Invisible Essence!

Ye shall be hindered from loving Me and souls shall be perturbed as they make mention of Me. For minds cannot grasp Me nor hearts contain Me.

Bahá'u'lláh, *The Hidden Words*, Arabic No. 66.

*B*eware, beware, lest thou be led to join partners with the Lord, thy God. He is, and hath from everlasting been, one and alone, without peer or equal, eternal in the past, eternal in the future, detached from all things, ever-abiding, unchangeable, and self-subsisting.

Bahá'u'lláh, *Gleanings from the Writings of Bahá'u'lláh*, section XCIV, p. 192.

O my servants! Let not your vain hopes and idle fancies sap the foundations of your belief in the All-Glorious God, inasmuch as such imaginings have been wholly unprofitable unto men, and failed to direct their steps unto the straight Path. Think ye, O My servants, that the Hand of My all-encompassing, My overshadowing, and transcendent sovereignty is chained up, that the flow of Mine ancient, My ceaseless, and all-pervasive mercy is checked, or that the clouds of My sublime and unsurpassed favours have ceased to rain their gifts upon men? Can ye imagine that the wondrous works that have proclaimed My divine and resistless power are withdrawn, or that the potency of My will and purpose hath been deterred from directing the destinies of mankind? If it be not so, wherefore, then, have ye striven to prevent the deathless Beauty of My sacred and gracious Countenance from being unveiled to men's eyes? Why have ye struggled to hinder the Manifestation of the Almighty and All-Glorious Being from shedding the radiance of His Revelation upon the earth?

Bahá'u'lláh, *Gleanings from the Writings of Bahá'u'lláh*, section CLIII, p. 324.

Progressive Revelation

O Salmán! The door of the knowledge of the Ancient Being hath ever been, and will continue for ever to be, closed in the face of men. No man's understanding shall ever gain access unto His holy court. As a token of His mercy, however, and as a proof of His loving-kindness, He hath manifested unto men the Day Stars of His divine guidance, the

Symbols of His divine unity, and hath ordained the knowledge of these sanctified Beings to be identical with the knowledge of His own Self. ... Every one of them is the Way of God that connecteth this world with the realms above, and the Standard of His Truth unto everyone in the kingdoms of earth and heaven. They are the Manifestations of God amidst men, the evidences of His Truth, and the signs of His glory.

Bahá'u'lláh, *Gleanings from the Writings of Bahá'u'lláh*, section XXI, p. 49-50.

*K*now thou assuredly that the essence of all the Prophets of God is one and the same. ... To prefer one in honour to another, to exalt certain ones above the rest, is in no wise to be permitted.

Bahá'u'lláh, *Gleanings from the Writings of Bahá'u'lláh*, section XXXIV, p. 78.

*E*very Prophet Whom the Almighty and Peerless Creator hath purposed to send to the peoples of the earth hath been entrusted with a Message, and charged to act in a manner that would best meet the requirements of the age in which He appeared.

Bahá'u'lláh, *Gleanings from the Writings of Bahá'u'lláh*, section XXXIV, p. 79.

*I*t should also be borne in mind that, great as is the power manifested by this Revelation and however vast the range of the Dispensation its Author has inaugurated, it emphatically repudiates the claim to be regarded as the final revelation of God's will and purpose for mankind. To hold such a conception of its character and functions would be tantamount to a betrayal of its cause and a denial of its truth. It must necessarily conflict with the fundamental principle which constitutes the bedrock of Bahá'í belief, the principle that religious truth is not absolute but relative, that Divine Revelation is orderly, continuous and progressive and not spasmodic or final.

Shoghi Effendi, The Dispensation of Bahá'u'lláh, *The World Order of Bahá'u'lláh*, p. 115.

The Purpose Underlying Creation

O Son of Man!

Veiled in My immemorial being and in the ancient eternity of My essence, I knew My love for thee; therefore I created thee, have engraved on thee Mine image and revealed to thee My beauty.

Bahá'u'lláh, *The Hidden Words*, Arabic No. 3.

*H*aving created the world and all that liveth and moveth therein, He, through the direct operation of His unconstrained and sovereign Will, chose to confer upon man the unique distinction and capacity to know Him and to love Him—a capacity that must needs be regarded as the generating impulse and the primary purpose underlying the whole of creation ...

Bahá'u'lláh, *Gleanings from the Writings of Bahá'u'lláh*, section XXVII, p. 65.

*T*he purpose of God in creating man hath been, and will ever be, to enable him to know his Creator and to attain His Presence. To this most excellent aim, this supreme objective, all the heavenly Books and the divinely-revealed and weighty Scriptures unequivocally bear witness. Whoso hath recognized the Day Spring of Divine guidance and entered His holy court hath drawn nigh unto God and attained His Presence, a Presence which is the real Paradise, and of which the loftiest mansions of heaven are but a symbol.

Bahá'u'lláh, *Gleanings from the Writings of Bahá'u'lláh*, section XXIX, p. 70.

"*W*hat is the purpose of our lives?"

'Abdu'l-Bahá: "To acquire virtues. We come from the earth; why were we transferred from the mineral to the vegetable kingdom—from the plant to the animal kingdom? So that we may attain perfection in each of these kingdoms, that we may possess the best qualities of the mineral, that we may acquire the power of growing as in the plant, that we may be adorned with the instincts of the animal and possess the faculties of sight, hearing, smell, touch and taste, until from the animal kingdom we step into the world of humanity and are gifted with reason, the power of invention, and the forces of the spirit."

Public Talk of 'Abdu'l-Bahá, *Paris Talks*, pp. 189-190.

Spiritual Development: God's Grace and Human Striving

*W*ho is there that hath cried after Thee, and whose prayer hath remained unanswered? Where is he to be found who hath reached forth towards Thee, and whom Thou hast failed to approach? Who is he that can claim to have fixed his gaze upon Thee, and toward whom the eye of Thy loving-kindness hath not been directed? I bear witness that Thou hadst turned toward Thy servants ere they had turned toward Thee, and hadst remembered them ere they had remembered Thee. All grace is Thine, O Thou in Whose hand is the kingdom of Divine gifts and the source of every irrevocable decree.

Bahá'u'lláh, *Prayers and Meditations*, section CLXI, p. 193-194 or 254.

*T*he incomparable Creator hath created all men from one same substance, and hath exalted their reality above the rest of His creatures. Success or failure, gain or loss, must, therefore, depend upon man's own exertions. The more he striveth, the greater will be his progress.

Bahá'u'lláh, *Gleanings from the Writings of Bahá'u'lláh*, section XXXIV, pp. 81-82.

*I*f, in the Day when all the peoples of the earth will be gathered together, any man should, whilst standing in the presence of God, be asked: "Wherefore hast thou disbelieved in My Beauty and turned away from My Self," and if such a man should reply and say: "Inasmuch as all men have erred, and none hath been found willing to turn his face to the Truth, I too, following their example, have grievously failed to recognize the Beauty of the Eternal," such a plea will, assuredly, be rejected. For the faith of no man can be conditioned by any one except himself.

Bahá'u'lláh, Gleanings from the Writings of Bahá'u'lláh, section LXXV, p. 143.

The Immortality of the Soul

*K*now, verily, that the soul is a sign of God, a heavenly gem whose reality the most learned of men hath failed to grasp, and whose mystery no mind, however acute, can ever hope to unravel.

Bahá'u'lláh, Gleanings from the Writings of Bahá'u'lláh, section LXXXII, pp. 158-159.

*K*now thou that the soul of man is exalted above, and is independent of all infirmities of body or mind. That a sick person showeth signs of weakness is due to the hindrances that interpose themselves between his soul and his body, for the soul itself remaineth unaffected by any bodily ailments.

Bahá'u'lláh, Gleanings from the Writings of Bahá'u'lláh, section LXXX, pp. 153-154.

The Next Life

*A*nd now concerning thy question regarding the soul of man and its survival after death. Know thou of a truth that the soul, after its separation from the body, will continue to progress until it attaineth the presence of God, in a state and condition which neither the revolution of ages and centuries, nor the changes and chances of this world, can alter. It will endure as long as the Kingdom of God, His sovereignty, His dominion and power will endure. It will manifest the signs of God and His attributes, and will reveal His loving kindness and bounty.

Bahá'u'lláh, Gleanings from the Writings of Bahá'u'lláh, section LXXXI, p. 155.

*T*he immortality of the spirit is mentioned in the Holy Books; it is the fundamental basis of the divine religions.

'Abdu'l-Bahá, Some Answered Questions, p. 223.

*T*he rewards of the other world are peace, the spiritual graces, the various spiritual gifts in the Kingdom of God, the gaining of the desires of the heart and the soul, and the meeting of God in the world of eternity. In the same way the punishments of the other world—that is to say, the torments of the other world—consist in being deprived of the special divine blessings and the absolute bounties, and falling into the lowest degrees of existence. He who is deprived of these divine favours, although he continues after death, is considered as dead by the people of truth.

'Abdu'l-Bahá, Some Answered Questions, pp. 224-225.

*I*t is even possible that the condition of those who have died in sin and unbelief may become changed—that is to say, they may become the object of pardon through the bounty of God, not through His justice—for bounty is giving without desert, and justice is giving what is deserved. As we have power to pray for these souls here, so likewise we shall possess the same power in the other world, which is the Kingdom of God. Are not all the people in that world the creatures of God? Therefore, in that world also they can make progress. As here they can receive light by their supplications, there also they can plead for forgiveness and receive light through entreaties and supplications.

'Abdu'l-Bahá, *Some Answered Questions*, p. 232.

... *T*he Kingdom of God is sanctified (or free) from time and place; it is another world and another universe. But the holy souls are promised the gift of intercession. And know thou for a certainty, that in the divine worlds, the spiritual beloved ones (believers) will recognize each other, and will seek union (with each other), but a spiritual union. Likewise, a love that one may have entertained for any one will not be forgotten in the world of the Kingdom. Likewise, thou wilt not forget (there) the life that thou hast had in the material world.

'Abdu'l-Bahá, *Tablets of Abdul-Baha Abbas*, Vol. I, pp. 205-206.

Part Two
Growing as a Bahá'í

Chapter Four
The Process of Spiritual Development

The Spiritual Reality of Human Beings

O son of man!
Veiled in My immemorial being and in the ancient eternity of My essence, I knew My love for thee; therefore I created thee, have engraved on thee Mine image and revealed to thee My beauty.

Bahá'u'lláh, The Hidden Words, Arabic No. 3.

O son of being!
Thou art My lamp and My light is in thee. Get thou from it thy radiance and seek none other than Me. For I have created thee rich and have bountifully shed My favour upon thee.

Bahá'u'lláh, The Hidden Words, Arabic No. 11.

O son of being!
With the hands of power I made thee and with the fingers of strength I created thee; and within thee have I placed the essence of My light. Be thou content with it and seek naught else, for My work is perfect and My command is binding. Question it not, nor have a doubt thereof.

Bahá'u'lláh, The Hidden Words, Arabic No. 12.

O son of spirit!
I created thee rich, why dost thou bring thyself down to poverty? Noble I made thee, wherewith dost thou abase thyself? Out of the essence of knowledge I gave thee being, why seekest thou enlightenment from anyone beside Me? Out of the clay of love I moulded thee, how dost thou busy thyself with another? Turn thy sight unto thyself, that thou mayest find Me standing within thee, mighty, powerful and self-subsisting.

Bahá'u'lláh, The Hidden Words, Arabic No. 13.

O son of man!
Thou art My dominion and My dominion perisheth not; wherefore fearest thou thy perishing? Thou art My light and My light shall never be extinguished, why dost thou dread extinction? Thou art My glory and My glory fadeth not; thou art My robe and My robe shall never be outworn. Abide then in thy love for Me, that thou mayest find Me in the realm of glory.

Bahá'u'lláh, The Hidden Words, Arabic No. 14.

O my servant!
Thou art even as a finely tempered sword concealed in the darkness of its sheath and its value hidden from the artificer's knowledge. Wherefore come forth from the sheath of self and desire that thy worth may be made resplendent and manifest unto all the world.

Bahá'u'lláh, The Hidden Words, Persian No. 72.

O my friend!
Thou art the day-star of the heavens of My holiness, let not the defilement of the world eclipse thy splendour. Rend asunder the veil of heedlessness, that from behind the clouds thou mayest emerge resplendent and array all things with the apparel of life.

Bahá'u'lláh, The Hidden Words, Persian No. 73.

*R*egard man as a mine rich in gems of inestimable value. Education can, alone, cause it to reveal its treasures, and enable mankind to benefit therefrom.

Bahá'u'lláh, Gleanings from the Writings of Bahá'u'lláh, section CXXII, p. 260.[34]

O My servants! Could ye apprehend with what wonders of My munificence and bounty I have willed to entrust your souls, ye would, of a truth, rid yourselves of attachment to all created things, and would gain a true knowledge of your own selves—a knowledge which is the same as the comprehension of Mine own Being. Ye would find yourselves independent of all else but Me, and would perceive, with your inner and outer eye, and as manifest as the revelation of My effulgent Name, the seas of My loving-kindness and bounty moving within you.

Bahá'u'lláh, Gleanings from the Writings of Bahá'u'lláh, section CLIII, pp. 326-327.

Relating to God and Developing Our Spiritual Powers

*W*hen a person becomes a Bahá'í, actually what takes place is that the seed of the spirit starts to grow in the human soul. This seed must be watered by the outpourings of the Holy Spirit. These gifts of the spirit are received through prayer, meditation, study of the Holy Utterances and service to the Cause of God. The fact of the matter is that service in the Cause is like the plough which ploughs the physical soil when seeds are sown. It is necessary that the soil be ploughed up, so that it can be enriched, and thus cause a stronger growth of the seed. In exactly the same way the evolution of the spirit takes place through ploughing up the soil of the heart so that it is a constant reflection of the Holy Spirit. In this way the human spirit grows and develops by leaps and bounds.

---

[34] Also *Tablets of Bahá'u'lláh*, p. 162.

Naturally there will be periods of distress and difficulty, and even severe tests; but if that person turns firmly towards the divine Manifestation, studies carefully His spiritual teachings and receives the blessings of the Holy Spirit, he will find that in reality these tests and difficulties have been the gifts of God to enable him to grow and develop.

Thus you might look upon your own difficulties in the path of service. They are the means of your spirit growing and developing. You will suddenly find that you have conquered many of the problems which upset you, and then you will wonder why they should have troubled you at all. An individual must centre his whole heart and mind on service to the Cause, in accordance with the high standards set by Bahá'u'lláh. When this is done, the Hosts of the Supreme Concourse will come to the assistance of the individual, and every difficulty and trial will gradually be overcome.

Letter dated 6 October 1954 written on behalf of Shoghi Effendi, The Compilation of Compilations,
Vol. II (Living the Life), No. 1334, pp. 24-25.

*R*egarding the questions you asked: self has really two meanings, or is used in two senses, in the Bahá'í writings; one is self, the identity of the individual created by God. This is the self mentioned in such passages as "he hath known God who hath known himself", etc. The other self is the ego, the dark, animalistic heritage each one of us has, the lower nature that can develop into a monster of selfishness, brutality, lust and so on. It is this self we must struggle against, or this side of our natures, in order to strengthen and free the spirit within us and help it to attain perfection.

Self-sacrifice means to subordinate this lower nature and its desires to the more Godly and noble side of our selves. Ultimately, in its highest sense, self-sacrifice means to give our will and our all to God to do with as He pleases. Then He purifies and glorifies our true self until it becomes a shining and wonderful reality.

Letter written on behalf of Shoghi Effendi, The Compilation of Compilations, Vol. II (Living the Life),
No.1318, pp. 18-19.

*T*he only people who are truly free of the "dross of self" are the Prophets, for to be free of one's ego is a hall-mark of perfection. We humans are never going to become perfect, for perfection belongs to a realm we are not destined to enter. However, we must constantly mount higher, seek to be more perfect.

The ego is the animal in us, the heritage of the flesh which is full of selfish desires. By obeying the laws of God, seeking to live the life laid down in our teachings, and prayer and struggle, we can subdue our egos. We call people "saints" who have achieved the highest degree of mastery over their egos.

There is no contradiction between *Gleanings* p. 66 and p. 262. In one place He says the mirror will never be free from dross, in the other place He says it will be "so cleared as to be able" etc. It is a relative thing; perfection will never be reached, but great and ever greater, progress can be made.

Shoghi Effendi, Unfolding Destiny, p. 453. (8 January 1949).

Faith and Steadfastness

*T*he supreme cause for creating the world and all that is therein is for man to know God. In this Day whosoever is guided by the fragrance of the raiment of His mercy to gain admittance into the pristine Abode, which is the station of recognizing the Source of divine commandments and the Dayspring of His Revelation, hath everlastingly attained unto all good. Having reached this lofty station a twofold obligation resteth upon every soul. One is to be steadfast in the Cause with such steadfastness that were all the peoples of the world to attempt to prevent him from turning to the Source of Revelation, they would be powerless to do so. The other is observance of the divine ordinances which have streamed forth from the wellspring of His heavenly-propelled Pen. For man's knowledge of God cannot develop fully and adequately save by observing whatsoever hath been ordained by Him and is set forth in His heavenly Book.

Bahá'u'lláh, *Tablets of Bahá'u'lláh*, p. 268.

*T*he first and foremost duty prescribed unto men, next to the recognition of Him Who is the Eternal Truth, is the duty of steadfastness in His Cause.

Bahá'u'lláh, *Gleanings from the Writings of Bahá'u'lláh*, section CXXXIV, p. 290.

O son of man!

For everything there is a sign. The sign of love is fortitude under My decree, and patience under My trials.

Bahá'u'lláh, *The Hidden Words,* Arabic No. 48.

*F*aith is the magnet which draws the confirmation of the Merciful One. Service is the magnet which attracts the heavenly strength. I hope thou wilt attain both.

'Abdu'l-Bahá, *Tablets of Abdul-Baha Abbas*, Vol. I, p. 62.

*O*h, trust in God! for His bounty is everlasting, and in His blessings, for they are superb. Oh! put your faith in the Almighty, for He faileth not and His goodness endureth forever! His Sun giveth Light continually, and the Clouds of His Mercy are full of the Waters of Compassion with which He waters the hearts of all who trust in Him. His refreshing Breeze ever carries healing in its wings to the parched souls of men!

Public Talk of 'Abdu'l-Bahá, *Paris Talks*, pp. 108-109.

*N*ever lose thy trust in God. Be thou ever hopeful, for the bounties of God never cease to flow upon man. If viewed from one perspective, they seem to decrease, but from another they are full and complete. Man is under all conditions immersed in a sea of God's blessings. Therefore, be thou not hopeless under any circumstances, but rather be firm in thy hope.

'Abdu'l-Bahá, *Selections from the Writings of 'Abdu'l-Bahá*, no. 178, p. 205.

O thou who art turning thy face towards God! Close thine eyes to all things else, and open them to the realm of the All-Glorious. Ask whatsoever thou wishest of Him alone; seek whatsoever thou seekest from Him alone. With a look He granteth a hundred thousand hopes, with a glance He healeth a hundred thousand incurable ills, with a nod He layeth balm on every wound, with a glimpse He freeth the hearts from the shackles of grief. He doeth as He doeth, and what recourse have we? He carrieth out His Will, He ordaineth what He pleaseth. Then better for thee to bow down thy head in submission, and put thy trust in the All-Merciful Lord.

'Abdu'l-Bahá, *Selections from the Writings of 'Abdu'l-Bahá*, no. 22, p. 51.

We must not only be patient with others, infinitely patient!, but also with our own poor selves, remembering that even the Prophets of God sometimes got tired and cried out in despair!

Letter dated 22 October 1946 written on behalf of Shoghi Effendi, *Unfolding Destiny*, p. 456.

He urges you to persevere and add up your accomplishments, rather than to dwell on the dark side of things. Everyone's life has both a dark and bright side. The Master said: turn your back to the darkness and your face to Me.

Letter dated 22 October 1946 written on behalf of Shoghi Effendi, *Unfolding Destiny*, p. 7.

Love and Sacrifice

O son of man!
I loved thy creation, hence I created thee. Wherefore, do thou love Me, that I may name thy name and fill thy soul with the spirit of life.

Bahá'u'lláh, *The Hidden Words*, Arabic No. 4.

O son of being!
Love Me, that I may love thee. If thou lovest Me not, My love can in no wise reach thee. Know this, O servant.

Bahá'u'lláh, *The Hidden Words*, Arabic No. 5.

O son of man!
If thou lovest Me, turn away from thyself; and if thou seekest My pleasure, regard not thine own; that thou mayest die in Me and I may eternally live in thee.

Bahá'u'lláh, *The Hidden Words*, Arabic No. 7.

O son of Spirit!
There is no peace for thee save by renouncing thyself and turning unto Me; for it behooveth thee to glory in My name, not in thine own; to put thy trust in Me and not in thyself, since I desire to be loved alone and above all that is.

Bahá'u'lláh, *The Hidden Words*, Arabic No. 8.

O son of utterance!

Thou art My stronghold; enter therein that thou mayest abide in safety. My love is in thee, know it, that thou mayest find Me near unto thee.

Bahá'u'lláh, *The Hidden Words,* Arabic No. 10.

*L*et the flame of the love of God burn brightly within your radiant hearts. Feed it with the oil of Divine guidance, and protect it within the shelter of your constancy. Guard it within the globe of trust and detachment from all else but God, so that the evil whisperings of the ungodly may not extinguish its light.

Bahá'u'lláh, *Gleanings from the Writings of Bahá'u'lláh,* section CLIII, pp. 325-326.

*K*now thou of a certainty that love is the secret of God's holy Dispensation, the manifestation of the All-Merciful, the fountain of spiritual outpourings. Love is heaven's kindly light, the Holy Spirit's eternal breath that vivifieth the human soul. Love is the cause of God's revelation unto man, the vital bond inherent, in accordance with the divine creation, in the realities of things. Love is the one means that ensureth true felicity both in this world and the next. Love is the light that guideth in darkness, the living link that uniteth God with man, that assureth the progress of every illumined soul. Love is the most great law that ruleth this mighty and heavenly cycle, the unique power that bindeth together the divers elements of this material world, the supreme magnetic force that directeth the movements of the spheres in the celestial realms. Love revealeth with unfailing and limitless power the mysteries latent in the universe. Love is the spirit of life unto the adorned body of mankind, the establisher of true civilization in this mortal world, and the shedder of imperishable glory upon every high-aiming race and nation.

'Abdu'l-Bahá, *Selections from the Writings of 'Abdu'l-Bahá,* no. 12, pp. 27-28.

*T*here are four kinds of love. The first is the love that flows from God to man; it consists of the inexhaustible graces, the Divine effulgence and heavenly illumination. Through this love the world of being receives life. Through this love man is endowed with physical existence, until, through the breath of the Holy Spirit—this same love—he receives eternal life and becomes the image of the Living God. This love is the origin of all the love in the world of creation.

The second is the love that flows from man to God. This is faith, attraction to the Divine, enkindlement, progress, entrance into the Kingdom of God, receiving the Bounties of God, illumination with the lights of the Kingdom. This love is the origin of all philanthropy; this love causes the hearts of men to reflect the rays of the Sun of Reality.

The third is the love of God towards the Self or Identity of God. This is the transfiguration of His Beauty, the reflection of Himself in the mirror of His Creation. This is the reality of love, the Ancient Love, the Eternal Love. Through one ray of this Love all other love exists.

The fourth is the love of man for man. The love which exists between the hearts of believers is prompted by the ideal of the unity of spirits. This love is attained through the knowledge of God, so that men see the Divine Love reflected in the heart. Each sees in the other the Beauty of God reflected in the soul, and finding this point of similarity, they are attracted to one another in love. This love will make all men the waves of one sea, this love will make them all the stars of one heaven and the fruits of one tree. This love will bring the realization of true accord, the foundation of real unity.

Public Talk of 'Abdu'l-Bahá, *Paris Talks*, pp. 193-194.

*F*or love of God and spiritual attraction do cleanse and purify the human heart and dress and adorn it with the spotless garment of holiness; and once the heart is entirely attached to the Lord, and bound over to the Blessed Perfection, then will the grace of God be revealed.

This love is not of the body but completely of the soul. And those souls whose inner being is lit by the love of God are even as spreading rays of light, and they shine out like stars of holiness in a pure and crystalline sky. For true love, real love, is the love for God, and this is sanctified beyond the notions and imaginings of men.

'Abdu'l-Bahá, *Selections from the Writings of 'Abdu'l-Bahá*, no. 174, pp. 202-203.

... *T*o make a sacrifice is to receive a gift ...

'Abdu'l-Bahá, *Selections from the Writings of 'Abdu'l-Bahá*, no. 200, p. 245.

*T*he mystery of sacrifice is a profound one, requiring detailed explanation, but briefly it may be stated that sacrificial love is the love shown by the moth towards the candle, by the parched wayfarer towards the living fountain, by the true lover towards his beloved, ... The sacrificial lover, in other words, should become entirely forgetful of self, ... he should seek the good pleasure of the True One, desire to gaze upon His countenance, and wish to follow in His way. ... This is the first degree of sacrifice.

As for the second degree, it is in man's becoming rid of all attachment to the human world .... In this degree, the radiance of the All-Merciful should so suffuse and permeate his being that this nether world may pale into non-existence before the reality of the Kingdom. When a lump of iron is cast into the forge, its ferrous qualities of blackness, coldness and solidity, which symbolize the attributes of the human world, are concealed and disappear, while the fire's distinctive qualities of redness, heat and fluidity, which symbolize the virtues of the Kingdom, become visibly apparent in it, so that the iron may be said to have sacrificed its own qualities and characteristics to the fire, and to have acquired the virtues of that element. Even so is it with man: when, released from earthly bonds, from human imperfections, and from the darkness of the animal world, he ... partaketh of the outpourings of the unseen world, and acquireth divine virtues and perfections, then will he become a sacrificial lover of the Sun of Truth, and make haste with heart and soul to reach the place of sacrifice.

'Abdu'l-Bahá, *Tablets of Abdul-Baha Abbas*, Vol II, p. 354-355. (revised.)

... nearness to God necessitates sacrifice of self, severance and the giving up of all to Him. Nearness is likeness.

Public Talk of 'Abdu'l-Bahá, *The Promulgation of Universal Peace*, p. 148.

Knowledge and Insight

*K*now thou that, according to what thy Lord, the Lord of all men, hath decreed in His Book, the favours vouchsafed by Him unto mankind have been, and will ever remain, limitless in their range. First and foremost among these favours, which the Almighty hath conferred upon man, is the gift of understanding. His purpose in conferring such a gift is none other except to enable His creature to know and recognize the one true God—exalted be His glory. This gift giveth man the power to discern the truth in all things, leadeth him to that which is right, and helpeth him to discover the secrets of creation.

Bahá'u'lláh, *Gleanings from the Writings of Bahá'u'lláh*, section XCV, p. 194.

... *T*hey that tread the path of faith, they that thirst for the wine of certitude, must cleanse themselves of all that is earthly—their ears from idle talk, their minds from vain imaginings, their hearts from worldly affections, their eyes from that which perisheth. They should put their trust in God, and, holding fast unto Him, follow in His way. Then will they be made worthy of the effulgent glories of the sun of divine knowledge and understanding, and become the recipients of a grace that is infinite and unseen, inasmuch as man can never hope to attain unto the knowledge of the All-Glorious, can never quaff from the stream of divine knowledge and wisdom, can never enter the abode of immortality, nor partake of the cup of divine nearness and favour, unless and until he ceases to regard the words and deeds of mortal men as a standard for the true understanding and recognition of God and His Prophets.

Bahá'u'lláh, *The Kitáb-i-Íqán* (The Book of Certitude), pp. 3-4.

*I*mmerse yourselves in the ocean of My words, that ye may unravel its secrets, and discover all the pearls of wisdom that lie hid in its depths.

Bahá'u'lláh, *The Kitáb-i-Aqdas* (The Most Holy Book), para. 182, p. 85.

O ye dwellers in the highest paradise!

Proclaim unto the children of assurance that within the realms of holiness, nigh unto the celestial paradise, a new garden hath appeared, round which circle the denizens of the realm on high and the immortal dwellers of the exalted paradise. Strive, then, that ye may attain that station, that ye may unravel the mysteries of love from its wind-flowers and learn the secret of divine and consummate wisdom from its eternal fruits. Solaced are the eyes of them that enter and abide therein!

Bahá'u'lláh, *The Hidden Words*, Persian No. 18.

O son of my handmaid!

Quaff from the tongue of the merciful the stream of divine mystery, and behold from the dayspring of divine utterance the unveiled splendour of the day-star of wisdom. Sow the seeds of My divine wisdom in the pure soil of the heart, and water them with the waters of certitude, that the hyacinths of knowledge and wisdom may spring up fresh and green from the holy city of the heart.

Bahá'u'lláh, *The Hidden Words*, Persian No. 78.

O son of the throne!

Thy hearing is My hearing, hear thou therewith. Thy sight is My sight, do thou see therewith, that in thine inmost soul thou mayest testify unto My exalted sanctity, and I within Myself may bear witness unto an exalted station for thee.

Bahá'u'lláh, *The Hidden Words*, Arabic No. 44.

*I*n sum, the differences in objects have now been made plain. Thus when the wayfarer gazeth only upon the place of appearance—that is, when he seeth only the many-coloured globes—he beholdeth yellow and red and white; hence it is that conflict hath prevailed among the creatures, and a darksome dust from limited souls hath hid the world. And some do gaze upon the effulgence of the light; and some have drunk of the wine of oneness and these see nothing but the sun itself.

Thus, for that they move on these three differing planes, the understanding and the words of the wayfarers have differed; and hence the sign of conflict doth continually appear on earth. For some there are who dwell upon the plane of oneness and speak of that world, and some inhabit the realms of limitation, and some the grades of self, while others are completely veiled. Thus do the ignorant people of the day, who have no portion of the radiance of Divine Beauty, make certain claims, and in every age and cycle inflict on the people of the sea of oneness what they themselves deserve.

Bahá'u'lláh, *The Seven Valleys and The Four Valleys*, pp. 20-21.

*T*he wayfarer in this Valley seeth in the fashionings of the True One nothing save clear providence, and at every moment saith: "No defect canst thou see in the creation of the God of Mercy: Repeat the gaze: Seest thou a single flaw?" He beholdeth justice in injustice, and in justice, grace. In ignorance he findeth many a knowledge hidden, and in knowledge a myriad wisdoms manifest. He breaketh the cage of the body and the passions, and consorteth with the people of the immortal realm. He mounteth on the ladders of inner truth and hasteneth to the heaven of inner significance. He rideth in the ark of "we shall show them our signs in the regions and in themselves," and journeyeth over the sea of "until it become plain to them that (this Book) is the truth." And if he meeteth with injustice he shall have patience, and if he cometh upon wrath he shall manifest love.

Bahá'u'lláh, *The Seven Valleys and the Four Valleys*, pp. 12-13.

O Thou the Compassionate God. Bestow upon me a heart which, like unto a glass, may be illumined with the light of Thy love, and confer upon me thoughts which may change this world into a rose-garden through the outpourings of heavenly grace.

'Abdu'l-Bahá, *A Selection of Bahá'í Prayers and Holy Writings*, no. 49, p. 53.

Choice and Action

*W*hatsoever instilleth assurance into the hearts of men, whatsoever exalteth their station or promoteth their contentment, is acceptable in the sight of God. How lofty is the station which man, if he but chooseth to fulfil his high destiny, can attain!

Bahá'u'lláh, *Gleanings from the Writings of Bahá'u'lláh*, section CI, p. 206.

*W*ert thou to consider this world, and realize how fleeting are the things that pertain unto it, thou wouldst choose to tread no path except the path of service to the Cause of thy Lord. None would have the power to deter thee from celebrating His praise, though all men should arise to oppose thee.

Go thou straight on and persevere in His service.

Bahá'u'lláh, *Gleanings from the Writings of Bahá'u'lláh*, section CXLIV, p. 314.

O son of love!
Thou art but one step away from the glorious heights above and from the celestial tree of love. Take thou one pace and with the next advance into the immortal realm and enter the pavilion of eternity. Give ear then to that which hath been revealed by the pen of glory.

Bahá'u'lláh, *The Hidden Words*, Persian No. 7.

O my friends!
Have ye forgotten that true and radiant morn, when in those hallowed and blessed surroundings ye were all gathered in My presence beneath the shade of the tree of life, which is planted in the all-glorious paradise? Awestruck ye listened as I gave utterance to these three most holy words: O friends! Prefer not your will to Mine, never desire that which I have not desired for you, and approach Me not with lifeless hearts, defiled with worldly desires and cravings. Would ye but sanctify your souls, ye would at this present hour recall that place and those surroundings, and the truth of My utterance should be made evident unto all of you.

Bahá'u'lláh, *The Hidden Words*, Persian No. 19.

O son of my handmaid!
Guidance hath ever been given by words, and now it is given by deeds. Every one must show forth deeds that are pure and holy, for words are the property of all alike, whereas such deeds as these belong only to Our loved ones. Strive then with heart and soul to distinguish yourselves by your deeds. In this wise We counsel you in this holy and resplendent tablet.

Bahá'u'lláh, *The Hidden Words*, Persian No. 76.

O my servants!

Ye are the trees of My garden; ye must give forth goodly and wondrous fruits, that ye yourselves and others may profit therefrom. Thus it is incumbent on every one to engage in crafts and professions, for therein lies the secret of wealth, O men of understanding! For results depend upon means, and the grace of God shall be all-sufficient unto you. Trees that yield no fruit have been and will ever be for the fire.

Bahá'u'lláh, *The Hidden Words*, Persian No. 80.

*H*ow often the beloved Master was heard to say. Should each one of the friends take upon himself to carry out, in all its integrity and implications, only one of the teachings of the Faith, with devotion, detachment, constancy and perseverance and exemplify it in all his deeds and pursuits of life, the world would become another world and the face of the earth would mirror forth the splendours of the Abhá Paradise. Consider what marvellous changes would be effected if the beloved of the Merciful conducted themselves, both in their individual and collective capacities, in accordance with the counsels and exhortations which have streamed from the Pen of Glory.

Letter dated 12 January 1923 written on behalf of Shoghi Effendi,
The Compilation of Compilations, Vol. II (Living the Life), no. 1266, p. 1.

*T*he great thing is to "live the life"—to have our lives so saturated with the Divine teachings and the Bahá'í Spirit that people cannot fail to see a joy, a power, a love, a purity, a radiance, and efficiency in our character and work that will distinguish us from worldly-minded people and make people wonder what is the secret of this new life in us. We must become entirely selfless and devoted to God so that every day and every moment we seek to do only what God would have us do and in the way He would have us do it. If we do this sincerely then we shall have perfect unity and harmony with each other. Where there is want of harmony, there is lack of the true Bahá'í Spirit. Unless we can show this transformation in our lives, this new power, this mutual love and harmony, then the Bahá'í teachings are but a name to us.

Letter dated 14 February 1925 written on behalf of Shoghi Effendi,
The Compilation of Compilations, Vol. II (Living the Life), no. 1271, p. 3.

A "best teacher" and an "exemplary believer" is ultimately neither more nor less than an ordinary Bahá'í who has consecrated himself to the work of the Faith, deepened his knowledge and understanding of its Teachings, placed his confidence in Bahá'u'lláh, and arisen to serve Him to the best of his ability. This door is one which we are assured will open before the face of every follower of the Faith who knocks hard enough, so to speak. When the will and the desire are strong enough, the means will be found and the way opened ...

Letter dated 21 September 1957 written on behalf of Shoghi Effendi, *The Compilation of Compilations*, Vol. II (Living the Life), no. 1340, p. 27; and no. 2012, p. 326. (revised July 1990.)

The Divine Education Programme

O people of God! That which traineth the world is Justice, for it is upheld by two pillars, reward and punishment. These two pillars are the sources of life to the world.

Bishárát (Glad-Tidings), Bahá'u'lláh, *Tablets of Bahá'u'lláh*, p. 27; and pp. 128-129.

*F*or every act performed there shall be a recompense according to the estimate of God, and unto this the very ordinances and prohibitions prescribed by the Almighty amply bear witness. For surely if deeds were not rewarded and yielded no fruit, then the Cause of God—exalted is He—would prove futile. ... However, unto them that are rid of all attachments a deed is, verily, its own reward.

Súrih-i-Vafá (Tablet to Vafá), Bahá'u'lláh, *Tablets of Bahá'u'lláh*, p. 189.

*I*n this day the breeze of God is wafted, and His Spirit hath pervaded all things. Such is the outpouring of His grace that the pen is stilled and the tongue is speechless.

Bahá'u'lláh, *The Kitáb-i-Íqán* (The Book of Certitude), pp. 180-181.

Bestowals and Blessings

... *W*hatever is in the heavens and whatever is on the earth is a direct evidence of the revelation within it of the attributes and names of God, inasmuch as within every atom are enshrined the signs that bear eloquent testimony to the revelation of that most great Light. Methinks, but for the potency of that revelation, no being could ever exist. How resplendent the luminaries of knowledge that shine in an atom, and how vast the oceans of wisdom that surge within a drop! To a supreme degree is this true of man, who, among all created things, hath been invested with the robe of such gifts, and hath been singled out for the glory of such distinction. For in him are potentially revealed all the attributes and names of God to a degree that no other created being hath excelled or surpassed. All these names and attributes are applicable to him. Even as He hath said: "Man is My mystery, and I am his mystery." Manifold are the verses that have been repeatedly revealed in all the heavenly Books and the holy Scriptures, expressive of this most subtle and lofty theme. Even as He hath revealed: "We will surely show them Our signs in the world and within themselves." Again He saith: "And also in your own selves: will ye not then behold the signs of God?" And yet again He revealeth: "And be ye not like those who forget God, and whom He hath therefore caused to forget their own selves." In this connection, He Who is the eternal King—may the souls of all that dwell within the mystic Tabernacle be a sacrifice unto Him—hath spoken: "He hath known God who hath known himself."

I swear by God, O esteemed and honoured friend! Shouldst thou ponder these words in thine heart, thou wilt of a certainty find the doors of divine wisdom and infinite knowledge flung open before thy face.

Bahá'u'lláh, *The Kitáb-i-Íqán* (The Book of Certitude), pp. 100-102.

*A*nd of all men, the most accomplished, the most distinguished and the most excellent are the Manifestations of the Sun of Truth. Nay, all else besides these Manifestations, live by the operation of their Will, and move and have their being through the outpourings of their grace. "But for Thee, I would have not created the heavens." Nay, all in their holy presence fade into utter nothingness, and are a thing forgotten. Human tongue can never befittingly sing their praise, and human speech can never unfold their mystery. These Tabernacles of holiness, these primal Mirrors which reflect the light of unfading glory, are but expressions of Him Who is the Invisible of the Invisibles. By the revelation of these gems of divine virtue all the names and attributes of God, such as knowledge and power, sovereignty and dominion, mercy and wisdom, glory, bounty and grace, are made manifest.

Bahá'u'lláh, *The Kitáb-i-Íqán* (The Book of Certitude), p. 103.

O son of bounty!

Out of the wastes of nothingness, with the clay of My command I made thee to appear, and have ordained for thy training every atom in existence and the essence of all created things. Thus, ere thou didst issue from thy mother's womb, I destined for thee two founts of gleaming milk, eyes to watch over thee, and hearts to love thee. Out of My loving-kindness, 'neath the shade of My mercy I nurtured thee, and guarded thee by the essence of My grace and favour. And My purpose in all this was that thou mightest attain My everlasting dominion and become worthy of My invisible bestowals. And yet heedless thou didst remain, and when fully grown, thou didst neglect all My bounties and occupied thyself with thine idle imaginings, in such wise that thou didst become wholly forgetful, and, turning away from the portals of the Friend, didst abide within the courts of My enemy.

Bahá'u'lláh, *The Hidden Words*, Persian No. 29.

... *G*od hath ordained every good thing, whether created in the heavens or in the earth, for such of His servants as truly believe in Him. Eat ye, O people, of the good things which God hath allowed you, and deprive not yourselves from His wondrous bounties.

Bahá'u'lláh, *Gleanings from the Writings of Bahá'u'lláh*, section CXXVIII, p. 276.

*B*eseech ye the one true God to grant that ye may taste the savour of such deeds as are performed in His path, and partake of the sweetness of such humility and submissiveness as are shown for His sake. Forget your own selves, and turn your eyes towards your neighbour. Bend your energies to whatever may foster the education of men. Nothing is, or can ever be, hidden from God. If ye follow in His way, His incalculable and imperishable blessings will be showered upon you.

Bahá'u'lláh, *Gleanings from the Writings of Bahá'u'lláh*, section V, p. 9.

*T*he blessings of Bahá'u'lláh are a shoreless sea, and even life everlasting is only a dewdrop therefrom. The waves of that sea are continually lapping against the hearts of the friends, and from those waves there come intimations of the spirit and ardent pulsings of the soul, until the heart giveth way, and willing or not, turneth humbly in prayer unto the Kingdom of the Lord. Wherefore do all ye can to disengage your inner selves, that ye may at every moment reflect new splendours from the Sun of Truth.

Ye live, all of you, within the heart of 'Abdu'l-Bahá, and with every breath do I turn my face toward the Threshold of Oneness and call down blessings upon you, each and all.

'Abdu'l-Bahá, Selections from the Writings of 'Abdu'l-Bahá, no. 162, pp. 192-193.

Tests and Difficulties

O son of man!
If adversity befall thee not in My path, how canst thou walk in the ways of them that are content with My pleasure? If trials afflict thee not in thy longing to meet Me, how wilt thou attain the light in thy love for My beauty?

Bahá'u'lláh, The Hidden Words, Arabic No. 50.

O son of man!
My calamity is My providence, outwardly it is fire and vengeance, but inwardly it is light and mercy. Hasten thereunto that thou mayest become an eternal light and an immortal spirit. This is My command unto thee, do thou observe it.

Bahá'u'lláh, The Hidden Words, Arabic No. 51.

O My servants! Sorrow not if, in these days and on this earthly plane, things contrary to your wishes have been ordained and manifested by God, for days of blissful joy, of heavenly delight, are assuredly in store for you. Worlds, holy and spiritually glorious, will be unveiled to your eyes. You are destined by Him, in this world and hereafter, to partake of their benefits, to share in their joys, and to obtain a portion of their sustaining grace. To each and every one of them you will, no doubt, attain.

Bahá'u'lláh, Gleanings from the Writings of Bahá'u'lláh, section CLIII, p. 329.

*T*ests are benefits from God, for which we should thank Him. Grief and sorrow do not come to us by chance, they are sent to us by the Divine mercy for our own perfecting.

While a man is happy he may forget his God; but when grief comes and sorrows overwhelm him, then will he remember his Father Who is in Heaven, and who is able to deliver him from his humiliations.

Men who suffer not, attain no perfection. The plant most pruned by the gardeners is that one which, when the summer comes, will have the most beautiful blossoms and the most abundant fruit.

The labourer cuts up the earth with his plough, and from that earth comes the rich and plentiful harvest. The more a man is chastened, the greater is the harvest of spiritual virtues shown forth by him. A soldier is no good general until he has been in the front of the fiercest battle and has received the deepest wounds.

Public Talk of 'Abdu'l-Bahá, Paris Talks, pp. 42-43.

*T*hou has written concerning the tests that have come upon thee. To the sincere ones, tests are as a gift from God, the Exalted, for a heroic person hasteneth, with the utmost joy and gladness, to the tests of a violent battlefield, but the coward is afraid and trembles and utters moaning and lamentation. Likewise, an expert student prepareth and memorizeth his lessons and exercises with the utmost effort, and in the day of examination he appears with infinite joy before the master. Likewise, the pure gold shines radiantly in the fire of test. Consequently, it is made clear that for holy souls, trials are as the gift of God, the Exalted; but for weak souls they are an unexpected calamity. This test is just as thou hast written: it removeth the rust of egotism from the mirror of the heart until the Sun of Truth may shine therein. For no veil is greater than egotism and no matter how thin that covering may be, yet it will finally veil man entirely and prevent him from receiving a portion from the eternal bounty.

'Abdu'l-Bahá, *Tablets of Abdul-Baha Abbas*, Vol. III, pp. 722-723.

*E*verything of importance in this world demands the close attention of its seeker. The one in pursuit of anything must undergo difficulties and hardships until the object in view is attained and the great success is obtained. This is the case of things pertaining to the world. How much higher is that which concerns the Supreme Concourse! That Cause involves every favour, glory and eternal bliss in the world of God.

'Abdu'l-Bahá, *Tablets of Abdul-Baha Abbas*, Vol. II, pp. 265-266.

*A*s to the subject of babes and infants and weak ones who are afflicted by the hands of oppressors: This contains great wisdom and this subject is of paramount importance. In brief, for those souls there is a recompense in another world and many details are connected with this matter. For those souls that suffering is the greatest mercy of God. Verily that mercy of the Lord is far better and preferable to all the comfort of this world and the growth and development of this place of mortality.

'Abdu'l-Bahá, *Bahá'í World Faith*, p. 372.

*H*e is very happy to see that you have put into practice one of the most encouraging precepts of 'Abdu'l-Bahá in which He said that we should try and make every stumbling-block a stepping-stone to progress. In the course of your past life you have all stumbled very gravely; but, far from being embittered or defeated by this experience, you are determined to make it a means of purifying your natures, improving your characters, and enabling you to become better citizens in the future. This is truly pleasing in the eyes of God.

Letter dated 26 March 1957 written on behalf of Shoghi Effendi, *The Compilation of Compilations*, Vol. II (Living the Life), no. 1338, p. 26.

Guidance and Confirmations

*T*hat which is pre-eminent above all other gifts, is incorruptible in nature, and pertaineth to God Himself, is the gift of Divine Revelation. Every bounty conferred by the Creator upon man, be it material or spiritual, is subservient unto this. It is, in its essence, and will ever so remain, the Bread which cometh down from Heaven. It is

God's supreme testimony, the clearest evidence of His truth, the sign of His consummate bounty, the token of His all-encompassing mercy, the proof of His most loving providence, the symbol of His most perfect grace. He hath, indeed, partaken of this highest gift of God who hath recognized His Manifestation in this Day.

    Bahá'u'lláh, *Gleanings from the Writings of Bahá'u'lláh*, section XCV, p. 195.

*B*y the righteousness of God! Whoso openeth his lips in this Day and maketh mention of the name of his Lord, the hosts of Divine inspiration shall descend upon him from the heaven of My name, the All-Knowing, the All-Wise. On him shall also descend the Concourse on high, each bearing aloft a chalice of pure light. Thus hath it been foreordained in the realm of God's Revelation, by the behest of Him Who is the All-Glorious, the Most Powerful.

    Bahá'u'lláh, *Gleanings from the Writings of Bahá'u'lláh*, section CXXIX, p. 280.

*H*e, verily, will aid everyone that aideth Him, and will remember everyone that remembereth Him. To this beareth witness this Tablet that hath shed the splendour of the loving-kindness of your Lord, the All-Glorious, the All-Compelling ...

  Bahá'u'lláh, *The Compilation of Compilations*, Vol. II (The Power of Divine Assistance), no. 1646, p. 203.[35]

O ye servants of the Sacred Threshold! The triumphant hosts of the Celestial Concourse, arrayed and marshalled in the Realms above, stand ready and expectant to assist and assure victory to that valiant horseman who with confidence spurs on his charger into the arena of service. Well is it with that fearless warrior, who armed with the power of true Knowledge, hastens unto the field, disperses the armies of ignorance, and scatters the hosts of error, who holds aloft the Standard of Divine Guidance, and sounds the Clarion of Victory. By the righteousness of the Lord! He hath achieved a glorious triumph and obtained the true victory.

    'Abdu'l-Bahá, *Selections from the Writings of 'Abdu'l-Bahá*, no. 208, p. 264.

*T*eaching is the source of Divine Confirmation. It is not sufficient to pray diligently for guidance, but this prayer must be followed by meditation as to the best methods of action and *then action itself.* Even if the action should not immediately produce results, or perhaps not be entirely correct, that does not make so much difference, because *prayers can only be answered through action* and if someone's action is wrong, God can use that method of showing the pathway which is right.

  Letter dated 22 August 1957 written on behalf of Shoghi Effendi, *The Compilation of Compilations*, Vol. II (Guidelines for Teaching), no. 2011, p. 325. (revised.)

*T*he invisible hosts of the Kingdom are ready to extend to you all the assistance you need, and through them you will no doubt succeed in removing every obstacle in your way, and in fulfilling this most cherished desire of your heart. Bahá'u'lláh has given us [a] promise that should we persevere in our efforts and repose all our confidence in Him the doors of success will be widely open before us ...

  Letter dated 22 September 1936 written on behalf of Shoghi Effendi, *The Compilation of Compilations*, Vol. II (The Power of Divine Assistance), no. 1705, p. 220.

---

35 Also cited by Shoghi Effendi, *The Advent of Divine Justice*, p. 76.

Chapter Five
Turning towards God

Requisites for Spiritual Growth

Bahá'u'lláh has stated quite clearly in His writings the essential requisites for our spiritual growth, and these are stressed again and again by 'Abdu'l-Bahá in His talks and Tablets. One can summarize them briefly in this way:

1. The recital each day of one of the Obligatory Prayers with pure-hearted devotion.
2. The regular reading of the Sacred Scriptures, specifically at least each morning and evening with reverence, attention and thought.
3. Prayerful meditation on the Teachings, so that we may understand them more deeply, fulfil them more faithfully, and convey them more accurately to others.
4. Striving every day to bring our behaviour more into accordance with the high standards that are set forth in the Teachings.
5. Teaching the Cause of God.
6. Selfless service in the work of the Cause and in the carrying on of our trade or profession.

Messages from the Universal House of Justice 1963–1986, para. 375.5, p. 589.

Prayer

O son of light!
Forget all save Me and commune with My Spirit. This is of the essence of My command; therefore turn unto it.

Bahá'u'lláh, *The Hidden Words*, Arabic No. 16.

Thou disappointest no one who hath sought Thee, nor dost Thou keep back from Thee any one who hath desired Thee.

Bahá'u'lláh, *Prayers and Meditations*, section CLVI, p. 250.

Worship thou God in such wise that if thy worship lead thee to the fire, no alteration in thine adoration would be produced, and so likewise if thy recompense should be paradise. Thus and thus alone should be the worship which befitteth the one True

114 PATHWAYS TO TRANSFORMATION

God. Shouldst thou worship Him because of fear, this would be unseemly in the sanctified Court of His presence, and could not be regarded as an act by thee dedicated to the Oneness of His Being. Or if thy gaze should be on paradise, and thou shouldst worship Him while cherishing such a hope, thou wouldst make God's creation a partner with Him, notwithstanding the fact that paradise is desired by men.

Fire and paradise both bow down and prostrate themselves before God. That which is worthy of His Essence is to worship Him for His sake, without fear of fire, or hope of paradise.

Although when true worship is offered, the worshipper is delivered from the fire, and entereth the paradise of God's good-pleasure, yet such should not be the motive of his act. However, God's favour and grace ever flow in accordance with the exigencies of His inscrutable wisdom.

The most acceptable prayer is the one offered with the utmost spirituality and radiance; its prolongation hath not been and is not beloved by God. The more detached and the purer the prayer, the more acceptable is it in the presence of God.

The Báb, Selections from the Writings of the Báb, pp. 77-78.

... *T*he core of religious faith is the mystic feeling which unites man with God. This state of spiritual communion can be brought about and maintained by means of meditation and prayer. And this is the reason why Bahá'u'lláh has so much stressed the importance of worship. It is not sufficient for a believer merely to accept and observe the teachings. He should, in addition, cultivate the sense of spirituality which he can acquire chiefly by means of prayer ...

... The believers, particularly the young ones, should therefore fully realize the necessity of praying. For prayer is absolutely indispensable to their inner spiritual development, and this, as already stated, is the very foundation and purpose of the religion of God.

Letter written on behalf of Shoghi Effendi, Directives from the Guardian, no. 223, pp. 86-87.

How to Pray

*I*f one friend feels love for another he will wish to say so. Though he knows that the friend is aware that he loves him, he will still wish to say so. ... God knows the wishes of all hearts, but the impulse to pray is a natural one, springing from man's love to God. ...

... Prayer need not be in words, but rather in thought and action. But if this love and this desire are lacking, it is useless to try to force them. Words without love mean nothing. If a person talks to you as an unpleasant duty, with no love or pleasure in his meeting with you, do you wish to converse with him?

Words of 'Abdu'l-Bahá, reported in Bahá'u'lláh and the New Era,
Prayer the Language of Love section, p. 94.

We must strive to attain to that condition[36] by being separated from all things and from the people of the world and by turning to God alone. It will take some effort on the part of man to attain to that condition, but he must work for it, strive for it. We can attain to it by thinking and caring less for material things and more for the spiritual. The further we go from the one, the nearer we are to the other. The choice is ours.

Our spiritual perception, our inward sight must be opened, so that we can see the signs and traces of God's spirit in everything. Everything can reflect to us the light of the Spirit.

Words of 'Abdu'l-Bahá, reported in *Bahá'u'lláh and the New Era*,
The Devotional Attitude section, p. 89.

The wisdom of obligatory prayer is this: That it causeth a connection between the servant and the True One, because at that time man with all his heart and soul turneth his face towards the Almighty, seeking His association and desiring His love and companionship. For a lover, there is no greater pleasure than to converse with his beloved, and for a seeker, there is no greater bounty than intimacy with the object of his desire. It is the greatest longing of every soul who is attracted to the Kingdom of God to find time to turn with entire devotion to his Beloved, so as to seek His bounty and blessing and immerse himself in the ocean of communion, entreaty and supplication.

'Abdu'l-Bahá, *The Importance of Obligatory Prayer and Fasting*, vii, pp. 14-15.

If you find you need to visualize some one when you pray, think of the Master. Through Him you can address Bahá'u'lláh. Gradually try to think of the qualities of the Manifestation, and in that way a mental form will fade out, for after all the body is not the thing, His Spirit is there and is the essential, everlasting element.

Letter dated 31 January 1939 written on behalf of Shoghi Effendi,
Directives from the Guardian, no. 159, p. 59.[37]

The Obligatory Prayers

I bear witness, O my God, that Thou hast created me to know Thee and to worship Thee. I testify, at this moment, to my powerlessness and to Thy might, to my poverty and to Thy wealth.

There is none other God but Thee, the Help in Peril, the Self-Subsisting.

Bahá'u'lláh, Short Obligatory Prayer, *Bahá'í Prayers (US)*, p. 4.

O My brother! How great, how very great, can the law of obligatory prayer be, when, through His mercy and loving kindness, one is enabled to observe it. When a man commenceth the recitation of the Obligatory Prayer, he should see himself severed from all created things and regard himself as utter nothingness before the will and purpose of God, in such wise that he seeth naught but Him in the world of being. This is the station of

---

36 Spiritual condition in which communion with God becomes possible.
37 Also *The Compilation of Compilations*, Vol. II (Prayer, Meditation and the Devotional Attitude), p. 242.

God's well-favoured ones and those who are wholly devoted to Him. Should one perform the Obligatory Prayer in this manner, he will be accounted by God and the Concourse on high among those who have truly offered the prayer.

Bahá'u'lláh, in *The Importance of Obligatory Prayer and Fasting*, p. 4.

*O*bligatory prayer causeth the heart to become attentive to the Divine kingdom. One is alone with God, converseth with Him, and acquireth bounties. Likewise, if one performeth the Obligatory Prayer with his heart in a state of utmost purity, he will obtain the confirmations of the Holy Spirit, and this will entirely obliterate love of self. I hope that thou wilt persevere in the recitation of the Obligatory Prayer, and thus will come to witness the power of entreaty and supplication.

'Abdu'l-Bahá, in *The Importance of Obligatory Prayer and Fasting*, p. 17.

*O*bligatory prayer and supplication cause man to reach the kingdom of mystery, and the worship of the Supreme One. They bestow nearness unto His threshold. There is a pleasure in offering prayers that transcendeth all other pleasures, and there is a sweetness in chanting and singing the verses of God which is the greatest desire of all the believers, men and women alike. While reciting the Obligatory Prayer, one converseth intimately and shareth secrets with the true Beloved. No pleasure is greater than this, if one proceedeth with a detached soul, with tears overflowing, with a trusting heart and an eager spirit. Every joy is earthly save this one, the sweetness of which is divine.

'Abdu'l-Bahá, in *The Importance of Obligatory Prayer and Fasting*, pp. 17-18.

*T*he daily obligatory prayers are three in number. The shortest one consists of a single verse which has to be recited once in every twenty-four hours at midday. The medium, which begins with the words, "The Lord is witness that there is none other God but He", has to be recited three times a day, in the morning, at noon, and in the evening. This prayer is accompanied by certain physical acts and gestures. The long prayer, which is the most elaborate of the three, has to be recited only once in every twenty-four hours, and at any time one feels inclined to do so.

The believer is entirely free to choose any one of these three prayers, but is under the obligation of reciting one of them, and in accordance with any specific directions with which it may be accompanied.

These daily obligatory prayers, together with a few other specific ones, such as the Healing Prayer, the Tablet of Aḥmad, have been invested by Bahá'u'lláh with a special potency and significance, and should therefore be accepted as such and be recited by the believers with unquestioning faith and confidence, that through them they may enter into a much closer communion with God, and identify themselves more fully with His laws and precepts.

Letter dated 10 January 1936 written on behalf of Shoghi Effendi to a National Spiritual Assembly, *Directives from the Guardian*, no. 160, p. 60. (revised.)

*T*he friends have long been familiar with the great importance which Bahá'u'lláh attaches to daily obligatory prayer and to the observance of the fast, but a number of aspects of the law, such as those concerning ablutions, travelling and the compensation for prayers missed, remained to be made universally applicable. This step is now taken.

Thus all elements of the laws dealing with obligatory prayer and fasting are, without any exception, now applicable.

> Letter dated 28 December of the Universal House of Justice to the Bahá'ís of the World, cited in *Australian Bahá'í Bulletin*, February 2000, p. 2.

The Dynamics of Prayer

O thou who art turning thy face towards God! Close thine eyes to all things else, and open them to the realm of the All-Glorious. Ask whatsoever thou wishest of Him alone; seek whatsoever thou seekest from Him alone. With a look He granteth a hundred thousand hopes, with a glance He healeth a hundred thousand incurable ills, with a nod He layeth balm on every wound, with a glimpse He freeth the hearts from the shackles of grief. He doeth as He doeth, and what recourse have we? He carrieth out His Will, He ordaineth what He pleaseth. Then better for thee to bow down thy head in submission, and put thy trust in the All-Merciful Lord.

> 'Abdu'l-Bahá, *Selections from the Writings of 'Abdu'l-Bahá*, no. 22, p. 51.

*G*od will answer the prayer of every servant if that prayer is urgent. His mercy is vast, illimitable. ...

But we ask for things which the divine wisdom does not desire for us, and there is no answer to our prayer.

> 'Abdu'l-Bahá, *The Promulgation of Universal Peace*, pp. 246-247. (5 August 1912).

*G*od is merciful. In His mercy He answers the prayers of all His servants when according to His supreme wisdom it is necessary.

> 'Abdu'l-Bahá, *The Promulgation of Universal Peace*, p. 247. (5 August 1912).

*A*lthough you seem to feel that your prayers have not so far been answered, and do no longer have any hope that your material conditions will ameliorate, the Guardian wishes you nevertheless not to allow such disappointments to undermine your faith in the power of prayer, but rather to continue entreating the Almighty to enable you to discover the great wisdom which may be hidden behind all these sufferings. For are not our sufferings often blessings in disguise, through which God wishes to test the sincerity and depth of our faith, and thereby make us firmer in His Cause?

... The true worshipper, while praying, should endeavour not so much to ask God to fulfil his wishes and desires, but rather to adjust these and make them conform to the Divine Will. Only through such an attitude can one derive that feeling of inner peace and contentment which the power of prayer alone can confer.

> Letter dated 26 October 1938 written on behalf of Shoghi Effendi, *The Compilation of Compilations*, Vol. II (Prayer, Mediation and the Devotional Attitude), no. 1768, pp. 239-240.

*W*e cannot clearly distinguish between personal desire and guidance, but if the way opens, when we have sought guidance, then we may presume God is helping us.

> Letter written on behalf of Shoghi Effendi, *Directives from the Guardian*, no. 205, pp. 77-78.

*Y*ou mention that the answers to your prayers never seem to have come through clearly. Mrs Ruth Moffett has published her recollection of five steps of prayer for guidance that she was told by the beloved Guardian. When asked about these notes, Shoghi Effendi replied, in letters written by his secretary on his behalf, that these notes should be regarded as "personal suggestions", that he considered them to be "quite sound", but that the friends need not adopt them "strictly and universally". The House feels that they may be helpful to you, and indeed, you may already be familiar with them. They are as follows:

... use these five steps if we have a problem of any kind for which we desire a solution, or wish help.

Pray and meditate about it. Use the prayers of the Manifestations, as they have the greatest power. Learn to remain in the silence of contemplation for a few moments. During this deepest communion take the next step.

Arrive at a decision and hold to this. This decision is usually born in a flash at the close or during contemplation. It may seem almost impossible of accomplishment, but if it seems to be an answer to prayer or a way of solving the problem, then immediately take the next step.

Have determination to carry the decision through. Many fail here. The decision, budding into determination, is blighted and instead becomes a wish or a vague longing. When determination is born, immediately take the next step.

Have faith and confidence, that the Power of the Holy Spirit will flow through you, the right message will appear, the door will open, the right message, and the right thing will come to meet your need. Then as you rise from prayer take immediately the fifth step.

Act as though it had all been answered. Then act with tireless, ceaseless energy. And, as you act, you yourself, will become a magnet which will attract more power to your being, until you become an unobstructed channel for the Divine Power to flow through you.

Messages of the Universal House of Justice 1963-1986, para. 214.5, pp. 384-385. (11 October 1978.)

Meditation and Reading of the Sacred Scriptures

Daily Reading of the Sacred Writings

*R*ecite ye the verses of God every morn and eventide. Whoso faileth to recite them hath not been faithful to the Covenant of God and His Testament, and whoso turneth away from these holy verses in this Day is of those who throughout eternity have turned away from God. Fear ye God, O My servants, one and all. Pride not yourselves on much reading of the verses or on a multitude of pious acts by night and day; for were a man to read a single verse with joy and radiance it would be better for him than to read with lassitude all the Holy Books of God, the Help in Peril, the Self-Subsisting.

Bahá'u'lláh, *The Kitáb-i-Aqdas* (The Most Holy Book), para. 149, pp. 73–74.

*I*ntone, O My servant, the verses of God that have been received by thee, as intoned by them who have drawn nigh unto Him, that the sweetness of thy melody may kindle thine own soul, and attract the hearts of all men. Whoso reciteth, in the privacy of his chamber, the verses revealed by God, the scattering angels of the Almighty shall scatter abroad the fragrance of the words uttered by his mouth, and shall cause the heart of every righteous man to throb. Though he may, at first, remain unaware of its effect, yet the virtue of the grace vouchsafed unto him must needs sooner of later exercise its influence upon his soul. Thus have the mysteries of the Revelation of God been decreed by virtue of the Will of Him Who is the Source of power and wisdom.

Bahá'u'lláh, *Gleanings from the Writings of Bahá'u'lláh*, section CXXXVI, p. 295.

Systematic Study of the Teachings

O My servants! My holy, My divinely ordained Revelation may be likened unto an ocean in whose depths are concealed innumerable pearls of great price, of surpassing lustre.

Bahá'u'lláh, *Gleanings from the Writings of Bahá'u'lláh*, CLIII, p. 325.

*B*etter is it for a person to write down but one of His verses than to transcribe the whole of the Bayán and all the books which have been written in the Dispensation of the Bayán. For everything shall be set aside except His Writings, which will endure until the following Revelation. And should anyone inscribe with true faith but one letter of that Revelation, his recompense would be greater than for inscribing all the heavenly Writings of the past and all that has been written during previous Dispensations. Likewise continue thou to ascend through one Revelation after another, knowing that thy progress in the Knowledge of God shall never come to an end, even as it can have no beginning.

The Báb, *Selections from the Writings of the Báb*, p. 91.

... *I*nvestigate and study the Holy Scriptures word by word so that you may attain knowledge of the mysteries hidden therein. Be not satisfied with words, but seek to understand the spiritual meanings hidden in the heart of the words.

'Abdu'l-Bahá, *The Promulgation of Universal Peace*, p. 459.

*T*he Guardian hopes that along with whatever other studies you take up, you will continually study the teachings and endeavour to acquire a profound knowledge of them. The importance of young Bahá'ís becoming thoroughly steeped in every branch of the teachings cannot be over-emphasized ....

Shoghi Effendi, *The Compilation of Compilations*, Vol. I (Deepening), no. 496, p. 226;
and Vol. II (Youth), no. 2274, p. 431. (22 January 1944.)

*T*o deepen in the Cause means to read the writings of Bahá'u'lláh, and the Master so thoroughly as to be able to give it to others in its pure form. There are many who have some superficial idea of what the Cause stands for. They, therefore, present it together with all sorts of ideas that are their own. As the Cause is still in its early days we must be most careful lest we fall into this error and injure the Movement we so much adore. There is no limit to the study of the Cause. The more we read the Writings, the more truths we can find in Them, the more we will see that our previous notions were erroneous.

Letter dated 25 August 1926 written on behalf of Shoghi Effendi, *The Compilation of Compilations*, Vol. I (Deepening), no. 451, p. 212.[38]

*T*hose who participate in such a campaign, whether in an organizing capacity, or as workers to whose care the execution of the task itself has been committed, must, as an essential preliminary to the discharge of their duties, thoroughly familiarize themselves with the various aspects of the history and teachings of their Faith. In their efforts to achieve this purpose they must study for themselves, conscientiously and painstakingly, the literature of their Faith, delve into its teachings, assimilate its laws and principles, ponder its admonitions, tenets and purposes, commit to memory certain of its exhortations and prayers, master the essentials of its administration, and keep abreast of its current affairs and latest developments. They must strive to obtain, from sources that are authoritative and unbiased, a sound knowledge of the history and tenets of Islám—the source and background of their Faith—and approach reverently and with a mind purged from pre-conceived ideas the study of the Qur'án which, apart from the sacred scriptures of the Bábí and Bahá'í Revelations, constitutes the only Book which can be regarded as an absolutely authenticated Repository of the Word of God. They must devote special attention to the investigation of those institutions and circumstances that are directly connected with the origin and birth of their Faith, with the station claimed by its Forerunner, and with the laws revealed by its Author.

Shoghi Effendi, *The Advent of Divine Justice*, p. 49.

Meditation

*O*ne hour's reflection is preferable to seventy years of pious worship ....

Bahá'u'lláh, *The Kitáb-i-Íqán* (The Book of Certitude), p. 238.

*I*t is an axiomatic fact that while you meditate you are speaking with your own spirit. In that state of mind you put certain questions to your spirit and the spirit answers: the light breaks forth and the reality is revealed.

You cannot apply the name 'man' to any being void of this faculty of meditation; without it he would be a mere animal, lower than the beasts.

Through the faculty of meditation man attains to eternal life; through it he receives the breath of the Holy Spirit—the bestowal of the Spirit is given in reflection and meditation.

---

38   Also *Lights of Guidance*, no. 1052, p. 312; and no. 1914, p. 566.

The spirit of man is itself informed and strengthened during meditation; through it affairs of which man knew nothing are unfolded before his view. Through it he receives Divine inspiration, through it he receives heavenly food.

Meditation is the key for opening the doors of mysteries. In that state man abstracts himself: in that state man withdraws himself from all outside objects; in that subjective mood he is immersed in the ocean of spiritual life and can unfold the secrets of things-in-themselves. To illustrate this, think of man as endowed with two kinds of sight; when the power of insight is being used the outward power of vision does not see.

This faculty of mediation frees man from the animal nature, discerns the reality of things, puts man in touch with God.

This faculty brings forth from the invisible plane the sciences and arts. Through the meditative faculty inventions are made possible, colossal undertakings are carried out; through it governments can run smoothly. Through this faculty man enters into the very Kingdom of God.

Nevertheless some thoughts are useless to man; they are like waves moving in the sea without result. But if the faculty of meditation is bathed in the inner light and characterized with divine attributes, the results will be confirmed.

The meditative faculty is akin to the mirror; if you put it before earthly objects it will reflect them. Therefore if the spirit of man is contemplating earthly subjects he will be informed of these.

But if you turn the mirror of your spirits heavenwards, the heavenly constellations and the rays of the Sun of Reality will be reflected in your hearts, and the virtues of the will be obtained.

Public Talk of 'Abdu'l-Bahá, *Paris Talks*, pp. 187-188.

*A*s to meditation: This also is a field in which the individual is free. There are no set forms of meditation prescribed in the teachings, no plan as such, for inner development. The friends are urged—nay enjoined—to pray, and they also should meditate, but the manner of doing the latter is left entirely to the individual.

Letter written on behalf of Shoghi Effendi, *Directives from the Guardian*, no. 90, p. 35.

*S*ome believers may find that it is beneficial to them to follow a particular method of meditation, and they may certainly do so, but such methods should not be taught at Bahá'í Summer Schools or be carried out during a session of the School because, while they may appeal to some people, they may repel others. They have nothing to do with the Faith and should be kept quite separate so that inquirers will not be confused.

Messages from the Universal House of Justice 1963-1986, para. 375.8, pp. 589-590.

Meditation on the Greatest Name

*I*t hath been ordained that every believer in God, the Lord of Judgement, shall, each day, having washed his hands and then his face, seat himself and, turning unto God, repeat "Alláh-u-Abhá" ninety-five times. Such was the decree of the Maker of the Heavens when, with majesty and power, He established Himself upon the thrones of His Names.

Bahá'u'lláh, *The Kitáb-i-Aqdas* (The Most Holy Book), para. 18, p. 26.

*S*ay, by reason of your remembering Him Whom God shall make manifest and by extolling His name, God will cause your hearts to be dilated with joy, and do ye not wish your hearts to be in such a blissful state? Indeed the hearts of them that truly believe in Him Whom God shall make manifest are vaster than the expanse of heaven and earth and whatever is between them. God hath left no hindrance in their hearts, were it but the size of a mustard seed. He will cheer their hearts, their spirits, their souls and their bodies and their days of prosperity or adversity, through the exaltation of the name of Him Who is the supreme Testimony of God and the promotion of the Word of Him Who is the Dayspring of the glory of their Creator.

The Báb, *Selections from the Writings of the Báb*, p. 145.

*T*he Greatest Name is the name of Bahá'u'lláh. "Yá Bahá'u'l-Abhá" is an invocation meaning: "O Thou Glory of Glories"! "Alláh-u-Abhá" is a greeting which means: "God the All-Glorious". Both refer to Bahá'u'lláh. By Greatest Name is meant that Bahá'u'lláh has appeared in God's greatest name, in other words, that He is the supreme Manifestation of God.

Shoghi Effendi, *Letters from the Guardian to Australia and New Zealand, 1923-1957*, p. 41.
(From a letter dated 26 December 1941 written on behalf of Shoghi Effendind.)[39]

*W*e have also decided that it is timely for Bahá'ís in every land to take to their hearts the words of the *Kitáb-i-Aqdas*: "It hath been ordained that every believer in God, the Lord of Judgement, shall, each day, having washed his hands and then his face, seat himself and, turning unto God, repeat 'Allah-u-Abhá' ninety-five times. Such was the decree of the Maker of the Heavens when, with majesty and power, He established Himself upon the thrones of His Names."

Let all experience the spiritual enrichment brought to their souls by this simple act of worshipful meditation.

Letter dated 28 December 1999 of the Universal House of Justice to the Bahá'ís of the World, cited in *Australian Bahá'í Bulletin*, February 2000, p. 2.

---

[39] Also *Lights of Guidance*, no. 894, p. 267.

Fasting

*A*s regards fasting, it constitutes, together with the obligatory prayers, the two pillars that sustain the revealed Law of God. They act as stimulants to the soul, strengthen, revive and purify it, and thus insure its steady development.
Letter written on behalf of Shoghi Effendi, *Directives from the Guardian*, no. 71, p. 27.

The Ordinance of Fasting

*W*e have commanded you to pray and fast from the beginning of maturity; this is ordained by God, your Lord and the Lord of your forefathers. He hath exempted from this those who are weak from illness or age, as a bounty from His presence, and He is the Forgiving, the Generous.
Bahá'u'lláh, *The Kitáb-i-Aqdas* (The Most Holy Book), para. 10, pp. 22-23.

*W*e have enjoined upon you fasting during a brief period, and at its close have designated for you Naw-Rúz as a feast. ...The traveller, the ailing, those who are with child or giving suck, are not bound by the fast ...
... Abstain from food and drink from sunrise to sundown, and beware lest desire deprive you of this grace that is appointed in the Book.
Bahá'u'lláh, *The Kitáb-i-Aqdas*, (The Most Holy Book), paras 16-17, pp. 24-25.

*I*n truth, I say that obligatory prayer and fasting occupy an exalted station in the sight of God. It is, however, in a state of health that their virtue can be realized. In time of ill-health it is not permissible to observe these obligations; such hath been the bidding of the Lord, exalted be His glory, at all times.
Bahá'u'lláh, *The Kitáb-i-Aqdas*, (The Most Holy Book), Questions and Answers 93, p. 134.

*T*he age of maturity is fifteen for both men and women.
Bahá'u'lláh, *The Kitáb-i-Aqdas*, (The Most Holy Book), Questions and Answers 20, p. 113.

The Spiritual Significance of the Fast

*A*ll praise be unto God, Who hath revealed the law of obligatory prayer as a reminder to His servants, and enjoined on them the Fast that those possessed of means may become apprised of the woes and sufferings of the destitute.
Bahá'u'lláh, in *The Importance of Obligatory Prayer and Fasting*, p. 2.

*T*hese are the days whereon Thou hast bidden all men to observe the fast, that through it they may purify their souls and rid themselves of all attachment to anyone but Thee ....
Bahá'u'lláh, *Prayers and Meditations*, section LVI, p. 78.

I have fasted for love of Thee and in pursuance of Thine injunction, and have broken my fast with Thy praise on my tongue and in conformity with Thy pleasure.

> Bahá'u'lláh, *Prayers and Meditations*, section LVI, p. 80.

*S*houldst Thou regard him who hath broken the fast as one who hath observed it, such a man would be reckoned among them who from eternity had been keeping the fast. And shouldst Thou decree that he who hath observed the fast hath broken it, that person would be numbered with such as have caused the Robe of Thy Revelation to be stained with dust, and been far removed from the crystal waters of this living Fountain.

> Bahá'u'lláh, *Prayers and Meditations*, section XLVI, pp. 67-68.

*I*t is essentially a period of meditation and prayer, of spiritual recuperation, during which the believer must strive to make the necessary readjustments in his inner life, and to refresh and reinvigorate the spiritual forces latent in his soul. Its significance and purpose are, therefore, fundamentally spiritual in character. Fasting is symbolic, and a reminder of abstinence from selfish and carnal desires.

> Shoghi Effendi, *Directives from the Guardian*, no. 71, pp.28-29.

Right Speech and Action

Striving to Bring Our Behaviour into Accordance with the Teachings

O children of Adam!
Holy words and pure and goodly deeds ascend unto the heaven of celestial glory. Strive that your deeds may be cleansed from the dust of self and hypocrisy and find favour at the court of glory; for ere long the assayers of mankind shall, in the holy presence of the Adored one, accept naught but absolute virtue and deeds of stainless purity. This is the day-star of wisdom and of divine mystery that hath shone above the horizon of the divine will. Blessed are they that turn thereunto.

> Bahá'u'lláh, *The Hidden Words*, Persian No. 69.

O son of my handmaid!
Guidance hath ever been given by words, and now it is given by deeds. Every one must show forth deeds that are pure and holy, for words are the property of all alike, whereas such deeds as these belong only to Our loved ones. Strive then with heart and soul to distinguish yourselves by your deeds. In this wise We counsel you in this holy and resplendent tablet.

> Bahá'u'lláh, *The Hidden Words*, Persian No. 76.

*E*very word is endowed with a spirit, therefore the speaker or expounder should carefully deliver his words at the appropriate time and place, for the impression which each word maketh is clearly evident and perceptible. The Great Being saith: One word may be likened unto fire, another unto light, and the influence which both exert is manifest in the world. Therefore an enlightened man of wisdom should primarily speak with words as mild as milk, that the children of men may be nurtured and edified thereby and may attain the ultimate goal of human existence which is the station of true understanding and nobility.

Lawḥ-i-Maqṣúd (Tablet of Maqṣúd), Bahá'u'lláh, *Tablets of Bahá'u'lláh*, pp. 172-173.

O emigrants!
The tongue I have designed for the mention of Me, defile it not with detraction. If the fire of self overcome you, remember your own faults and not the faults of My creatures, inasmuch as every one of you knoweth his own self better than he knoweth others.

Bahá'u'lláh, *The Hidden Words*, Persian No. 66.

O son of being!
Bring thyself to account each day ere thou art summoned to a reckoning; for death, unheralded, shall come upon thee and thou shalt be called to give account for thy deeds.

Bahá'u'lláh, *The Hidden Words*, Arabic No. 31.

*R*educe not the ordinances of God to fanciful imaginations of your own; rather observe all the things which God hath created at His behest with the eye of the spirit, even as ye see things with the eyes of your bodies.

The Báb, *Selections from the Writings of the Báb*, p. 146.

*T*ruthfulness is the foundation of all the virtues of the world of humanity. Without truthfulness, progress and success in all of the worlds of God are impossible for a soul. When this holy attribute is established in man, all the divine qualities will also become realized.

'Abdu'l-Bahá, *The Compilation of Compilations*, Vol. II (Trustworthiness), no. 2052, p. 338.

*I*t is our duty and privilege to translate the love and devotion we have for our beloved Cause into deeds and actions that will be conducive to the highest good of mankind.

Letter dated 20 November 1920 written on behalf of Shoghi Effendi, *The Compilation of Compilations*, Vol. II (Living the Life), no. 1269, p. 2.

*T*he chosen ones of God ... should not look at the depraved condition of the society in which they live, nor at the evidences of moral degradation and frivolous conduct which the people around them display. They should not content themselves merely with relative distinction and excellence. Rather they should fix their gaze upon nobler heights by setting the counsels and exhortations of the Pen of Glory as their supreme goal. Then it will be readily realized how numerous are the stages that still remain to be traversed, how far off the goal lies—a goal which is none other than exemplifying heavenly morals and virtues.

> Letter dated 30 October 1924 written on behalf of Shoghi Effendi, *The Compilation of Compilations,* Vol. I (Chaste and Holy Life), no. 122, p. 49; and Vol. II (Living the Life), no. 1268, p. 2.

*T*he great thing is to 'live the life'—to have our lives so saturated with the Divine teachings and the Bahá'í Spirit that people cannot fail to see a joy, a power, a love, a purity, a radiance, an efficiency in our character and work that will distinguish us from worldly-minded people and make people wonder what is the secret of this new life in us. We must become entirely selfless and devoted to God so that every day and every moment we seek to do only what God would have us do and in the way He would have us do it. If we do this sincerely then we shall have perfect unity and harmony with each other. Where there is want of harmony, there is lack of true Bahá'í Spirit. Unless we can show forth this transformation in our lives, this new power, this mutual love and harmony, then the Bahá'í teachings are but a name to us.

> Letter written on behalf of Shoghi Effendi, *The Compilation of Compilations,* Vol. II (Living the Life), no. 1271, p. 3.

*I*f we Bahá'ís cannot attain to cordial unity among ourselves, then we fail to realize the main purpose for which the Báb, Bahá'u'lláh and the Beloved Master lived and suffered.

> Letter dated 12 May 1925 written on behalf of Shoghi Effendi, *The Compilation of Compilations,* Vol. II (Living the Life), no. 1272, p. 3.

Teaching the Cause of God

*B*ehold how the generality of mankind hath been endued with the capacity to hearken unto God's most exalted Word—the Word upon which must depend the gathering together and spiritual resurrection of all men ....

> Bahá'u'lláh, *Gleanings from the Writings of Bahá'u'lláh,* section XLIII, p. 96.[40]

O son of man!
Magnify My cause that I may reveal unto thee the mysteries of My greatness and shine upon thee with the light of eternity.

> Bahá'u'lláh, *The Hidden Words,* Arabic No. 41.

O son of being!
Make mention of Me on My earth, that in My heaven I may remember thee, thus shall Mine eyes and thine be solaced.

> Bahá'u'lláh, *The Hidden Words,* Arabic No. 43.

*T*his Day a door is open wider than both heaven and earth. The eye of the mercy of Him Who is the Desire of the worlds is turned towards all men. An act, however

---

40   Also *Tablets of Bahá'u'lláh,* p. 89.

infinitesimal, is, when viewed in the mirror of the knowledge of God, mightier than a mountain. Every drop proffered in His path is as the sea in that mirror. For this is the Day which the one true God, glorified be He, hath announced in all His Books, unto His Prophets and His Messengers.

Bahá'u'lláh, cited by Shoghi Effendi, *The Advent of Divine Justice*, p. 78.

*O*f all the gifts of God the greatest is the gift of Teaching. It draweth unto us the Grace of God and is our first obligation. Of such a gift how can we deprive ourselves? Nay, our lives, our goods, our comforts, our rest, we offer them all as a sacrifice for the Abhá Beauty and teach the Cause of God.

'Abdu'l-Bahá, *The Will and Testament of 'Abdu'l-Bahá*, p. 25.

*W*hen the friends do not endeavour to spread the message, they fail to remember God befittingly, and will not witness the tokens of assistance and confirmation from the Abhá Kingdom nor comprehend the divine mysteries. However, when the tongue of the teacher is engaged in teaching, he will naturally himself be stimulated, will become a magnet attracting the divine aid and bounty of the Kingdom, and will be like unto the bird at the hour of dawn, which itself becometh exhilarated by its own singing, its warbling and its melody.

'Abdu'l-Bahá, *Selections from the Writings of 'Abdu'l-Bahá*, no. 211, pp. 267-268.

... *O*utside this Divine Refuge the people will not, we firmly believe, find inner conviction, peace and security.

Letter dated 24 April 1949 written on behalf of Shoghi Effendi, *Directives from the Guardian*, no. 195, p. 73.[41]

Selfless Service in the Work of the Cause and One's Trade or Profession

*I*t is enjoined upon every one of you to engage in some form of occupation, such as crafts, trades and the like. We have graciously exalted your engagement in such work to the rank of worship unto God, the True One. Ponder ye in your hearts the grace and the blessings of God and render thanks unto Him at eventide and at dawn. Waste not your time in idleness and sloth. Occupy yourselves with that which profiteth yourselves and others. Thus hath it been decreed in this Tablet from whose horizon the daystar of wisdom and utterance shineth resplendent.

Bishárát (Glad-Tidings), Bahá'u'lláh, *Tablets of Bahá'u'lláh*, p. 26.

*I*t is incumbent upon every man of insight and understanding to strive to translate that which hath been written into reality and action. ... That one indeed is a man who, today, dedicateth himself to the service of the entire human race. The Great Being saith:

---

[41] Also *The Compilation of Compilations*, Vol. II (The Use of Radio and Television), no. 1891, p. 283.

Blessed and happy is he that ariseth to promote the best interests of the peoples and kindreds of the earth. In another passage He hath proclaimed: It is not for him to pride himself who loveth his own country, but rather for him who loveth the whole world. The earth is but one country, and mankind its citizens.

Bahá'u'lláh, Gleanings from the Writings of Bahá'u'lláh, section CXVII, p. 250.[42]

Such hindrances, no matter how severe and insuperable they may at first seem, can and should be effectively overcome through the combined and sustained power of prayer and of continued effort. For have not Bahá'u'lláh and 'Abdu'l-Bahá both repeatedly assured us that the Divine and unseen hosts of victory will ever reinforce and strengthen those who valiantly and confidently labour in their name? This assurance should indeed enable you to overcome any feeling of unworthiness, of incapacity to serve, and any inner or outer limitation which threatens to handicap your labours for the Cause. You should therefore arise, and with a heart filled with joy and confidence endeavour to contribute any share that is in your power toward the wider diffusion and greater consolidation of our beloved Faith.

Whatever the particular field of service you may choose, whether teaching or administrative, the essential is for you to persevere, and not to allow any consciousness of your limitations to dampen your zeal, much less deter you from serving joyously and actively.

Letter dated 6 February 1939 written on behalf of Shoghi Effendi,
The Compilation of Compilations, Vol. II (Living the Life), no. 1284, pp. 7-8.

Voluntary Sharing of Wealth

O children of dust!

Tell the rich of the midnight sighing of the poor, lest heedlessness lead them into the path of destruction, and deprive them of the Tree of Wealth. To give and to be generous are attributes of Mine; well is it with him that adornest himself with My virtues.

Bahá'u'lláh, The Hidden Words, Persian No. 49.

O my servant!

The best of men are they that earn a livelihood by their calling and spend upon themselves and upon their kindred for the love of God, the Lord of all worlds.

Bahá'u'lláh, The Hidden Words, Persian No. 82.

O ye rich on earth!

The poor in your midst are My trust; guard ye My trust, and be not intent only on your own ease.

Bahá'u'lláh, The Hidden Words, Persian No. 54.

---

[42] Also The Proclamation of Bahá'u'lláh, pp. 115-116.

O ye that pride yourselves on mortal riches!

Know ye in truth that wealth is a mighty barrier between the seeker and his desire, the lover and his beloved. The rich, but for a few, shall in no wise attain the court of His presence nor enter the city of content and resignation. Well is it then with him, who, being rich, is not hindered by his riches from the eternal kingdom, nor deprived by them of imperishable dominion. By the Most Great Name! The splendour of such a wealthy man shall illuminate the dwellers of heaven, even as the sun enlightens the people of the earth!

Bahá'u'lláh, *The Hidden Words,* Persian No. 53.

*N*othing that existeth in the world of being hath ever been or ever will be worthy of mention. However, if a person be graciously favoured to offer a penny-worth—nay even less—in the path of God, this would in His sight be preferable and superior to all the treasures of the earth. It is for this reason that the one true God—exalted be His glory—hath in all His heavenly Scriptures praised those who observe His precepts and bestow their wealth for His sake.

Bahá'u'lláh, *The Compilation of Compilations,* Vol. I (Ḥuqúqu'lláh), 1099, p. 489.

*T*hou has written that they have pledged themselves to observe maximum austerity in their lives with a view to forwarding the remainder of their income to His exalted presence. This matter was mentioned at His holy court. He said: Let them act with moderation and not impose hardship upon themselves. We would like them both to enjoy a life that is well-pleasing.

'Abdu'l-Bahá, *The Compilation of Compilations,* Vol. I (Ḥuqúqu'lláh), 1155, p. 508.

*W*e must be like the fountain or spring that is continually emptying itself of all that it has and is continually being refilled from an invisible source. To be continually giving out for the good of our fellows undeterred by fear of poverty and reliant on the unfailing bounty of the Source of all wealth and all good—this is the secret of right living.

Shoghi Effendi, *Directives from the Guardian*, no. 83, p. 32.[43]

Ḥuqúqu'lláh

*I*n surveying the vast range of creation thou shalt perceive that the higher a kingdom of created things is on the arc of ascent, the more conspicuous are the signs and evidences of the truth that co-operation and reciprocity at the level of a higher order are greater than those that exist at the level of a lower order. For example the evident signs of this fundamental reality are more discernible in the vegetable kingdom than in the mineral, and still more manifest in the animal world than in the vegetable.

And thus when contemplating the human world thou beholdest this wondrous phenomenon shining resplendent from all sides with the utmost perfection, inasmuch as in

---

[43] Also *The Compilation of Compilations,* Vol. I (Bahá'í Funds and Contributions), no. 1212, p. 529.

this station acts of co-operation, mutual assistance and reciprocity are not confined to the body and to things that pertain to the material world, but for all conditions, whether physical or spiritual, such as those related to the minds, thoughts, opinions, manners, customs, attitudes, understandings, feelings or other human susceptibilities. In all these thou shouldst find these binding relationships securely established. The more this inter-relationship is strengthened and expanded, the more will human society advance in progress and prosperity. Indeed without these vital ties it would be wholly impossible for the world of humanity to attain true felicity and success.

Now consider, if among the people who are merely the manifestations of the world of being this significant matter is of such importance, how much greater must be the spirit of co-operation and mutual assistance among those who are the essences of the world of creation, who have sought the sheltering shadow of the heavenly Tree, and are favoured by the manifestations of divine grace; and how the evidences of this spirit should, through their earnest endeavour, their fellowship and concord, become manifest in every sphere of their inner and outer lives, in the realm of the spirit and divine mysteries and in all things related to this world and the next. Thus there can be no doubt that they must be willing even to offer up their lives for each other.

This is the basic principle on which the institution of Ḥuqúqu'lláh is established, inasmuch as its proceeds are dedicated to the furtherance of these ends. Otherwise the one true God hath ever been and will always be independent of all else beside Him. Even as He hath enabled all created things to partake of His boundless grace and loving-kindness, likewise is He able to bestow riches upon His loved ones out of the treasuries of His power. However, the wisdom of this command is that the act of giving is well-pleasing in the sight of God. Consider how well-pleasing must this mighty act be in His estimation that He hath ascribed it unto His Own Self. Rejoice ye then, O people of generosity!

We earnestly hope that in this Most Great Cycle the wondrous attributes of the All-Merciful may, through the infinite bounty and blessings of the King of Glory, find expression in the lives of the servants of God in such wise that the sweet savours thereof will shed fragrance upon all regions.

This matter needeth further details, but We have treated in brief.

'Abdu'l-Bahá, *The Compilation of Compilations*, Vol. I (Ḥuqúqu'lláh), no. 1159, pp. 509-510.

*T*he question of the Huqúq dependeth on the willingness of the individuals themselves. From every true believer who is willing to tender the Right of God spontaneously and with the utmost joy and radiance, the offering is graciously accepted, but not otherwise. Verily, thy Lord is independent of all mankind. Consider that which the All-Merciful hath revealed in the Qur'án: "O men! Ye are but paupers in need of God, but God is the Self-Sufficient, the All-Praised."

At all times one must have the utmost regard for the dignity and honour of the Cause of God.

Bahá'u'lláh, *The Compilation of Compilations*, Vol. I (Ḥuqúqu'lláh), no. 1148, pp. 505-506.

*T*hou hast enquired about the Huqúq. From one's annual income, all expenses during the year are deductible, and on what is left 19% is payable to the Huqúq.

'Abdu'l-Bahá, *The Compilation of Compilations,* Vol. I (Ḥuqúqu'lláh), no. 1163, p. 511.

Pilgrimage

*T*he Lord hath ordained that those of you who are able shall make pilgrimage to the sacred House, and from this He hath exempted women as a mercy on His part. He, of a truth, is the All-Bountiful, the Most Generous.

Bahá'u'lláh, *The Kitáb-i-Aqdas* (The Most Holy Book), para. 32, p. 30.

*T*wo sacred Houses are covered by this ordinance, the House of the Báb in Shíráz and the House of Bahá'u'lláh in Baghdád. Bahá'u'lláh has specified that pilgrimage to either of these two Houses fulfils the requirement of this passage (Q & A 25, 29). In two separate Tablets, known as Súriy-i-Hajj (Q & A 10), Bahá'u'lláh has prescribed specific rites for each of these pilgrimages. In this sense, the performance of a pilgrimage is more than simply visiting these two Houses.

After the passing of Bahá'u'lláh, 'Abdu'l-Bahá designated the Shrine of Bahá'u'lláh at Bahjí as a place of pilgrimage. In a Tablet, He indicates that the *"Most Holy Shrine, the Blessed House in Baghdád and the venerated House of the Báb in Shíráz"* are *"consecrated to pilgrimage"*, and that it is *"obligatory"* to visit these places *"if one can afford it and is able to do so, and if no obstacle stands in one's way"*. No rites have been prescribed for pilgrimage to the Most Holy Shrine.

In the *Bayán*, the Báb enjoined the ordinance of pilgrimage once in a lifetime upon those of His followers who were financially able to undertake the journey. He stated that the obligation was not binding on women in order to spare them the rigours of travel.

Bahá'u'lláh likewise exempts women from His pilgrimage requirements. The Universal House of Justice has clarified that this exemption is not a prohibition, and that women are free to perform the pilgrimage.

Bahá'u'lláh, *The Kitáb-i-Aqdas* (The Most Holy Book), Notes nos 54–55, pp. 191–192.

*E*qually significant has been the founding on Mt. Carmel of two international Archives, the one adjoining the shrine of the Báb, the other in the immediate vicinity of the resting-place of the Greatest Holy Leaf, where, for the first time in Bahá'í history, priceless treasures, hitherto scattered and often hidden for safekeeping, have been collected and are now displayed to visiting pilgrims. These treasures include portraits of both the Báb and Bahá'u'lláh; personal relics such as the hair, the dust and garments of the Báb; the locks and blood of Bahá'u'lláh and such articles as His pen-case, His garments, His brocaded tájes (head dresses), the kashkúl of His Sulaymáníyyih days, His watch and His Qur'án; manuscripts and Tablets of inestimable value, some of them illuminated, such as part of the Hidden Words written in Bahá'u'lláh's own hand, the *Persian Bayán*, in the handwriting of Siyyid Ḥusayn, the Báb's amanuensis, the original Tablets to the Letters of the Living penned by the Báb, and the manuscript of *Some Answered Questions*. This precious collection, moreover, includes objects and effects associated with 'Abdu'l-Bahá; the blood-stained garment of the Purest Branch, the ring of Quddús, the sword of Mullá Ḥusayn, the seals of the Vazír, the father of Bahá'u'lláh, the brooch presented by the Queen of Rumania to Martha Root, the originals of the Queen's letters to her and to others, and of her tributes to the Faith, as well as no less than twenty volumes of prayers and Tablets revealed by the Founders of the Faith, authenticated and transcribed by Bahá'í Assemblies throughout the Orient, and supplementing the vast collection of their published writings.

Moreover, as a further testimony to the majestic unfoldment and progressive consolidation of the stupendous undertaking launched by Bahá'u'lláh on that holy mountain, may be mentioned the selection of a portion of the school property situated in the precincts of the Shrine of the Báb as a permanent resting-place for the Greatest Holy Leaf, the *"well-beloved"* sister of 'Abdu'l-Bahá, the *"Leaf that hath sprung"* from the *"Pre-existent Root,"* the *"fragrance"* of Bahá'u'lláh's *"shining robe,"* elevated by Him to a *"station such as none other woman hath surpassed,"* and comparable in rank to those immortal heroines such as Sarah, Ásíyih, the Virgin Mary, Fáṭimih and Ṭáhirih, each of whom has outshone every member of her sex in previous Dispensations. And lastly, there should be mentioned, as a further evidence of the blessings flowing from the Divine Plan, the transfer, a few years later, to that same hallowed spot, after a separation in death of above half a century, and notwithstanding the protests voiced by the brother and lieutenant of the arch-breaker of Bahá'u'lláh's Covenant, of the remains of the Purest Branch, the martyred son of Bahá'u'lláh, *"created of the light of Bahá,"* the *"Trust of God"* and His *"Treasure"* in the Holy Land, and offered up by his Father as a *"ransom"* for the regeneration of the world and the unification of its peoples. To this same burial-ground, and on the same day the remains of the Purest Branch were interred, was transferred the body of his mother, the saintly Navváb, she to whose dire afflictions, as attested by 'Abdu'l-Bahá in a Tablet, the 54th chapter of the Book of Isaiah has, in its entirety, borne witness, whose *"Husband,"* in the words of that Prophet, is *"the Lord of Hosts,"* whose *"seed shall inherit the Gentiles,"* and whom Bahá'u'lláh in His Tablet, has destined to be *"His consort in every one of His worlds."*

The conjunction of these three resting-places, under the shadow of the Báb's own Tomb, embosomed in the heart of Carmel, facing the snow-white city across the bay of 'Akká, the Qiblih of the Bahá'í world, set in a garden of exquisite beauty, reinforces, if we would correctly estimate its significance, the spiritual potencies of a spot, designated by Bahá'u'lláh Himself the seat of God's throne. It marks, too, a further milestone in the road leading eventually to the establishment of that permanent world Administrative Centre of the future Bahá'í Commonwealth, destined never to be separated from, and to function in the proximity of, the Spiritual Centre of that Faith, in a land already revered and held sacred alike by the adherents of three of the world's outstanding religious systems.

Shoghi Effendi, *God Passes By*, pp. 347–348.

The Spiritual Meaning of Pilgrimage

*I*n all the Divine Books the promise of the Divine Presence hath been explicitly recorded. By this Presence is meant the Presence of Him Who is the Dayspring of the signs, and the Dawning-Place of the clear tokens, and the Manifestation of the Excellent Names, and the Source of the attributes, of the true God, exalted be His glory. God in His Essence and in His own Self hath ever been unseen, inaccessible, and unknowable. By Presence, therefore, is meant the Presence of the One Who is His Viceregent amongst men.

Bahá'u'lláh, Epistle to the Son of the Wolf, p. 118.

*T*he purpose of God in creating man hath been, and will ever be, to enable him to know his Creator and to attain His Presence. To this most excellent aim, this supreme objective, all the heavenly Books and the divinely-revealed and weighty Scriptures unequivocally bear witness. Whoso hath recognized the Day Spring of Divine guidance and entered His holy court hath drawn nigh unto God and attained His Presence, a Presence which is the real Paradise, and of which the loftiest mansions of heaven are but a symbol.

Bahá'u'lláh, Gleanings from the Writings of Bahá'u'lláh, section XXIX, p. 70.

I bear witness that he who hath known Thee hath known God, and he who hath attained unto Thy presence hath attained unto the presence of God. Great, therefore, is the blessedness of him who hath believed in Thee, and in Thy signs, and hath humbled himself before Thy sovereignty, and hath been honoured with meeting Thee, and hath attained the good pleasure of Thy will, and circled around Thee, and stood before Thy throne.

Bahá'u'lláh, Prayers and Meditations, section CLXXX, p. 311.

*P*raise be to God that through His gracious bounty you were enabled to visit His exalted, His sacred and luminous Threshold, to refresh and perfume your nostrils with the sweet-scented fragrances of God diffused from these imperishable, holy Places. This wondrous gift calls for thanksgiving, and this heavenly bestowal warrants praise and glorification. And such praise is best expressed when one's pilgrimage, one's honour at attaining His holy Court and becoming the recipient of His favours and loving-kindness produce a profound effect and influence upon every aspect of one's life, upon one's bearing and demeanour, and one's activities. There is no doubt that it will be so.

Shoghi Effendi, Bahíyyih Khánum, p. 220.

Chapter Six
Deveoping Character and Spiritual Relationships

He heartily agrees with you that unless we *practise* the Teachings we cannot possibly expect the Faith to grow, because the fundamental purpose of all religions—including our own—is to bring man nearer to God, and to change his character, which is of the utmost importance. Too much emphasis is often laid on the social and economic aspects of the Teachings; but the moral aspect cannot be over-emphasized.

> Letter dated 6 September 1946 written on behalf of Shoghi Effendi, *The Compilation of Compilations*, Vol. I (A Chaste and Holy Life), no. 159, p. 61; Vol. II (Living the Life), no. 1311, p. 16; and Vol. II (Youth), no. 2285, p. 434.

*I*ndeed when we see the increasing darkness in the world today we can fully realize that unless the Message of Bahá'u'lláh reaches into the hearts of men and transforms them, there can be no peace and no spiritual progress in the future.

His constant hope is that the believers will conduct themselves, individually and in their Bahá'í Community life, in such a manner as to attract the attention of others to the Cause. The world is not only starving for lofty principles and ideals, it is, above all, starving for a shining example which the Bahá'ís can and must provide.

> Letter dated 22 February 1945 written on behalf of Shoghi Effendi, *The Compilation of Compilations*, Vol. II (Living the Life), no. 1304, p. 14.[44]

He was very happy to hear from you, and to learn that Green Acre this year was pervaded with a love and harmony that was instrumental in confirming many new souls in the Faith. This love among the believers is the magnet which will, above all else, attract the hearts and bring new souls into the Cause. Because obviously the teachings—however wonderful—cannot change the world unless the Spirit of Bahá'u'lláh's love is mirrored in the Bahá'í Communities.

> Letter dated 22 October 1944 written on behalf of Shoghi Effendi, *The Compilation of Compilations*, Vol. II (Living the Life), no. 1302, p. 13.

---

44 Also *Lights of Guidance*, no. 1413, p. 432.

Happiness

O son of spirit!

My first counsel is this: Possess a pure, kindly and radiant heart, that thine may be a sovereignty ancient, imperishable and everlasting.

Bahá'u'lláh, *The Hidden Words*, Arabic No. 1.

O son of spirit!

The spirit of holiness beareth unto thee the joyful tidings of reunion; wherefore dost thou grieve? The spirit of power confirmeth thee in His cause; why dost thou veil thyself? The light of His countenance doth lead thee; how canst thou go astray?

Bahá'u'lláh, *The Hidden Words*, Arabic No. 34.

O son of man!

Rejoice in the gladness of thine heart, that thou mayest be worthy to meet Me and to mirror forth My beauty.

Bahá'u'lláh, *The Hidden Words*, Arabic No. 36.

*L*et not the happenings of the world sadden you. I swear by God! The sea of joy yearneth to attain your presence, for every good thing hath been created for you, and will, according to the needs of the times, be revealed unto you.

Bahá'u'lláh, cited by Shoghi Effendi, *The Advent of Divine Justice*, p. 82.

I myself was in prison forty years—one year alone would have been impossible to bear—nobody survived that imprisonment more than a year! But, thank God, during all those forty years I was supremely happy! Every day, on waking, it was like hearing good tidings, and every night infinite joy was mine. Spirituality was my comfort, and turning to God was my greatest joy. If this had not been so, do you think it possible that I could have lived through those forty years in prison?

Thus, Spirituality is the greatest of God's gifts, and "Life Everlasting" means "Turning to God". May you, one and all, increase daily in spirituality, may you be strengthened in all goodness, may you be helped more and more by the Divine consolation, be made free by the Holy Spirit of God, and may the power of the Heavenly Kingdom live and work among you.

Public Talk of 'Abdu'l-Bahá, *Paris Talks*, pp. 112-113.

*L*et God's beloved, each and every one, be the essence of purity, the very life of holiness, so that in every country they may become famed for their sanctity, independence of spirit, and meekness. Let them be cheered by draughts from the eternal cup of love for God, and make merry as they drink from the wine-vaults of Heaven. Let them behold the Blessed Beauty, and feel the flame and rapture of that meeting, and be struck dumb with awe and wonder. This is the station of the sincere; this is the way of the loyal; this is the brightness that shineth on the faces of those nigh unto God.

'Abdu'l-Bahá, *Selections from the Writings of 'Abdu'l-Bahá*, no. 174, p. 203.

*K*now thou that there are two kinds of happiness—spiritual and material.

As to material happiness, it never exists; nay, it is but imagination, an image reflected in mirrors, a spectre and shadow. Consider the nature of material happiness. It is something, which but slightly removes one's afflictions; yet the people imagine it to be joy, delight, exultation and blessing. All the material blessings, including food, drink, etc., tend only to allay thirst, hunger and fatigue. They bestow no delight on the mind nor pleasure on the soul; nay, they furnish only the bodily wants. So this kind of happiness has no real existence.

As to spiritual happiness, this is the true basis of the life of man because life is created for happiness, not for sorrow; for pleasure, not for grief. Happiness is life; sorrow is death. Spiritual happiness is life eternal. This is a light which is not followed by darkness. This is an honour which is not followed by shame. This is a life that is not followed by death. This is an existence that is not followed by annihilation. This great blessing and precious gift is obtained by man only through the guidance of God.

... This happiness is the fundamental basis from which man is created, worlds are originated, the contingent beings have existence and the world of God appears like unto the appearance of the sun at mid-day.

This happiness is but the love of God.

... Were it not for this happiness the world of existence would not have been created.

'Abdu'l-Bahá, *Star of the West*, Vol. VII:16, 31 December 1916, p. 163.

... *W*hat pleasure can compare the pleasure of bringing joy and hope to other hearts. The more we make others happy the greater will be our own happiness and the deeper our sense of having served humanity.

Shoghi Effendi, *Light of Divine Guidance*, Vol. I, p. 45.

Gratitude

*Y*our eyes have been illumined, your ears are attentive, your hearts knowing. You must be free from prejudice and fanaticism, beholding no differences between the races and religions. You must look to God, for He is the real Shepherd, and all humanity are His sheep. He loves them and loves them equally. As this is true, should the sheep quarrel among themselves? They should manifest gratitude and thankfulness to God, and the best way to thank God is to love one another.

Public Talk of 'Abdu'l-Bahá, *The Promulgation of Universal Peace*, pp. 468–469.

*D*ay and night I entreat and supplicate to the Kingdom of God and beg for you infinite assistance and confirmation. Do not take into consideration your own aptitudes and capacities, but fix your gaze on the consummate bounty, the divine bestowal and the power of the Holy Spirit—the power that converteth the drop into a sea and the star into a sun.

Praise be to God, the hosts of the Supreme Concourse secure the victory and the power of the Kingdom is ready to assist and to support. Should ye at every instant unloosen the tongue in thanksgiving and gratitude, ye would not be able to discharge yourselves of the obligation of gratitude for these bestowals.

Consider: eminent personages whose fame hath spread all over the world shall, erelong, fade into utter nothingness as the result of their deprivation of this heavenly bounty; no name and no fame shall they leave behind, and of them no fruit and trace shall survive. But as the effulgences of the Sun of Truth have dawned forth upon you and ye have attained everlasting life, ye shall shine and sparkle forevermore from the horizon of existence.

'Abdu'l-Bahá, *Selections from the Writings of 'Abdu'l-Bahá*, no. 68, pp. 104-105.

*T*he glories of that Sun are shining now from out the high, immortal realms, and His glance is resting on His loved ones. The portals of everlasting blessings are opened wide. The succouring armies are standing ready, waiting to behold what efforts the loved ones will exert as they carry out the holy Will, as they boil up and roar like waves of the sea. Let them rest not for a moment, nor wish for quiet and repose; let them carry out all His behests and thus prove their loyal gratitude for all His endless grace.

Shoghi Effendi, *Bahíyyih Khánum*, p. 130.

Inner Peace and Certitude

O son of spirit!

With the joyful tidings of light I hail thee: rejoice! To the court of holiness I summon thee; abide therein that thou mayest live in peace for evermore.

Bahá'u'lláh, *The Hidden Words*, Arabic No. 33.

O son of man!

Wert thou to speed through the immensity of space and traverse the expanse of heaven, yet thou wouldst find no rest save in submission to Our command and humbleness before Our Face.

Bahá'u'lláh, *The Hidden Words*, Arabic No. 40.

O son of my handmaid!

Quaff from the tongue of the merciful the stream of divine mystery, and behold from the day-spring of divine utterance the unveiled splendour of the day-star of wisdom. Sow the seeds of My divine wisdom in the pure soil of the heart, and water them with the waters of certitude, that the hyacinths of knowledge and wisdom may spring up fresh and green from the holy city of the heart.

Bahá'u'lláh, *The Hidden Words*, Persian No. 78.

*W*ere men to meditate upon the lives of the Prophets of old, so easily would they come to know and understand the ways of these Prophets that they would cease to be veiled by such deeds and words as are contrary to their own worldly desires, and thus consume every intervening veil with the fire burning in the Bush of divine knowledge, and abide secure upon the throne of peace and certitude.

Bahá'u'lláh, *The Kitáb-i-Íqán* (The Book of Certitude), p. 53.

... *P*eace of mind is gained by the centring of the spiritual consciousness on the Prophet of God; therefore you should study the spiritual Teachings, and receive the Water of Life from the Holy Utterances. Then by translating these high ideals into action, your entire character will be changed, and your mind will not only find peace, but your entire being will find joy and enthusiasm.

Letter dated 15 October 1952 written on behalf of Shoghi Effendi, *Lights of Guidance*, no. 381, p. 112.

Purity and Detachment

O son of man!
The temple of being is My throne; cleanse it of all things, that there I may be established and there I may abide.

Bahá'u'lláh, *The Hidden Words*, Arabic No. 58.

O son of being!
Thy heart is My home; sanctify it for My descent. Thy spirit is My place of revelation; cleanse it for My manifestation.

Bahá'u'lláh, *The Hidden Words*, Arabic No. 59.

... *C*hrist has addressed the world, saying, "Except ye be converted, and become as little children, ye shall not enter into the kingdom of heaven"—that is, men must become pure in heart to know God. ... The hearts of all children are of the utmost purity. They are mirrors upon which no dust has fallen. But this purity is on account of weakness and innocence, not on account of any strength and testing, for as this is the early period of their childhood, their hearts and minds are unsullied by the world. They cannot display any great intelligence. They have neither hypocrisy nor deceit. This is on account of the child's weakness, whereas the man becomes pure through his strength. Through the power of intelligence he becomes simple; through the great power of reason and understanding and not through the power of weakness he becomes sincere. When he attains to the state of perfection, he will receive these qualities; his heart becomes purified, his spirit enlightened, his soul is sensitized and tender—all through his great strength. This is the difference between the perfect man and the child. Both have the underlying qualities of simplicity and sincerity.....

'Abdu'l-Bahá, The Promulgation of Universal Peace, p. 53.

Purity of Motive

*F*irst and foremost, one should resort to every possible means to purge one's heart and motives, otherwise, engaging in any form of enterprise would be futile. It is also essential to abstain from hypocrisy and blind imitation, inasmuch as their foul odour is soon detected by every man of understanding and wisdom. ... One can hardly imagine what a great influence genuine love, truthfulness and purity of motives exert on the souls of men. But these traits cannot be acquired by any believer unless he makes a daily effort to gain them ...

Shoghi Effendi, The Compilation of Compilations, Vol. II (Living the Life), no. 1267, pp. 1-2; and Vol. II (Guidelines for Teaching), no. 1928, p. 301.

Physical Cleanliness

O Friends of the Pure and Omnipotent God! To be pure and holy in all things is an attribute of the consecrated soul and a necessary characteristic of the unenslaved mind. The best of perfections is immaculacy and the freeing of oneself from every defect. Once the individual is, in every respect, cleansed and purified, then will he become a focal Centre reflecting the Manifest Light.

First in a human being's way of life must be purity, then freshness, cleanliness, and independence of spirit. First must the stream bed be cleansed; then may the sweet river waters be led into it. Chaste eyes enjoy the beatific vision of the Lord and know what this encounter meaneth; a pure sense inhaleth the fragrances that blow from the rose gardens of His grace; a burnished heart will mirror forth the comely face of truth.

... My meaning is this, that in every aspect of life, purity and holiness, cleanliness and refinement, exalt the human condition and further the development of man's inner reality. Even in the physical realm, cleanliness will conduce to spirituality, as the Holy Writings clearly state.

'Abdu'l-Bahá, Selections from the Writings of 'Abdu'l-Bahá, no. 129, pp. 146-147.

Chastity

*T*he brightness of the light of chastity sheddeth its illumination upon the worlds of the spirit, and its fragrance is wafted even unto the Most Exalted Paradise.

Bahá'u'lláh, cited by Shoghi Effendi, The Advent of Divine Justice, p. 32.

*I*t[45] demands daily vigilance in the control of one's carnal desires and corrupt inclinations. It calls for the abandonment of a frivolous conduct, with its excessive attachment to trivial and often misdirected pleasures.

Shoghi Effendi, *The Advent of Divine Justice*, p. 30.

*I*t[46] condemns the prostitution of art and of literature, the practices of nudism and of companionate marriage, infidelity in marital relationships, and all manner of promiscuity, of easy familiarity, and of sexual vices.

Shoghi Effendi, *The Advent of Divine Justice*, p. 30.

*W*e must reach a spiritual plane where God comes first and great human passions are unable to turn us away from Him. All the time we see people who either through the force of hate or the passionate attachment they have to another person, sacrifice principle or bar themselves from the Path of God.

We must love God, and in this state, a general love for all men becomes possible. We cannot love each human being for himself, but our feeling towards humanity should be motivated by our love for the Father Who created all men.

Letter dated 4 October 1950 written on behalf of Shoghi Effendi, *The Compilation of Compilations*, Vol. II (Living the Life), no.1327, p. 22.

*W*e have received your letter of 19 June 1973 and can sympathize with the problems that Bahá'í youth face when trying to live up to the Bahá'í standards of behaviour. It is, perhaps, natural that in the bewildering amoral environment in which Bahá'í youth are growing up they feel the need for specific instructions on which intimacies are permissible and which are not. However, we feel it would be most unwise for any Bahá'í institution to issue detailed instructions about this.

The Bahá'í youth should study the teachings on chastity and, with these in mind, should avoid any behaviour which would arouse passions which would tempt them to violate them. In deciding what acts are permissible to them in the light of these considerations the youth must use their own judgement, following the guidance of their consciences and the advice of their parents.

If Bahá'í youth combine such personal purity with an attitude of uncensorious forbearance towards others they will find that those who have criticized or even mocked them will come, it time, to respect them. They will, moreover, be laying a firm foundation for future married happiness.

Messages from the Universal House of Justice 1963-1986, paras 133.1-3, p. 253. (Letter dated 9 July 1973 from The Universal House of Justice.)[47]

---

45   A chaste and holy life.
46   A chaste and holy life.
47   Also *Lights of Guidance*, no. 1213, p. 362.

Avoidance of Alcohol and Habit Forming Drugs

*I*t is inadmissible that man, who hath been endowed with reason, should consume that which stealeth it away. Nay, rather it behoveth him to comport himself in a manner worthy of the human station, and not in accordance with the misdeeds of every heedless and wavering soul.

Bahá'u'lláh, *The Kitáb-i-Aqdas* (The Most Holy Book), para. 119, p. 62.

*I*t[48] requires total abstinence from all alcoholic drinks, from opium and from similar habit-forming drugs.

Shoghi Effendi, *The Advent of Divine Justice*, p. 30.

*C*oncerning smoking: It is not forbidden in the Bahá'í teachings and no one can enforce its prohibition. It is strongly discouraged as a habit which is not very clean or very healthy. But it is a matter left entirely to the conscience of the individual and not of major importance, whereas the use of alcohol is definitely forbidden and thus not left optional to the conscience of the believer.

Letter written on behalf of Shoghi Effendi, *Lights of Guidance*, no. 1189, pp. 355-356.

... *B*ahá'ís should not use hallucinogenic agents, including LSD, peyote and similar substances, except when prescribed for medical treatment. Neither should they become involved in experiments with such substances.

Letter from The Universal House of Justice, *Lights of Guidance*, no. 1184, p. 354. (11 November 1967.)

Moderation

*W*hoso cleaveth to justice, can, under no circumstances, transgress the limits of moderation. He discerneth the truth in all things, through the guidance of Him Who is the All-Seeing. The civilization, so often vaunted by the learned exponents of arts and sciences, will, if allowed to overleap the bounds of moderation, bring great evil upon men. Thus warneth you He Who is the All-Knowing. If carried to excess, civilization will prove as prolific a source of evil as it had been of goodness when kept within the restraints of moderation. Meditate on this, O people, and be not of them that wander distraught in the wilderness of error.

Bahá'u'lláh, *Gleanings from the Writings of Bahá'u'lláh*, section CLXIV, pp. 342-343.

*S*uch a chaste and holy life, with its implications of modesty, purity, temperance, decency, and clean-mindedness, involves no less than the exercise of moderation in all that pertains to dress, language, amusements, and all artistic and literary avocations.

Shoghi Effendi, *The Advent of Divine Justice*, p. 30.

---

48   A chaste and holy life.

Love and Unity

... *C*onsort with the followers of all religions in a spirit of friendliness and fellowship ....

They that are endued with sincerity and faithfulness should associate with all the peoples and kindreds of the earth with joy and radiance, inasmuch as consorting with people hath promoted and will continue to promote unity and concord, which in turn are conducive to the maintenance of order in the world and to the regeneration of nations. Blessed are such as hold fast to the cord of kindliness and tender mercy and are free from animosity and hatred.

Tarázát (Ornaments), Bahá'u'lláh, *Tablets of Bahá'u'lláh*, pp. 35-36.

*R*eal love is impossible unless one turn his face towards God and be attracted to His beauty.

'Abdu'l-Bahá, *Bahá'í World Faith*, p. 364.[49]

*T*he love which exists between the hearts of believers is prompted by the ideal of the unity of spirits. This love is attained through the knowledge of God, so that men see the Divine love reflected in the heart. Each sees in the other the beauty of God reflected in the soul, and finding this point of similarity, they are attracted to one another in love.

Public Talk of 'Abdu'l-Bahá, *Paris Talks*, p. 193-194.

... *T*hat love of God, and consequently of men, is the essential foundation of every religion, our own included. A greater degree of love will produce a greater unity, because it enables people to bear with each other, to be patient and forgiving.

Letter written on behalf of Shoghi Effendi, *Directives from the Guardian*, no. 199, p. 75.[50]

... *W*hen you meet those whose opinions differ from your own, do not turn away your face from them. All are seeking truth, and there are many roads leading thereto. Truth has many aspects, but it remains always and forever one.

Do not allow difference of opinion, or diversity of thought to separate you from your fellow-men, or to be the cause of dispute, hatred and strife in your hearts. Rather, search diligently for the truth, and make all men your friends.

Public Talk of 'Abdu'l-Bahá, *Paris Talks*, p. 46.

---

49   Also *Tablets of Abdul-Baha Abbas*, Vol. III, p. 505.
50   Also The Compilation of Compilations, Vol. II (Living the Life), no. 1299, p. 12.

Friendship

O son of My handmaid!
Wouldst thou seek the grace of the Holy Spirit, enter into fellowship with the righteous, for he hath drunk the cup of eternal life at the hands of the immortal Cup-bearer and even as the true morn doth quicken and illumine the hearts of the dead.

Bahá'u'lláh, *The Hidden Words,* Persian No. 58.

*T*he second condition:[51] Fellowship and love amongst the believers. The divine friends must be attracted to and enamoured of each other and ever be ready and willing to sacrifice their own lives for each other. Should one soul from amongst the believers meet another, it must be as though a thirsty one with parched lips has reached to the fountain of the water of life, or a lover has met his true beloved. For one of the greatest divine wisdoms regarding the appearance of the Holy Manifestations is this: The souls may come to know each other and become intimate with each other; the power of the love of God may make all of them the waves of one sea, the flowers of one rose garden, and the stars of one heaven. This is the wisdom for the appearance of the Holy Manifestations! When the most great bestowal reveals itself in the hearts of the believers, the world of nature will be transformed, the darkness of the contingent being will vanish, and heavenly illumination will be obtained. Then the whole world will become the Paradise of Abhá, every one of the believers of God will become a blessed tree, producing wonderful fruits.

'Abdu'l-Bahá, *The Tablets of the Divine Plan,* pp. 52-53.

*T*here is no teaching in the Bahá'í Faith that "soul mates" exist. What is meant is that marriage should lead to a profound friendship of spirit, which will endure in the next world, where there is no sex, and no giving and taking in marriage; just the way we should establish with our parents, our children, our brothers and sisters and friends a deep spiritual bond which will be everlasting, and not merely physical bonds of human relationship.

Letter dated 4 December 1954 written on behalf of Shoghi Effendi, *The Compilation of Compilations,* Vol. II (Preserving Marriages), no. 2332, p. 452.

*W*e know absence of light is darkness, but no one would assert darkness was not a fact. It exists even though it is only the absence of something else. So evil exists too, and we cannot close our eyes to it, even though it is a negative existence. We must seek to supplant it by good, and if we see an evil person is not influenceable by us, then we should shun his company for it is unhealthy.

Letter dated 4 October 1950 written on behalf of Shoghi Effendi, *Unfolding Destiny,* p. 458.

---

51   Conditions to attain the station of an Apostle of Bahá'u'lláh.

Kindness

*W*hen a man turns his face to God he finds sunshine everywhere. All men are his brothers. Let not conventionality cause you to seem cold and unsympathetic when you meet strange people from other countries. Do not look at them as though you suspected them of being evil-doers, thieves and boors. You think it necessary to be very careful, not to expose yourselves to the risk of making acquaintance with such, possibly, undesirable people.

I ask you not to think only of yourselves. Be kind to the strangers, whether they come from Turkey, Japan, Persia, Russia, China or any other country of the world.

Help to make them feel at home; find out where they are staying, ask if you may render them any service; try to make their lives a little happier.

In this way, even if, sometimes, what you at first suspected should be true, still go out of your way to be kind to them—this kindness will help them to become better.

... Let those who meet you know, without your proclaiming the fact, that you are indeed a Bahá'í.

Put into practice the Teaching of Bahá'u'lláh, that of kindness to all nations. Do not be content with showing friendship in words alone; let your heart burn with loving kindness for all who may cross your path.

Public Talk of 'Abdu'l-Bahá, *Paris Talks*, pp. 1-2.

*E*very human creature is the servant of God. All have been created and reared by the power and favour of God; all have been blessed with the bounties of the same Sun of Divine truth; all have quaffed from the fountain of the infinite mercy of God; and all in His estimation and love are equal as servants. He is beneficent and kind to all. Therefore no one should glorify himself over another; no one should manifest pride or superiority toward another; no one should look upon another with scorn and contempt; and no one should deprive or oppress a fellow creature. All must be considered as submerged in the ocean of God's mercy. We must associate with all humanity with gentleness and kindliness. We must love all with love of the heart. Some are ignorant; they must be trained and educated. One is sick; he must be healed. Another is as a child; we must assist him to attain maturity. We must not detest him who is ailing, neither shun him, scorn nor curse him; but care for him with the utmost kindness and tenderness. An infant must not be treated with disdain simply because it is an infant. Our responsibility is to train, educate and develop it in order that it may advance toward maturity.

Public Talk of 'Abdu'l-Bahá, *The Promulgation of Universal Peace*, p. 63.

*B*e in perfect unity. Never become angry with one another. ... Love the creatures for the sake of God and not for themselves. You will never become angry or impatient if you love them for the sake of God. Humanity is not perfect. There are imperfections in every human being, and you will always become unhappy if you look toward the people themselves. But if you look toward God, you will love them and be kind to them, for the world of God is the world of perfection and complete mercy. Therefore, do not look at the shortcomings of anybody; see with the sight of forgiveness. The imperfect eye beholds imperfections. The eye that covers faults looks towards the Creator of souls. He created them, trains and provides for them, endows them with capacity and life, sight and hearing; therefore, they are the signs of His grandeur.

Public Talk of 'Abdu'l-Bahá, The Promulgation of Universal Peace, p. 93.

*T*o look always at the good and not at the bad. If a man has ten good qualities and one bad one, to look at the ten and forget the one; and if a man has ten bad qualities and one good one, to look at the one and forget the ten.

Words of 'Abdu'l-Bahá, reported by J. E. Esselmont, Bahá'u'lláh and the New Era,
The Sincovering Eye section, p. 80.

*W*e should all visit the sick. When they are in sorrow and suffering, it is a real help and benefit to have a friend come. Happiness is a great healer to those who are ill. ... The people in the East show the utmost kindness and compassion to the sick and suffering. This has greater effect than the remedy itself. You must always have this thought of love and affection when you visit the ailing and afflicted.

Public Talk of 'Abdu'l-Bahá, The Promulgation of Universal Peace, p. 204. (17 June 1912).

*B*riefly, it is not only their fellow human beings that the beloved of God must treat with mercy and compassion, rather must they show forth the utmost loving-kindness to every living creature. For in all physical respects, and where the animal spirit is concerned, the selfsame feelings are shared by animal and man. Man hath not grasped this truth, however, and he believeth that physical sensations are confined to human beings, wherefore is he unjust to the animals, and cruel.

And yet in truth, what difference is there when it cometh to physical sensations? The feelings are one and the same, whether ye inflict pain on man or on beast. There is no difference here whatever. ...

Train your children from their earliest days to be infinitely tender and loving to animals. If an animal be sick, let the children try to heal it, if it be hungry, let them feed it, if thirsty, let them quench its thirst, if weary, let them see that it rests.

'Abdu'l-Bahá, Selections from the Writings of 'Abdu'l-Bahá, no. 138, pp. 158-159.

Courtesy

O My friends!

Walk ye in the ways of the good pleasure of the Friend, and know that His pleasure is in the pleasure of His creatures. That is: no man should enter the house of his friend save at his friend's pleasure, nor lay hands upon his treasures nor prefer his own will to his friends, and in no wise seek an advantage over him. Ponder this, ye that have insight!

Bahá'u'lláh, The Hidden Words, Persian No. 43.

O people of God! I admonish you to observe courtesy, for above all else it is the prince of virtues. Well is it with him who is illumined with the light of courtesy and is attired with the vesture of uprightness.

Law<u>h</u>-i-Dunyá (Tablet of the World), *Tablets of Bahá'u'lláh,* p. 88.

Justice

O son of spirit!
The best beloved of all things in My sight is Justice; turn not away therefrom if thou desirest Me, and neglect it not that I may confide in thee. By its aid thou shalt see with thine own eyes and not through the eyes of others, and shalt know of thine own knowledge and not through the knowledge of thy neighbour. Ponder this in thy heart; how it behoveth thee to be. Verily justice is My gift to thee and the sign of My loving-kindness. Set it then before thine eyes.

Bahá'u'lláh, *The Hidden Words,* Arabic No. 2.

*T*he light of men is Justice. Quench it not with the contrary winds of oppression and tyranny. The purpose of justice is the appearance of unity among men.

Kalimát-Firdawsíyyih (Words of Paradise), Bahá'u'lláh, *Tablets of Bahá'u'lláh,* pp. 66-67.

*T*hat which traineth the world is Justice, for it is upheld by two pillars, reward and punishment. These two pillars are the sources of life to the world.

Ishráqát (Splendours), Bahá'u'lláh, *Tablets of Bahá'u'lláh,* pp. 27, and 128-129.

Not Causing Harm

... beware lest your hands or tongues cause harm unto anyone among mankind.

Law<u>h</u>-i-Dunyá (Tablet of the World), Bahá'u'lláh, *Tablets of Bahá'u'lláh,* p. 85.

O army of God! Beware lest ye harm any soul, or make any heart to sorrow; lest ye wound any man with your words, be he known to you or a stranger, be he friend or foe. Pray ye for all; ask ye that all be blessed, all be forgiven. Beware, beware, lest any of you seek vengeance, even against one who is thirsting for your blood. Beware, beware, lest ye offend the feelings of another, even though he be an evil-doer, and he wish you ill. Look ye not upon the creatures, turn ye to their Creator. See ye not the never-yielding people, see but the Lord of Hosts. Gaze ye not down upon the dust, gaze upward at the shining sun, which hath caused every patch of darksome earth to glow with light.

'Abdu'l-Bahá, *Selections from the Writings of 'Abdu'l-Bahá,* no. 35, p. 73.

Prohibitions

Asceticism
Mendicancy
Arson
Adultery
Murder
Theft
Gambling
Homosexuality
Cruelty to animals
Backbiting
Calumny
Striking or wounding a person
Carrying arms unless essential
Contention and conflict
Idleness and sloth

Bahá'u'lláh, The Kitáb-i-Aqdas (The Most Holy Book), Synopsis and Codification, section IV.D.1.y, pp. 157-158.

Truthfulness

Truthfulness is the foundation of all human virtues. Without truthfulness progress and success, in all the worlds of God, are impossible for any soul. When this holy attribute is established in man, all the divine qualities will also be acquired.

'Abdu'l-Bahá, cited by Shoghi Effendi, The Advent of Divine Justice, p. 26.

Consider that the worst of qualities and most odious of attributes, which is the foundation of all evil, is lying. No worse or more blameworthy quality than this can be imagined to exist; it is the destroyer of all human perfections and the cause of innumerable vices. There is no worse characteristic than this; it is the foundation of all evils.

'Abdu'l-Bahá, Some Answered Questions, p. 215.

As to the question whether it is right to tell an untruth in order to save another, he feels that under no condition should we tell an untruth but at the same time try and help the person in a more legitimate manner. Of course it is not necessary to be too outspoken until the question is directly put to us.

Letter dated 21 December 1927 written on behalf of Shoghi Effendi, The Compilation of Compilations, Vol. II (Living the Life), no. 1273, p. 4.

Not Backbiting

O son of man!
Breathe not the sins of others so long as thou art thyself a sinner. Shouldst thou transgress this command, accursed wouldst thou be, and to this I bear witness.

Bahá'u'lláh, *The Hidden Words,* Arabic No. 27.

*D*o not complain of others. Refrain from reprimanding them, and if you wish to give admonition or advice, let it be offered in such a way that it will not burden the bearer.

Public Talk of 'Abdu'l-Bahá, *The Promulgation of Universal Peace,* p. 453. (2 December 1912.)

*A*s regards backbiting, i.e. discussing the faults of others, in their absence, the teachings are very emphatic. In a Tablet to an American friend the Master wrote: "The worst human quality and the most great sin is backbiting, more especially when it emanates from the tongues of the believers of God. If some means were devised so that the doors of backbiting were shut eternally and each one of the believers unsealed his lips in praise of others, then the teachings of His Holiness Bahá'u'lláh would spread, the hearts be illumined, the spirits glorified, and the human world would attain to everlasting felicity." (Quoted in *Star of the West,* Vol. IV, p. 192.) Bahá'u'lláh says in the *Hidden Words*: "Breathe not the sins of others so long as thou art a sinner. Shouldst thou transgress this command ACCURSED ART THOU." The condemnation of backbiting could hardly be couched in stronger language than in these passages, and it is obviously one of the foremost obligations for Bahá'ís to set their faces against this practice. Even if what is said against another person be true, the mentioning of his faults to others still comes under the category of backbiting, and is forbidden.

Letter dated 11 February 1925 written on behalf of Shoghi Effendi, *Lights of Guidance,* no. 305, p. 88.

Honesty

*T*his wronged one enjoineth on you honesty and piety.

Bahá'u'lláh, *Epistle to the Son of the Wolf,* p. 23.

*K*indness cannot be shown the tyrant, the deceiver, or the thief, because, far from awakening them to the error of their ways, it maketh them to continue in their perversity as before.

'Abdu'l-Bahá, *Selections from the Writings of 'Abdu'l-Bahá,* no. 138, p. 158

Fairness

*B*e fair to yourselves and to others, that the evidences of justice may be revealed, through your deeds, among Our faithful servants.

Bahá'u'lláh, *Gleanings from the Writings of Bahá'u'lláh*, section CXXVIII, p. 278.

... *E*quity is the most fundamental among human virtues. The evaluation of all things must needs depend upon it.

Bahá'u'lláh, *Gleanings from the Writings of Bahá'u'lláh*, section C, p. 203.

*O*bserve equity in your judgement, ye men of understanding heart! He that is unjust in his judgement is destitute of the characteristics that distinguish man's station.

Bahá'u'lláh, *Gleanings from the Writings of Bahá'u'lláh*, section C, p. 204.

... *I*f thine eyes be turned towards justice, choose thou for thy neighbour that which thou choosest for thyself.

Kalimát-i-Firdawsíyyih (Words of Paradise), *Epistle to the Son of the Wolf*, p. 30.[52]

*S*uch rectitude of conduct must manifest itself, with ever-increasing potency, in every verdict which the elected representatives of the Bahá'í community, in whatever capacity they may find themselves, may be called upon to pronounce. It must be constantly reflected in the business dealings of all its members, in their domestic lives, in all manner of employment, and in any service they may, in the future, render their government or people. It must be exemplified in the conduct of all Bahá'í electors, when exercising their sacred rights and functions. ... It must be demonstrated in the impartiality of every defender of the Faith against its enemies, in his fair-mindedness in recognizing any merits that enemy may possess, and in his honesty in discharging any obligations he may have towards him.

Shoghi Effendi, *The Advent of Divine Justice*, pp. 26–27.

*T*o discriminate against any race, on the ground of its being socially backward, politically immature, and numerically in a minority, is a flagrant violation of the spirit that animates the Faith of Bahá'u'lláh.

Shoghi Effendi, *The Advent of Divine Justice*, p. 35.

---

[52] Also *Tablets of Bahá'u'lláh*, p. 64.

Trustworthiness

... *We* gazed on one of the Beauties of the Most Sublime Paradise, standing on a pillar of light, and calling aloud saying: "O inmates of earth and heaven! Behold ye My beauty, and My radiance, and My revelation, and My effulgence. By God, the True One! I am Trustworthiness and the revelation thereof, and the beauty thereof. I will recompense whosoever will cleave unto Me, and recognize My rank and station, and hold fast unto My hem. I am the most great ornament of the people of Bahá, and the vesture of glory unto all who are in the kingdom of creation. I am the supreme instrument for the prosperity of the world, and the horizon of assurance unto all beings."

Ṭarázát (Ornaments), Epistle to the Son of the Wolf, pp. 136-137.[53]

O son of being!
Ascribe not to any soul that which thou wouldst not have ascribed to thee, and say not that which thou doest not. This is My command unto thee, do thou observe it.

Bahá'u'lláh, The Hidden Words, Arabic No. 29.

It[54] must characterize the attitude of every loyal believer towards non-acceptance of political posts, non-identification with political parties, non-participation in political controversies, and non-membership in political organizations and ecclesiastical institutions. It must reveal itself in the uncompromising adherence of all, whether young or old, to the clearly enunciated and fundamental principles laid down by 'Abdu'l-Bahá in His addresses, and to the laws and ordinances revealed by Bahá'u'lláh in His Most Holy Book.

Shoghi Effendi, The Advent of Divine Justice, pp. 26-27.

... *Every* organized community, enlisted under the banner of Bahá'u'lláh should feel it to be its first and inescapable obligation to nurture, encourage, and safeguard every minority belonging to any faith, race, class, or nation within it.

Shoghi Effendi, The Advent of Divine Justice, p. 35.

---

53 Also Tablets of Bahá'u'lláh, p. 38.
54 Rectitude of conduct.

Chapter Seven
Teaching the Bahá'í Faith: Learning about Growth

Orientation to Teaching

Valuing Teaching

O son of man!
Magnify My cause that I may reveal unto thee the mysteries of My greatness and shine upon thee with the light of eternity.

Bahá'u'lláh, The Hidden Words, Arabic No. 41.

It is better to guide one soul than to possess all that is on earth, for as long as that guided soul is under the shadow of the Tree of Divine Unity, he and the one who hath guided him will both be recipients of God's tender mercy, whereas possession of earthly things will cease at the time of death. The path to guidance is one of love and compassion, not of force and coercion. This hath been God's method in the past, and shall continue to be in the future!

The Báb, Selections from the Writings of the Báb, p. 77.

Of all the gifts of God the greatest is the gift of Teaching. It draweth unto us the Grace of God and is our first obligation. Of such a gift how can we deprive ourselves?

'Abdu'l-Bahá, The Will and Testament of 'Abdu'l-Bahá, p. 25.

The greatest glory and honour which can come to an individual is to bring the light of guidance to some new soul. The quickening power of the Holy Spirit, which has come into the world through Bahá'u'lláh, is the source of immortal life; and those who are quickened by this spirit in this world will find themselves in great honour and glory in the next world. The most meritorious service which anyone could render is to bring the light of divine guidance and the quickening power of the spirit to an entirely new area. Humanity is crying for salvation; and it is only by the Bahá'ís going into the various areas of the world, that it can be brought to them. This is the reason the Guardian has encouraged all of the friends to disperse to new territories, for this is the hour for the quickening of the world.

Letter dated 11 March 1956 written on behalf of Shoghi Effendi, The Compilation of Compilations, Vol. II (Guidelines for Teaching), no. 1994, p. 321.

*T*he Bahá'ís are the leaven of God, which must leaven the lump of their nation. In direct ratio to their success will be the protection vouchsafed, not only to them but to their country. These are the immutable laws of God, from which there is no escape: "For unto whomsoever much is given, of him shall be much required."

Letter dated 21 September 1957 written on behalf of Shoghi Effendi, *The Compilation of Compilations*, Vol. II (Living the Life), no. 1340, p. 27; and Vol. II (Guidelines for Teaching), no. 2012, p. 326.

*O*ur lot, dear brothers and sisters, is to be consciously involved in a vast historic process the like of which has not ever been experienced before by any people. As a global community, we have, thus far, attained a unique and magnificent success in being representative of the full spectrum of the human race—thanks to the inestimable expenditure of life, effort and treasure willingly made by thousands of our spiritual forebears. There is no other aggregation of human beings who can claim to have raised up a system with the demonstrated capacity to unite all of God's children in one world-embracing Order. This achievement places us not only in a position of incomparable strength, but more particularly in one of inescapable responsibility. Does not every one of us therefore have a divine obligation to fulfil, a sacred duty to perform towards every other one who is not yet aware of the call of God's latest Manifestation? Time does not stop, does not wait. With every passing hour a fresh affliction strikes at a distracted humanity. Dare we linger?

The Universal House of Justice, *Riḍván Message to the Bahá'ís of the World*, BE 155/AD 1998, para. 18.

Teaching for the Sake of God

*T*each ye the Cause of God, O people of Bahá, for God hath prescribed unto every one the duty of proclaiming His Message, and regardeth it as the most meritorious of all deeds.

Bahá'u'lláh, *Gleanings from the Writings of Bahá'u'lláh*, CXXVIII, p. 278.

*C*entre your energies in the propagation of the Faith of God. Whoso is worthy of so high a calling, let him arise and promote it. Whoso is unable, it is his duty to appoint him who will, in his stead, proclaim this Revelation, whose power hath caused the foundations of the mightiest structures to quake, every mountain to be crushed into dust, and every soul to be dumbfounded.

Bahá'u'lláh, *Gleanings from the Writings of Bahá'u'lláh*, section XCVI, pp. 196-197.

Sustaining Expectancies of Success

*W*hen the victory arriveth, every man shall profess himself as believer and shall hasten to the shelter of God's Faith. Happy are they who in the days of world-encompassing trials have stood fast in the Cause and refused to swerve from its truth.

Bahá'u'lláh, *Gleanings from the Writings of Bahá'u'lláh*, section CL, p. 319.

*B*y the Lord of the Kingdom! If one arise to promote the Word of God with a pure heart, overflowing with the love of God and severed from the world, the Lord of Hosts will assist him with such a power as will penetrate the core of the existent beings.

> 'Abdu'l-Bahá, *The Compilation of Compilations,* Vol. II (The Power of Divine Assistance), no. 1676, p. 211; and Vol. II (Guidelines for Teaching), no. 1913, p. 297.[55]

*T*rials and sufferings, Bahá'u'lláh has repeatedly warned us in His Tablets, are even as the oil that feeds the lamp. The Cause cannot reveal its full splendour unless and until it encounters and successfully overcomes the very obstacles that every now and then stand in its way, and for some time appear to threaten its very foundations. Such obstacles, tests and trials are indeed blessings in disguise, and as such are bound to help in promoting the Faith.

> Letter dated 31 July 1935 written on behalf of Shoghi Effendi, *The Compilation of Compilations,* Vol. I (Crisis and Victory), no. 286, p. 147.

*D*o not feel discouraged if your labours do not always yield an abundant fruitage. For a quick and rapidly-won success is not always the best and the most lasting. The harder you strive to attain your goal, the greater will be the confirmations of Bahá'u'lláh, and the more certain you can feel to attain success. Be cheerful, therefore, and exert yourself with full faith and confidence. For Bahá'u'lláh has promised His Divine assistance to everyone who arises with a pure and detached heart to spread His holy Word, even though he may be bereft of every human knowledge and capacity, and notwithstanding the forces of darkness and of opposition which may be arrayed against him. The goal is clear, the path safe and certain, and the assurances of Bahá'u'lláh as to the eventual success of our efforts quite emphatic. Let us keep firm, and whole-heartedly carry on the great work which He has entrusted into our hands.

> Letter dated 3 February 1937 written on behalf of Shoghi Effendi, *Unfolding Destiny*, p. 436.[56]

*I*t is not enough for the friends to make the excuse that their best teachers and their exemplary believers have arisen and answered the call to pioneer. A "best teacher" and an "exemplary believer" is ultimately neither more nor less than an ordinary Bahá'í who has consecrated himself to the work of the Faith, deepened his knowledge and understanding of its Teachings, placed his confidence in Bahá'u'lláh, and arisen to serve Him to the best of his ability. This door is one which we are assured will open before the face of every follower of the Faith who knocks hard enough, so to speak. When the will and the desire are strong enough, the means will be found and the way opened either to do more work locally, to go to a new goal town ... or to enter the foreign pioneer field ....

> Letter dated 21 September 1957 written on behalf of Shoghi Effendi, *The Compilation of Compilations*, Vol. II (Living the Life), no. 1340, p. 27; and Vol. II (Guidelines for Teaching), no. 2012, p. 326.

*T*o be most effective, teaching needs more than proclamation. The message needs to be conveyed personally from one soul to another in a spirit of love. Shoghi Effendi

---

[55]   Also *Tablets of Abdul-Baha Abbas*, Vol. II, p. 348.
[56]   Also *The Compilation of Compilations*, Vol. II (Guidelines for Teaching), no. 1947, pp. 309-310.

talks about the "art" of teaching. To excel in such an art requires courage, effort, constant application, the pain of uncertainty, and an enormous willingness to take risks and suffer rebuffs ... To them must be added audacity, joy, and confident reliance on the Holy Spirit. Ingenuity is also required and perseverance. Although it may not be easy to meet people to teach them the Faith, let the friends never lose heart. There are ways if one seeks them with sufficient determination.

Letter written on behalf of the Universal House of Justice to a National Spiritual Assembly, C. Samimi, Firesides, p. ix.

Preparing for Teaching

Memorizing Points from the Writings

*T*he sanctified souls should ponder and meditate in their hearts regarding the methods of teaching. From the texts of the wondrous, heavenly Scriptures they should memorize phrases and passages bearing on various instances, so that in the course of their speech they may recite divine verses whenever the occasion demandeth it, inasmuch as these holy verses are the most potent elixir, the greatest and mightiest talisman. So potent is their influence that the hearer will have no cause for vacillation. I swear by My life! This Revelation is endowed with such a power that it will act as the lodestone for all nations and kindreds of the earth. Should one pause to meditate attentively he would recognize that no place is there, nor can there be, for anyone to flee to.

Lawḥ-i-Siyyid-Mihdíy-i-Dahají (Tablet to Siyyid Mihdíy-Dahají), Bahá'u'lláh, Tablets of Bahá'u'lláh, p. 200.

Planning Ways to Contact People

*H*aving on his own initiative, and undaunted by any hindrances with which either friend or foe may, unwittingly or deliberately, obstruct his path, resolved to arise and respond to the call of teaching, let him carefully consider every avenue of approach which he might utilize in his personal attempts to capture the attention, maintain the interest, and deepen the faith, of those whom he seeks to bring into the fold of his Faith. Let him survey the possibilities which the particular circumstances in which he lives offer him, evaluate their advantages, and proceed intelligently and systematically to utilize them for the achievement of the object he has in mind. Let him also attempt to devise such methods as association with clubs, exhibitions, and societies, lectures on subjects akin to the teachings and ideals of his Cause such as temperance, morality, social welfare, religious and racial tolerance, economic co-operation, Islám, and Comparative Religion, or participation in social, cultural, humanitarian, charitable, and educational organizations and enterprises which, while safeguarding the integrity of his Faith, will open up to him a multitude of ways and means whereby he can enlist successively the sympathy, the support, and ultimately the allegiance of those with whom he comes in contact.

Shoghi Effendi, The Advent of Divine Justice, p. 51.

*T*he believers ought to give the Message even to those who do not seem to be ready for it, because they can never judge the real extent to which the Word of God can influence the hearts and minds of the people, even those who appear to lack any power of receptivity to the Teachings.

Letter dated 14 January 1948 written on behalf of Shoghi Effendi, *Directives from the Guardian*, no. 198, pp. 74-75.[57]

Preparing Oneself for Teaching Opportunities

O God, my God! Aid Thou Thy trusted servants to have loving and tender hearts. Help them to spread, amongst all the nations of the earth, the light of guidance that cometh from the Company on high. Verily Thou art the Strong, the Powerful, the Mighty, the All-Subduing, the Ever-Giving. Verily Thou art the Generous, the Gentle, the Tender, the Most Bountiful.

'Abdu'l-Bahá, *Selections from the Writings of 'Abdu'l-Bahá*, p. 22.

... make a special point of praying ardently not only for success in general, but that God may send to you the souls that are ready. There are such souls in every city ....

Letter dated 18 March 1950 written on behalf of Shoghi Effendi, *The Compilation of Compilations*, Vol. II (Guidelines for Teaching), no. 1975, p. 316.

Learning from Experience

*T*eaching is the source of Divine Confirmation. It is not sufficient to pray diligently for guidance, but this prayer must be followed by meditation as to the best methods of action and then action itself. Even if the action should not immediately produce results, or perhaps not be entirely correct, that does not make so much difference, because prayers can only be answered through action and if someone's action is wrong, God can use that method of showing the pathway which is right ....

Letter dated 22 August 1957 written on behalf of Shoghi Effendi, *The Compilation of Compilations*, Vol. II (Guidelines for Teaching), no. 2011, p. 325.

*P*erhaps the reason why you have not accomplished so much in the field of teaching is the extent you looked upon your own weaknesses and inabilities to spread the message. Bahá'u'lláh and the Master have both urged us repeatedly to disregard our own handicaps and lay our whole reliance upon God. He will come to our help if we only arise and become an active channel for God's grace. Do you think it is the teachers who make converts and change human hearts? No, surely not. They are only pure souls who take the first step, and then let the spirit of Bahá'u'lláh move them and make use of them. If any one of them should even for a second consider his achievements as due to his own capacities, his work is ended and his fall starts. This is in fact the reason why so many competent souls have after wonderful services suddenly found themselves absolutely

---

57 Also *The Compilation of Compilations*, Vol. II (Guidelines for Teaching), no. 1950, p. 310.

impotent and perhaps thrown aside by the Spirit of the Cause as useless souls. The criterion is the extent to which we are ready to have the will of God operate through us.

Stop being conscious of your frailties, therefore; have a perfect reliance upon God; let your heart burn with the desire to serve His mission and proclaim His call; and you will observe how eloquence and the power to change human hearts will come as a matter of course.

Shoghi Effendi will surely pray for your success if you should arise and start to teach. In fact the mere act of arising will win for you God's help and blessings.

> Letter dated 31 March 1932 written on behalf of Shoghi Effendi, *The Compilation of Compilations*, Vol. II (The Power of Divine Assistance), no. 1703, pp. 219-220; and Vol. II (Guidelines for Teaching), no. 1939, p. 307.

*T*he House of Justice is sure that ways will be found through prayer, intelligent analysis, and dedicated consultation to increase the rate of enrolment of believers in Australia.

> The Universal House of Justice, *Bahá'í Scholarship: A Compilation and Essays*, pp. 44-45. (28 July 1992.)

The Practice of Personal Teaching

Setting an Example of Bahá'í Life

*W*hoso ariseth among you to teach the Cause of his Lord, let him, before all else, teach his own self, that his speech may attract the hearts of them that hear him. Unless he teacheth his own self, the words of his mouth will not influence the heart of the seeker.

> Bahá'u'lláh, *Gleanings from the Writings of Bahá'u'lláh*, section CXXVIII, p. 277.

*N*ot all of us are capable of serving in the same way, but the one way every Bahá'í can spread the Faith is by example. This moves the hearts of people far more deeply than words ever can.

The love we show others, the hospitality and understanding, the willingness to help them, these are the very best advertisements of the Faith.. They will want to hear about it when they see these things in our lives.

> Letter dated 14 October 1943 written on behalf of Shoghi Effendi, *The Compilation of Compilations*, Vol. II (Living the Life), no. 1291, p. 10.

*U*ntil the public sees in the Bahá'í Community a true pattern, in action, of something better than it already has, it will not respond to the Faith in large numbers.

> Letter dated 13 March 1944 written on behalf of Shoghi Effendi, *Promoting Entry by Troops*, Letter no.10, p. 26.

*O*f these spiritual prerequisites of success, which constitute the bedrock on which the security of all teaching plans, Temple projects, and financial schemes, must ultimately rest, the following stand out as pre-eminent and vital, which the members of the American Bahá'í community will do well to ponder. ... These requirements are none other than a high sense of moral rectitude in their social and administrative activities, absolute chastity in their individual lives, and complete freedom from prejudice in their dealings with peoples of a different race, class, creed, or colour.

Shoghi Effendi, The Advent of Divine Justice, pp. 21-22.

Not by the force of numbers, not by the mere exposition of a set of new and noble principles, not by an organized campaign of teaching—no matter how world-wide and elaborate in its character—not even by the staunchness of our faith or the exaltation of our enthusiasm, can we ultimately hope to vindicate in the eyes of a critical and sceptical age the supreme claim of the Abhá Revelation. One thing and only one thing will unfailingly and alone secure the undoubted triumph of this sacred Cause, namely, the extent to which our own inner life and private character mirror forth in their manifold aspects the splendour of those eternal principles proclaimed by Bahá'u'lláh.

Shoghi Effendi, Unfolding Destiny, p. 28.[58]

Showing Sincere Friendship to All

The friends of God should weave bonds of fellowship with others and show absolute love and affection towards them. These links have a deep influence on people and they will listen. When the friends sense receptivity to the Word of God, they should deliver the Message with wisdom. They must first try and remove any apprehensions in the people they teach.

'Abdu'l-Bahá, The Compilation of Compilations, Vol. II (Guidelines for Teaching), no. 1924, p. 300.

Let him remember the example set by 'Abdu'l-Bahá, and His constant admonition to shower such kindness upon the seeker, and exemplify to such a degree the spirit of the teachings he hopes to instil into him, that the recipient will be spontaneously impelled to identify himself with the Cause embodying such teachings.

Shoghi Effendi, The Advent of Divine Justice, p. 52.

The role of the individual is of unique importance in the work of the Cause. It is the individual who manifests the vitality of faith upon which the success of the teaching work and the development of the community depend. Bahá'u'lláh's command to each believer to teach His Faith confers an inescapable responsibility which cannot be transferred to, or assumed by, any institution of the Cause. The individual alone can exercise those capacities which include the ability to take initiative, to seize opportunities, to form friendships, to interact personally with others, to build relationships, to win the co-operation of others in common service to the Faith and society, and to convert into action the decisions made by consultative bodies . It is the individual's duty to "consider every avenue

---

58   Also Bahá'í Administration, p. 66.

of approach which he might utilize in his personal attempts to capture the attention, maintain the interest, and deepen the faith, of those whom he seeks to bring into the fold of his Faith."[59]

> The Universal House of Justice, *Riḍván Message to the Bahá'ís of the World*, BE 153/AD 1996, para. 20.

Interesting People in the Faith

*T*his is the day in which to speak. It is incumbent upon the people of Bahá to strive, with the utmost patience and forbearance, to guide the peoples of the world to the Most Great Horizon.

> Bahá'u'lláh, cited by Shoghi Effendi, *The Advent of Divine Justice*, p. 82.

*O*ne word may be likened unto fire, another unto light, and the influence which both exert is manifest in the world. Therefore an enlightened man of wisdom should primarily speak with words as mild as milk, that the children of men may be nurtured and edified thereby and may attain the ultimate goal of human existence which is the station of true understanding and nobility. And likewise He saith: One word is like unto springtime causing the tender saplings of the rose-garden of knowledge to become verdant and flourishing, while another word is even as a deadly poison. It behoveth a prudent man of wisdom to speak with utmost leniency and forbearance so that the sweetness of his words may induce everyone to attain that which befitteth man's station.

> *Lawḥ-i-Maqṣúd* (Tablet of Maqṣúd), Bahá'u'lláh, *Tablets of Bahá'u'lláh*, p. 173.

*I*n accordance with the divine teachings in this glorious dispensation we should not belittle anyone and call him ignorant, saying: "You know not, but I know". Rather, we should look upon others with respect, and when attempting to explain and demonstrate, we should speak as if we are investigating the truth, saying: "Here these things are before us. Let us investigate to determine where and in what form the truth can be found." The teacher should not consider himself as learned and others ignorant. Such a thought breedeth pride, and pride is not conducive to influence. The teacher should not see in himself any superiority; he should speak with the utmost kindliness, lowliness and humility, for such speech exerteth influence and educateth the souls.

> 'Abdu'l-Bahá, *Selections from the Writings of 'Abdu'l-Bahá*, no. 15, p. 30.

*T*o optimize the use of these capacities, the individual draws upon his love for Bahá'u'lláh, the power of the Covenant, the dynamics of prayer, the inspiration and education derived from regular reading and study of the Holy Texts, and the transformative forces that operate upon his soul as he strives to behave in accordance with the divine laws and principles. In addition to these, the individual, having been given the duty to teach the Cause, is endowed with the capacity to attract particular blessings promised

---

59 Shoghi Effendi, *The Advent of Divine Justice*, p. 51.

by Bahá'u'lláh. "Whoso openeth his lips in this Day," the Blessed Beauty asserts, "and maketh mention of the name of his Lord, the hosts of Divine inspiration shall descend upon him from the heaven of My name, the All-Knowing, the All-Wise. On him shall also descend the Concourse on high, each bearing aloft a chalice of pure light."[60]

The Universal House of Justice, *Riḍván Message to the Bahá'ís of the World,* BE 153/AD 1996, para. 21.

*L*et him consider the degree of his hearer's receptivity, and decide for himself the suitability of either the direct or indirect method of teaching, whereby he can impress upon the seeker the vital importance of the Divine Message, and persuade him to throw in his lot with those who have already embraced it. Let him remember the example set by 'Abdu'l-Bahá, and His constant admonition to shower such kindness upon the seeker, and exemplify to such a degree the spirit of the teachings he hopes to instil into him, that the recipient will be spontaneously impelled to identify himself with the Cause embodying such teachings.

Shoghi Effendi, *The Advent of Divine Justice,* pp. 51-52.

*Y*et, if we but call to mind the practice generally adopted by 'Abdu'l-Bahá, we cannot fail to perceive the wisdom, nay the necessity, of gradually and cautiously disclosing to the eyes of an unbelieving world the implications of a Truth which, by its own challenging nature, it is so difficult for it to comprehend and embrace.

It was He, our beloved 'Abdu'l-Bahá, our true and shining Exemplar, who with infinite tact and patience, whether in His public utterances or in private converse, adapted the presentation of the fundamentals of the Cause to the varying capacities and the spiritual receptiveness of His hearers. He never hesitated, however, to tear the veil asunder and reveal to the spiritually ripened those challenging verities that set forth in its true light the relationship of this Supreme Revelation with the Dispensations of the past.

Shoghi Effendi, *Bahá'í Administration,* p. 125.

*I*n teaching the Cause, much depends on the personality of the teacher and on the method he chooses for presenting the message. Different personalities and different classes and types of individuals need different methods of approach. And it is the sign of an able teacher to know how to best adapt his methods to various types of people whom he happens to meet. There is no one method one can follow all through. But there should be as many ways of approach as there are types of individual seekers. Flexibility and variety of method is, therefore, an essential prerequisite for the success of every teaching activity.

Letter dated 31 May 1934 written on behalf of Shoghi Effendi, *The Compilation of Compilations,* Vol. II (Guidelines for Teaching), no. 1941, p. 308.

---

60   Bahá'u'lláh, Gleanings from the Writings of Bahá'u'lláh, section CXXIX, p. 280.

Attracting Seekers to the Spiritual World

O Friends! You must all be so ablaze in this day with the fire of the love of God that the heat thereof may be manifest in all your veins, your limbs and members of your body, and the peoples of the world may be ignited by this heat and turn to the horizon of the Beloved.

Bahá'u'lláh, *The Compilation of Compilations,* Vol. II (Guidelines for Teaching), no. 1898, p. 293.

*T*hey must be baptized with the water of life, the fire of the love of God and the breaths of the Holy Spirit; be satisfied with little food, but take a large portion from the heavenly table. They must disengage themselves from temptation and covetousness, and be filled with the spirit. Through the effect of their pure breath, they must change the stone into the brilliant ruby and the shell into pearl. Like unto the cloud of vernal shower, they must transform the black soil into the rose garden and orchard. They must make the blind seeing, the deaf hearing, the extinguished one enkindled and set aglow, and the dead quickened.

'Abdu'l-Bahá, *Tablets of the Divine Plan,* no. 7, p. 96.

*T*he teacher, when teaching, must be himself fully enkindled, so that his utterance, like unto a flame of fire, may exert influence and consume the veil of self and passion. He must also be utterly humble and lowly so that others may be edified, and be totally self-effaced and evanescent so that he may teach with the melody of the Concourse on high—otherwise his teaching will have no effect.

'Abdu'l-Bahá, *Selections from the Writings of 'Abdu'l-Bahá,* no. 217, p. 270.

*S*peak, therefore; speak out with great courage at every meeting. When thou art about to begin thine address, turn first to Bahá'u'lláh, and ask for the confirmations of the Holy Spirit, then open thy lips and say whatever is suggested to thy heart; this, however, with the utmost courage, dignity and conviction. It is my hope that from day to day your gatherings will grow and flourish, and that those who are seeking after truth will hearken therein to reasoned arguments and conclusive proofs.

'Abdu'l-Bahá, *Selections from the Writings of 'Abdu'l-Bahá,* no. 216, pp. 269-270.

*T*he first and most important qualification of a Bahá'í teacher is, indeed, unqualified loyalty and attachment to the Cause. Knowledge is, of course, essential, but compared to devotion it is secondary in importance.

Letter dated 14 November 1935 written on behalf of Shoghi Effendi, *Directives from the Guardian,* no. 186, p. 70. (revised.)

Setting Forth Reasons for Accepting the Faith

*T*he first and foremost testimony establishing His truth is His own Self. Next to this testimony is His Revelation. For whoso faileth to recognize either the one or the other He hath established the words He hath revealed as proof of His reality and truth. This is, verily, an evidence of His tender mercy unto men. He hath endowed every soul with the capacity to recognize the signs of God. How could He, otherwise, have fulfilled His testimony unto men, if ye be of them that ponder His Cause in their hearts.

Bahá'u'lláh, *Gleanings from the Writings of Bahá'u'lláh*, section LII, pp. 105-106.

*B*eware of false prophets, who come to you in sheep's clothing, but inwardly are ravenous wolves. You will know them by their fruits. Are grapes gathered from thorns, or figs from thistles? So, every sound tree bears good fruit, but the bad tree bears evil fruit. A sound tree cannot bear evil fruit, nor can a bad tree bear good fruit. Every tree that does not bear good fruit is cut down and thrown into the fire. Thus you will know them by their fruits.

Words of Jesus, *The New Testament*, Matthew 7:15-20.

*E*very proof and prophecy, every manner of evidence, whether based on reason or on the text of the scriptures and traditions, are to be regarded as centred in the persons of Bahá'u'lláh and the Báb. In them is to be found their complete fulfilment.

'Abdu'l-Bahá, cited in The Dispensation of Bahá'u'lláh, Shoghi Effendi, *The World Order of Bahá'u'lláh*, pp. 127-128.

*O*ne Holy Soul gives life to the world of humanity, changes the aspect of the terrestrial globe, causes intelligence to progress, vivifies souls, lays the basis of a new life, establishes new foundations, organizes the world, brings nations and religions under the shadow of one standard, delivers man from the world of imperfections and vices, and inspires him with the desire and need of natural and acquired perfections. Certainly nothing short of a divine power could accomplish so great a work. We ought to consider this with justice, for this is the office of justice.

'Abdu'l-Bahá, *Some Answered Questions*, pp. 9-10.

The Life of Bahá'u'lláh

*H*e Who is everlastingly hidden from the eyes of men can never be known except through His Manifestation, and His Manifestation can adduce no greater proof of the truth of His Mission than the proof of His own Person.

Bahá'u'lláh, *Gleanings from the Writings of Bahá'u'lláh*, section XX, p. 49.

The Teachings of Bahá'u'lláh

*T*hat which hath been made manifest in this pre-eminent, this most exalted Revelation, stands unparalleled in the annals of the past, nor will future ages witness its like.

Bahá'u'lláh, cited by Shoghi Effendi, *The World Order of Bahá'u'lláh*, pp. 103-104, and 167.[61]

The Influence of Bahá'u'lláh

....*I*s not the object of every Revelation to effect a transformation in the whole character of mankind, a transformation that shall manifest itself both outwardly and inwardly, that shall affect both its inner life and external conditions? For if the character of mankind be not changed, the futility of God's universal Manifestations would be apparent.

Bahá'u'lláh, *The Kitáb-i-Íqán* (The Book of Certitude), pp. 240-241.

The Prophecies of Bahá'u'lláh

*A*nd if you say in your heart, "How may we know the word which the LORD has not spoken?"—when a prophet speaks in the name of the LORD, if the word does not come to pass or come true, that is a word which the LORD has not spoken; the prophet has spoken it presumptuously, you need not be afraid of him.

Deuteronomy, *The Old Testament*, 18:21-22.

Prophecies in Previous Scripture

*T*he Revelation which, from time immemorial, hath been acclaimed as the Purpose and Promise of all the Prophets of God, and the most cherished Desire of His Messengers, hath now, by virtue of the pervasive Will of the Almighty and at His irresistible bidding, been revealed unto men. The advent of such a Revelation hath been heralded in all the sacred Scriptures.

Bahá'u'lláh, *Gleanings from the Writings of Bahá'u'lláh*, section III, p. 5.

Accepting the Response of the Hearer

*B*e unrestrained as the wind, while carrying the Message of Him Who hath caused the Dawn of Divine Guidance to break. Consider, how the wind, faithful to that which God hath ordained, bloweth upon all the regions of the earth, be they inhabited or desolate. Neither the sight of desolation, nor the evidences of prosperity, can either pain or please it. It bloweth in every direction, as bidden by its Creator. So should be every one that claimeth to be a lover of the one true God. It behoveth him to fix his gaze upon the fundamentals of His Faith, and to labour diligently for its propagation. Wholly

---

[61] Also *The Advent of Divine Justice*, p. 77.

for the sake of God he should proclaim His Message, and with that same spirit accept whatever response his words may evoke in his hearer. He who shall accept and believe, shall receive his reward; and he who shall turn away, shall receive none other than his own punishment.

Bahá'u'lláh, *Gleanings from the Writings of Bahá'u'lláh*, section CLXI, p. 339.

O son of dust!

The wise are they that speak not unless they obtain a hearing, even as the cup-bearer, who proffereth not his cup till he findeth a seeker, and the lover who crieth not out from the depths of his heart until he gazeth upon the beauty of his beloved.

Bahá'u'lláh, *The Hidden Words*, Persian No. 36.

*B*eware lest ye contend with any one, nay, strive to make him aware of the truth with kindly manner and most convincing exhortation. If your hearer respond, he will have responded to his own behoof, and if not, turn ye away from him, and set your faces towards God's sacred Court, the seat of resplendent holiness.

Bahá'u'lláh, *Gleanings from the Writings of Bahá'u'lláh*, section CXXVIII, p. 279.

*C*onsort with all men, O people of Bahá, in a spirit of friendliness and fellowship. If ye be aware of a certain truth, if ye possess a jewel, of which others are deprived, share it with them in a language of utmost kindliness and good-will. If it be accepted, if it fulfil its purpose, your object is attained. If any one should refuse it, leave him unto himself, and beseech God to guide him. Beware lest ye deal unkindly with him. A kindly tongue is the lodestone of the hearts of men. It is the bread of the spirit, it clotheth the words with meaning, it is the fountain of the light of wisdom and understanding.

Bahá'u'lláh, *Epistle to the Son of the Wolf*, p. 15.[62]

Using Various Teaching Methods

Firesides

*B*lessed art thou for having opened the door of thy home unto the people to come and hear of the Kingdom.

'Abdu'l-Bahá, *Tablets of Abdul-Baha Abbas*, Vol. I, pp. 68–69.

*K*now that in every home where God is praised and prayed to, and His Kingdom proclaimed, that home is a garden of God and a paradise of His happiness.

'Abdu'l-Bahá, *Tablets of Abdul-Baha Abbas*, Vol. I, p. 69.

---

[62] Also Gleanings from the Writings of Bahá'u'lláh, section CXXXII, p. 289.

*I*t should not be overlooked, however, that the most powerful and effective teaching medium that has been found so far is the fireside meeting, because in the fireside meeting, intimate personal questions can be answered, and the student find the spirit of the Faith more abundant there.

Letter dated 11 December 1952 written on behalf of Shoghi Effendi, *The Compilation of Compilations*, Vol. II (Guidelines for Teaching), no. 1983, pp. 317-318.

*T*he most effective method of teaching is the Fireside group, where new people can be shown Bahá'í hospitality, and ask all questions which bother them. They can feel there the true Bahá'í spirit—and it is the spirit that quickeneth.

Letter dated 20 October 1956 written on behalf of Shoghi Effendi, *The Compilation of Compilations*, Vol. II (Guidelines for Teaching), no. 2000, p. 323.

*T*he Guardian hopes the Friends ... will display the loving spirit of the Master in their contacts, and then win those souls to the Faith. The fireside method of teaching seems to produce the greatest results, when each one invites friends into their homes once in nineteen days, and introduces them to the Faith. Close association and loving service affects the hearts; and when the heart is affected, then the spirit can enter. It is the Holy Spirit that quickens, and the Friends must become channels for its diffusion.

Letter dated 27 January 1957 written on behalf of Shoghi Effendi, *The Compilation of Compilations*, Vol. II (Guidelines for Teaching), no. 2005, p. 324.

Travelling

*T*he movement itself from place to place, when undertaken for the sake of God hath always exerted, and can now exert, its influence in the world. In the Books of old the station of them that have voyaged far and near in order to guide the servants of God hath been set forth and written down.

Bahá'u'lláh cited by Shoghi Effendi, *The Advent of Divine Justice*, p. 84.

Pioneering

*T*hey that have forsaken their country for the purpose of teaching Our Cause—these shall the Faithful Spirit strengthen through its power. A company of Our chosen angels shall go forth with them, as bidden by Him Who is the Almighty, the All-Wise. How great the blessedness that awaiteth him that hath attained the honour of serving the Almighty! By My life! No act, however great, can compare with it, except such deeds as have been ordained by God, the All-Powerful, the Most Mighty. Such a service is, indeed, the prince of all goodly deeds, and the ornament of every goodly act.

Bahá'u'lláh, *Gleanings from the Writings of Bahá'u'lláh*, section CLVII, p. 334.

Arts and Music

*I*n this Cause the art of music is of paramount importance. The Blessed Perfection, when He first came to the barracks ('Akká) repeated this statement: "If among the immediate followers there had been those who could have played some musical instrument, i.e., flute or harp, or could have sung, it would have charmed every one." In short, musical melodies form an important role in the associations, or outward and inward characteristics, or qualities of man, for it is the inspirer or motive power of both the material and spiritual susceptibilities. What a motive power it is in all feelings of love! When man is attached to the Love of God, music has a great effect upon him.

'Abdu'l-Bahá, *The Compilation of Compilations*, Vol. II (Music), no. 1421, pp. 77-78.

*S*hoghi Effendi was very much interested to learn of the success of the "Pageant of the Nations" you produced. He sincerely hopes that all those who attended it were inspired by the same spirit that animated you while arranging it.

It is through such presentations that we can arouse the interest of the greatest number of people in the spirit of the Cause. The day will come when the Cause will spread like wildfire when its spirit and teachings will be presented on the stage or in art and literature as a whole. Art can better awaken such noble sentiments than cold rationalizing, especially among the mass of the people.

We have to wait only a few years to see how the spirit breathed by Bahá'u'lláh will find expression in the work of the artists. What you and some other Bahá'ís are attempting are only faint rays that precede the effulgent light of a glorious morn. We cannot yet value the part the Cause is destined to play in the life of society. We have to give it time. The material this spirit has to mould is too crude and unworthy, but it will at last give way and the Cause of Bahá'u'lláh will reveal itself in its full splendour.

Letter dated 10 October 1932 written on behalf of Shoghi Effendi, *The Compilation of Compilations*, Vol. I (Arts and Craft), no. 26, pp. 7-8.

Writing

*I*f any man were to arise to defend, in his writings, the Cause of God against its assailants, such a man, however inconsiderable his share, shall be so honoured in the world to come that the Concourse on high would envy his glory. No pen can depict the loftiness of his station, neither can any tongue describe its splendour.

Bahá'u'lláh, *Gleanings from the Writings of Bahá'u'lláh*, section CLIV, p. 330.

*A*t this early stage of the Cause all works by Bahá'ís which deal with the Faith, whether in the form of books, pamphlets, translations, poems, songs, radio and television scripts, films, recordings, etc. must be approved before submission for publication, whether to a Bahá'í or non-Bahá'í publisher. In the case of material for purely local consumption the competent authority is the Local Spiritual Assembly, otherwise the National Spiritual Assembly (through its Reviewing Committee) is the approving authority.

... this measure is both obligatory and temporary ...

Messages from the Universal House of Justice 1963–1986, paras 94.3a–94.3b, pp. 185–186. (Riḍván 1971.)

Bahá'í authors may submit their works for review to any National Spiritual Assembly, and may send their works, once approved, to any publisher they like, Bahá'í or non-Bahá'í, at home or abroad. It should be remembered, however, that the approval should be given by the National Spiritual Assembly of the country where the work is to be first published. And in the case of a non-Bahá'í publisher the author should insist on use of the system of transliteration at present used by the Faith for languages employing the Roman alphabet.

It is hoped that Bahá'í authors will provide a constant stream of new works. Introductory books, commentaries, dissertations on various aspects of the Revelation, text books, histories, reviews, audio-visual material are all needed to stimulate study of the Faith and to promote the vital teaching work.

Messages from the Universal House of Justice 1963–1986, paras 94.3p–94.3q, p. 188. (Riḍván 1971.)

Supporting New Believers

Receiving Declarations of Belief

The first duty prescribed by God for His servants is the recognition of Him Who is the Dayspring of His Revelation and the Fountain of His laws, Who representeth the Godhead in both the Kingdom of His Cause and the world of creation. Whoso achieveth this duty hath attained unto all good; and whoso is deprived thereof hath gone astray, though he be the author of every righteous deed.

Bahá'u'lláh, *The Kitáb-i-Aqdas* (The Most Holy Book), para. 1, p. 19.

The Bahá'í Community shall consist of all persons recognized by the Universal House of Justice as possessing the qualifications of Bahá'í faith and practice.

The Constitution of the Universal House of Justice, By-Laws, Section I, p. 8.

When enrolling new believers, we must be wise and gentle, and not place so many obstacles in their way that they feel it impossible to accept the Faith.

Letter dated 25 June 1953 written on behalf of Shoghi Effendi, *Unfolding Destiny*, p. 308.

The prime motive should always be the response of man to God's Message, and the recognition of His Messenger. Those who declare themselves as Bahá'ís should become enchanted with the beauty of the Teachings; and touched by the love of Bahá'u'lláh. The declarants need not know all the proofs, history, laws, and principles of the Faith, but in the process of declaring themselves they must, in addition to catching the spark of faith, become basically informed about the Central Figures of the Faith, as well as the existence of laws they must follow and an administration they must obey.

Messages from the Universal House of Justice 1963-1986, para. 18.4, p. 39. (13 July 1964.)

What one believes is an internal and personal matter, and it is not for any person or institution to insist upon what others should believe. Since there is a wide range of meanings in the Sacred Scriptures, there are bound to be different ways in which individuals understand many of the Bahá'í teachings. However, it is necessary for the viability of the Bahá'í community that its members share a common understanding of fundamentals. This implies a commitment by each member to function within the framework established by such an understanding.

This framework includes, for example, cognizance of the existence of a Divine Revelation brought by Bahá'u'lláh, the Manifestation of God for this age, and acceptance of the two primary duties prescribed by God, as expressed in the *Kitáb-i-Aqdas*, the Most Holy Book of the Bahá'í Revelation. These are: "recognition of Him Who is the Dayspring of His Revelation and the Fountain of His laws," and observance of "every ordinance of Him Who is the Desire of the world." "These twin duties," the Aqdas firmly states, "are inseparable. Neither is acceptable without the other."

Furthermore, 'Abdu'l-Bahá, Whom Bahá'u'lláh appointed as the Interpreter of His writings, reaffirms these fundamentals of Bahá'í belief. In His Will and Testament He writes: "This is the foundation of the belief of the people of Bahá (may my life be offered up for them): 'His Holiness, the Exalted One (the Báb), is the Manifestation of the Unity and Oneness of God and the Forerunner of the Ancient Beauty. His Holiness the Abhá Beauty (may my life be a sacrifice for His steadfast friends) is the Supreme Manifestation of God and the Dayspring of His Most Divine Essence. All others are servants unto Him and do His bidding.'"

It is within the context of these statements of basic belief that membership in the Bahá'í Faith is determined. Acknowledging that the matter of ascertaining the qualification of a true believer is a "delicate and complex question", Shoghi Effendi, the appointee of 'Abdu'l-Bahá as Guardian of the Cause and authorized interpreter of its teachings, set down for Spiritual Assembles the "principal factors that must be taken into consideration before deciding whether a person may be regarded as a true believer or not": "Full recognition of the station of the Forerunner, the Author, and the True Exemplar of the Bahá'í Cause, as set forth in 'Abdu'l-Bahá's Testament; unreserved acceptance of, and submission to, whatsoever has been revealed by their Pen; loyal and steadfast adherence to every clause of our Beloved's sacred Will; and close association with the spirit as well as the form of the present day Bahá'í administration throughout the world."

Letter dated 28 February 1997 written on behalf of
The Universal House of Justice to a National Spiritual Assembly.

Nurturing New Believers

Let him refrain, at the outset, from insisting on such laws and observances as might impose too severe a strain on the seeker's newly awakened faith, and endeavour to nurse him, patiently, tactfully, and yet determinedly, into full maturity, and aid him to proclaim his unqualified acceptance of whatever has been ordained by Bahá'u'lláh. Let him, as soon as that stage has been attained, introduce him to the body of his fellow-believers, and seek, through constant fellowship and active participation in the local activities of his community, to enable him to contribute his share to the enrichment of its life, the furtherance of its tasks, the consolidations of its interests, and the co-ordination of its activities with those of its sister communities. Let him not be content until he has infused into his spiritual child so deep a longing as to impel him to arise independently, in his turn, and devote his energies to the quickening of other souls, and the upholding of the laws and principles laid down by his newly-adopted Faith.

Shoghi Effendi, *The Advent of Divine Justice*, p. 52.

Maintaining Love and Unity in the Community

Too great emphasis cannot be laid on the importance of the unity of the friends, for only by manifesting the greatness of their love for and patience with each other can they hope to attract large numbers to their ranks.

Letter dated 2 August 1942 written on behalf of Shoghi Effendi, *Promoting Entry by Troops*, no. 8, p. 26.

The thing the world needs today is the Bahá'í spirit. People are craving for love, for a high standard to look up to, as well as for solutions to their many grave problems. The Bahá'ís should shower on those whom they meet the warm and living spirit of the Cause, and this, combined with teaching, cannot but attract the sincere truth-seekers to the Faith.

Letter dated 18 December 1943 written on behalf of Shoghi Effendi, *The Compilation of Compilations*, Vol. II (Living the Life), no. 1298, p. 12.

Teaching the Masses

The Process of Entry by Troops

It is also recorded in the blessed Gospel: *Travel ye throughout the world and call ye the people to the Kingdom of God.*[63] Now this is the time that you may arise and perform this most great service and become the cause of the guidance of innumerable souls. Thus

---

63   Mark 16:15

through this superhuman service the rays of peace and conciliation may illumine and enlighten all the regions and the world of humanity may find peace and composure.

'Abdu'l-Bahá, *The Tablets of the Divine Plan*, no. 4, p. 22.

... *A* steady flow of reinforcements is absolutely vital and is of extreme urgency ...

This flow, moreover, will presage and hasten the advent of the day which, as prophesied by 'Abdu'l-Bahá, will witness the entry by troops of peoples of divers nations and races into the Bahá'í world—a day which, viewed in its proper perspective, will be the prelude to that long-awaited hour when a mass conversion on the part of these same nations and races, and as a direct result of a chain of events, momentous and possibly catastrophic in nature, and which cannot as yet be dimly visualized, will suddenly revolutionize the fortunes of the Faith, derange the equilibrium of the world, and reinforce a thousand-fold the numerical strength as well as the material power and the spiritual authority of the Faith of Bahá'u'lláh.

Shoghi Effendi, *Citadel of Faith*, p. 117.

*W*hen the masses of mankind are awakened and enter the Faith of God, a new process is set in motion and the growth of a new civilization begins. Witness the emergence of Christianity and of Islám. These masses are the rank and file, steeped in traditions of their own, but receptive to the new Word of God, by which, when they truly respond to it, they become so influenced as to transform those who come in contact with them.

Messages from the Universal House of Justice 1963-1986, para. 18.1, p. 38. (13 July 1964.)

The Principle of Universality: Reaching all Strata of Society

*T*o gather jewels have I come to this world. If one speck of a jewel lie hid in a stone and that stone be beyond the seven seas, until I have found and secured that jewel, my hand shall not stay from its search.

Bahá'u'lláh, cited in *"Gems of Nabíl"*, Trans. Shoghi Effendi and J. E. Esselmont, *The Bahá'í World*, Vol. VIII (1938-1940), p. 934; and *The Bahá'í World*, Vol. XI (1946-1950), p. 775.

*W*e fain would hope that the people of Bahá may be guided by the blessed words: "Say: all things are of God." This exalted utterance is like unto water for quenching the fire of hate and enmity which smouldereth within the hearts and breasts of men. By this single utterance contending peoples and kindreds will attain the light of true unity.

Kitáb-i-'Ahd, (Book of the Covenant), Bahá'u'lláh, *Tablets of Bahá'u'lláh*, p. 222.

*D*iversity of hues, form and shape, enricheth and adorneth the garden, and heighteneth the effect thereof. In like manner, when divers shades of thought, temperament and character, are brought together under the power and influence of one central agency, the beauty and glory of human perfection will be revealed and made manifest. Naught but

the celestial potency of the Word of God, which ruleth and transcendeth the realities of all things, is capable of harmonizing the divergent thoughts, sentiments, ideas, and convictions of the children of men.
'Abdu'l-Bahá, *Selections from the Writings of 'Abdu'l-Bahá*, no. 225, p. 291.[64]

*T*he Guardian attaches the utmost importance, as you know, to the teaching of the natives of America.

In the *Tablets of the Divine Plan*, the Master pays the utmost attention to this most important matter. He states that if the Power of the Holy Spirit today properly enters into the minds and the hearts of the natives of the great American continents that they will become great standard bearers of the Faith, similar to the Nomads (Arabians) who became the most cultured and enlightened people under the Mohammedan civilization.
Letter written on behalf of Shoghi Effendi, *Lights of Guidance*, no. 1776, p. 524.

*H*e attaches great importance to teaching the aboriginal Australians, and also in converting more Maoris to the Faith, and hopes that the Bahá'ís will devote some attention to contacting both of these minority groups.
Letter dated 16 June 1954 written on behalf of Shoghi Effendi, *Letters from the Guardian to Australia and New Zealand*, p. 119.[65]

*T*he Cause of God has room for all. It would, indeed, not be the Cause of God if it did not take in and welcome everyone—poor and rich, educated and ignorant, the unknown, and the prominent—God surely wants them all, as He created them all.
Letter dated 10 December 1942 written on behalf of Shoghi Effendi, *The Compilation of Compilations*, Vol. II (Prominent People), no. 1828, p. 261; and Vol. II (Guidelines for Teaching), no. 1953, p. 311.

Reaching People of Capacity

*T*hus far, we have achieved a marvellous diversity in the large numbers of ethnic groups represented in the faith, and everything should be done to fortify it through larger enrolments from among groups already represented and the attraction of members from groups not yet reached. However, there is another category of diversity which must be built up and without which the Cause will not be able adequately to meet the challenges being thrust upon it. Its membership, regardless of ethnic variety, needs now to embrace increasing numbers of people of capacity, including persons of accomplishment and prominence in the various fields of human endeavour. Enrolling significant numbers of such persons is an indispensable aspect of teaching the masses, an aspect which cannot any longer be neglected and which must be consciously and deliberately incorporated into our teaching work, so as to broaden its base and accelerate the process of entry by troops.
The Universal House of Justice, *Riḍván Message to the Bahá'ís of the World*, BE 147/AD 1990, para. 18.

---

[64] Also Tablets of the Divine Plan, no. 5, p. 103.
[65] Also Arohanui: Letters to New Zealand, p. 67.

Flexible Teaching Plans

The International Teaching centre has concluded that the Bahá'í institutions in ... seem to be placing too much reliance on large, expensive projects, involving a great deal of successful public relations and proclamation. These are, in their own way, very useful activities, but it must be realized that they cannot be expected to produce large numbers of new believers. The key to the conversion of people to the Faith is the action of the individual Bahá'í conveying the spark of faith to individual seekers, answering their questions and deepening their understanding of the teachings.

> Letter written on behalf of the Universal House of Justice, *Promoting Entry by Troops*, no. 43, pp. 43-44.

An expansion of thought and action in certain aspects of our work would enhance our possibilities for success in meeting our aforementioned commitments. Since change, ever more rapid change, is a constant characteristic of life at this time, and since our growth, size and external relations demand much of us, our community must be ready to adapt. In a sense this means that the community must become more adept at accommodating a wide range of actions without losing concentration on the primary objectives of teaching, namely, expansion and consolidation. A unity in diversity of actions is called for, a condition in which different individuals will concentrate on different activities, appreciating the salutary effect of the aggregate on the growth and development of the Faith, because each person cannot do everything and all persons cannot do the same thing. This understanding is important to the maturity which, by the many demands being made upon it, the community is being forced to attain.

> The Universal House of Justice, *Riḍván Message to the Bahá'ís of the World*, BE 147/AD 1990, para. 16.

Relating the Faith to Contemporary Social and Humanitarian Issues

The Cause has the remedy for all the world's ills. The reason why more people don't accept it is because the Bahá'ís are not always capable of presenting it to them in a way that meets the immediate needs of their minds. Young Bahá'ís like yourself must prepare themselves to really bring the Message to their generation, who need it so desperately and who can understand the language it speaks so well.

> Letter 21 October 1943 written on behalf of Shoghi Effendi, *The Compilation of Compilations*, Vol. I (The importance of Deepening), no. 495, p. 226; and Vol. II (Youth), no. 2273, p. 431.[66]

It is apparent that Australian society is under marked stress as a consequence of the economic difficulties the nation is facing, and that there is public concern about such issues as morality, ethics in political life and business, the relationship between the racial components of society, the role of women in religious activities, social disintegration evident through marriage breakdown, youth delinquency, crime and violence. If they

---

[66] Also *Bahá'í Scholarship: A Compilation and Essays*, no. 6, p. 5.

persist, such conditions must inevitably lead the Australian people, sooner or later, to a determined search for effective solutions to these manifold problems.

It is abundantly evident that the only fundamental and enduring resolution to the distress of the people of Australia, or any other part of the world, lies in acceptance of the claim of Bahá'u'lláh and the implementation of His Teachings. One might well inquire whether the manner in which the Teachings are being presented in Australia is such as to relate these principles to the current issues of concern to the public.

Although it is vital that the Faith does not involve itself in partisan political issues or that it arouse unnecessary controversy, there is ample room for it to address the pressing issues of concern at a more fundamental level than that illustrated by the calls for political action, law enforcement, and economic policy which feature in the debate about these issues in the wider community. The solution offered by the Bahá'í Teachings is aimed at the most basic level, that of human values and motivation; it is founded on the capacity of the Faith to effect a profound spiritual transformation in its adherents, and is rooted in the recognition that irreligion and disunity have given rise to the lamentable disintegration now occurring all over the world.

The House of Justice is sure that ways will be found through prayer, intelligent analysis, and dedicated consultation to increase the rate of enrolment of believers in Australia.

The Universal House of Justice, *Bahá'í Scholarship: A Compilation and Essays*, pp. 44–45. (28 July 1992.)

*T*he media are giving increasing attention to the Bahá'í world community; authors are acknowledging its existence in a growing number of articles, books and reference works, one of the most highly respected of which recently listed the Faith as the most widely spread religion after Christianity. A remarkable display of interest in this community by governments, civil authorities, prominent personalities and humanitarian organizations is increasingly apparent. Not only are the community's laws and principles, organization and way of life being investigated, but its advice and active help are also being sought for the alleviation of social problems and the carrying out of humanitarian activities.

The Universal House of Justice, *Riḍván Message to the Bahá'ís of the World*, BE 145/AD 1988, para. 2.

Expansion and Consolidation Go Hand in Hand

*E*very outward thrust into new fields, every multiplication of Bahá'í institutions, must be paralleled by a deeper thrust of the roots which sustain the spiritual life of the community and ensure its sound development. From this vital, this ever-present need, attention must at no time be diverted; nor must it be, under any circumstances, neglected, or subordinated to the no less vital and urgent task of ensuring the outer expansion of Bahá'í administrative institutions. That this community, so alive, so devoted, so strikingly and rapidly developing, may maintain a proper balance between these two essential aspects of its development, and march forward with rapid strides and along sound lines toward the goal of the Plan it has adopted, is the ardent hope of my heart and my constant prayer.

Shoghi Effendi, *Letters from the Guardian to Australia and New Zealand*, p. 76.

*H*e feels sure that your Assembly is capable of carrying on its work in this spirit, and of fanning the hearts to flame through the fire of the love of God, rather than putting out the first sparks with buckets-full of administrative information and regulations.

    Letter dated 9 July 1957 written on behalf of Shoghi Effendi, *Lights of Guidance*, no. 274, p. 78.

*A*fter declaration, the new believers must not be left to their own devices. Through correspondence and dispatch of visitors, through conferences and training courses these friends must be patiently strengthened and lovingly helped to develop into full Bahá'í maturity. The beloved Guardian, referring to the duties of Bahá'í Assemblies in assisting the newly declared believer, has written: "... the members of each and every assembly should endeavour, by their patience, their love, their tact and wisdom, to nurse, subsequent to his admission, the newcomer into Bahá'í maturity, and win him over gradually to the unreserved acceptance of whatever has been ordained in the teachings."

    Messages from the Universal House of Justice 1963-1986, para. 18.5, pp. 39-40. (13 July 1964.)

*I*n the visits made to the villages, the visiting teacher meets with the Local Communities to give them basic Bahá'í knowledge, such as living the Bahá'í life, the importance of teaching, prayer, fasting, Nineteen Day Feasts, Bahá'í elections, and contributions to the Fund. The question of contributions to the Fund is of utmost importance, so that the new believers may quickly feel themselves to be responsible members of the Community. Each National Assembly must find ways and means to stimulate the offering of contributions, in cash or kind, to make it easy for the friends to contribute and to give proper receipts to the donors.

    Messages from the Universal House of Justice 1963-1986, para. 18.14, p. 41. (13 July 1964, Annex.)

*T*he Order brought by Bahá'u'lláh is intended to guide the progress and resolve the problems of society. Our numbers are as yet too small to effect an adequate demonstration of the potentialities inherent in the administrative system we are building, and the efficacy of this system will not be appreciated without a vast expansion of our membership. With the prevailing situation in the world the necessity to effect such a demonstration becomes more compelling. It is all too obvious that even those who rail against the defects of the old order, and would even tear it down, are themselves bereft of any viable alternative to put in its place. Since the Administrative Order is designed to be a pattern for future society, the visibility of such a pattern will be a signal of hope to those who despair.

... The affairs of mankind have reached a stage at which increasing calls will be made upon our community to assist, through advice and practical measures, in solving critical social problems. It is a service that we will gladly render, but this means that our Local and National Spiritual Assemblies must adhere more scrupulously to principle. With increasing public attention being focused on the Cause of God, it becomes imperative for Bahá'í institutions to improve their performance, through a closer identification with the fundamental verities of the Faith, through greater conformity to the spirit and form of Bahá'í administration and through a keener reliance on the beneficial effects of proper consultation, so that the communities they guide will reflect a pattern of life that will offer hope to the disillusioned members of society.

The Universal House of Justice, Riḍván Message to the Bahá'ís of the World, BE 147/AD 1990, paras 17 and 19.

Summary

1. Teaching the waiting masses is a reality facing each National Assembly.

2. The friends must teach with conviction, determination, genuine love, lack of prejudice, and a simple language addressed to the heart.

3. Teaching must be followed up by training courses, conferences, and regular visits to deepen the believers in their knowledge of the Teachings.

4. The close touch of the National Office or Teaching Committees with the work is most essential, so that through reports and correspondence not only is information obtained and verified, but stimulation and encouragement is given.

5. Expansion and consolidation go hand in hand.

Messages from the Universal House of Justice 1963-1986, no. 18.18, p. 42. (13 July 1964, Annex.)

Part Three
Community Building

Chapter Eight
Bahá'í Marriage and Family Life

Shaping Spiritual Identity

... *Man* should know his own self and recognize that which leadeth unto loftiness or lowliness, glory or abasement, wealth or poverty.

Ṭarázát (Ornaments), *Tablets of Bahá'u'lláh*, p. 35.

Bahá'í marriage is the commitment of the two parties one to the other, and their mutual attachment of mind and heart. Each must, however, exercise the utmost care to become thoroughly acquainted with the character of the other, that the binding covenant between them may be a tie that will endure forever. Their purpose must be this: to become loving companions and comrades and at one with each other for time and eternity ...

'Abdu'l-Bahá, *Selections from the Writings of 'Abdu'l-Bahá*, no. 86, p. 118.

Marriage, among the mass of the people, is a physical bond, and this union can only be temporary, since it is foredoomed to a physical separation at the close.

Among the people of Bahá, however, marriage must be a union of the body and of the spirit as well, for here both husband and wife are aglow with the same wine, both are enamoured of the same matchless Face, both live and move through the same spirit, both are illumined by the same glory. This connection between them is a spiritual one, hence it is a bond that will abide forever. Likewise do they enjoy strong and lasting ties in the physical world as well, for if the marriage is based both on the spirit and the body, that union is a true one, hence it will endure. If, however, the bond is physical and nothing more, it is sure to be only temporary, and must inexorably end in separation.

'Abdu'l-Bahá, *Selections from the Writings of 'Abdu'l-Bahá*, no. 84, p. 117.

There is no teaching in the Bahá'í Faith that "soul mates" exist. What is meant is that marriage should lead to a profound friendship of spirit, which will endure in the next world, where there is no sex, and no giving and taking in marriage; just the way we should establish with our parents, our children, our brothers and sisters and friends a deep spiritual bond which will be everlasting, and not merely physical bonds of human relationship.

Letter dated 4 December 1954 written on behalf of Shoghi Effendi, *The Compilation of Compilations*, Vol. II (Preserving Bahá'í Marriages), no. 2332, p. 452.

*T*here is a difference between character and faith; it is often very hard to accept this fact and put up with it, but the fact remains that a person may believe in and love the Cause—even to being ready to die for it—and yet not have a good personal character, or possess traits at variance with the teachings. We should try to change, to let the Power of God help recreate us and make us true Bahá'ís in deed as well as in belief. But sometimes the process is slow, sometimes it never happens because the individual does not try hard enough.

Letter dated 17 October 1944 written on behalf of Shoghi Effendi, *Unfolding Destiny*, p. 440.[67]

A couple should study each other's character and spend time getting to know each other before they decide to marry, and when they do marry it should be with the intention of establishing an eternal bond.

Letter dated 3 November 1982 written on behalf of the Universal House of Justice, *Lights of Guidance*, no. 1269, p. 380.

Bahá'í Marriage

The Nature of Bahá'í Marriage

*A*nd when He desired to manifest grace and beneficence to men, and to set the world in order, He revealed observances and created laws; among them He established the law of marriage, made it as a fortress for well-being and salvation, and enjoined it upon us in that which was sent down out of the heaven of sanctity in His Most Holy Book. He saith, great is His glory: "Marry, O people, that from you may appear he who will remember Me amongst My servants; this is one of My commandments unto you; obey it as an assistance to yourselves.

Bahá'u'lláh, *Bahá'í Prayers (US)*, p. 105.

*T*he true marriage of Bahá'ís is this, that husband and wife should be united both physically and spiritually, that they may ever improve the spiritual life of each other, and may enjoy everlasting unity throughout all the worlds of God. This is Bahá'í marriage.

'Abdu'l-Bahá, *Selections from the Writings of 'Abdu'l-Bahá*, no. 86, p. 118.

Laws of Bahá'í Marriage

*I*t hath been laid down ... that marriage is dependent upon the consent of both parties. Desiring to establish love, unity and harmony amidst Our servants, We have conditioned it, once the couple's wish is known, upon the permission of their parents, lest enmity and rancour should arise amongst them. And in this We have yet other purposes. Thus hath Our commandment been ordained.

Bahá'u'lláh, *The Kitáb-i-Aqdas* (The Most Holy Book), para. 65, p. 42.

---

[67] Also *Lights of Guidance*, no. 264, p. 76.

𝒜s for the question regarding marriage under the Law of God: first thou must choose one who is pleasing to thee, and then the matter is subject to the consent of father and mother. Before thou makest thy choice, they have no right to interfere.

'Abdu'l-Bahá, *Selections from the Writings of 'Abdu'l-Bahá*, no. 85, p. 118.

ℬahá'u'lláh has clearly stated the consent of all living parents is required for a Bahá'í marriage. This applies whether the parents are Bahá'ís or non-Bahá'ís, divorced for years or not. This great law He has laid down to strengthen the social fabric, to knit closer the ties of the home, to place a certain gratitude and respect in the hearts of children for those who have given them life and sent their souls out on the eternal journey towards their Creator. We Bahá'ís must realize that in present-day society the exact opposite process is taking place: young people care less and less for their parents' wishes, divorce is considered a natural right, and obtained on the flimsiest and most unwarrantable and shabby pretexts. ... The Bahá'ís must, through rigid adherence to the Bahá'í laws and teachings, combat these corrosive forces which are so rapidly destroying home life and the beauty of family relationships, and tearing down the moral structure of society.

Letter dated 25 October 1947 written on behalf of Shoghi Effendi, *The Compilation of Compilations*, Vol. I (Divorce), no. 544, p. 242; Vol. I (Family Life), no. 892, p. 406; and Vol. II (Preserving Marriages), no. 2326, p. 449.

... 𝒯he bride and groom, before two witnesses, must state "We will all, verily, abide by the Will of God."

... The witnesses can be any two trustworthy people whose testimony is acceptable to the Spiritual Assembly under whose jurisdiction the marriage is performed.

The Universal House of Justice, *Local Spiritual Assembly Handbook*, no. 10.6.1, 10.10.2, p. 274, 282. (8 August 1969.)[68]

The Marriage Relationship

Love

𝒪 ye two believers in God! The Lord, peerless is He, hath made woman and man to abide with each other in the closest companionship, and to be even as a single soul. They are two helpmates, two intimate friends, who should be concerned about the welfare of each other.

If they live thus, they will pass through this world with perfect contentment, bliss, and peace of heart, and become the object of divine grace and favour in the Kingdom of heaven. But if they do other than this, they will live out their lives in great bitterness, longing at every moment for death, and will be shamefaced in the heavenly realm.

Strive, then, to abide, heart and soul, with each other as two doves in the nest, for this is to be blessed in both worlds.

'Abdu'l-Bahá, *Selections from the Writings of 'Abdu'l-Bahá*, no. 92, p. 122.

---

68   Also *Lights of Guidance*, no. 1296, p. 389.

Equality and Mutual Respect

All should know, and in this regard attain the splendours of the sun of certitude, and be illumined thereby: Women and men have been and will always be equal in the sight of God. The Dawning-Place of the Light of God sheddeth its radiance upon all with the same effulgence. Verily God created women for men, and men for women. The most beloved of people before God are the most steadfast and those who have surpassed others in their love for God, exalted be His glory ....

The friends of God must be adorned with the ornament of justice, equity, kindness and love. As they do not allow themselves to be the object of cruelty and transgression, in like manner they should not allow such tyranny to visit the handmaidens of God. He, verily, speaketh the truth and commandeth that which benefitteth His servants and handmaidens. He is the Protector of all in this world and the next.

Bahá'u'lláh, The Compilation of Compilations, Vol. II (Women), no. 2145, p. 379.

The happiness of mankind will be realized when women and men co-ordinate and advance equally, for each is the complement and helpmeet of the other.

Public Talk of 'Abdu'l-Bahá, The Promulgation of Universal Peace, p. 182.

According to the spirit of this age, women must advance and fulfil their mission in all departments of life, becoming equal to men. They must be on the same level as men and enjoy equal rights. This is my earnest prayer and it is one of the fundamental principles of Bahá'u'lláh.

Words of 'Abdu'l-Bahá, reported by J. E. Esslemont, Bahá'u'lláh and the New Era, p. 147.[69]

It is also evident from Bahá'í teachings that no husband should subject his wife to abuse of any kind, and that such a reprehensible action is the antithesis of the relationship of mutual respect and equality enjoined by the Bahá'í writings—a relationship governed by the principles of consultation and devoid of the use of force to compel obedience to one's will.

Letter written on behalf of the Universal House of Justice, The Compilation of Compilations, Vol. II (Women), no. 2344, p. 458.

Chastity and Fidelity

Let your eye be chaste, your hand faithful, your tongue truthful and your heart enlightened.

Lawḥ-i-Ḥikmat (Tablet of Wisdom), Bahá'u'lláh, Tablets of Bahá'u'lláh, p. 138.

---

[69] Also <i>The Compilation of Compilations</i>, Vol. II (Women), no. 2177, p. 391.

It is clear that the Bahá'í teachings call for an absolute standard of fidelity in the relationship between husband and wife. An excerpt from a letter dated 28 September 1941 to an individual believer written on behalf of Shoghi Effendi, quoted in "Messages from The Universal House of Justice, 1968-1973", page 108, states:

> The question you raise as to the place in one's life that a deep bond of love with someone we meet other than our husband or wife can have is easily defined in view of the teachings. Chastity implies both before and after marriage an unsullied, chaste sex life. Before marriage absolutely chaste, after marriage absolutely faithful to one's chosen companion. Faithful in all sexual acts, faithful in word and in deed.

Letter dated 22 July 1987 written on behalf of the Universal House of Justice, *The Compilation of Compilations*, Vol. II (Women), no. 2344, p. 458.

The Bahá'í Family

Children and Family Planning

As to thy question concerning the husband and wife, the tie between them and the children given to them by God: Know thou, verily, the husband is one who hath sincerely turned unto God, is awakened by the call of the Beauty of El-Bahá and chanteth the verses of Oneness in the great assemblies; the wife is a being who wisheth to be overflowing with and seeketh after the attributes of God and His names; and the tie between them is none other than the Word of God. Verily, it [the Word of God] causeth the multitudes to assemble together and the remote ones to be united. Thus the husband and wife are brought into affinity, are united and harmonized, even as though they were one person. Through their mutual union, companionship and love great results are produced in the world, both material and spiritual. The spiritual result is the appearance of divine bounties. The material result is the children who are born in the cradle of the love of God, who are nurtured by the breast of the knowledge of God, who are brought up in the bosom of the gift of God, and who are fostered in the lap of the training of God. Such children are those of whom it was said by Christ, "Verily, they are the children of the Kingdom!"

'Abdu'l-Bahá, *The Compilation of Compilations*, Vol. I (Family Life), no. 839, p. 390-391.[70]

... It was for the husband and wife to decide how many children they would have. A decision to have no children at all would vitiate the primary purpose of marriage unless, of course, there were some medical reason why such a decision would be required.

Letter dated 28 January 1977 written on behalf of the Universal House of Justice, *Lights of Guidance*, no. 1163, p. 347.

---

[70] Also *Tablets of 'Abdu'l-Bahá Abbás*, Vol. III, pp. 605-606.

As you know, abortion and irreversible surgical operations for the purpose of preventing the birth of unwanted children are forbidden in the Cause unless there are circumstances which justify such actions on medical grounds, in which case the decision, at present, is left to the consciences of those concerned who must carefully weigh the medical advice in the light of the general guidance given in the Teachings. Although the primary purpose of marriage is, as Bahá'u'lláh indicates, the procreation of children, this is not the only purpose of marriage; it would be entirely permissible for a Bahá'í couple to use birth-control methods, provided they do not choose a method which has the effect of aborting the fertilized ovum after conception has taken place.

Letter dated 11 January 1988 written on behalf of the Universal House of Justice to an individual believer.

Family Roles, Relationships and Responsibilities

The fruits that best befit the tree of human life are trustworthiness and godliness, truthfulness and sincerity; but greater than all, after recognition of the unity of God, praised and glorified be He, is regard for the rights that are due to one's parents. This teaching hath been mentioned in all the Books of God, and reaffirmed by the Most Exalted Pen.

Bahá'u'lláh, *The Kitáb-i-Aqdas* (The Most Holy Book), Questions and Answers section, no. 106, p. 139.

Beware lest ye commit that which would sadden the hearts of your fathers and mothers. ... Should anyone give you a choice between the opportunity to render a service to Me and a service to them, choose ye to serve them, and let such service be a path leading you to Me.

Bahá'u'lláh, *The Compilation of Compilations*, Vol. I (Family Life), no. 824, p. 387.

Unto every father hath been enjoined the instruction of his son and daughter in the art of reading and writing and in all that hath been laid down in the Holy Tablet. He that putteth away that which is commanded unto him, the Trustees are then to take from him that which is required for their instruction if he be wealthy and, if not, the matter devolveth upon the House of Justice. Verily have We made it a shelter for the poor and needy. He that bringeth up his son or the son of another, it is as though he hath brought up a son of Mine; upon him rest My glory, My loving-kindness, My mercy, that have compassed the world.

Bahá'u'lláh, *The Kitáb-i-Aqdas* (The Most Holy Book), para. 48, p. 37.

If love and agreement are manifest in a single family, that family will advance, become illumined and spiritual ...

Public Talk of 'Abdu'l-Bahá, *The Promulgation of Universal Peace*, pp. 144-145. (25 May 1912.)

According to the teachings of Bahá'u'lláh, the family, being a human unit, must be educated according to the rules of sanctity. All the virtues must be taught the family.

The integrity of the family bond must be constantly considered, and the rights of the individual members must not be transgressed. The rights of the son, the father, the mother—none of them must be transgressed, none of them must be arbitrary. Just as the son has certain obligations to his father, the father, likewise, has certain obligations to his son. The mother, the sister and other members of the household have their certain prerogatives. All these rights and prerogatives must be conserved, yet the unity of the family must be sustained. The injury of one shall be considered the injury of all; the comfort of each, the comfort of all; the honour of one, the honour of all.

Public Talk of 'Abdu'l-Bahá, *The Promulgation of Universal Peace*, p. 168. (2 June 1912.)

*T*he mother is the first teacher of the child. For children, at the beginning of life, are fresh and tender as a young twig, and can be trained in any fashion you desire. If you rear the child to be straight, he will grow straight, in perfect symmetry. It is clear that the mother is the first teacher and that it is she who establisheth the character and conduct of the child.

Wherefore, O ye loving mothers, know ye that in God's sight, the best of all ways to worship Him is to educate the children and train them in all the perfections of humankind; and no nobler deed than this can be imagined.

'Abdu'l-Bahá, *The Compilation of Compilations*, Vol. I (Bahá'í Education), no. 639, pp. 288–289.

Prayers for Family Members

*T*hou seest, O Lord, our suppliant hands lifted up towards the heaven of Thy favour and bounty. Grant that they may be filled with the treasures of Thy munificence and bountiful favour. Forgive us, and our fathers and our mothers, and fulfil whatsoever we have desired from the ocean of Thy grace and Divine generosity. Accept, O Beloved of our hearts, all our works in Thy path. Thou art, verily, the Most Powerful, the Most Exalted, the Incomparable, the One, the Forgiving, the Gracious.

Bahá'u'lláh, *Gleanings from the Writings of Bahá'u'lláh*, CXXXVIII, pp. 301-302.

*I*t is seemly that the servant should, after each prayer, supplicate God to bestow mercy and forgiveness upon his parents. Thereupon God's call will be raised: "Thousand upon thousand of what thou hast asked for thy parents shall be thy recompense!" Blessed is he who remembereth his parents when communing with God. There is, verily, no God but Him, the Mighty, the Well-Beloved.

The Báb, *Selections from the Writings of the Báb*, p. 94.

*G*lory be unto Thee, O my God! Verily, this Thy servant and this Thy maid-servant have gathered under the shadow of Thy mercy and they are united through Thy favour and generosity. O Lord! Assist them in this Thy world and Thy Kingdom and destine for them every good through Thy bounty and grace. O Lord! Confirm them in Thy servitude and assist them in Thy service. Suffer them to become the signs of Thy Name in

Thy world and protect them through Thy bestowals, which are inexhaustible in this world and in the world to come. O Lord! They are supplicating the kingdom of Thy mercifulness and invoking the realm of Thy singleness. Verily they are married in obedience to Thy command. Cause them to become the signs of harmony and unity until the end of time. Verily, Thou art the Omnipotent, the Omnipresent and the Almighty!

'Abdu'l-Bahá, *Bahá'í Prayers (US)*, p. 107.

O Thou kind Lord! These lovely children are the handiwork of the fingers of Thy might and the wondrous signs of Thy greatness. O God! Protect these children, graciously assist them to be educated and enable them to render service to the world of humanity. O God! These children are pearls, cause them to be nurtured within the shell of Thy loving-kindness.

Thou art the Bountiful, the All-Loving.

'Abdu'l-Bahá, *Bahá'í Prayers (US)*, no. 13, p. 36.

O Thou most glorious Lord! Make this little maidservant of Thine blessed and happy; cause her to be cherished at the threshold of Thy oneness and let her drink deep from the cup of Thy love so that she may be filled with rapture and ecstasy and diffuse sweet-scented fragrance. Thou art the Mighty and the Powerful, and Thou art the All-Knowing, the All-Seeing.

'Abdu'l-Bahá, *A Selection of Bahá'í Prayers and Holy Writings*, p. 25.

O Lord! Make this youth radiant, and confer Thy bounty upon this poor creature. Bestow upon him knowledge, grant him added strength at the break of every morn and guard him within the shelter of Thy protection so that he may be freed from error, may devote himself to the service of Thy Cause, may guide the wayward, lead the hapless, free the captives and awaken the heedless, that all may be blessed with Thy remembrance and praise. Thou art the Mighty and the Powerful.

'Abdu'l-Bahá, *Bahá'í Prayers (US)*, pp. 38-39.

Rearing and Educating Children

Developing Spirituality

Strain every nerve to acquire both inner and outer perfections, for the fruit of the human tree hath ever been and will ever be perfections both within and without. It is not desirable that a man be left without knowledge or skills, for he is then but a barren tree. Then, so much as capacity and capability allow, ye needs must deck the tree of being with fruits such as knowledge, wisdom, spiritual perception and eloquent speech.

Bahá'u'lláh, *The Compilation of Compilations*, Vol. I (Bahá'í Education), 560, p. 247; and Vol. I (Excellence in all Things), no. 770, p. 368.

*T*each ye your children the verses that have been divinely revealed, that they may recite them in most melodious voices. This is what hath been set down in His mighty book.

Bahá'u'lláh, *The Compilation of Compilations*, Vol. I (Bahá'í Education), no. 572, p. 250.

... from the very beginning, the children must receive divine education and must continually be reminded to remember their God. Let the love of God pervade their inmost being, commingled with their mother's milk.

'Abdu'l-Bahá, *Selections from the Writings of 'Abdu'l-Bahá*, no. 99, p. 127.

*I*t is the hope of 'Abdu'l-Bahá that those youthful souls in the schoolroom of the deeper knowledge will be tended by one who traineth them to love.

'Abdu'l-Bahá, *Selections from the Writings of 'Abdu'l-Bahá*, no. 107, p. 134.

*T*hrough the power and charm of music the spirit of man is uplifted. It has wonderful sway and effect in the hearts of children, for their hearts are pure, and melodies have great influence in them.

Public Talk of 'Abdu'l-Bahá, *The Promulgation of Universal Peace*, p. 52. (24 April 1912.)

*F*rom their childhood instil in their hearts the love of God so they may manifest in their lives the fear of God and have confidence in the bestowals of God.

Public Talk of 'Abdu'l-Bahá, *The Promulgation of Universal Peace*, p. 54. (24 April 1912.)

Moral Education

*T*hat which is of paramount importance for the children, that which must precede all else, is to teach them the oneness of God and the Laws of God. ...

The parents must exert every effort to rear their offspring to be religious, for should the children not attain this greatest of adornments, they will not obey their parents, which in a certain sense means they will not obey God.

Bahá'u'lláh, *The Compilation of Compilations*, Vol. I (Bahá'í Education), no. 565, p. 248.

*I*t is incumbent on every father and mother to counsel their children over a long period, and guide them unto those things which lead to everlasting honour.

'Abdu'l-Bahá, *Selections from the Writings of 'Abdu'l-Bahá*, no. 108, p. 134.

*H*e [the child] should be trained, his natural inclinations harmonized, adjusted and controlled, and if necessary suppressed or regulated, so as to ensure his healthy physical and moral development.

Letter written on behalf of Shoghi Effendi, *The Compilation of Compilations*, Vol. I (Bahá'í Education), no. 673, p. 303.

*W*hensoever a mother seeth that her child hath done well, let her praise and applaud him and cheer his heart; and if the slightest undesirable trait should manifest itself, let her counsel the child and punish him, and use means based on reason, even a slight verbal chastisement should this be necessary. It is not, however, permissible to strike a child, or vilify him, for the child's character will be totally perverted if he be subjected to blows or verbal abuse.

'Abdu'l-Bahá, *Selections from the Writings of 'Abdu'l-Bahá*, no. 95, p. 125.

*T*he child must not be oppressed or censured because it is undeveloped; it must be patiently trained.

'Abdu'l-Bahá, *The Promulgation of Universal Peace*, pp. 180-181. (9 June 1912.)

*T*he children must be carefully trained to be most courteous and well-behaved.

'Abdu'l-Bahá, *Selections from the Writings of 'Abdu'l-Bahá*, no. 110, p. 135.

Fostering Learning

*E*ncourage the children from their earliest years to master every kind of learning, and make them eager to become skilled in every art—the aim being that through the favouring grace of God, the heart of each one may become even as a mirror disclosing the secrets of the universe, penetrating the innermost reality of all things; and that each may earn world-wide fame in all branches of knowledge, science and the arts.

Certainly, certainly, neglect not the education of the children. Rear them to be possessed of spiritual qualities, and be assured of the gifts and favours of the Lord.

'Abdu'l-Bahá, *The Compilation of Compilations*, Vol. I (Bahá'í Education), no. 601, pp. 267-268; and Vol I (Excellence in all Things), no. 791, pp. 374-375.

*I*t is for this reason that, in this new cycle, education and training are recorded in the Book of God as obligatory and not voluntary. That is, it is enjoined upon the father and mother, as a duty, to strive with all effort to train the daughter and the son, to nurse them from the breast of knowledge and to rear them in the bosom of sciences and arts. Should they neglect this matter, they shall be held responsible and worthy of reproach in the presence of the stern Lord.

'Abdu'l-Bahá, *Selections from the Writings of 'Abdu'l-Bahá*, no. 98, pp. 126-127.

I hope thou wilt acquire great proficiency in writing literature, composition, eloquence of tongue and fluency of speech ... becoming an esteemed servant in the Threshold of Oneness and partaking of a share of the heavenly gifts, and progressing day by day until thou attain to the apex of the excellencies of this human world.

'Abdu'l-Bahá, *Tablets of Abdul-Baha Abbas*, Vol. III, pp. 501-502.

... consider how much the art of music is admired and praised. Try, if thou canst, to use spiritual melodies, songs and tunes, and to bring the earthly music into harmony with the celestial melody. Then thou wilt notice what a great influence music hath and what heavenly joy and life it conferreth.

'Abdu'l-Bahá, *The Compilation of Compilations*, Vol. II (Music), no. 1419, p. 76.

*T*each them to dedicate their lives to matters of great import, and inspire them to undertake studies that will benefit mankind.

'Abdu'l-Bahá, *Selections from the Writings of 'Abdu'l-Bahá*, no. 102, p. 129.

Creating and Maintaining Harmony

*M*y home is the home of peace. My home is the home of joy and delight. My home is the home of laughter and exultation. Whosoever enters through the portals of this home, must go out with gladsome heart. This is the home of light; whosoever enters here must become illumined ...

'Abdu'l-Bahá, *The Compilation of Compilations*, Vol. I (Family Life), no. 859, p. 397. (28 April 1918).

*I*t is highly important for man to raise a family. So long as he is young, because of youthful self-complacency, he does not realize its significance, but this will be a source of regret when he grows old ... In this glorious Cause the life of a married couple should resemble the life of the angels in heaven—a life full of joy and spiritual delight, a life of unity and concord, a friendship both mental and physical. The home should be orderly and well-organized. Their ideas and thoughts should be like the rays of the sun of truth and the radiance of the brilliant stars in the heavens. Even as two birds they should warble melodies upon the branches of the tree of fellowship and harmony. They should always be elated with joy and gladness and be a source of happiness to the hearts of others. They should set an example to their fellow-men, manifest a true and sincere love towards each other and educate their children in such a manner as to blazon the fame and glory of their family.

'Abdu'l-Bahá, *The Compilation of Compilations*, Vol. I (Family Life), no. 860, p. 397.

*S*urely Shoghi Effendi would like to see you and the other friends give their whole time and energy to the Cause, for we are in great need for competent workers, but the home is an institution that Bahá'u'lláh has come to strengthen and not to weaken. Many unfortunate things have happened in Bahá'í homes just for neglecting this point. Serve the Cause but also remember your duties towards your home. It is for you to find the balance and see that neither makes you neglect the other.

Letter dated 14 May 1929 written on behalf of Shoghi Effendi, *The Compilation of Compilations*, Vol. I (Family Life), no. 865, p. 399.

*T*he members of a family all have duties and responsibilities towards one another and to the family as a whole, and these duties and responsibilities vary from member to member because of their natural relationships.

> Letter dated 28 December 1980 written on behalf of the Universal House of Justice, *Messages from the Universal House of Justice 1963-1986*, para. 272.4, p. 471.[71]

*I*n considering the problems that you and your wife are experiencing, the House of Justice points out that the unity of your family should take priority over any other consideration. ... For example, service to the Cause should not produce neglect of the family. It is important for you to arrange your time so that your family life is harmonious and your household receives the attention it requires.

> Letter dated 1 August 1978 written on behalf of the Universal House of Justice, *The Compilation of Compilations*, Vol. I (Family Life), no. 914, p. 412; Vol. II (Women), no. 2160, p. 383; and Vol. II (Writers and Writing), no. 2336, p. 453.

*Y*ou ask how to deal with anger. The House of Justice suggests that you call to mind the admonitions found in our Writings on the need to overlook the shortcomings of others; to forgive and conceal their misdeeds, not to expose their bad qualities, but to search for and affirm their praiseworthy ones, and to endeavour to be always forbearing, patient, and merciful. Such passages as the following extracts from letters written on behalf of the beloved Guardian will be helpful:

There are qualities in everyone which we can appreciate and admire, and for which we can love them; and perhaps, if you determine to think only of these qualities which your husband possesses, this will help to improve the situation ... You should turn your thoughts away from the things which upset you, and constantly pray to Bahá'u'lláh to help you. Then you will find how that pure love, enkindled by God, which burns in the soul when we read and study the Teachings, will warm and heal, more than anything else. Each of us is responsible for one life only, and that is our own. Each of us is immeasurably far from being "perfect as our heavenly father is perfect" and the task of perfecting our own life and character is one that requires all our attention, our will-power and energy ...

> Letter dated 17 July 1979 written on behalf of the Universal House of Justice, *The Compilation of Compilations*, Vol. II (Preserving Bahá'í Marriages), no. 2339, p. 455.

Consultation

*T*he prime requisites for them that take counsel together are purity of motive, radiance of spirit, detachment from all else save God, attraction to His Divine Fragrances, humility and lowliness amongst His loved ones, patience and long-suffering in difficulties and servitude to His exalted Threshold. Should they be graciously aided to acquire these attributes, victory from the unseen Kingdom of Bahá shall be vouchsafed to them.

---

71 Also *The Compilation of Compilations*, Vol. I (Family Life), no. 916, p. 414; and *Lights of Guidance*, no. 730, p. 219.

The members thereof must take counsel together in such wise that no occasion for ill-feeling or discord may arise. This can be attained when every member expresseth with absolute freedom his own opinion and setteth forth his argument. Should any one oppose, he must on no account feel hurt for not until matters are fully discussed can the right way be revealed. The shining spark of truth cometh forth only after the clash of differing opinions.

'Abdu'l-Bahá, Selections from the Writings of 'Abdu'l-Bahá, nos 43-44, p. 87.

*T*hey must then proceed with the utmost devotion, courtesy, dignity, care and moderation to express their views. They must in every matter search out the truth and not insist upon their own opinion, for stubbornness and persistence in one's views will lead ultimately to discord and wrangling and the truth will remain hidden.

'Abdu'l-Bahá, Selections from the Writings of 'Abdu'l-Bahá, no. 45, p. 88.

... if such differences do occur, they should not reach the point of causing conflict, hatred and antagonism ... you should immediately postpone discussion of the subject, until wranglings, disputations, and loud talk vanish, and a propitious time is at hand.

'Abdu'l-Bahá, The Compilation of Compilations, Vol. I (Consultation), no. 184, p. 98.

*B*ahá'u'lláh also stressed the importance of consultation. We should not think this worthwhile method of seeking solutions is confined to the administrative institutions of the Cause. Family consultation employing full and frank discussion, and animated by awareness of the need for moderation and balance, can be the panacea for domestic conflict. Wives should not attempt to dominate their husbands, nor husbands their wives ...

Letter dated 1 August 1978 written on behalf of the Universal House of Justice, The Compilation of Compilations, Vol. II (Women), no. 2160, p. 383; and Vol. II (Preserving Marriages), no. 2336, p. 453.

*I*n any group, however loving the consultation, there are nevertheless points on which, from time to time, agreement cannot be reached. In a Spiritual Assembly this dilemma is resolved by a majority vote. There can, however, be no majority where only two parties are involved, as in the case of a husband and wife. There are, therefore, times when a wife should defer to her husband, and times when a husband should defer to his wife, but neither should ever unjustly dominate the other.

Letter dated 18 February 1982 written on behalf of the Universal House of Justice, The Compilation of Compilations, Vol. I (Family Life), no. 916, p. 415; Vol. II (Women), no. 2162, p. 384; and Vol. II (Preserving Marriages), no. 2340, p. 456. (revised July 1990).

*Y*ou have asked, however, for specific rules of conduct to govern the relationships of husbands and wives. This the House of Justice does not wish to do, and it feels that there is already adequate guidance included in the compilation on this subject; for example, the principle that the rights of each and all in the family unit must be upheld, and the advice that loving consultation should be the keynote, that all matters must be settled in harmony and love, and that there are times when the husband and wife should defer to the wishes of the other. Exactly under what circumstances such deference should take place is a matter for each couple to determine.

<blockquote>Letter dated 16 May 1982 written on behalf of the Universal House of Justice, The Compilation of Compilations, Vol. II (Women), no. 2163, p. 385; and Vol. II (Preserving Marriages), no. 2341, p. 456.</blockquote>

*B*ahá'ís should be profoundly aware of the sanctity of marriage and should strive to make their marriages an eternal bond of unity and harmony. This requires effort and sacrifice and wisdom and self-abnegation.

<blockquote>Letter dated 3 November 1982 written on behalf of the Universal House of Justice, The Compilation of Compilations, Vol. II (Preserving Bahá'í Marriages), no. 2342, p. 457.</blockquote>

Seeking Outside Help Before Problems Become Too Great

*I*t is a great pity that two believers ... should not be able to live together really harmoniously, and he feels you should take constructive action and not allow the situation to get worse. When the shadow of separation hangs over a husband and wife they should leave no stone unturned in their effort to avert its becoming a reality.

<blockquote>Letter dated 5 July 1949 written on behalf of Shoghi Effendi, The Compilation of Compilations, Vol. II (Preserving Bahá'í Marriages), no. 2329, p. 451.</blockquote>

... *N*o husband should subject his wife to abuse of any kind, whether emotional, mental or physical ...

When a Bahá'í wife finds herself in such a situation and feels it cannot be resolved through consultation with her husband, she could well turn to the Local Spiritual Assembly for advice and guidance, and might also find it highly advantageous to seek the assistance of competent professional counsellors. If the husband is also a Bahá'í, the Local Spiritual Assembly can bring to his attention the need to avoid abusive behaviour and can, if necessary, take firm measures to encourage him to conform to the admonitions of the teachings.

<blockquote>Letter dated 6 August 1989 written on behalf of the Universal House of Justice, The Compilation of Compilations, Vol. II (Preserving Bahá'í Marriages), no. 2347, p. 459.</blockquote>

*T*he House of Justice is distressed to learn that you and your husband are continuing to experience marital difficulties. It has frequently advised believers in such situations to turn to the Spiritual Assemblies for advice and counsel, and to follow this advice in their efforts to preserve the unity for their marital relationship. It has been found useful in many instances to also seek the assistance of competent professional marriage counsellors, who can provide useful insights and guidance in the use of constructive measures to bring about a greater degree of unity.

<blockquote>Letter dated 17 July 1989 written on behalf of the Universal House of Justice, The Compilation of Compilations, Vol. II (Preserving Bahá'í Marriages), no. 2346, p. 459.</blockquote>

Divorce

*T*ruly, the Lord loveth union and harmony and abhorreth separation and divorce. Live ye one with another, O people, in radiance and joy. By My life! All that are on earth shall pass away, while good deeds alone shall endure; to the truth of My words God doth Himself bear witness. Compose your differences, O My servants; then heed ye the admonition of Our Pen of Glory and follow not the arrogant and wayward.

> Bahá'u'lláh, *The Kitáb-i-Aqdas* (The Most Holy Book), para. 70, pp. 44–45.

*F*or while, according to the Bahá'í law, divorce is permissible, yet it is highly discouraged, and should be resorted to only when every effort to prevent it has proved to be vain and ineffective.

> Letter dated 11 September 1938 written on behalf of Shoghi Effendi, *The Compilation of Compilations*, Vol. I (Divorce), no. 536, p. 239; Vol. II (Preserving Bahá'í Marriages), no. 2314, p. 445.

*B*ahá'u'lláh came to bring unity to the world and a fundamental unity is that of the family. Divorce disrupts the family and leads to the disintegration of society:

> Regarding the Bahá'í Teachings on divorce. While the latter has been made permissible by Bahá'u'lláh yet He has strongly discouraged its practice, for if not checked and seriously controlled it leads gradually to the disruption of family life and to the disintegration of society.
>
> Letter written on behalf of Shoghi Effendi, *Local Spiritual Assembly Handbook*, no. 11.1.2, p. 286.

*H*e feels that you should by all means make every effort to hold your marriage together, especially for the sake of your children, who, like all children of divorced parents, cannot but suffer from conflicting loyalties, for they are deprived of the blessings of a father and mother in one home, to look after their interests and love them jointly.

> Letter dated 6 March 1953 written on behalf of Shoghi Effendi, *The Compilation of Compilations*, Vol. I (Family Life), no. 898, p. 408; and Vol. II (Preserving Bahá'í Marriages), no. 2331, p. 452.

The Year of Patience

*I*f, however, antipathy or resentment develop between the marriage partners, divorce is permissible after the lapse of one full year. During this year of patience, the husband is obliged to provide for the financial support of his wife and children, and the couple is urged to reconcile their differences.

> The Universal House of Justice, added to: Bahá'u'lláh, *The Kitáb-i-Aqdas* (The Most Holy Book), Notes no.100, pp. 210-211.

*T*he Bahá'í Law requires that the parties separate for one full year before the divorce may be realized. This contemplates complete physical separation in the sense that they should not reside in the same dwelling.
> Letter from The Universal House of Justice, *Local Spiritual Assembly Handbook*, no. 11.3.4, p. 291.

*I*n the strict legal sense there are no 'grounds' for a Bahá'í divorce. No question of misbehaviour of either party is involved and the only condition under which a Bahá'í divorce may be considered is the irreconcilable antipathy of the parties.
> Letter from The Universal House of Justice, *Local Spiritual Assembly Handbook*, no. 11.2.4, p. 289.

*E*ither party may apply for the year of waiting without the consent of the other.
> Letter from The Universal House of Justice, *Local Spiritual Assembly Handbook*, no. 11.2.3, p. 288.

... *B*ahá'ís who apply for divorce should be so counselled and left in no doubt that it is the duty of the Spiritual Assembly concerned, according to the emphatic command of our Scripture, to do everything possible to bring about a reconciliation.
> Letter from The Universal House of Justice, *Local Spiritual Assembly Handbook*, no. 11.24, p. 288.

*I*rreconcilable antipathy arising between the parties to a marriage is not merely a lack of love for one's spouse but an antipathy which cannot be resolved.
> Letter from The Universal House of Justice, *Local Spiritual Assembly Handbook*, no. 11.2.4, p. 289.

... *I*f the Assembly finds that it is unable to persuade the party concerned to withdraw the application for divorce, it must conclude that, from its point of view, there appears to be an irreconcilable antipathy, and it has no alternative to setting the date for the beginning of the year of waiting.
> Letter written on behalf of the Universal House of Justice, *Local Spiritual Assembly Handbook*, no. 11.2.4, p. 290.

*O*ne party to a divorce, acting alone, cannot petition for a termination of the year of waiting.
> Letter written on behalf of the Universal House of Justice, *Local Spiritual Assembly Handbook*, no. 11.3.13, p. 293.

... *I*f, at the end of the year, harmony is not established, the Bahá'í divorce becomes effective, unless further waiting is necessary before the civil divorce is granted since the Bahá'í divorce cannot be granted before the civil divorce is finalized. Other than this, there is no possibility for extending the period of waiting. Moreover, Bahá'ís should not prolong the process longer than is necessary.
> Letter written on behalf of the Universal House of Justice, *Local Spiritual Assembly Handbook*, no. 11.3.12, p. 293.

Sexual Relationships

*C*oncerning your question whether there are any legitimate forms of expression of the sex instinct outside of marriage; according to the Bahá'í Teachings no sexual act can be considered lawful unless performed between lawfully married persons. Outside of marital life there can be no lawful or healthy use of the sex impulse. The Bahá'í youth should, on the one hand, be taught the lesson of self-control which, when exercised, undoubtedly has a salutary effect on the development of character and of personality in general, and on the other should be advised, nay even encouraged, to contract marriage while still young and in full possession of their physical vigour. Economic factors, no doubt, are often a serious hindrance to early marriage, but in most cases are only an excuse, and as such should not be overstressed.

Letter dated 13 December 1940 written on behalf of Shoghi Effendi, *The Compilation of Compilations*, Vol. I (A Chaste and Holy Life), no. 146, p. 56.

The Bahá'í Attitude to Same Sex Relationships

*T*he Universal House of Justice has considered your letters of 27 August 1993 and 19 September 1994 in which you describe the impact of the changing sexual mores and the public debate on homosexuality on some of the members of the American Bahá'í community who are homosexuals...

It is important to understand that there is a difference between the Bahá'í attitude toward, on the one hand, the condition of homosexuality and those who are affected by it and, on the other, the practice of homosexual relations by members of the Bahá'í community.

As you know, the Bahá'í Faith strongly condemns all blatant acts of immorality, and it includes among them the expression of sexual love between individuals of the same sex. With regard to homosexual practices, Bahá'u'lláh, in the *Kitáb-i-Aqdas*, paragraph 107, and Questions and Answers, number 49, forbids paederasty and sodomy. The following extract from one of His Tablets reveals the strength of His condemnation:

"Ye are forbidden to commit adultery, sodomy and lechery. Avoid them, O concourse of the faithful. By the righteousness of God! Ye have been called into being to purge the world from the defilement of evil passions. This is what the Lord of all mankind hath enjoined upon you, could ye but perceive it. He who relateth himself to the All-Merciful and committeth satanic deeds, verily he is not of Me. Unto this beareth witness every atom, pebble, tree and fruit, and beyond them this ever-proclaiming, truthful and trustworthy Tongue."[72]

---

[72] Bahá'u'lláh, *The Compilation of Compilations*, Vol. I (A Chaste and Holy Life), no. 148, p. 57; and Vol. II (Preserving Bahá'í Marriages), no. 2332, p. 452.

In a letter dated 26 March 1950, written on his behalf, Shoghi Effendi, the authorized interpreter of the Bahá'í Teachings, further explicates the Bahá'í attitude toward homosexuality. It should be noted that the Guardian's interpretation of this subject is based on his infallible understanding of the Texts. It represents both a statement of moral principle and unerring guidance to Bahá'ís who are homosexuals. The letter states:

"No matter how devoted and fine the love may be between people of the same sex, to let it find expression in sexual acts is wrong. To say that it is ideal is no excuse. Immorality of every sort is really forbidden by Bahá'u'lláh, and homosexual relationships he looks upon as such, besides being against nature.

"To be afflicted this way is a great burden to a conscientious soul. But through the advice and help of doctors, through a strong and determined effort, and through prayer, a soul can overcome this handicap."[73]

It is evident, therefore, that the prohibition against Bahá'ís engaging in homosexual behaviour is an explicit Teaching of the Cause. The Universal House of Justice is authorized to change or repeal its own legislation as conditions change, thus providing Bahá'í law with an essential element of flexibility, but it cannot abrogate or change any of the laws which are explicitly laid down in the sacred Texts. It follows, then, that the House of Justice has no authority to change this clear teaching on homosexual practice ...

The view that homosexuality is a condition that is not amenable to change is to be questioned by Bahá'ís. There are, of course, many kinds and degrees of homosexuality, and overcoming extreme conditions is sure to be more difficult than overcoming others. Nevertheless, as noted earlier, the Guardian has stated, that "through the advice and help of doctors, through a strong and determined effort, and through prayer, a soul can overcome this handicap."

The statistics which indicate that homosexuality is incurable are undoubtedly distorted by the fact that many of those who overcome the problem never speak about it in public, and others solve their problems without even consulting professional counsellors.

Nevertheless there are undoubtedly cases in which the individual finds himself (or herself) unable to eliminate a physical attraction to members of the same sex, even though he succeeds in controlling his behaviour. This is but one of the many trials and temptations to which human beings are subject in this life. For Bahá'ís, it cannot alter the basic concept taught by Bahá'u'lláh, that the kind of sexuality purposed by God is the love between a man and a woman, and that its primary (but not its only) purpose is the bringing of children into this world and providing them with a loving and protective environment in which they can be reared to know and love God. If, therefore, a homosexual cannot overcome his or her condition to the extent of being able to have a heterosexual marriage, he or she must remain single, and abstain from sexual relations. These are the same requirements as for a heterosexual person who does not marry. While Bahá'u'lláh encourages the believers to marry, it is important to note that marriage is by no means an obligation. It is for the individual to decide whether he or she wishes to

---

73   Shoghi Effendi, *Lights of Guidance*, no. 1223, p. 366.

lead a family life or to live in a state of celibacy ...

To regard homosexuals with prejudice and disdain would be entirely against the spirit of Bahá'í Teachings. The doors are open for all of humanity to enter the Cause of God, irrespective of their present circumstance; this invitation applies to homosexuals as well as to any others who are engaged in practices contrary to the Bahá'í Teachings. Associated with this invitation is the expectation that all believers will make a sincere and persistent effort to eradicate those aspects of their conduct which are not in conformity with Divine Law. It is through such adherence to the Bahá'í Teachings that a true and enduring unity of the diverse elements of the Bahá'í community is achieved and safeguarded.

When a person wishes to join the Faith and it is generally known that he or she has a problem such as drinking, homosexuality, taking drugs, adultery, etc., the individual should be told in a patient and loving way of the Bahá'í Teachings on these matters. If it is later discovered that a believer is violating Bahá'í standards, it is the duty of the Spiritual Assembly to determine whether the immoral conduct is flagrant and can bring the name of the Faith into disrepute, in which case the Assembly must take action to counsel the believer and require him or her to make every effort to mend his ways. If the individual fails to rectify his conduct in spite of repeated warnings, sanctions should be imposed. Assemblies, of course, must exercise care not to pry into the private lives of the believers to ensure that they are behaving properly, but should not hesitate to take action in cases of blatant misbehaviour.

The Spiritual Assemblies should, to a certain extent, be forbearing in the matter of people's moral conduct, such as homosexuality, in view of the terrible deterioration of society in general. The Assemblies must also bear in mind that while awareness of contemporary social and moral values may well enhance their understanding of the situation of the homosexual, the standard which they are called upon to uphold is the Bahá'í standard. A flagrant violation of this standard disgraces the Bahá'í community in its own eyes even if the surrounding society finds the transgression tolerable.

Letter written on behalf of the Universal House of Justice, *The American Bahá'í*, Qawl 152.[74]

Death, Burial and Inheritance

Wills

According to the Teachings of Bahá'u'lláh, the making of a will is essentially an obligation of the individual Bahá'í. Each believer is free to dispose of his estate in whatever manner he chooses, within the limits imposed by civil law and after payment of burial expenses and other debts and obligations.

Letter written on behalf of the Universal House of Justice, *Local Spiritual Assembly Handbook*, no. 12.1.4, p. 310.

---

74   23 November–11 December 1995.

The Bahá'í laws of inheritance apply only in case of intestacy, that is, when the individual dies without leaving a will. In the *Kitáb-i-Aqdas*, Bahá'u'lláh instructs every believer to write a will. He elsewhere clearly states that the individual has full jurisdiction over his property and is free to determine the manner in which his or her estate is to be divided and to designate, in the will, those, whether Bahá'í or non-Bahá'í, who should inherit. In this connection, a letter written on behalf of Shoghi Effendi explains that:

... even though a Bahá'í is permitted in his will to dispose of his wealth in the way he wishes, yet he is morally and conscientiously bound to always bear in mind, while writing his will, the necessity of his upholding the principle of Bahá'u'lláh regarding the social function of wealth, and the consequent necessity of avoiding its over-accumulation and concentration in a few individuals or groups of individuals.

The Universal House of Justice, added to: Bahá'u'lláh, *The Kitáb-i-Aqdas* (The Most Holy Book), Notes no. 38, p. 182.

The civil law in relation to the making of wills is sometimes quite complex. It is, therefore, highly advisable for an individual to consult a lawyer when he makes his will to ensure that his intention is not nullified by some possible breach of the requirements of the law in the drawing up or execution of the will.

Letter written on behalf of the Universal House of Justice, *Local Spiritual Assembly Handbook*, no. 12.1.6, p. 311.

The friends should be strongly advised to make Wills specifying that they want their funerals to be conducted under the auspices of the Bahá'í Faith or at least in conformity with its requirements and they should make this known both to the Local Spiritual Assembly and to their own relatives, while they are still alive. In this way it is quite possible that agreements may be reached with non-Bahá'í relatives before death takes place.

Letter from The Universal House of Justice, *Local Spiritual Assembly Handbook*, no. 12.1.10, p. 312.

Bahá'í Burial

In brief, the Bahá'í law for the burial of the dead states that it is forbidden to carry the body for more than one hour's journey from the place of death; that the body should be wrapped in a shroud of white silk or cotton, and on its finger should be placed a ring bearing the inscription *"I came forth from God, and return unto Him, detached from all save Him, holding fast to His Name, the Merciful, the Compassionate"*; and that the coffin should be of crystal, stone or hard fine wood. A specific Prayer for the Dead is ordained, to be said before interment. As affirmed by 'Abdu'l-Bahá and the Guardian, this law precludes cremation of the dead. The formal prayer and the ring are meant to be used for those who have attained the age of maturity ....

The Universal House of Justice, added to: Bahá'u'lláh, *The Kitáb-i-Aqdas* (The Most Holy Book), Notes no. 149, p. 229.

*F*or the burial of the dead the only requirements now binding in the West are to bury the body (not to cremate it), not to carry it more than a distance of one hour's journey from the place of death, and to say the Prayer for the Dead if the deceased is a believer over the age of 15.

> Letter 9 June 1974 written on behalf of the Universal House of Justice, *The Compilation of Compilations*, Vol. I (Bahá'í Burial), no. 39, p. 12.

*R*egarding the Bahá'í funeral service: it is extremely simple, as it consists only of a congregational prayer to be read before burial. ... your National Spiritual Assembly should take great care lest any uniform procedure or ritual in this matter be adopted or imposed upon the friends. The danger in this, as in some other cases regarding Bahá'í worship, is that a definite system of rigid rituals and practices be developed among the believers. The utmost simplicity and flexibility should be observed, and a selection from the Bahá'í Sacred Writing[s] should serve the purpose at the present time, provided this selection is not rigidly and uniformly adopted on all such occasions.

> Letter written on behalf of Shoghi Effendi, *Directives from the Guardian*, no. 85, pp. 32-33.

*T*he Prayer for the Dead is ... the only Bahá'í obligatory prayer which is to be recited in congregation; it is to be recited by one believer while all present stand in silence ... there is no requirement to face the Qiblih when reciting this prayer.

> The Universal House of Justice, added to: Bahá'u'lláh, *The Kitáb-i-Aqdas* (The Most Holy Book), Notes no. 10, pp. 169-170.

*A*s a funeral is not a legal ceremony ... the family of the deceased may want some particular Bahá'í friend to officiate.

> Letter written on behalf of Shoghi Effendi, *Directives from the Guardian*, no. 121, p. 45.[75]

---

75 Also *The Compilation of Compilations*, Vol. I (Bahá'í Burial), no. 34, p. 11; and *Lights of Guidance*, no. 1301, p. 391.

Chapter Nine
The Bahá'í Administrative Order: The Primary Agency for Spiritual and Social Change

> ... the purpose underlying this most mighty Revelation is none other than the rehabilitation of the world and its nations: that perchance the power of utterance may prevail over the power of arms, and the world's affairs be administered through the potency of love.
>
> Bahá'u'lláh, *The Compilation of Compilations*, Vol. II (Trustworthiness), no. 2032, p. 332.

> No machinery falling short of the standard inculcated by the Bahá'í Revelation, and at variance with the sublime pattern ordained in His teachings ... can ever hope to achieve anything above or beyond that "Lesser Peace" to which the Author of our Faith has Himself alluded in His writings. ...
>
> The Most Great Peace, on the other hand, as conceived by Bahá'u'lláh—a peace that must inevitably follow as the practical consequence of the spiritualization of the world and the fusion of all its races, creeds, classes and nations—can rest on no other basis, and can be preserved through no other agency, except the divinely appointed ordinances that are implicit in the World Order that stands associated with His Holy Name.
>
> Shoghi Effendi, The Unfoldment of World Civilization, *The World Order of Bahá'u'lláh*, pp. 162-163.

The Nature of the Bahá'í Administrative Order

The Universal House of Justice is the supreme institution of an Administrative Order whose salient features, whose authority and whose principles of operation are clearly enunciated in the Sacred Writings of the Bahá'í Faith and their authorized interpretations. This Administrative Order consists, on the one hand, of a series of elected councils, universal, secondary and local, in which are vested legislative, executive and judicial powers over the Bahá'í community and, on the other, of eminent and devoted believers appointed for the specific purposes of protecting and propagating the Faith of Bahá'u'lláh under the guidance of the Head of that Faith.

The Constitution of the Universal House of Justice, preamble, para. 1, p. 8.

Its Animating Purpose

*A*nd now, it behooves us to reflect on the animating purpose and the primary functions of these divinely-established institutions, the sacred character and the universal efficacy of which can be demonstrated only by the spirit they diffuse and the work they actually achieve. I need not dwell upon what I have already reiterated and emphasized that the administration of the Cause is to be conceived as an instrument and not a substitute for the Faith of Bahá'u'lláh, that it should be regarded as a channel through which His promised blessings may flow, that it should guard against such rigidity as would clog and fetter the liberating forces released by His Revelation. ... Who, I may ask, when viewing the international character of the Cause, its far-flung ramifications, the increasing complexity of its affairs, the diversity of its adherents, and the state of confusion that assails on every side the infant Faith of God, can for a moment question the necessity of some sort of administrative machinery that will insure, amid the storm and stress of a struggling civilization, the unity of the Faith, the preservation of its identity, and the protection of its interests?

Shoghi Effendi, *The World Order of Bahá'u'lláh*, pp. 9-10.

Abolition of a Professional Clergy and Leadership

*C*ollateral with His summons to the pursuit of knowledge, Bahá'u'lláh has abolished entirely that feature of all past religions by which a special caste of persons such as the Christian priesthood or the Islamic 'ulamá came to exercise authority over the religious understanding and practice of their fellow believers. In a letter written in Persian on his behalf to the Spiritual Assembly of the Bahá'ís of Istanbul, the Guardian is at some pains to underline the importance of this marked departure from past religious history:

> But praise be to God that the Pen of Glory has done away with the unyielding and dictatorial views of the learned and the wise, dismissed the assertions of individuals as an authoritative criterion, even though they were recognized as the most accomplished and learned among men, and ordained that all matters be referred to authorized centres and specified assemblies.

The Bahá'í Dispensation is described in the words of its Founder as "a day that shall not be followed by night". Through His Covenant, Bahá'u'lláh has provided an unfailing source of divine guidance that will endure throughout the Dispensation. Authority to administer the affairs of the community and to ensure both the integrity of the Word of God and the promotion of the Faith's message is conferred upon the Administrative Order to which the Covenant has given birth. It is solely by the process of free election or by unsought appointment that the members of the institutions of this Order are assigned to their positions in it. There is no profession in either the teaching of the Faith or its administration for which one can train or to which a believer can properly aspire. Cautionary words of Bahá'u'lláh are particularly relevant:

> Ever since the seeking of preference and distinction came into play, the world hath

been laid waste. It has become desolate ....

Indeed, man is noble, inasmuch as each one is a repository of the sign of God. Nevertheless, to regard oneself as superior in knowledge, learning or virtue, or to exalt oneself or seek preference is a grievous transgression.

Letter dated 14 March 1996 written on behalf of the Universal House of Justice, *Issues Related to the Study of the Bahá'í Faith*, pp. 20-21.

The Distinctive Character of the Bahá'í Administrative Order

The Bahá'í Commonwealth of the future, of which this vast Administrative Order is the sole framework, is, both in theory and practice, not only unique in the entire history of political institutions, but can find no parallel in the annals of any of the world's recognized religious systems. No form of democratic government; no system of autocracy or of dictatorship, whether monarchical or republican; no intermediary scheme of a purely aristocratic order; nor even any of the recognized types of theocracy, whether it be the Hebrew Commonwealth, or the various Christian ecclesiastical organizations, or the Imámate or the Caliphate in Islám—none of these can be identified or be said to conform with the Administrative Order which the master-hand of its perfect Architect has fashioned.

This new-born Administrative Order incorporates within its structure certain elements which are to be found in each of the three recognized forms of secular government, without being in any sense a mere replica of any one of them, and without introducing within its machinery any of the objectionable features which they inherently possess. It blends and harmonizes, as no government fashioned by mortal hands has as yet accomplished, the salutary truths which each of these systems undoubtedly contains without vitiating the integrity of those God-given verities on which it is ultimately founded.

The Administrative Order of the Faith of Bahá'u'lláh must in no wise be regarded as purely democratic in character inasmuch as the basic assumption which requires all democracies to depend fundamentally upon getting their mandate from the people is altogether lacking in this Dispensation. In the conduct of the administrative affairs of the Faith, in the enactment of the legislation necessary to supplement the laws of the *Kitáb-i-Aqdas*, the members of the Universal House of Justice, it should be borne in mind, are not, as Bahá'u'lláh's utterances clearly imply, responsible to those whom they represent, nor are they allowed to be governed by the feelings, the general opinion, and even the convictions of the mass of the faithful, or of those who directly elect them. They are to follow, in a prayerful attitude, the dictates and promptings of their conscience. They may, indeed they must, acquaint themselves with the conditions prevailing among the community, must weigh dispassionately in their minds the merits of any case presented for their consideration, but must reserve for themselves the right of an unfettered decision. "God will verily inspire them with whatsoever He willeth," is Bahá'u'lláh's incontrovertible assurance. They, and not the body of those who either directly or indirectly elect them, have thus been made the recipients of the divine guidance which is at once the life-blood and ultimate safeguard of this Revelation. Moreover, he who symbolizes the hereditary principle in this Dispensation has been made the interpreter of the words of its Author, and ceases consequently, by virtue of the actual authority vested in him, to be the figurehead invariably associated with the prevailing systems of constitutional monarchies.

Shoghi Effendi, The Dispensation of Bahá'u'lláh, *The World Order of Bahá'u'lláh*, pp. 152–153.

Its Source and Foundation

*I*n His Will and Testament 'Abdu'l-Bahá conferred the mantle of Guardian of the Cause and infallible Interpreter of its teachings upon His eldest grandson, Shoghi Effendi, and confirmed the authority and guarantee of divine guidance decreed by Bahá'u'lláh for the Universal House of Justice on all matters *"which have not outwardly been revealed in the Book"*. The Guardianship and the Universal House of Justice can thus be seen to be, in the words of Shoghi Effendi, the "Twin Successors" of Bahá'u'lláh and 'Abdu'l-Bahá. They are the supreme institutions of the Administrative Order which was founded and anticipated in the *Kitáb-i-Aqdas* and elaborated by 'Abdu'l-Bahá in His Will.

During the thirty-six years of his ministry, Shoghi Effendi raised up the structure of elected Spiritual Assemblies—the Houses of Justice referred to in the *Kitáb-i-Aqdas*, now in their embryonic stage—and with their collaboration initiated the systematic implementation of the Divine Plan that 'Abdu'l-Bahá had laid out for the diffusion of the Faith throughout the world. He also set in motion, on the basis of the strong administrative structure that had been established, the processes which were an essential preparation for the election of the Universal House of Justice. This body, which came into existence in April 1963, is elected through secret ballot and plurality vote in a three-stage election by adult Bahá'ís throughout the world. The revealed Word of Bahá'u'lláh, together with the interpretations and expositions of the Centre of the Covenant and the Guardian of the Cause, constitute the binding terms of reference of the Universal House of Justice and are its bedrock foundation.

The Universal House of Justice, added to: Bahá'u'lláh, *The Kitáb-i-Aqdas* (The Most Holy Book), Introduction, p. 3–4.

*I*t should be carefully borne in mind that the local as well as the international Houses of Justice have been expressly enjoined by the *Kitáb-i-Aqdas*; that the institution of the National Spiritual Assembly, as an intermediary body, and referred to in the Master's Will as the "Secondary House of Justice," has the express sanction of 'Abdu'l-Bahá; and that the method to be pursued for the election of the International and National Houses of Justice has been set forth by Him in His Will, as well as in a number of His Tablets. Moreover, the institutions of the local and national Funds, that are now the necessary adjuncts to all local and national spiritual assemblies, have not only been established by 'Abdu'l-Bahá in the Tablets He revealed to the Bahá'ís of the Orient, but their importance and necessity have been repeatedly emphasized by Him in His utterances and writings. The concentration of authority in the hands of the elected representatives of the believers; the necessity of the submission of every adherent of the Faith to the considered judgement of Bahá'í Assemblies; His preference for unanimity in decision; the decisive character of the majority vote; and even the desirability for the exercise of close supervision over all Bahá'í publications, have been sedulously instilled by 'Abdu'l-Bahá, as evidenced by His authenticated and widely-scattered Tablets. To accept His broad and humanitarian Teachings on one hand, and to reject and dismiss with neglectful indifference His more challenging and distinguishing precepts, would be an act of manifest disloyalty to that which He has cherished most in His life.

Shoghi Effendi, *The World Order of Bahá'u'lláh*, pp. 5-6.

This Administrative Order, as it expands and consolidates itself, will no doubt manifest the potentialities and reveal the full implications of this momentous Document—this most remarkable expression of the Will of One of the most remarkable Figures of the Dispensation of Bahá'u'lláh. It will, as its component parts, its organic institutions, begin to function with efficiency and vigour, assert its claim and demonstrate its capacity to be regarded not only as the nucleus but the very pattern of the New World Order destined to embrace in the fullness of time the whole of mankind.

It should be noted that in this connection that this Administrative Order is fundamentally different from anything that any Prophet has previously established, inasmuch as Bahá'u'lláh has Himself revealed its principles, established its institutions, appointed the person to interpret His Word and conferred the necessary authority on the body designed to supplement and apply His legislative ordinances. Therein lies the secret of its strength, its fundamental distinction, and the guarantee against disintegration and schism.

Shoghi Effendi, The Dispensation of Bahá'u'lláh, *The World Order of Bahá'u'lláh*, pp. 144-145.

The Guardianship and the Universal House of Justice

Authority and Divine Guidance

The sacred and youthful branch, the Guardian of the Cause of God, as well as the Universal House of Justice, to be universally elected and established, are both under the care and protection of the Abhá Beauty ... Whatsoever they decide is of God. Whoso obeyeth him not, neither obeyeth them, hath not obeyed God ....

'Abdu'l-Bahá, *The Will and Testament of 'Abdu'l Bahá*, p. 11.

Their common, their fundamental object is to insure the continuity of that divinely-appointed authority which flows from the Source of our Faith, to safeguard the unity of its followers and to maintain the integrity and flexibility of its teachings. Acting in conjunction with each other these two inseparable institutions administer its affairs, co-ordinate its activities, promote its interests, execute its laws and defend its subsidiary institutions.

Shoghi Effendi, The Dispensation of Bahá'u'lláh, *The World Order of Bahá'u'lláh*, p. 148.

Shoghi Effendi was asked several times during his ministry to define the sphere of his operation and his infallibility. The replies he gave and which were written on his behalf are most illuminating. He explains that he is not an infallible authority on subjects such as economics and science, nor does he go into technical matters since his infallibility is confined to "matters which are related strictly to the Cause". He further points out that "he is not, like the Prophet, omniscient at will", that his "infallibility covers interpretation of the revealed word, and its application", and that he is also "infallible in the protection of the Faith". Furthermore, in one of the letters, the following guideline is set forth:

> It is not for individual believers to limit the sphere of the Guardian's authority, or to judge when they have to obey the Guardian and when they are free to reject his judgement. Such an attitude would evidently lead to confusion and to schism. The Guardian being the appointed interpreter of the Teachings, it is his responsibility to state what matters, affecting the interests of the Faith, demand on the part of the believers complete and unqualified obedience to his instructions.

It must always be remembered that authoritative interpretation of the Teachings was, after 'Abdu'l-Bahá, the exclusive right of the Guardian, and fell within the "sacred and prescribed domain" of the Guardianship, and therefore the Universal House of Justice cannot and will not infringe upon that domain. The exclusive sphere of the Universal House of Justice is to "pronounce upon and deliver the final judgement on such laws and ordinances as Bahá'u'lláh has not expressly revealed". Apart from this fundamental difference in the functions of the twin pillars of the Order of Bahá'u'lláh, insofar as the other duties of the Head of the Faith are concerned, the Universal House of Justice shares with the Guardian the responsibility for the application of the revealed word, the protection of the Faith, as well as the duty "to insure the continuity of that divinely-appointed authority which flows from the Source of our Faith, to safeguard the unity of its followers and to maintain the integrity and flexibility of its Teachings". However, the Universal House of Justice is not omniscient; like the Guardian, it wants to be provided with facts when called upon to render a decision, and like him, it may well change its decision when new facts emerge.

Letter dated 22 August 1977 written on behalf of the Universal House of Justice to an individual believer, *Lights of Guidance*, nos 1050-1051, p. 312.

Appointment of Shoghi Effendi as Guardian

O my loving friends! After the passing away of this wronged one, it is incumbent upon the Aghsán (Branches), the Afnán (Twigs) of the Sacred Lote-Tree, the Hands (pillars of the Cause of God and loved ones of the Abhá Beauty to turn unto Shoghi Effendi—the youthful branch branched from the two hallowed and sacred Lote-Trees and the fruit grown from the union of the two offshoots of the Tree of Holiness, —as he is the sign of God, the chosen branch, the Guardian of the Cause of God, he unto whom all the Aghsán, the Afnán, the Hands of the Cause of God and His loved ones must turn. He is the Interpreter of the Word of God and after him will succeed the first-born of his lineal descendants.

'Abdu'l-Bahá, *The Will and Testament of 'Abdu'l-Bahá*, p. 11.

O ye the faithful loved ones of 'Abdu'l-Bahá! It is incumbent upon you to take the greatest care of Shoghi Effendi ...

For he is, after 'Abdu'l-Bahá, the Guardian of the Cause of God, the Afnán, the Hands (pillars) of the Cause and the beloved of the Lord must obey him and turn unto him. He that obeyeth him not, hath not obeyed God ... All must seek guidance and turn unto the Centre of the Cause and the House of Justice. And he that turneth unto whatsoever else is indeed in grievous error.

'Abdu'l-Bahá, *The Will and Testament of 'Abdu'l-Bahá*, p. 25–26.

Events Following the Passing of Shoghi Effendi

*O*n the following morning, 19 November, nine Hands of the Cause, selected from the Holy Land and the several continents of East and West, with Amatu'l-Bahá Rúhíyyih Khánum, broke the seals placed upon the beloved Guardian's safe and desk and made careful examination of their precious contents. These same Hands, rejoicing the other Hands assembled in the Mansion of Bahá'u'lláh at Bahjí, certified that Shoghi Effendi had left no Will and Testament. It was likewise certified that the beloved Guardian had left no heir. The Aghsán (branches) one and all are either dead or have been declared violators of the Covenant by the Guardian for their faithlessness to the Master's *Will and Testament* and their hostility to him named first Guardian in that sacred document.

The first effect of the realization that no successor to Shoghi Effendi could have been appointed by him was to plunge the Hands of the Cause into the very abyss of despair. ...

From this dark abyss, however, contemplation of the Guardian's own life of complete sacrifice and his peerless services gradually redeemed our anguished hearts.

First Conclave of the Hands of the Cause, *Ministry of the Custodians*, pp. 35–36.

*A*fter prayerful and careful study of the Holy Texts bearing upon the question of the appointment of the successor to Shoghi Effendi as Guardian of the Cause of God, and after prolonged consideration of the views of the Hands of the Cause of God residing in the Holy Land, the Universal House of Justice finds that there is no way to appoint or legislate to make it possible to appoint a second Guardian to succeed Shoghi Effendi.

Messages from the Universal House of Justice 1963–1986, para. 5.1, p. 14. (6 October 1963.)

*T*he Covenant of Bahá'u'lláh is unbroken, its all-encompassing power inviolate. The two unique features which distinguish it from all religious covenants of the past are unchanged and operative. The revealed Word, in its original purity, amplified by the divinely guided interpretations of 'Abdu'l-Bahá and Shoghi Effendi, remains immutable, unadulterated by any man-made creeds or dogmas, unwarrantable inferences or unauthorized interpretations. The channel of Divine guidance, providing flexibility in all the affairs of mankind, remains open through that Institution which was founded by Bahá'u'lláh and endowed by Him with supreme authority and unfailing guidance, and of which the Master wrote: "Unto this body all things must be referred." How clearly we can see the truth of Bahá'u'lláh's assertion: "The Hand of Omnipotence hath established His Revelation upon an unassailable, an enduring foundation. Storms of human strife are powerless to undermine its basis, nor will men's fanciful theories succeed in damaging its structure."

Messages from the Universal House of Justice 1963–1986, para. 6.3, p. 15.

The Universal House Of Justice

*I*t is incumbent upon the Trustees of the House of Justice to take counsel together regarding those things which have not outwardly been revealed in the Book, and to enforce that which is agreeable to them. God will verily inspire them with whatsoever He willeth, and He, verily, is the Provider, the Omniscient.

Kalimát-i-Firdawsíyyih, (Words of Paradise), Bahá'u'lláh, *Tablets of Bahá'u'lláh*, p. 68.

*A*t whatever time all the beloved of God in each country appoint their delegates, and these in turn elect their representatives, and these representatives elect a body, that body shall be regarded as the Supreme House of Justice.

'Abdu'l-Bahá, cited in *Messages from the Universal House of Justice 1963–1986*, para. 23.13, p. 53.

*U*nto the Most Holy Book every one must turn, and all that is not expressly recorded therein must be referred to the Universal House of Justice. That which this body, whether unanimously or by a majority doth carry, that is verily the Truth and the Purpose of God Himself. ...

It is incumbent upon these members (of the Universal House of Justice) to gather in a certain place and deliberate upon all problems which have caused difference, questions that are obscure and matters that are not expressly recorded in the Book. Whatsoever they decide has the same effect as the Text itself. Inasmuch as the House of Justice hath power to enact laws that are not expressly recorded in the Book and bear upon daily transactions, so also it hath power to repeal the same. ... The House of Justice is both the initiator and the abrogator of its own laws.

'Abdu'l-Bahá, *The Will and Testament of 'Abdu'l-Bahá*, pp. 19–20.

The provenance, the authority, the duties, the sphere of action of the Universal House of Justice all derive from the revealed Word of Bahá'u'lláh which, together with the interpretations and expositions of the Centre of the Covenant and of the Guardian of the Cause—who, after 'Abdu'l-Bahá, is the sole authority in the interpretation of Bahá'í Scripture—constitute the binding terms of reference of the Universal House of Justice and are its bedrock foundation. The authority of these Texts is absolute and immutable until such time as Almighty God shall reveal His new Manifestation to Whom will belong all authority and power.

There being no successor to Shoghi Effendi as Guardian of the Cause of God, the Universal House of Justice is the Head of the Faith and its supreme institution, to which all must turn, and on it rests the ultimate responsibility for ensuring the unity and progress of the Cause of God.

The Constitution of the Universal House of Justice, Declaration of Trust, p. 4.

Election of The Universal House of Justice

The Universal House of Justice shall consist of nine men ...

The members of the Universal House of Justice shall be elected by secret ballot by the members of all National Spiritual Assemblies at a meeting to be known as the International Bahá'í Convention.

An election of the Universal House of Justice shall be held once every five years unless otherwise decided by the Universal House of Justice, and those elected shall continue in office until such time as their successors shall be elected and the first meeting of these successors is duly held.

The Constitution of the Universal House of Justice, By-Laws, Section V, p. 11.

According to the ordinances of the Faith of God, women are the equals of men in all rights save only that of membership on the Universal House of Justice, for as hath been stated in the text of the Book, both the head and the members of the House of Justice are men. However, in all other bodies, such as the Temple Construction Committee, the Teaching Committee, the Spiritual Assembly, and in charitable and scientific associations, women share equally in all rights with men.

'Abdu'l-Bahá, J. & P. Khan, *Advancement of Women*, pp. 123-124.

As regards your question concerning the membership of the Universal House of Justice: there is a Tablet from 'Abdu'l-Bahá in which He definitely states that the membership of the Universal House is confined to men, and that the wisdom of it will be fully revealed and appreciated in the future. In the local as well as the national Houses of Justice, however, women have the full right of membership. It is, therefore, only to the International House that they cannot be elected. The Bahá'ís should accept this statement of the Master in a spirit of deep faith, confident that there is a divine guidance and wisdom behind it which will be gradually unfolded to the eyes of the world.

Letter dated 28 July 1936 written on behalf of Shoghi Effendi, 28 July 1936, *Directives from the Guardian*, no. 211, pp. 79–80.[76]

While individuals are free to speculate on the reason for the membership of the Universal House of Justice being confined to men, there is no authoritative text to support the assertion that it is due to women being so compassionate as to be unable to make objective decisions. Indeed, it might well be argued that if this were the reason, the teachings would have provided also for the exclusion of women from Local and National Spiritual Assemblies ...

Letter written on behalf of the Universal House of Justice, J. & P. Khan, *Advancement of Women*, p. 129.

Bahá'ís believe that to gain a fuller understanding of the reason women are excused from membership of the Universal House of Justice, we must await the evolution of society, and we are confident that the wisdom of women's exclusion will become manifest as society develops and becomes more united.

Letter written on behalf of the Universal House of Justice, J. & P. Khan, *Advancement of Women*, p. 127.

Signature of The Universal House of Justice

The signature of the Universal House of Justice shall be the words 'The Universal House of Justice' or in Persian 'Baytu'l-'Adl-i-A'ẓam' written by hand by any one of its members upon authority of the Universal House of Justice, to which shall be affixed in each case the Seal of the Universal House of Justice.

The Constitution of the Universal House of Justice, By-Laws, Section V.5, p. 13.

Bahá'í International Community

Under the guidance of the Universal House of Justice, its governing authority, the Bahá'í International Community comprises 148 national affiliates (the National Spiritual Assemblies). At the international level it operates through branches specialized for different aspects of its work. At the present time these are three in number: the Secretariat, located at the World Centre of the Faith in Israel; the United Nations Office, based in New York City with a branch in Geneva; and the Office of Public Information, with its headquarters in Israel and a bureau in New York. Both the United Nations Office and the Office of Public Information have representatives in a number of major centres of the world.

The Bahá'í International Community, cited in *A Basic Bahá'í Dictionary*, p. 37.

---

76 Also *The Compilation of Compilations*, Vol. II (Women), no. 2118, p. 369.

*J*OYFULLY ANNOUNCE BAHÁ'Í WORLD ATTAINMENT CONSULTATIVE STATUS UNITED NATIONS ECONOMIC AND SOCIAL COUNCIL THEREBY FULFILLING LONG CHERISHED HOPE BELOVED GUARDIAN AND WORLD CENTRE GOAL NINE YEAR PLAN. SUSTAINED PERSISTENT EFFORTS MORE THAN TWENTY YEARS ACCREDITED REPRESENTATIVES BAHÁ'Í INTERNATIONAL COMMUNITY UNITED NATIONS DEVOTED SUPPORT BAHÁ'Í COMMUNITIES THROUGHOUT WORLD FINALLY REWARDED. SIGNIFICANT ACHIEVEMENT ADDS PRESTIGE INFLUENCE RECOGNITION EVER ADVANCING FAITH BAHÁ'U'LLÁH. OFFERING PRAYERS GRATITUDE HOLY SHRINES.

Messages from the Universal House of Justice, para. 78.1, p. 167. (18 February 1970.)

The Hands of the Cause of God, Boards of Counsellors and Auxiliary Boards

*I*n the *Kitáb-i-'Ahd* (the Book of His Covenant) Bahá'u'lláh wrote *"Blessed are the rulers and the learned amoung the people of Bahá,"* and referring to this very passage the beloved Guardian wrote on 4 November 1931:

In this holy cycle the "learned" are, on the one hand, the Hands of the Cause of God, and, on the other, the teachers and diffusers of His teachings who do not rank as Hands, but who have attained an eminent position in the teaching work. As to the "rulers" they refer to the members of the Local, National and International Houses of Justice. The duties of each of these souls will be determined in the future. (Translated from the Persian.)

The Hands of the Cause of God, the Counsellors and the members of the Auxiliary Boards fall within the definition of the "learned" given by the beloved Guardian. Thus they are all intimately interrelated and it is not incorrect to refer to the three ranks collectively as one institution.

However, each is also a separate institution in itself.

Messages from the Universal House of Justice, paras 111.3–111.5, pp. 214–215. (24 April 1972.)

*T*he existence of institutions of such exalted rank, comprising individuals who play such a vital role, who yet have no legislative, administrative or judicial authority, and are entirely devoid of priestly functions or the right to make authoritative interpretations, is a feature of Bahá'í administration unparalleled in the religions of the past. The newness and uniqueness of this concept make it difficult to grasp; only as the Bahá'í Community grows and the believers are increasingly able to contemplate its administrative structure uninfluenced by concepts of past ages, will the vital interdependence of the "rulers" and "learned" in the Faith be properly understood, and the inestimable value of their interaction be fully recognized.

Messages from the Universal House of Justice, para. 111.14, p. 217. (24 April 1972.)

The Hands of the Cause of God

*L*ight and glory, greeting and praise be upon the Hands of His Cause, through whom the light of fortitude hath shone forth and the truth hath been established that the authority to choose rests with God, the Powerful, the Mighty, the Unconstrained, through whom the ocean of bounty hath surged and the fragrance of the gracious favours of God, the Lord of mankind, hath been diffused.

Lawḥ-i-Dunyá (Tablet of the World), Bahá'u'lláh, Tablets of Bahá'u'lláh, p. 83.

O friends! The Hands of the Cause of God must be nominated and appointed by the Guardian of the Cause of God. All must be under his shadow and obey his command. Should any, within or without the company of the Hands of the Cause of God disobey and seek division, the wrath of God and His vengeance will be upon him, for he will have caused a breach in the true Faith of God.

The obligations of the Hands of the Cause of God are to diffuse the Divine Fragrances, to edify the souls of men, to promote learning, to improve the character of all men and to be, at all times and under all conditions, sanctified and detached from earthly things. They must manifest the fear of God by their conduct, their manners, their deeds and their words.

This body of the Hands of the Cause of God is under the direction of the Guardian of the Cause of God. He must continually urge them to strive and endeavour to the utmost of their ability to diffuse the sweet savours of God, and to guide all the peoples of the world, for it is the light of Divine Guidance that causeth all the universe to be illumined.

'Abdu'l-Bahá, The Will and Testament of 'Abdu'l-Bahá, pp. 12–13.

... *T*he Hands of the Cause of God must be ever watchful and so soon as they find anyone beginning to oppose and protest against the Guardian of the Cause of God, cast him out from the congregation of the people of Bahá and in no wise accept any excuse from him.

'Abdu'l-Bahá, The Will and Testament of 'Abdu'l-Bahá, p. 12.

*T*he rank and position of the Hands of the Cause are superior to the position of the National Assemblies.

Shoghi Effendi, Lights of Guidance, no. 1086, p. 324. (30 April 1957).

The International Teaching Centre

*A*NNOUNCE ESTABLISHMENT HOLY LAND LONG ANTICIPATED INTERNATIONAL TEACHING CENTRE DESTINED EVOLVE INTO ONE THOSE WORLD-SHAKING WORLD-EMBRACING WORLD-DIRECTING ADMINISTRATIVE INSTITUTIONS ORDAINED BY BAHÁ'U'LLÁH ANTICIPATED BY 'ABDU'L-BAHÁ ELUCIDATED BY SHOGHI EFFENDI. MEMBERSHIP THIS NASCENT INSTITUTION COMPRISES ALL HANDS CAUSE GOD AND INITIALLY THREE COUNSELLORS WHO WITH HANDS PRESENT HOLY LAND WILL CONSTITUTE

NUCLEUS ITS VITAL OPERATIONS. CALLING UPON HOOPER DUNBAR FLORENCE MAYBERRY 'AZÍZ YAZDÍ PROCEED HOLY LAND ASSUME THIS HIGHLY MERITORIOUS SERVICE. OFFERING PRAYERS HEARTFELT GRATITUDE SACRED THRESHOLD THIS FURTHER EVIDENCE ORGANIC EVOLUTION ADMINISTRATIVE ORDER BAHÁ'U'LLAH.

Messages from the Universal House of Justice, para. 131.1, p. 246. (5 June 1973.)

*T*his International Teaching Centre now established will, in due course, operate from that building designated by the Guardian as the Seat for the Hands of the Cause, which must be raised on the arc on Mount Carmel in close proximity to the Seat of the Universal House of Justice.

The duties now assigned to this nascent institution are:
- To co-ordinate, stimulate and direct the activities of the Continental Boards of Counsellors and to act as liaison between them and the Universal House of Justice.
- To be fully informed of the situation of the Cause in all parts of the world and to be able, from the background of this knowledge, to make reports and recommendations to the Universal House of Justice and give advice to the Continental Boards of Counsellors.
- To be alert to possibilities, both within and without the Bahá'í community, for the extension of the teaching work into receptive or needy areas, and to draw the attention of the Universal House of Justice and the Continental Boards of Counsellors to such possibilities, making recommendations for action.
- To determine and anticipate needs for literature, pioneers and travelling teachers and to work out teaching plans, both regional and global, for the approval of the Universal House of Justice.

Messages from the Universal House of Justice, paras 132.2-132.3d, pp. 246-247. (8 June 1973.)

The Continental Boards of Counsellors

... *T*he Universal House of Justice decided, as announced in its recent cable, to establish Continental Boards of Counsellors for the protection and propagation of the Faith. Their duties will include directing the Auxiliary Boards in their respective areas, consulting and collaborating with National Spiritual Assemblies, and keeping the Hands of the Cause and the Universal House of Justice informed concerning the conditions of the Cause in their areas.

... One member of each Continental Board of Counsellors has been designated as Trustee of the Continental Fund for its area.

The Auxiliary Boards for Protection and Propagation will henceforth report to the Continental Boards of Counsellors, who will appoint or replace members of the Auxiliary Boards as circumstances may require.

Messages from the Universal House of Justice 1963-1986, paras 59.2, 59.4, and 59.5, pp. 131-132. (24 June 1968.)

*T*he institution of the Boards of Counsellors was brought into being by the Universal House of Justice to extend into the future the specific functions of protection and propagation conferred upon the Hands of the Cause of God. The members of these boards are appointed by the Universal House of Justice.

1. The term of office of a Counsellor, the number of Counsellors on each Board, and the boundaries of the zone in which each Board of Counsellors shall operate, shall be decided by the Universal House of Justice.
2. A Counsellor functions as such only within his zone and should he move his residence out of the zone for which he is appointed he automatically relinquishes his appointment.
3. The rank and specific duties of a Counsellor render him ineligible for service on local or national administrative bodies. If elected to the Universal House of Justice he ceases to be a Counsellor.

The Constitution of The Universal House of Justice, By-Laws, Section IX, pp. 15-16.

*T*he members of these Boards of Counsellors will serve for a term, or terms, the length of which will be determined and announced at a later date, and while serving in this capacity, will not be eligible for membership on national or local administrative bodies.

Messages from the Universal House of Justice 1963-1986, para. 59.4, p. 132. (24 June 1968.)

The Auxiliary Boards

*I*n each zone there shall be two Auxiliary Boards, one for the protection and one for the propagation of the Faith, the numbers of whose members shall be set by the Universal House of Justice. The members of these Auxiliary Boards shall serve under the direction of the Continental Boards of Counsellors and shall act as their deputies, assistants and advisers.

1. The members of the Auxiliary Boards shall be appointed from among the believers of that zone by the Continental Board of Counsellors.
2. Each Auxiliary Board member shall be allotted a specific area in which to serve and, unless specifically deputized by the Counsellors, shall not function as a member of the Auxiliary Board outside that area.
3. An Auxiliary Board member is eligible for any elective office but if elected to an administrative post on a national or local level must decide whether to retain membership on the Board or accept the administrative post, since he may not serve in both capacities at the same time. If elected to the Universal House of Justice he ceases to be a member of the Auxiliary Board.

The Constitution of The Universal House of Justice, By-Laws, Section X, p. 16.

*A*uthority and direction flow from the Assemblies, whereas the power to accomplish the tasks resides primarily in the entire body of the believers. It is the principal task of the Auxiliary Boards to assist in arousing and releasing this power. This is a vital activity, and if they are to be able to perform it adequately they must avoid becoming involved in the work of administration. For example, when Auxiliary Board members arouse believers to pioneer, any believer who expresses his desire to do so should be referred to the appropriate committee which will then organize the project. Counsellors and Auxiliary Board members should not, themselves, organize pioneering or travel teaching projects. Thus it is seen that the Auxiliary Boards should work closely with the grass roots of the community: the individual believers, groups and Local Spiritual Assemblies, advising, stimulating and assisting them. The Counsellors are responsible for stimulating, counselling and assisting National Spiritual Assemblies, and also work with individuals, groups, and Local Assemblies.

Messages from the Universal House of Justice 1963-1986, para. 72.3, pp. 150-151. (1 October 1969.)

... *We* have decided to take a further step in the development of the institution by giving to each Continental Board of Counsellors the discretion to authorize individual Auxiliary Board members to appoint assistants. ...

The exact nature of the duties and the duration of the appointment of the assistants is also left to each Continental Board to decide for itself. Their aims should be to activate and encourage Local Spiritual Assemblies, to call the attention of Local Spiritual Assembly members to the importance of holding regular meetings, to encourage local communities to meet for the Nineteen Day Feasts and Holy Days, to help deepen their fellow-believers' understanding of the Teachings, and generally to assist the Auxiliary Board members in the discharge of their duties. Appointments may be made for a limited period, such as a year or two, with the possibility of re-appointment. Believers can serve at the same time both as assistants to Auxiliary Board members and on administrative institutions.

Messages from the Universal House of Justice 1963-1986, paras 137.3-137.4, pp. 255-256. (7 October 1973.)

National Institutions of the Faith

The National Spiritual Assembly

... the Guardian wishes me to again affirm his view that the authority of the National Spiritual Assembly is undivided and unchallengeable in all matters pertaining to the administration of the Faith ... and that, therefore, the obedience of individual Bahá'ís, delegates, groups, and Assemblies to that authority is imperative, and should be whole-hearted and unqualified.

Letter dated 11 June 1934 written on behalf of Shoghi Effendi, *The Compilation of Compilations*, Vol. II (National Spiritual Assembly), no. 1458, p. 105.[77]

---

77 Also *Lights of Guidance*, no. 127, p. 36.

*I*ts immediate purpose is to stimulate, unify and co-ordinate by frequent personal consultations, the manifold activities of the friends as well as the local Assemblies; and by keeping in close and constant touch with the Holy Land, initiate measures, and direct in general the affairs of the Cause in that country.

It serves also another purpose, no less essential than the first, as in the course of time it shall evolve into the National House of Justice (referred to in 'Abdu'l-Bahá's Will as the "secondary House of Justice"), which according to the explicit text of the Testament will have, in conjunction with the other National Assemblies throughout the Bahá'í world, to elect directly the members of the International House of Justice, that Supreme Council that will guide, organize and unify the affairs of the Movement throughout the world.

Shoghi Effendi, *Bahá'í Administration*, p. 39. (12 March 1923.)

*L*et it be made clear to every inquiring reader that among the most outstanding and sacred duties incumbent upon those who have been called upon to initiate, direct and co-ordinate the affairs of the Cause, are those that require them to win by every means in their power the confidence and affection of those whom it is their privilege to serve.

Shoghi Effendi, *Bahá'í Administration*, p. 143. (18 October 1927.)

*A*bove all, the National Spiritual Assembly shall ever seek to attain that station of unity in devotion to the Revelation of Bahá'u'lláh which will attract the confirmations of the Holy Spirit and enable the Assembly to serve the founding of the Most Great Peace. In all its deliberation and action the National Assembly shall have constantly before it as Divine guide and standard the utterance of Bahá'u'lláh:

"It behooveth them (i.e., members of the Spiritual Assemblies) to be the trusted ones of the Merciful among men and to regard themselves as the guardians appointed of God for all that dwell on earth. It is incumbent upon them to take counsel together and to have regard for the interests of the servants of God, for His sake, even as they regard their own interests, and to choose that which is meet and seemly."

Declaration of Trust and By-Laws of a National Spiritual Assembly, By-Laws of a Local Spiritual Assembly, By-Laws of the National Spiritual Assembly, Article 1, pp. 6–7.[78]

Role in Expansion and Consolidation

*T*he evolution of the Plan imposes a three-fold obligation, which all individual believers, all Local Assemblies, as well as the National Assembly itself, must respectively recognize and conscientiously fulfil. Each and every believer, undaunted by the uncertainties, the perils and the financial stringency afflicting the nation, must arise and insure, to the full measure of his or her capacity, that continuous and abundant flow of funds into the national Treasury, on which the successful prosecution of the Plan must chiefly depend. Upon the local Assemblies, whose special function and high privilege is to facilitate the admission of new believers into the community, and thereby stimulate the infusion of fresh blood into its organic institutions, a duty no less binding in character

---

78 Also *The Bahá'í World*, Vol. XIV, p. 503.

devolves. To them I wish particularly to appeal, at this present hour, when the call of God is being raised throughout the length and breadth of both continents in the New World, to desist from insisting too rigidly on the minor observances and beliefs, which might prove a stumbling block in the way of any sincere applicant, whose eager desire is to enlist under the banner of Bahá'u'lláh. While conscientiously adhering to the fundamental qualifications already laid down, the members of each and every Assembly should endeavour, by their patience, their love, their tact and wisdom to nurse, subsequent to his admission, the new-comer into Bahá'í maturity, and win him over gradually to the unreserved acceptance of whatever has been ordained in the teachings. As to the National Assembly, whose inescapable responsibility is to guard the integrity, co-ordinate the activities, and stimulate the life, of the entire community, its chief concern at the present moment should be to anxiously deliberate as how best to enable both individual believers and local Assemblies to fulfil their respective tasks. Through their repeated appeals, through their readiness to dispel all misunderstandings and remove all obstacles, through the example of their lives, and their unrelaxing vigilance, their high sense of justice, their humility, consecration and courage, they must demonstrate to those whom they represent their capacity to play their part in the progress of the Plan in which they, no less than the rest of the community, are involved. May the all-conquering Spirit of Bahá'u'lláh be so infused into each component part of this harmoniously functioning System as to enable it to contribute its proper share to the consummation of the Plan.

Shoghi Effendi, *Messages to America*, pp. 11-12; and *The Compilation of Compilations*, Vol. II (The National Spiritual Assembly), no. 1445, pp. 92-93. (30 January 1938.)

*T*raining of the friends and their striving, through serious individual study, to acquire knowledge of the Faith, to apply its principles and administer its affairs, are indispensable to developing the human resources necessary to the progress of the Cause. But knowledge alone is not adequate; it is vital that training be given in a manner that inspires love and devotion, fosters firmness in the Covenant, prompts the individual to active participation in the work of the Cause and to taking sound initiatives in the promotion of its interests. Special efforts to attract people of capacity to the Faith will also go far towards providing the human resources so greatly needed at this time. Moreover, these endeavours will stimulate and strengthen the ability of Spiritual Assemblies to meet their weighty responsibilities.

The proper functioning of these institutions depends largely on the efforts of their members to familiarize themselves with their duties and to adhere scrupulously to principle in their personal behaviour and in the conduct of their official responsibilities. Of relevant importance, too, are their resolve to remove all traces of estrangement and sectarian tendencies from their midst, their ability to win the affection and support of the friends under their care and to involve as many individuals as possible in the work of the Cause. By their constantly aiming at improving their performance, the communities they guide will reflect a pattern of life that will be a credit to the Faith and will, as a welcome consequence, rekindle hope among the increasingly disillusioned members of society.

The Universal House of Justice, *Riḍván Message to the Bahá'ís of the World*, BE 150/AD 1993, paras 9-10.

*A*lthough Spiritual Assemblies are good at specifying goals, they have not yet mastered the art of making use of the talents of individuals and rousing the mass of the friends to action in fulfilment of such goals. Removing this deficiency would be a mark of the maturation of these institutions. May your Assembly lead the way.

The Universal House of Justice, *Rights and Responsibilities*, p. 47. (19 May 1994.)

Maintenance of Harmony and Bahá'í Standards

*S*uch a rectitude of conduct must manifest itself, with ever-increasing potency, in every verdict which the elected representatives of the Bahá'í community, in whatever capacity they may find themselves, may be called upon to pronounce. ... It must be exemplified in the conduct of all Bahá'í electors, when exercising their sacred rights and functions. ... It must constitute the brightest ornament of the life, the pursuits, the exertions, and the utterances of every Bahá'í teacher, whether labouring at home or abroad, whether in the front ranks of the teaching force, or occupying a less active and responsible position. It must be made the hallmark of that numerically small, yet intensely dynamic and highly responsible body of the elected national representatives of every Bahá'í community, which constitutes the sustaining pillar, and the sole instrument for the election, in every community, of that Universal House whose very name and title, as ordained by Bahá'u'lláh, symbolizes that rectitude of conduct which is its highest mission to safeguard and enforce.

Shoghi Effendi, *The Advent of Divine Justice*, pp. 26-27.

*A*nything whatsoever affecting the interests of the Cause and in which the National Assembly as a body is involved should, if regarded as unsatisfactory by Local Assemblies or individual believers, be immediately referred to the National Assembly itself. Neither the general body of the believers, nor any Local Assembly, nor even the delegates to the annual Convention, should be regarded as having any authority to entertain appeals against the decision of the National Assembly. Should the matter be referred to the Guardian it will be his duty to consider it with the utmost care and to decide whether the issues involved justify him to consider it in person, or to leave it entirely to the discretion of the National Assembly.

Shoghi Effendi, *Directives from the Guardian*, no. 137, p. 50; and *The Compilation of Compilations*, Vol. II (The National Spiritual Assembly), no. 1506, pp. 129-130. (10 September 1934.)

*E*xcommunication is a spiritual thing and up until now the Guardian has always been the one who exerted this power, and he feels for the present he must continue to be. Only actual enemies of the Cause are excommunicated. On the other hand, those who conspicuously disgrace the Faith or refuse to abide by its laws can be deprived, as a punishment, of their voting rights; this in itself is a severe action, and he therefore always urges all National Assemblies (who can take such action) to first warn and repeatedly warn the evil-doer before taking the step of depriving him of his voting rights. He feels your Assembly must act with the greatest wisdom in such matters, and only impose this sanction if a believer is seriously injuring the Faith in the eyes of the public through his conduct or flagrantly breaching the laws of God. If such a sanction were lightly used the friends would come to attach no importance to it, or to feel the National Spiritual Assembly used it every time they got angry with some individual's disobedience to them. We must always remember that, sad and often childish, as it seems, some of those who make the worst nuisances of themselves to their National Bodies are often very loyal believers, who think they are protecting the true interests of their Faith by attacking National Spiritual Assembly decisions!

<blockquote>Letter dated 8 May 1948 written on behalf of Shoghi Effendi, *Dawn of a New Day*, pp. 128-129.</blockquote>

*T*he Guardian feels very strongly that everywhere, throughout the entire Bahá'í world, the believers have got to master and follow the principles of their divinely laid down Administrative Order. They will never solve their problems by departing from the correct procedure ... The Bahá'ís have got to learn to live up to the laws of Bahá'u'lláh which are infinitely higher, more exacting and more perfect than those the world is at present familiar with. Running away, fighting with each other, fostering dissension, is not going to advance the Indian or any other Community; all it is going to do is to bring Bahá'u'lláh's plans and work to a standstill until such time as the believers *unite* to serve Him, or new and more dedicated souls arise to take their place.

<blockquote>Letter dated 8 May 1948 written on behalf of Shoghi Effendi, *Dawn of a New Day*, p. 129.</blockquote>

*I*t would be impossible to overestimate the obligation resting upon you to refine your dealings with the community in the ways already described. You cannot at any time afford to forget that the manner of the use of authority is critical to the success of your work. With this in mind, you must also attend seriously to the behaviour of those, more particularly your officers, who must of necessity act on your behalf in carrying out your decisions and conveying your instructions to others. Further, it is sometimes the case that staff members at your National Centre, in their eagerness to be exactly and completely obedient, carry out the instruction of your Assembly with a sharpness of manner and tone that hurts people and provokes resentment against the very body the staff are striving to serve with loyalty and devotion. The staff should be sensitized to the situation and made to realize, through your loving and persistent guidance, that the spiritual requisites for good and respectful relations with others must be conscientiously applied in their interactions with the friends because to do so is not only virtuous in itself but will also minimize the incidence of bad feeling towards your Assembly.

The temperament of authority in the administration of justice varies according to the degree of gravity of each case. Some cases require that the Assembly take action that is firm or drastic. Even so, Assembly members have always to be mindful that the authority they wield must in general be expressed with love, humility and a genuine respect for others. Thus exercised, authority strikes a natural note and accords with that which is acceptable to spiritually attuned and fair-minded souls. The following guidance of Shoghi Effendi, as conveyed by his secretary, is especially relevant: "The administrators of the Faith of God must be like unto shepherds. Their aim should be to dispel all the doubts, misunderstandings and harmful differences which may arise in the community of the believers. And this they can adequately achieve provided they are motivated by a true sense of love for their fellow-brethren coupled with firm determination to act with justice in all cases which are submitted to them for consideration."

The Universal House of Justice, *Rights and Responsibilities*, pp. 44-45. (19 May 1994.)

Avoidance of Over-Administration

Over-administration can be even worse for the Faith at this time than under-administration. The believers are, for the most part, young in the Cause, and if they make mistakes it is not half as important as if their spirit is crushed by being told all the time—do this and don't do that! The new National Body should be like a loving parent, watching over and helping its children, and not like a stern judge, waiting for an opportunity to display his judicial powers. The reason he points this out to you is that constantly, for the past twenty years and more, he has been pointing this out to the old and tried National Assemblies, and he does not want the younger bodies to make the same mistakes. Individual cases should be dealt with as they arise, according to the Teachings, of which the believers have quite sufficient available to handle all of their problems at this time, and no more additional rules and regulations need be introduced.

Letter dated 30 June 1957 written on behalf of Shoghi Effendi, *High Endeavours*, p. 35.[79]

National and Unit Conventions

In view of the growth of the Faith and the developing life of the Bahá'í communities, the Universal House of Justice has decided that, notwithstanding that in some countries the number of believers and of Local Spiritual Assemblies is still small, the time has come for delegates to National Conventions everywhere to be elected on the basis of electoral units, but with the option of introducing certain differences from the procedures followed to date. These differences are explained below and are designed to make the system adaptable to the variations in the make-up of the many Bahá'í communities and in the geography of the lands in which they are situated.

... When establishing the electoral unit basis for the election of delegates, a National Spiritual Assembly should divide the territory under its jurisdiction into electoral units, based on the number of adult Bahá'ís in each area, in such a way that each unit will be responsible for electing preferably one delegate only.

Letter dated 21 July 1985 written on behalf of the Universal House of Justice, *Messages from the Universal House of Justice*, paras 433.2 and 433.4, pp. 671-672.[80]

... The assembled accredited representatives of the ... believers should exercise not only the vital and responsible right of electing the National Assembly, but should also

---

[79] Also *Lights of Guidance,* no. 136, p. 38.
[80] Also *Lights of Guidance,* no. 53, p. 15.

fulfil the functions of an enlightened, consultative and co-operative body that will enrich the experience, enhance the prestige, support the authority, and assist the deliberations of the National Spiritual Assembly. It is my firm conviction that it is the bounden duty, in the interest of the Cause we all love and serve, of the members of the incoming National Assembly, once elected by the delegates at Convention time, to seek and have the utmost regard, individually as well as collectively, for the advice, the considered opinion and the true sentiments of the assembled delegates. Banishing every vestige of secrecy, of undue reticence, of dictatorial aloofness, from their midst, they should radiantly unfold to the eyes of the delegates, by whom they are elected, their plans, their hopes, and their cares. They should familiarize the delegates with the various matters that will have to be considered in the current year, and calmly and conscientiously study and weigh the opinions and judgements of the delegates.

Shoghi Effendi, Bahá'í Administration, p. 79. (29 January 1925.)

Consultation, frank and unfettered, is the bedrock of this unique Order. Authority is concentrated in the hands of the elected members of the National Assembly. Power and initiative are primarily vested in the entire body of the believers acting through their local representatives. To generate those forces which must give birth to the body of their national administrators, and to confer, freely and fully and at fixed intervals, with both the incoming and outgoing National Assemblies, are the twofold functions, the supreme responsibility and sole prerogative of the delegates assembled in Convention. Nothing short of close and constant interaction between these various organs of Bahá'í administration can enable it to fulfil its high destiny.

Letter dated 18 November 1933 written on behalf of Shoghi Effendi, *The Compilation of Compilations*, Vol. II (The National Spiritual Assembly), no. 1456, p. 103.

Concerning the status of members of the National Spiritual Assembly at Convention sessions the Guardian feels that the members of both the incoming and the outgoing Assemblies should be given the full right to participate in the Convention discussions. Those members of the National Spiritual Assembly who have been elected delegates will, in addition to the right of participation, be entitled to vote. The Guardian wishes thereby to render more effective the deliberations and the recommendations of the national representatives. He feels that the exercise of such a right by the members of the National Spiritual Assembly will enable them to consult more fully with the assembled delegates, to exchange fully and frankly with them their views, and to consider collectively the interests, needs and requirements of the Cause. This, he believes, is one of the primary functions of the Convention.

Letter dated 25 December 1933 written on behalf of Shoghi Effendi, *The Compilation of Compilations*, Vol. II (The National Spiritual Assembly), no. 1457, pp. 104-105.[81]

Direction comes from Assembly decisions, but its effectiveness depends not only on the clarity with which it is given but also on a number of spiritual and moral factors

---

81   Also *Lights of Guidance*, no. 60, pp. 18-19.

which must be blended in the general attitude of the individual believers, on the one hand, and the manner and style of functioning of the Assembly, on the other. The following advice of Shoghi Effendi, addressed in an early letter to the Western friends, deals with these two aspects:

"Let us also bear in mind that the keynote of the Cause of God is not dictatorial authority but humble fellowship, not arbitrary power, but the spirit of frank and loving consultation. Nothing short of the spirit of a true Bahá'í can hope to reconcile the principles of mercy and justice, of freedom and submission, of the sanctity of the right of the individual and of self-surrender, of vigilance, discretion and prudence on the one hand, and fellowship, candour and courage on the other.

"The duties of those whom the friends have freely and conscientiously elected as their representatives are no less vital and binding than the obligations of those who have chosen them. Their function is not to dictate, but to consult, and to consult not only among themselves, but as much as possible with the friends whom they represent. ... They should never be led to suppose that they are the central ornaments of the body of the Cause, intrinsically superior to others in capacity or merit, and sole promoters of its teachings and principles. They should approach their task with extreme humility, and endeavour, by their open-mindedness, their high sense of justice and duty, their candour, their modesty, their entire devotion to the welfare and interests of the friends, the Cause, and humanity, to win not only the confidence and the genuine support and respect of those whom they should serve, but also their esteem and real affection."[82]

These instructions of the beloved Guardian get to the very heart of what must be more deeply internalized by the members of your Assembly at this time. We repeat for emphasis the terms "extreme humility", "open-mindedness", "candour", "modesty"; and we underscore the openness which is implicit in candour, because the co-operation which must be fostered between your Assembly and the friends will depend significantly on the degree to which, with wise discretion, you share your concerns with the community. Your greatest opportunity for this is the annual National Convention, when the representatives of the entire community come together to consult with you. It is not sufficient that you give only good news and encouraging statistics to the delegates. Do as Shoghi Effendi advised you: "Banishing every vestige of secrecy, of undue reticence, of dictatorial aloofness, from their midst, they should radiantly and abundantly unfold to the eyes of the delegates, by whom they are elected, their plans, their hopes, and their cares. They should familiarize the delegates with the various matters that will have to be considered in the current year, and calmly and conscientiously study and weigh the opinions and judgements of the delegates."

Even if the delegates find themselves unable to offer useful recommendations toward the resolution of particular issues, by your bringing them into your confidence, they will develop an appreciation, as would be impossible otherwise, of the serious matters confronting the cause. With this understanding, they will be equipped to assist the

---

82   Shoghi Effendi, *Bahá'í Administration*, pp. 63–64. (23 February 1924.)

community to respond effectively to your decisions, no matter how challenging these may turn out to be. Moreover, it will relieve you of any overwhelming sense of burden to know that such a responsible body of believers shares your innermost concerns; and even more than that, the effect of your openness will be to strengthen the delegates' support for your authority, which it is their sacred duty to give. Besides, as it is neither possible nor practicable for your Assembly to meet with all the believers, nor for the members to be constantly travelling throughout the community, the friends' feeling that you are remote can be ameliorated, though not entirely removed, by the effectiveness of your interactions with the delegates.

The Universal House of Justice, *Rights and Responsibilities*, pp. 42-44. (19 May 1994.)

National Committees and Institutes

Large issues in such spiritual activities that affect the Cause in general in that land, ... far from being under the exclusive jurisdiction of any local assembly or group of friends, must each be minutely and fully directed by a special board, elected by the National Body, constituted as a committee thereof, responsible to it and upon which the National Body shall exercise constant and general supervision.

Shoghi Effendi, *Bahá'í Administration*, p. 24. (5 March 1922.)

As it has been observed already, the role of these committees set up by the National Spiritual Assembly, the renewal, the membership and functions of which should be reconsidered separately each year by the incoming National Assembly, is chiefly to make thorough and expert study of the issue entrusted to their charge, advise by their reports, and assist in the execution of the decisions which in vital matters are to be exclusively and directly rendered by the National Assembly.

Shoghi Effendi, *Bahá'í Administration*, p. 141. (18 October 1927.)

National Teaching Committee

Whether it be the body of their elected national representatives, or its chief auxiliary institution, the National Teaching Committee, or its subsidiary organs, the regional teaching committees, or the local Spiritual Assemblies and their respective teaching committees, they who labour for the spread of the Cause of Bahá'u'lláh should, through constant interchange of ideas, through letters, circulars, reports, bulletins and other means of communication with these established instruments designed for the propagation of the Faith, insure the smooth and speedy functioning of the teaching machinery of their Administrative Order. Confusion, delay, duplication of efforts, dissipation of energy will, thereby, be completely avoided, and the mighty flood of the grace of Bahá'u'lláh, flowing abundantly and without the least obstruction through these essential channels will so inundate the hearts and souls of men as to enable them to bring forth the harvest repeatedly predicted by 'Abdu'l-Bahá.

Shoghi Effendi, *The Advent of Divine Justice*, pp. 52-53.

*T*he function of a National Teaching Committee is to take charge, under the direction of the National Spiritual Assembly, of the entire teaching programme of the country. It should be given its terms of reference which will specifically define the general objectives and methods of the teaching on the homefront; it should be provided with a budget and be required to submit to the National Spiritual Assembly an overall plan for the accomplishment of its tasks. Once this plan has been approved, the Committee should be allowed to carry out its work, although of course you should receive regular reports of its progress and of its financial position.

One of the great benefits deriving from such an arrangement is that the National Spiritual Assembly is freed from the day-to-day details of the teaching work and while retaining supervision of this most important method in its own hand, has an executive arm in its National Teaching Committee, which should be given the full confidence and support of the National Spiritual Assembly.

The Universal House of Justice, *Lights of Guidance*, no. 555, p. 168. (12 November 1971.)

*I*f a National Spiritual Assembly finds that its National Teaching Committee cannot devote sufficient attention to the work of consolidation, it should not hesitate to appoint, in addition, special committees whose tasks would be the conduct of the various activities which are essential for consolidation. Activities falling within this category include the organization of circuits of travelling teachers skilled in consolidation work; the holding of summer and winter schools, weekend institutes and conferences; the initiation and operation of tutorial schools; the dissemination of Bahá'í literature and the encouragement of its study by the friends; and the organization of special courses and institutes for Local Spiritual Assembly members.

Letter dated 17 April 1981 written on behalf of the Universal House of Justice, *Messages from the Universal House of Justice 1963-1986*, para. 280.5, p. 485.[83]

Institutes

*Y*our Institutes should not only be seats of Bahá'í learning but also centres from which mass teaching and consolidation work over a large area must be inspired and conducted. The Institute is not merely a building, nor solely a place where Bahá'í classes can be held for a few days. It should be the centre of complex activities which systematically assist your Assembly in the achievement of its goal in teaching and consolidation.

The Universal House of Justice, *Lights of Guidance*, no. 1909, p. 564. (23 June 1966.)

*T*o effect the possibilities of expansion and consolidation implied by entry by troops, a determined, world-wide effort to develop human resources must be made. The endeavour of individuals to conduct study classes in their homes, the sponsorship by the institutions of occasional courses of instruction, and the informal activities of the community, though important, are not adequate for the education and training of a rapidly expanding

---

[83] Also *Lights of Guidance*, no. 566, p. 171.

community. It is therefore of paramount importance that systematic attention be given to devising methods for educating large numbers of believers in the fundamental verities of the Faith and for training and assisting them to serve the Cause as their God-given talents allow. There should be no delay in establishing permanent institutes designed to provide well-organized, formally conducted programmes of training on a regular schedule. Access of the institute to physical facilities will of course be necessary, but it may not require a building of its own.

This matter calls for an intensification of the collaboration between the Continental Counsellors and National Spiritual Assemblies. For the success of these training institutes will depend in very large measure on the active involvement of the Continental Counsellors and the Auxiliary Board members in their operation. Particularly will it be necessary for Auxiliary Board members to have a close working relationship with institutes and, of course, with the Local Spiritual Assemblies whose communities will benefit from institute programmes. Since institutes are to be regarded as centres of learning, and since their character harmonizes with, and provides scope for the exercise of, the educational responsibilities of the Auxiliary Board members, the intimate involvement in institute operations should now become a part of the evolving functions of these officers of the Faith. Drawing on the talents and abilities of increasing numbers of believers will also be crucial to the development and execution of institute programmes.

As the term "institute" has assumed various uses in the Bahá'í community, a word of clarification is needed. The next four years[84] will represent an extraordinary period in the history of our Faith, a turning point of epochal magnitude. What the friends throughout the world are now being asked to do is to commit themselves, their material resources, their abilities and their time to the development of a network of training institutes on a scale never before attempted. These centres of Bahá'í learning will have as their goal one very practical outcome, namely, the raising up of large numbers of believers who are trained to foster and facilitate the process of entry by troops with efficiency and love.

The Universal House of Justice, *Riḍván Message to the Bahá'ís of the World*, BE 153/AD 1996, paras 27–29.

Regional Agencies

... *T*he Guardian has ... re-emphasized the necessity of avoiding over-centralization in the conduct of the affairs of the Cause, thereby relieving your Assembly of an unmanageable amount of detail and routine work, which would interfere with its clear and paramount duty of maintaining a thorough and vigilant supervision over the work of the Cause as a whole. Excessive decentralization, on the other hand, would tend to nullify the principle which places ultimate authority and responsibility in the hands of the National Spiritual Assembly. His recent instruction regarding the relationship of the Regional Teaching Committees to the National Teaching Committee safeguards this principle which lies at the very basis of the Administrative Order. The Regional

---

84 Riḍván 1996 to Riḍván 2000.

Committees, although appointed by the National Spiritual Assembly, should, unlike all other Committees, be viewed as special adjuncts created specifically for the purpose of helping directly the National Teaching Committee in its all-important task of stimulating the teaching activities of the Faith. ... In a sense they are sub-Committees of the National Teaching Committee, to whom their reports and all details of the National Teaching activity should be constantly and directly referred.

    Letter dated 25 May 1941 on behalf of Shoghi Effendi, *Lights of Guidance*, no. 568, p. 172.

Regional Bahá'í Councils

*T*he expansion of the Bahá'í community and the growing complexity of the issues which are facing National Spiritual Assemblies in certain countries have brought the Cause to a new stage in its development. They have caused us in recent years to examine various aspects of the balance between centralization and decentralization. In a few countries we have authorized the National Spiritual Assemblies to establish State Bahá'í Councils or Regional Teaching and Administrative Committees. From the experience gained in the operation of these bodies, and from detailed examination of the principles set forth by Shoghi Effendi, we have reached the conclusion that the time has arrived for us to formalize a new element of Bahá'í administration, between the local and national levels, comprising institutions of a special kind, to be designated as "Regional Bahá'í Councils".

Regional Bahá'í Councils will be brought into being only with our permission and only in countries where conditions make this step necessary. Nevertheless, we find it desirable to inform all National Spiritual Assemblies of the nature of this historic development, and to make clear its place in the evolution of national and local Bahá'í institutions.

The institutions of the Administrative Order of Bahá'u'lláh, rooted in the provisions of His Revelation, have emerged gradually and organically, as the Bahá'í community has grown through the power of the divine impulse imparted to humankind in this age. The characteristics and functions of each of these institutions have evolved, and are still evolving, as are the relationships between them. The writings of the beloved Guardian expound the fundamental elements of this mighty System and make it clear that the Administrative Order, although different in many ways from the World Order which it is the destiny of the Bahá'í Revelation to call into being, is both the "nucleus" and "pattern" of that World Order. Thus, the evolution of the institutions of the Administrative Order, while following many variants to meet changing conditions in different times and places, should strictly follow the essential principles of Bahá'í administration which have been laid down in the Sacred Text and in the interpretations provided by 'Abdu'l-Bahá and the Guardian.

One of the subtle qualities of the Bahá'í Administrative Order is the balance between centralization and decentralization. This balance must be correctly maintained, but different factors enter into the equation, depending upon the institutions involved. For example, the relationship between a National or Local Spiritual Assembly and its committees is of a different nature from that between National and Local Spiritual Assemblies. The former is a relationship between a central administrative body and "its assisting organs of executive and legislative action",[85] while the latter is a relationship between national and local levels of the House of Justice, each of which is a divinely ordained institution with clearly prescribed jurisdiction, duties and prerogatives.

Regional Bahá'í Councils partake of some, but not all, characteristics of Spiritual Assemblies, and thus provide a means of carrying forward the teaching work and administering related affairs of a rapidly growing Bahá'í community in a number of situations. Without such an institution, the development of a national committee structure required to cover the needs in some countries would run the danger of over-complexity through adding a further layer of committees under the regional committees, or the danger of excessive decentralization through conferring too much autonomy on committees which are characterized by the Guardian as "bodies that should be regarded in no other light than that of expert advisers and executive assistants."

The distinguishing effects of the establishment of Regional Bahá'í Councils are the following:
- It provides for a level of autonomous decision making on both teaching and administrative matters, as distinct from merely executive action, below the National Assembly and above the Local Assemblies.
- It involves the members of Local Spiritual Assemblies of the area in the choice of the members of the Council, thus reinforcing the bond between it and the local believers while, at the same time, bringing into public service capable believers who are known to the friends in their own region.
- It establishes direct consultative relationships between the Continental Counsellors and the Regional Bahá'í Councils.
- It offers the possibility of forming a Regional Bahá'í Council in an ethnically distinct region which covers parts of two or more countries. In such a situation the Council is designated to work directly under one of the National Assemblies involved, providing copies of its reports and minutes to the other National Assembly.
- The greater degree of decentralization involved in the devolution of authority upon Regional Bahá'í Councils requires a corresponding increase in the capacity of the National Spiritual Assembly itself to keep fully informed of what is proceeding in all parts of the territory over which it has ultimate jurisdiction.

The Universal House of Justice to all National Spiritual Assemblies, 30 May 1997.

The Local Spiritual Assembly

*T*he Lord hath ordained that in every city a House of Justice be established wherein shall gather counsellors to the number of Bahá[86], and should it exceed this number it does not matter. ... It behoveth them to be the trusted ones of the Merciful among men and to regard themselves as the guardians appointed of God for all that dwell on earth.

Bahá'u'lláh, *The Kitáb-i-Aqdas* (The Most Holy Book), para. 30, p. 29.

---

85   Letter of 18 October, 1927 to the National Spiritual Assembly of the Bahá'ís of the United States and Canada.
86   Nine

*A*ddressing the nations, the Ancient Beauty ordaineth that in every city in the world a house be established in the name of justice wherein shall gather pure and steadfast souls to the number of the Most Great Name. At this meeting they should feel as if they were entering the Presence of God, inasmuch as this binding command hath flowed from the Pen of Him Who is the Ancient of Days. The glances of God are directed towards this Assembly.

> Bahá'u'lláh, *The Compilation of Compilations*, Vol. II (Local Spiritual Assemblies), no. 1356, p. 39.

'*A*bdu'l-Bahá is constantly engaged in ideal communication with any Spiritual Assembly which is instituted through the divine bounty, and the members of which, in the utmost devotion, turn to the divine Kingdom and are firm in the Covenant. To them he is whole-heartedly attached and with them he is linked by everlasting ties.

> 'Abdu'l-Bahá, *Selections from the Writings of 'Abdu'l-Bahá*, no. 46, p. 89.

*T*hese Spiritual Assemblies are aided by the Spirit of God. Their defender is 'Abdu'l-Bahá. Over them He spreadeth His wings. What bounty is there greater than this? These Spiritual Assemblies are shining lamps and heavenly gardens, from which the fragrances of holiness are diffused over all regions, and the lights of knowledge are shed abroad over all created things. From them the spirit of life streameth in every direction. They, indeed, are the potent sources of the progress of man, at all times and under all conditions.

> 'Abdu'l-Bahá, *Selections from the Writings of 'Abdu'l-Bahá*, no. 38, p. 80.

*T*he Spiritual Assembly, in the fulfilment of its obligations and responsibilities under this Corporation, shall have exclusive jurisdiction and authority over all the local activities and affairs of the Bahá'í community of [city, shire, etc.], including paramount authority in the administration of this Corporation. It shall be responsible for maintaining the integrity and accuracy of all Bahá'í teaching, whether written or oral, undertaken throughout the local community. It shall make available the published literature of the Faith. It shall represent the community in its relations to the National Spiritual Assembly, in its relations to the Universal House of Justice, to other local Bahá'í communities, and to the general public in [city, shire, etc.]. It shall be charged with the recognition of all applicants requesting membership in the local Bahá'í community. It shall pass upon the right of any and all members of the community whose membership is in question to retain their status as voting members of the community. It shall call the meetings of the community, including the Bahá'í Anniversaries and Feasts, the Meetings of consultation, and the annual meeting at which the members of the Assembly are elected. It shall appoint and supervise all committees of the Bahá'í community. It shall collect and disburse all funds intended for the maintenance of this Corporation. It shall have full and complete custody of the headquarters or meeting place of the Bahá'í community. It shall have exclusive authority to conduct Bahá'í marriage ceremonies and issue Bahá'í marriage certificates within the area of its jurisdiction. It shall report to the National Spiritual Assembly annually, or when requested, the membership roll of the Bahá'í community, for the information and approval of the National Spiritual Assembly.

> *Declaration of Trust and By-Laws of a National Spiritual Assembly, By-Laws of a Local Spiritual Assembly,*
> By-Laws of a Local Spiritual Assembly, Article 111, pp. 15-16.

𝒜mong the more salient objectives to be attained by the Local Spiritual Assembly in its process of development to full maturity are to act as a loving shepherd to the Bahá'í flock, promote unity and concord among the friends, direct the teaching work, protect the Cause of God, arrange for Feasts, Anniversaries and regular meetings of the community, familiarize the Bahá'ís with its plans, invite the community to offer its recommendations, promote the welfare of youth and children, and participate, as circumstances permit, in humanitarian activities. In its relationship to the individual believer, the Assembly should continuously invite and encourage him to study the Faith, to deliver its glorious message, to live in accordance with its teachings, to contribute freely and regularly to the Fund, to participate in community activities and to seek refuge in the Assembly for advice and help, when needed.

Letter dated 30 July 1972 to the National Spiritual Assembly of Bolivia, *Messages from the Universal House of Justice 1963-1986*, para. 118.4, pp. 223-224.[87]

*I*n its own meetings it must endeavour to develop skill in the difficult but highly rewarding art of Bahá'í consultation, a process which will require great self-discipline on the part of all members and complete reliance on the power of Bahá'u'lláh. It should hold regular meetings and ensure that all its members are currently informed of the activities of the Assembly, that its Secretary carries out his duties, and its Treasurer holds and disburses the funds of the Faith to its satisfaction, keeping proper accounts and issuing receipts for all contributions. Many Assemblies find that some of their activities such as teaching, observance of Feasts and Anniversaries, solution of personal problems, and other duties are best dealt with by committees appointed by the Assembly and responsible to it.

Letter dated 30 July 1972 to the National Spiritual Assembly of Bolivia, *Messages from the Universal House of Justice 1963-1986*, para. 118.5, p. 224.[88]

*I*n all cases submitted for its consideration the Assembly must uphold the standard of justice in delivering its verdict, and in all its dealings with the community and the outside world it must strive to evince the qualities of leadership. The following quotation from a letter of the Guardian summarizes in simple terms the immediate goal every Assembly should set for itself in its efforts to pursue the exalted standard of perfection inculcated in our writings:

"The first quality for leadership both among individuals and Assemblies, is the capacity to use the energy and competence that exists amongst the rank and file of its followers. Otherwise the more competent members of the group will go at a tangent and try to find elsewhere a field of work and where they could use their energy.

"Shoghi Effendi hopes that the Assemblies will do their utmost in planning such teaching activities that every single soul will be kept busy."[89]

Letter dated 30 July 1972 to the National Spiritual Assembly of Bolivia, *Messages from the Universal House of Justice 1963-1986*, paras 118.6-118.6b, p. 224.[90]

---

87   Also *Lights of Guidance*, no. 149, p. 42.
88   Also *Lights of Guidance*, no. 167, p. 47.
89   From letter dated 30 August 1930 written on behalf of the Guardian to the National Spiritual Assembly of the United States and Canada.
90   Also *Lights of Guidance*, no. 118, p. 33.

*I*n the compilation of texts we sent to all National Spiritual Assemblies in August 1970, and in the By-Laws of a Local Spiritual Assembly, you will find all the objectives Local Spiritual Assemblies must aim at achieving in their process of growth and development.

Letter dated 30 July 1972 to the National Spiritual Assembly of Bolivia, *Messages from the Universal House of Justice 1963-1986*, para. 118.7, pp. 224–225.

*T*he evolution of local and national Bahá'í Assemblies at this time calls for a new state of mind on the part of their members as well as on the part of those who elect them, for the Bahá'í community is engaged in an immense historical process that is entering a critical stage. Bahá'u'lláh has given to the world institutions to operate in an Order designed to canalize the forces of a new civilization. Progress towards that glorious realization requires a great and continuous expansion of the Bahá'í community, so that adequate scope is provided for the maturation of these institutions. This is a matter of immediate importance to Bahá'u'lláh's avowed supporters in all lands.

For such an expansion to be stimulated and accommodated, the Spiritual Assemblies must rise to a new stage in the exercise of their responsibilities as channels of divine guidance, planners of the teaching work, developers of human resources, builders of communities, and loving shepherds of the multitudes. They can realize these prospects through increasing the ability of their members to take counsel together in accordance with the principles of the Faith and to consult with the friends under their jurisdiction, through fostering the spirit of service, through spontaneously collaborating with the Continental Counsellors and their auxiliaries, and through cultivating their external relations. Particularly must the progress in the evolution of the institutions be manifest in the multiplication of localities in which the functioning of the Spiritual Assembly enhances the individual believers' capacity to serve the Cause and fosters unified action. In sum, the maturity of the Spiritual Assembly must be measured not only by the regularity of its meetings and the efficiency of its functioning, but also by the continuity of the growth of Bahá'í membership, the effectiveness of the interaction between the Assembly and the members of its community, the quality of the spiritual and social life of the community, and the overall sense of vitality of a community in the process of dynamic, ever-advancing development.

The Universal House of Justice, *Riḍván Message to the Bahá'ís of the World*, BE 153/AD 1996, paras 23–24.

The Bahá'í Funds

*A*nd as the progress and execution of spiritual activities is dependent and conditioned upon material means, it is of absolute necessity that immediately after the establishment of local as well as national Spiritual Assemblies, a Bahá'í Fund be established, to be placed under the exclusive control of the Spiritual Assembly. All donations and contributions should be offered to the Treasurer of the Assembly, for the express purpose of promoting the interests of the Cause, throughout that locality or country. It is the sacred obligation of every conscientious and faithful servant of Bahá'u'lláh who desires to see His Cause advance, to contribute freely and generously for the increase of that Fund. The members of the Spiritual Assembly will at their own discretion expend it to promote the Teaching Campaign, to help the needy, to establish educational Bahá'í institutions, to extend in every way possible their sphere of service.

Shoghi Effendi, *Bahá'í Administration*, pp. 41-42. (12 March 1923.)

... *T*he Guardian would advise your Assembly to continue impressing upon the believers the necessity of their contributing regularly to the national fund, irrespective of whether there is an emergency to be met or not. Nothing short of a continuous flow of contributions to that fund can, indeed, ensure the financial stability upon which so much of the progress of the institutions of the Faith must now inevitably depend.

Letter dated 29 July 1935 written on behalf of Shoghi Effendi, *The Compilation of Compilations*, Vol. I (Funds), no. 1230, p. 538.

*A*s the activities of the American Bahá'í community expand, and its world-wide prestige correspondingly increases, the institution of the national Fund, the bedrock on which all other institutions must necessarily rest and be established, acquires added importance, and should be increasingly supported by the entire body of the believers, both in their individual capacities, and through their collective efforts, whether organized as groups or as Local Assemblies. The supply of funds, in support of the national Treasury, constitutes, at the present time, the life-blood of these nascent institutions which you are labouring to erect. Its importance cannot surely be overestimated. Untold blessings shall no doubt crown every effort directed to that end. I am eagerly and prayerfully awaiting the news of an unprecedented expansion in so vital an organ of the Administrative Order of our Faith.

Appended by to the letter dated 29 July 1935 by Shoghi Effendi, *The Compilation of Compilations*, Vol. I (Funds), no. 1231, pp. 538-539.

*R*egarding your question about contributions: it is up to the individual to decide; if he wishes to denote a sum to a specific purpose, he is free to do so; but the friends should recognize the fact that too much labelling of contributions will tie the hands of the Assembly and prevent it from meeting its many obligations in various fields of Bahá'í activity.

Letter dated 23 June 1950 written on behalf of Shoghi Effendi, *Messages to Canada*, p. 15.

The Spirit of Giving

*Y*ou asked concerning some plans whereby funds could be gathered for the Temple. Shoghi Effendi believes that the best and noblest method is to have free donations that are made spontaneously and with the sense of making some sacrifice in furthering the Cause. It is with sacrifice that this Temple is to be built. That is the truly worthy method.

Letter dated 14 April 1932 written on behalf of Shoghi Effendi, *The Compilation of Compilations*, Vol. I (Funds), no. 1225, p. 536.

... *I* feel urged to remind you of the necessity of ever bearing in mind the cardinal principle that all contributions to the Fund are to be purely and strictly voluntary in character. It should be made clear and evident to every one that any form of compulsion, however slight and indirect, strikes at the very root of the principle underlying the formation of the Fund ever since its inception.

Shoghi Effendi, Directives from the Guardian, no. 42, p. 15.

We must be like the fountain or spring that is continually emptying itself of all that it has and is continually being refilled from an invisible source. To be continually giving out for the good of our fellows undeterred by the fear of poverty and reliant on the unfailing bounty of the Source of all wealth and all good—that is the secret of right living.

Letter written on behalf of Shoghi Effendi, Directives from the Guardian, no. 83, p. 32.

Only Bahá'ís May Contribute

He wishes me to stress again that under no circumstances the believers should accept any financial help from non-Bahá'ís for use in connection with specific administrative activities of the Faith such as the Temple construction fund, and other local or national Bahá'í administrative funds. The reason for this is two-fold: First because the Institutions which the Bahá'ís are gradually building are in the nature of gifts from Bahá'u'lláh to the world; and secondly the acceptance of funds from non-believers for specific Bahá'í use would, sooner or later, involve the Bahá'ís into unforeseen complications and difficulties with others, and thus cause incalculable harm to the body of the Cause.

Letter dated 14 April 1934 written on behalf of Shoghi Effendi, The Compilation of Compilations, Vol. I (Funds), no. 1259, p. 548.

Ḥuqúqu'lláh

*S*hould a person acquire one hundred mithqáls of gold, nineteen mithqáls thereof belong unto God, the Creator of earth and heaven. Take heed, O people, lest ye deprive yourselves of this great bounty. We have prescribed this law unto you while We are wholly independent of you and of all that are in the heavens and on the earth. Indeed there lie concealed in this command, mysteries and benefits which are beyond the comprehension of anyone save God, the All-Knowing, the All-Informed. Say, through this injunction God desireth to purify your possessions and enable you to draw nigh unto such stations as none can attain, except those whom God may please. Verily, He is the Generous, the Gracious, the Bountiful.

O people! Act not treacherously in the matter of Ḥuqúqu'lláh and dispose not of it, except by his leave. Thus hath it been ordained in His Epistles as well as in this glorious Tablet.

Whoso dealeth dishonestly with God will in justice be exposed, and whoso fulfilleth the things he hath been commanded, divine blessings will descend upon him from the heaven of the bounty of his Lord, the Bestower, the Bountiful, the Most Generous, the

Ancient of Days. Verily, He desireth for you the things that are inscrutable to you at present, though the people themselves will readily discover them when their souls take their flight and the trappings of their earthly gaieties are rolled up. Thus warneth you the Author of the Preserved tablet.

<blockquote>Bahá'u'lláh, The Compilation of Compilations, Vol. I (Ḥuqúqu'lláh), no. 1108, pp. 491–492.[91]</blockquote>

To discharge one's obligations is highly praiseworthy in the sight of God. However, it is not permitted to solicit Huqúq from anyone. Beseech ye the one true God to enable His loved ones to offer that which is the Right of God, inasmuch as the observance of this injunction would cause one's possessions to be purified and protected and would become the means of attracting goodly gifts and heavenly blessings.

<blockquote>Bahá'u'lláh, The Compilation of Compilations, Vol. I (Ḥuqúqu'lláh), no. 1144, p. 504.</blockquote>

Ḥuqúqu'lláh is indeed a great law. It is incumbent upon all to make this offering, because it is the source of grace, abundance, and of all good. It is a bounty which shall remain with every soul in every world of the worlds of God, the All-Possessing, the All-Bountiful.

<blockquote>Bahá'u'lláh, The Compilation of Compilations, Vol. I (Ḥuqúqu'lláh), no. 1105, p. 490.[92]</blockquote>

The benefits accruing from benevolent works shall fall to the individuals concerned. In such matters only a word would suffice. Should anyone offer Huqúq with utmost joy and radiance, manifesting a spirit of resignation and content, his offering shall be acceptable before God, otherwise He can dispense with all the peoples of the earth ... Well is it with them that have fulfilled that which is prescribed in the Book of God. It is incumbent upon everyone to observe that which God hath purposed, for whatsoever hath been set forth in the Book by the Pen of Glory is an effective means for the purging, the purification and sanctification of the souls of men and a source of prosperity and blessing. Happy are they that have observed His commandments.

<blockquote>Bahá'u'lláh, The Compilation of Compilations, Vol. I (Ḥuqúqu'lláh), no. 1138, p. 502.</blockquote>

It is clear and evident that the payment of the Right of God is conducive to prosperity, to blessing, and to honour and divine protection.

<blockquote>Bahá'u'lláh, The Compilation of Compilations, Vol. I (Ḥuqúqu'lláh), no. 1104, p. 490.[93]</blockquote>

For a number of years Huqúq was not accepted. How numerous the offerings that on reaching Our presence were returned to the donors, because they were not needed then. However in recent years We have, in view of the exigencies of the times, accepted the payment of the Huqúq, but have forbidden solicitation thereof. Everyone must have the utmost regard for the dignity of the Word of God and for the exaltation of His Cause. Were a person to offer all the treasures of the earth at the cost of debasing the honour

---

[91] Also <i>Lights of Guidance</i>, no. 1035, p. 306.
[92] Also <i>Lights of Guidance</i>, no. 1032, p. 305.
[93] Also <i>Lights of Guidance</i>, no. 1031, p. 305.

of the Cause of God, were it even less than a grain of mustard, such an offering would not be permissible. All the world hath belonged and will always belong to God. If one spontaneously offereth Huqúq with the utmost joy and radiance it will be acceptable, and not otherwise. The benefit of such deeds reverteth unto the individuals themselves. This measure hath been ordained in view of the necessity for material means, for "averse is God from putting aught into effect through its means." Thus instructions were given to receive the Huqúq.

Bahá'u'lláh, The Compilation of Compilations, Vol. I (Ḥuqúqu'lláh), no. 1125, pp. 497-498.

O my heavenly friends! It is certain and evident that the Incomparable One is always praised for His absolute wealth, distinguished for His all-embracing mercy, characterized by His eternal grace, and known for His gifts to the world of existence. Nonetheless, in accordance with His inscrutable wisdom and in order to apply a unique test to distinguish the friend from the stranger, He hath enjoined the Huqúq upon His servants and made it obligatory.

Those who have observed this weighty ordinance have received heavenly blessings and in both worlds their faces shone radiantly and their nostrils perfumed by the sweet savours of God's tender mercy. One of the tokens of His consummate wisdom is that the payment of the Huqúq will enable the donors to become firm and steadfast and will exert a great influence on their hearts and souls. Furthermore the Huqúq will be used for charitable purposes.

'Abdu'l-Bahá, The Compilation of Compilations, Vol. I (Ḥuqúqu'lláh), no. 1160, pp. 510-511.

*T*he Blessed Beauty—may my life be offered up for His Dust—hath emphasized through His decisive Word that the utmost honesty hath to be observed in matters related to the Huqúq. The institution of Huqúq is sacred.

'Abdu'l-Bahá, The Compilation of Compilations, Vol. I (Ḥuqúqu'lláh), no. 1170, p. 513.

*R*egarding the Ḥuqúqu'lláh ... this is applied to one's merchandise, property and income. After deducting the necessary expenses, whatever is left as profit, and is an addition to one's capital, such a sum is subject to Huqúq. When one has paid Huqúq once on a particular sum, that sum is no longer subject to Huqúq, unless it should pass from one person to another. One's residence, and the household furnishings are exempt from Huqúq ... Ḥuqúqu'lláh is paid to the Centre of the Cause.

Letter dated 4 April-3 May 1927 written on behalf of Shoghi Effendi, The Compilation of Compilations, Vol. I (Ḥuqúqu'lláh), no. 1178, p. 515.

*I*t is clear from the Writings that a person is exempt from paying Ḥuqúqu'lláh on his residence and such household and professional equipment as are needful. It is left to the discretion of the individual to decide which items are necessary and which are not. It is obvious that the friends should not spend lavishly on residences and furnishings and rationalize on these expenditures in their desire to avoid payment of Ḥuqúqu'lláh. No specific text has been found exempting capital used to earn income. The Universal House of Justice leaves such matters to the consciences of the individual believers.

The Universal House of Justice, *The Compilation of Compilations*, Vol. I (Ḥuqúqu'lláh), no. 1204, p. 524.
(9 April 1980.)

... many details in the computation of Ḥuqúqu'lláh have been left by Bahá'u'lláh to the judgement and conscience of the individual believer. For example, He exempts such household equipment and furnishings as are needful, but He leaves it to the individual to decide which items are necessary and which are not. Contributions to the funds of the Faith cannot be considered as part of one's payment of Ḥuqúqu'lláh; moreover, if one owes Ḥuqúqu'lláh and cannot afford to both pay it and to make contributions to the Fund, the payment of Ḥuqúqu'lláh should take priority over making contributions. But as to whether contributions to the Fund may be treated as expenses in calculating the amount of one's assets on which Ḥuqúqu'lláh is payable; this is left to the judgement of each individual in the light of his own circumstances.

The Guardian's secretary wrote on his behalf that "one mithqál consists of nineteen nákhuds. The weight of twenty-four nákhuds equals four and three-fifths grammes. Calculations may be made on this basis". Nineteen mithqáls therefore equal 69.191667 grammes. One troy ounce equals 31.103486 grammes, thus 19 mithqáls equal 2.224563 oz. At the current rate of $339.10 per ounce, 19 mithqáls of gold would amount to $754.35. Thus on a savings of $754.35 an amount of $143.33 (i.e. 19%) would be payable as Ḥuqúqu'lláh.

The Universal House of Justice, *The Compilation of Compilations*, Vol. I (Ḥuqúqu'lláh), no. 1203, pp. 523-524. (16 September 1979.)

*T*he House of Justice further points out that however weighty are the obligations resting upon the believers to pay the Ḥuqúqu'lláh and to support other funds of the Faith, these are spiritual obligations which are to be fulfilled voluntarily, and under no circumstances may contributions to any of these funds, even the Ḥuqúqu'lláh, be demanded or solicited from individual believers. Appeals and exhortations must always be made to the generality of the friends, not to individuals.

The Universal House of Justice, *The Compilation of Compilations*, Vol. I (Ḥuqúqu'lláh), no. 1205, p. 524.
(7 May 1980.)

Bahá'í Elections

*I*n order to preserve the spiritual character and purpose of Bahá'í elections the practices of nomination or electioneering, or any other procedure or activity detrimental to that character and purpose shall be eschewed. A silent and prayerful atmosphere shall prevail during the election so that each elector may vote for none but those whom prayer and reflection inspire him to uphold.

1. All Bahá'í elections, except elections of officers of Local and National Spiritual Assemblies and committees, shall be by plurality vote taken by secret ballot.

2. Election of the officers of a Spiritual Assembly or committee shall be by majority vote of the Assembly or committee taken by secret ballot.
3. In case by reason of a tie vote or votes the full membership of an elected body is not determined on the first ballot, then one or more additional ballots shall be taken on the persons tied until all members are elected.
4. The duties and rights of a Bahá'í elector may not be assigned nor may they be exercised by proxy.

The Constitution of The Universal House of Justice, By-Laws, Section VI, p. 14.

*I*n order to be eligible to vote and hold elective office, a Bahá'í must have attained the age of twenty-one years.

The Constitution of The Universal House of Justice, By-Laws, Section I (1), p. 8.

*O*n the election day, the friends must wholeheartedly participate in the elections, in unity and amity, turning their hearts to God, detached from all things but Him, seeking His guidance and supplicating His aid and bounty.

Shoghi Effendi, *The Compilation of Compilations*, Vol. I (The Spiritual Character of Bahá'í Elections), no. 706, p. 315. (27 February 1923.)

... *I* earnestly appeal to every one of you ... to make ... yet another effort, this time more spontaneous and selfless than before, and endeavour to approach your task ... with that purity of spirit that can alone obtain our Beloved's most cherished desire. Let us recall His explicit and often repeated assurances that every Assembly elected in that rarefied atmosphere of selflessness and detachment is in truth appointed of God ....

Shoghi Effendi, *The Compilation of Compilations*, Vol. I (The Spiritual Character of Bahá'í Elections), no. 707, p. 315. (23 February 1924.)[94]

*I*f we but turn our gaze to the high qualifications of the members of Bahá'í Assemblies, ... we are filled with feelings of unworthiness and dismay, and would feel truly disheartened but for the comforting thought that if we rise to play nobly our part every deficiency in our lives will be more than compensated by the all-conquering spirit of His grace and power. Hence it is incumbent upon the chosen delegates to consider without the least trace of passion and prejudice, and irrespective of any material consideration, the names of only those who can best combine the necessary qualities of unquestioned loyalty, of selfless devotion, of a well-trained mind, of recognized ability and mature experience.

Shoghi Effendi, *The Compilation of Compilations*, Vol. I (The Spiritual Character of Bahá'í Elections), no. 708, pp. 315-316; Vol II (The Local Spiritual Assembly), no. 1363, p. 42; and Vol. II (The National Spiritual Assembly), no. 1436, p. 88. (3 June 1925.)[95]

---

[94] Also *Bahá'í Administration*, p. 65.
[95] Also *Bahá'í Administration*, p. 88.

I feel that reference to personalities before the election would give rise to misunderstanding and differences. What the friends should do is to get thoroughly acquainted with one another, to exchange views, to mix freely and discuss among themselves the requirements and qualifications for such a membership without reference or application, however indirect, to particular individuals. We should refrain from influencing the opinion of others, of canvassing for any particular individual, but should stress the necessity of getting fully acquainted with the qualifications of membership referred to in our Beloved's Tablets and of learning more about one another through direct, personal experience rather than through the reports and opinions of our friends.

> Shoghi Effendi, *Directives from the Guardian*, no. 60, p. 23. (14 May 1927.)[96]

*T*he strength and progress of the Bahá'í community depend upon the election of pure, faithful and active souls ... Canvassing is deprecated ....

> Letter dated 9 April 1932 written on behalf of Shoghi Effendi, *The Compilation of Compilations*, Vol. I (The Spiritual Character of Bahá'í Elections), no. 715, p. 317.

*T*he electors ... must prayerfully and devotedly and after meditation and reflection elect faithful, sincere, experienced, capable and competent souls who are worthy of membership ....

> Letter dated 1 July 1943 written on behalf of Shoghi Effendi, *The Compilation of Compilations*, Vol. I (The Spiritual Character of Bahá'í Elections), no. 716, p. 317.

Bahá'í Consultation and Decision Making

*C*onsultation He (Bahá'u'lláh) establishes as one of the fundamental principles of His Faith, describes it as "the lamp of guidance," as "the bestower of understanding," and as one of the two "luminaries" of the "heaven of Divine wisdom."

> Shoghi Effendi, *God Passes By*, p. 218.

*T*he prime requisites for them that take counsel together are purity of motive, radiance of spirit, detachment from all else save God, attraction to His Divine Fragrances, humility and lowliness amongst His loved ones, patience and long-suffering in difficulties and servitude to His exalted Threshold.

> 'Abdu'l-Bahá, *Selections from the Writings of 'Abdu'l-Bahá*, no. 43, p. 87.

---

[96] Also *The Compilation of Compilations*, Vol. I (The Spiritual Character of Bahá'í Elections), no. 709, p. 316; and Vol. II (The Local Spiritual Assembly), no. 1365, p. 43.

How to Consult

With love and unity

The first condition is absolute love and harmony amongst the members of the assembly. They must be wholly free from estrangement and must manifest in themselves the Unity of God .... Should harmony of thought and absolute unity be non-existent, that gathering shall be dispersed and that Assembly be brought to naught.

'Abdu'l-Bahá, *Selections from the Writings of 'Abdu'l-Bahá*, no. 45, pp. 87-88.

Seek Divine guidance

The second condition is that ... They must, when coming together, turn their faces to the on High and ask aid from the Realm of Glory.

'Abdu'l-Bahá, *Selections from the Writings of 'Abdu'l-Bahá*, no. 45, pp. 87-88.

With frankness and courtesy

They must then proceed with the utmost devotion, courtesy, dignity, care, and moderation to express their views. ... The honoured members must with all freedom express their own thoughts, and it is in no wise permissible for one to belittle the thought of another, nay, he must with moderation set forth the truth ....

'Abdu'l-Bahá, *Selections from the Writings of 'Abdu'l-Bahá*, no. 45, pp. 87-88.

Not feeling hurt

Should any one oppose, he must on no account feel hurt for not until matters are fully discussed can the right way be revealed. The shining spark of truth cometh forth only after the clash of differing opinions.

'Abdu'l-Bahá, *Selections from the Writings of 'Abdu'l-Bahá*, no. 44, p. 87.

Seek out the truth

They must in every matter search out the truth and not insist upon their own opinion, for stubbornness and persistence in one's views will lead ultimately to discord and wrangling and the truth will remain hidden.

'Abdu'l-Bahá, *Selections from the Writings of 'Abdu'l-Bahá*, no. 45, p. 88.

Consult the Writings

...Refer to the Holy Writ when differences arise.

The Universal House of Justice, added to: Bahá'u'lláh, *The Kitáb-i-Aqdas* (The Most Holy Book), Synopsis Codification, IV.D.3.g, p. 160.

The reconciliation of opposites

Nothing short of the spirit of a true Bahá'í can hope to reconcile the principles of mercy and justice, of freedom and submission, of the sanctity of the right of the individual and of self-surrender, of vigilance, discretion and prudence on the one hand, and fellowship, candour, and courage on the other.

Shoghi Effendi, *Bahá'í Administration*, pp. 63-64.

Making Decisions

The ideal of Bahá'í consultation is to arrive at a unanimous decision. When this is not possible a vote must be taken. In the words of the beloved Guardian: "... when they are called upon to arrive at a certain decision, they should, after dispassionate, anxious, and cordial consultation, turn to God in prayer, and with earnestness and conviction and courage record their vote and abide by the voice of the majority, which we are told by the Master to be the voice of truth, never to be challenged, and always to be whole-heartedly enforced."

As soon as a decision is reached it becomes the decision of the whole Assembly, not merely of those members who happened to be among the majority.

When it is proposed to put a matter to the vote, a member of the Assembly may feel that there are additional facts or views which must be sought before he can make up his mind and intelligently vote on the proposition. He should express this feeling to the Assembly, and it is for the Assembly to decide whether or not further consultation is needed before voting.

Whenever it is decided to vote on a proposition all that is required is to ascertain how many of the members are in favour of it; if this is a majority of those present, the motion is carried; if it is a minority the motion is defeated. Thus the whole question of "abstaining" does not arise in Bahá'í voting. A member who does not vote in favour of a proposition is, in effect, voting against it, even if at that moment he himself feels that he has been unable to make up his mind on the matter.

Messages from the Universal House of Justice 1963-1986, paras 79.3-79.6, pp. 167-168. (6 March 1970.)

Carrying out Decisions

It is again not permitted that any one of the honoured members object to or censure, whether in or out of the meeting, any decision arrived at previously, though that decision be not right, for such criticism would prevent any decision from being enforced.

'Abdu'l-Bahá, *Selections from the Writings of 'Abdu'l-Bahá*, no. 45, p. 88.

But once the opinion of the majority has been ascertained, all the members should automatically and unreservedly obey it, and faithfully carry it out.

Letter dated 18 April 1939 written on behalf of Shoghi Effendi to an individual believer, *The Compilation of Compilations*, Vol. I (Consultation), no. 198, pp. 104-105.

*I*n short, whatsoever thing is arranged in harmony and with love and purity of motive, its result is light, and should the least trace of estrangement prevail the result shall be darkness upon darkness ....

'Abdu'l-Bahá, *Selections from the Writings of 'Abdu'l-Bahá*, no. 45, p. 88.[97]

*S*o strong is the emphasis on unity that, for example, once a decision has been made by an Assembly, everyone is expected to support that decision wholeheartedly, relying confidently on 'Abdu'l-Bahá's assurance that, even if the decision is wrong, "as it is in unity the truth will be revealed and the wrong made right". This principle of unity is supplemented by other, related guidelines covering such issues as how criticism can be expressed, how the wrongdoing of members of the community is to be corrected, how the principle of justice is to be applied and appeals admitted, and how the integrity of individuals, the institutions and the Cause is to be upheld.

Letter dated 2 July 1996 written on behalf of the Universal House of Justice, *Rights and Responsibilities*, p. 51.

*T*he functioning of one's conscience, then, depends upon one's understanding of right and wrong; the conscience of one person may be established upon a disinterested striving after truth and justice, while that of another may rest on an unthinking predisposition to act in accordance with that pattern of standards, principles and prohibitions which is a product of his social environment. Conscience, therefore, can serve either as a bulwark of an upright character or can represent an accumulation of prejudices learned from one's forebears or absorbed from a limited social code.

A Bahá'í recognizes that one aspect of his spiritual and intellectual growth is to foster the development of his conscience in the light of divine Revelation—a Revelation which, in addition to providing a wealth of spiritual and ethical principles, exhorts man "to free himself from idle fancy and imitation, discern with the eye of oneness His glorious handiwork, and look into all things with a searching eye." This process of development, therefore, involves a clear-sighted examination of the conditions of the world with both heart and mind. A Bahá'í will understand that an upright life is based upon observance of certain principles which stem from Divine Revelation and which he recognizes as essential for the well-being of both the individual and society. In order to uphold such principles, he knows that, in certain cases, the voluntary submission of the promptings of his own personal conscience to the decision of the majority is a conscientious requirement, as in wholeheartedly accepting the majority decision of an Assembly at the outcome of consultation.

Letter dated 8 February 1998 written on behalf of the Universal House of Justice, *Issues Related to the Study of the Bahá'í Faith*, p. 40.

---

97   Also cited by Shoghi Effendi, *Unfolding Destiny*, p. 7.

Appeals and Criticism

*A*ppeal can be made from the Local Assembly's decision to the National Assembly, and from the National Assembly's decision to the Guardian. But the principle of authority invested in our elected bodies must be upheld. This is not something which can be learned without trial and test.

> Letter dated 30 June 1949 written on behalf of Shoghi Effendi, *Light of Divine Guidance*, Vol. I, p. 151.[98]

*T*he Guardian believes that a great deal of the difficulties from which the believers ... feel themselves to be suffering are caused by their neither correctly understanding nor putting into practice the administration. They seem—many of them—to be prone to continually challenging and criticizing the decisions of their Assemblies. If the Bahá'ís undermine the very bodies which are, however immaturely, seeking to co-ordinate Bahá'í activities and administer Bahá'í affairs, if they continually criticize their acts and challenge or belittle their decisions, they not only prevent any real rapid progress in the Faith's development from taking place, but they repel outsiders who quite rightly may ask how we ever expect to unite the whole world when we are so disunited among ourselves!

There is only one remedy for this: to study the administration, to obey the Assemblies, and each believer seek to perfect his own character as a Bahá'í. We can never exert the influence over others which we can exert over ourselves. If we are better, if we show love, patience, and understanding of the weaknesses of others; if we seek to never criticize but rather encourage, others will do likewise, and we can really help the Cause through our example and spiritual strength. The Bahá'ís everywhere, when the administration is first established, find it very difficult to adjust themselves. They have to learn to obey, even when the Assembly may be wrong, for the sake of unity. They have to sacrifice their personalities, to a certain extent, in order that the community life may grow and develop as a whole. These things are difficult—but we must realize that they will lead us to a very much greater, more perfect, way of life when the Faith is properly established according to the administration.

> Letter dated 26 October 1943 written on behalf of Shoghi Effendi, *The Compilation of Compilations*, Vol. II (The National Spiritual Assembly), no. 1469, pp. 111-112.

- *B*ahá'ís are "fully entitled to address criticisms to their Assemblies" and offer their recommendations. When Bahá'ís have addressed their criticisms, suggestions and advice to their Assemblies, including their views "about policies or individual members of elected bodies", they must "whole-heartedly accept the advice or decision of the Assembly".

- There is a clear distinction between, on the one hand, the prohibition of backbiting, which would include adverse comments about individuals or institutions made to

---

[98] Also *Lights of Guidance*, no. 282, p. 81; and *The Compilation of Compilations*, Vol. II (The National Spiritual Assembly), no. 1511, p. 131.

other individuals privately or publicly, and, on the other hand, the encouragement to unburden oneself of one's concerns to a Spiritual Assembly, Local or National (or now, also, to confide in a Counsellor or Auxiliary Board member). Thus, although one of the principal functions of the Nineteen Day Feast is to provide a forum for "open and constructive criticism and deliberation regarding the state of affairs within the local Bahá'í community", complaints about the actions of an individual member of an Assembly should be made directly and confidentially to the Assembly itself, not made to other individuals or even raised at a Nineteen Day Feast.

- While constructive criticism is encouraged, destructive criticism, such as the pattern of "continually challenging and criticizing the decisions" of the Assemblies, prevents the rapid growth of the Faith and repels those who are yet outside the community. Indeed "all criticisms and discussions of a negative character which may result in undermining the authority of the Assembly as a body should be strictly avoided. For otherwise the order of the Cause itself will be endangered, and confusion and discord will reign in the community." "Vicious criticism is indeed a calamity", the root of which is "lack of faith in the system of Bahá'u'lláh" and failure to follow the "Bahá'í laws in voting, in electing, in serving, and in abiding by Assembly decisions".

The questions of how criticism is expressed and acted upon in the Bahá'í community, and how the Spiritual Assemblies administer justice in regard to individual believers, are but elements of far greater concepts and should become second nature in the social discourse of Bahá'ís. The Bahá'í community is an association of individuals who have voluntarily come together, on recognizing Bahá'u'lláh's claim to be the Manifestation of God for this age, to establish certain patterns of personal and social behaviour and to build the institutions that are to promote these patterns. There are numerous individuals who share the ideals of the Faith and draw inspiration from its Teachings, while disagreeing with certain of its features, but those who actually enter the Bahá'í community have accepted, by their own free will, to follow the Teachings in their entirety, understanding that, if doubts and disagreements arise in the process of translating the Teachings into practice, the final arbiter is, by the explicit authority of the Revealed Text, the Universal House of Justice.

It is the ardent prayer of the Universal House of Justice that any friends who find themselves at odds in this endeavour will have confidence in the guidance it provides for them, will renew their study of the Teachings and, for the sake of Bahá'u'lláh, strengthen their love for one another. As the beloved Guardian's secretary wrote on his behalf to an individual believer on 25 October 1949: "Without the spirit of real love for Bahá'u'lláh, for His Faith and its Institutions, and the believers for each other, the Cause can never really bring in large numbers of people. For it is not preaching and rules the world wants, but love and action." The world-wide undertakings on which the Cause of God is embarked are far too significant, the need of the peoples of the world for the Message of Bahá'u'lláh far too urgent, the perils facing mankind far too grave, the progress of events far too swift, to permit His followers to squander their time and efforts in fruitless contention. Now, if ever, is the time for love among the friends, for unity of understanding and endeavour, for self-sacrifice and service by Bahá'ís in every part of the world.

> Letter dated 2 July 1996 written on behalf of the Universal House of Justice, *Issues Related to the Study of the Bahá'í Faith*, pp. 26-28.

Re-visioning Relationships: The Administrative Institutions and the Community

The great emphasis on the distinctiveness of the Order of Bahá'u'lláh is not meant to belittle existing systems of government. Indeed, they are to be recognized as the fruit of a vast period of social evolution, representing an advanced stage in the development of social organization. What motivates us is the knowledge that the supreme mission of the Revelation of Bahá'u'lláh, the Bearer of that Order, is, as Shoghi Effendi pointed out, "none other but the achievement of this organic and spiritual unity of the whole body of nations," indicating the "coming of age of the entire human race." The astounding implication of this is the near prospect of attaining an age-old hope, now made possible at last by the coming of Bahá'u'lláh. In practical terms, His mission signals the advent of "an organic change in the structure of present-day society, a change such as the world has not yet experienced." It is a fresh manifestation of the direct involvement of God in history, a reassurance that His children have not been left to drift, a sign of the outpouring of a heavenly grace that will enable all humanity to be free at last from conflict and contention to ascend the heights of world peace and divine civilization. Beyond all else, it is a demonstration of that love for His children, which He knew in the depth of His "immemorial being" and in the "ancient eternity" of His Essence, and which caused Him to create us all. In the noblest sense, then, attention to the requirements of His World Order is a reciprocation of that love.

> The Universal House of Justice, *Rights and Responsibilities*, pp. 6-7. (29 December 1988.)

The aggressiveness and competitiveness which animate a dominantly capitalistic culture; the partisanship inherent in a fervidly democratic system; the suspicion of public-policy institutions and the scepticism towards established authority ingrained in the political attitude of the people and which trace their origins to the genesis of American society; the cynical disregard of the moderating principles and rules of civilized human relationships resulting from an excessive liberalism and its immoral consequences—such unsavoury characteristics inform entrenched habits of American life, which imperceptibly at first but more obviously in the long run have come to exert too great a sway over the manner of management of the Bahá'í community and over the behaviour of portions of its rank and file in relation to the Cause. This unwholesome influence must be arrested by immediate, deliberate effort—an effort which must surely begin within your Assembly itself. Further accommodation of it will severely impede the progress of your community, despite the abundant possibilities of an imminent breakthrough. It was due to this concern in particular that we welcomed your request for a meeting with us.

The guarantee of well-being and success in all your endeavours to serve the Cause of God can be stated in one word: unity. It is the alpha and omega of all Bahá'í objectives. Among the first admonitions addressed to National Spiritual Assemblies by Shoghi Effendi was the following assertion: "It is, I firmly believe, of the utmost urgent importance that, with unity of purpose and action firmly established in our midst, and with every trace of animosity and mistrust of the past banished from their hearts, we should form one united front, and combat, wisely and tactfully, every force that might darken the spirit of the Movement, cause division in its ranks, and narrow it by dogmatic and sectarian belief." He then stated that "it is primarily upon the elected members of the National Spiritual Assemblies throughout the Bahá'í world that this highly important duty devolves", warning that, "should such a representative and responsible body fail to realize this fundamental requisite for all successful achievement, the whole structure is sure to crumble".

Unity within the Assembly itself is, of course, of immediate importance to the wider unity your actions are intended to foster and sustain. At no time can any member of your Assembly afford to be unmindful of this basic requirement nor neglect to work towards upholding it. Of particular relevance is the attitude that the members adopt towards their membership on that exalted body. There needs to be a recognition on their part of the Assembly's spiritual character and a feeling in their hearts of respect for the institution based upon a perception of it as something beyond or apart from themselves, as a sacred entity whose powers they have the privilege to engage and canalize by coming together in harmony and acting in accordance with divinely revealed principles. With such a perspective the members will be able better to acquire an appropriate posture in relation to the Assembly itself, to appreciate their role as Trustees of the Merciful and to counteract any impression that they have assumed ownership and control of the institution in the manner of major stockholders of a business enterprise.

Also relevant to effecting unity is the attitude of the friends, whether serving on any Assembly or not, towards the exercise of authority in the Bahá'í community. People generally tend to be suspicious of those in authority. The reason is not difficult to understand, since human history is replete with examples of the disastrous misuse of authority and power. A reversal of this tendency is not easily achievable, but the Bahá'í friends must be freed of suspicion towards their institutions if the wheels of progress are to turn with uninterrupted speed. A rigorous discipline of thought and action on the part of both the friends and the National Assembly will succeed in meeting this challenge; both must live up to their responsibilities in this regard by recognizing some fundamental realities.

The oneness of humanity, which is the primary principle and ultimate goal of the Cause of Bahá'u'lláh, implies, as Shoghi Effendi said, an "organic change in the structure of present-day society". So fundamental a change in the structural conception of society must imply a new pattern for the administration of community affairs in a Bahá'í context. The insights offered by the beloved Guardian, as conveyed by his secretary in a letter dated 14 October 1941, shed light on this critical subject:

> The friends must never mistake the Bahá'í administration for an end in itself. It is merely the instrument of the spirit of the Faith. This Cause is a Cause which God has revealed to humanity as a whole. It is designed to benefit the entire human race, and the only way it can do this is to reform the community life of mankind, as well as seeking to regenerate the individual. The Bahá'í Administration is only the first shaping of what in future will come to be the social life and laws of community living.

Shoghi Effendi's advice to an individual in another instance provides a further perspective: "He urges you to do all you can to promote unity and love amongst the members of the Community there, as this seems to be their greatest need. So often young communities, in their desire to administer the Cause, lose sight of the fact that these spiritual relationships are far more important and fundamental than the rules and regulations which must govern the conduct of community affairs."

It can therefore be deduced that the importance of the Bahá'í administration is its value in serving as a facilitator of the emergence and maintenance of community life in a wholly new mode, and in catering to the requirements of the spiritual relationships which flow from love and unity among the friends. This touches upon a distinguishing characteristic of Bahá'í life which such spiritual relationships foster, namely, the spirit of servitude to God, expressed in service to the Cause, to the friends and to humanity as a whole. The attitude of the individual as a servant, an attitude pre-eminently exemplified in the life and person of 'Abdu'l-Bahá, is a dynamic that permeates the activities of the Faith; it acquires collective, transformative force in the normal functioning of a community. In this regard, the institutions of the Faith stand as channels for the promotion of this salient characteristic. It is in this framework that the concepts of rulership and leadership, authority and power are properly understood and actualized.

The appearance of a united, firmly based and self-sustaining community must be a major goal of a Spiritual Assembly. Composed of a membership reflecting a diversity of personalities, talents, abilities and interests, such a community requires a level of internal interaction between the Assembly and the body of the believers based on a commonly recognized commitment to service, and in which a sense of partnership based on appreciation of each other's distinctive sphere of action is fully recognized and unfailingly upheld, and no semblance of a dichotomy between the two appears. In such a community leadership is that expression of service by which the Spiritual Assembly invites and encourages the use of the manifold talents and abilities with which the community is endowed, and stimulates and guides the diverse elements of the community towards goals and strategies by which the effects of a coherent force for progress can be realized.

The maintenance of a climate of love and unity depends largely upon the feeling among the individuals composing the community that the Assembly is part of themselves, that their co-operative interactions with that divinely ordained body allow them a fair latitude for initiative and that the quality of their relationships with both the institution and their fellow believers encourages a spirit of enterprise invigorated by an awareness of the revolutionizing purpose of Bahá'u'lláh's Revelation, by a consciousness of the high privilege of their being associated with efforts to realize that purpose, and by a consequent, ever-present sense of joy. In such a climate, the community is transformed from being the mere sum of its parts to assuming a wholly new personality as an entity in which its members blend without losing their individual uniqueness. The possibilities for manifesting such a transformation exist most immediately at the local level, but it is a major responsibility of the National Assembly to nurture the conditions in which they may flourish.

The authority to direct the affairs of the Faith locally, nationally and internationally, is divinely conferred on elected institutions. However, the power to accomplish the tasks of the community resides primarily in the mass of the believers. The authority of the institutions is an irrevocable necessity for the progress of humanity; its exercise is an art to be mastered. The power of action in the believers is unlocked at the level of individual initiative and surges at the level of collective volition. In its potential, this mass power, this mix of individual potentialities, exists in a malleable form susceptible to the multiple reactions of individuals to the sundry influences at work in the world. To realize its highest purpose, this power needs to express itself through orderly avenues of activity. Even though individuals may strive to be guided in their actions by their personal understanding of the Divine Texts, and much can be accomplished thereby, such actions, untempered by the overall direction provided by authorized institutions, are incapable of attaining the thrust necessary for the unencumbered advancement of civilization.

Individual initiative is a pre-eminent aspect of this power; it is therefore a major responsibility of the institutions to safeguard and stimulate it. Similarly, it is important for individuals to recognize and accept that the institutions must act as a guiding and moderating influence on the march of civilization. In this sense, the divine requirement that individuals obey the decisions of their Assemblies can clearly be seen as being indispensable to the progress of society. Indeed, individuals must not be abandoned entirely to their own devices with respect to the welfare of society as a whole, neither should they be stifled by the assumption of a dictatorial posture by members of the institutions.

The successful exercise of authority in the Bahá'í community implies the recognition of separate but mutually reinforcing rights and responsibilities between the institutions and the friends in general, a recognition that in turn welcomes the need for co-operation between these two interactive forces of society. As was stated in advice given by Shoghi Effendi: "The individuals and Assemblies must learn to co-operate, and to co-operate intelligently, if they desire to adequately discharge their duties and obligations towards the Faith. And no such co-operation is possible without mutual confidence and trust."

The Universal House of Justice, *Rights and Responsibilities*, pp. 36–42. (19 May 1994.)

Chapter Ten
The Bahá'í Community: The Matrix of transformation

*T*he community, as distinguished from the individual and the institutions, assumes its own character and identity as it grows in size. This is a necessary development to which much attention is required both with respect to places where large-scale enrolment has occurred and in anticipation of more numerous instances of entry by troops. A community is of course more than the sum of its membership; it is a comprehensive unit of civilization composed of individuals, families and institutions that are originators and encouragers of systems, agencies and organizations working together with a common purpose for the welfare of people both within and beyond its own borders; it is a composition of diverse, interacting participants that are achieving unity in an unremitting quest for spiritual and social progress. Since Bahá'ís everywhere are at the very beginning of the process of community building, enormous effort must be devoted to the tasks at hand.

As we have said in an earlier message, the flourishing of the community, especially at the local level, demands a significant enhancement in patterns of behaviour: those patterns by which the collective expression of the virtues of the individual members and the functioning of the Spiritual Assembly are manifest in the unity and fellowship of the community and the dynamism of its activity and growth. This calls for the integration of the component elements—adults, youth and children—in spiritual, social, educational and administrative activities; and their engagement in local plans of teaching and development. It implies a collective will and sense of purpose to perpetuate the Spiritual Assembly through annual elections. It involves the practice of collective worship of God. Hence, it is essential to the spiritual life of the community that the friends hold regular devotional meetings in local Bahá'í centres, where available, or elsewhere, including the homes of believers.

To effect the possibilities of expansion and consolidation implied by entry by troops, a determined, world-wide effort to develop human resources must be made. The endeavour of individuals to conduct study classes in their homes, the sponsorship by the institutions of occasional courses of instruction, and the informal activities of the community, though important, are not adequate for the education and training of a rapidly expanding community. It is therefore of paramount importance that systematic attention be given to devising methods for educating large numbers of believers in the fundamental verities of the Faith and for training and assisting them to serve the Cause as their God-given talents allow. There should be no delay in establishing permanent institutes designed to provide well-organized, formally conducted programmes of training on a regular schedule.

The Universal House of Justice, *Riḍván Message to the Bahá'ís of the World*, BE 153/AD 1996, paras 25-27.

At the heart of all activities, the spiritual, intellectual and community life of the believers must be developed and fostered, requiring: the prosecution with increased vigour of the development of Local Spiritual Assemblies so that they may exercise their beneficial influence and guidance on the life of Bahá'í communities; the nurturing of a deeper understanding of Bahá'í family life; the Bahá'í education of children, including the holding of regular Bahá'í classes and, where necessary, the establishment of tutorial schools for the provision of elementary education; the encouragement of Bahá'í youth in study and service; and the encouragement of Bahá'í women to exercise to the full their privileges and responsibilities in the work of the community—may they befittingly bear witness to the memory of the Greatest Holy Leaf, the immortal heroine of the Bahá'í Dispensation, as we approach the fiftieth anniversary of her passing.

The Universal House of Justice, *The Compilation of Compilations*, Vol. II (Women), no. 2207, p. 404. (Naw-Rúz 1979.)

Fostering Universal Participation

In our message to you of April, 1964, announcing the Nine Year Plan, we called attention to two major themes of that Plan, namely "a huge expansion of the Cause of God and universal participation by all believers in the life of that Cause."

... In that same message we indicated the meaning of universal participation: "the dedicated effort of every believer in teaching, in living the Bahá'í life, in contributing to the Fund, and particularly in the persistent effort to understand more and more the significance of Bahá'u'lláh's Revelation. In the words of the beloved Guardian, 'One thing and only one thing will unfailingly and alone secure the undoubted triumph of this sacred Cause, namely the extent to which our own inner life and private character mirror forth in their manifold aspects the splendour of those eternal principles proclaimed by Bahá'u'lláh.'"

"Regard the world as the human body," wrote Bahá'u'lláh to Queen Victoria. We can surely regard the Bahá'í world, the army of God, in the same way. In the human body, every cell, every organ, every nerve has its part to play. When all do so the body is healthy, vigorous, radiant, ready for every call made upon it. No cell, however humble, lives apart from the body, whether it is serving it or receiving from it. This is true of the body of mankind in which God "hast endowed each and all with talents and faculties," and is supremely true of the body of the Bahá'í World Community, for this body is already an organism, united in its aspirations, unified in its methods, seeking assistance and confirmation from the same Source, and illumined with the conscious knowledge of its unity. Therefore, in this organic, divinely guided, blessed and illumined body the participation of every believer is of the utmost importance, and is a source of power and vitality as yet unknown to us. For extensive and deep as has been the sharing in the glorious work of the Cause, who would claim that every single believer has succeeded in finding his or her fullest satisfaction in the life of the Cause? The Bahá'í World Community, growing like a healthy new body, develops new cells, new organs, new functions and powers as it presses on to its maturity, when every soul, living for the Cause of God, will receive from that Cause, health, assurance and the overflowing bounties of Bahá'u'lláh which are diffused through His divinely ordained order.

In addition to teaching every believer can pray. Every believer can strive to make his "own inner life and private character mirror forth in their manifold aspects the splendour of those eternal principles proclaimed by Bahá'u'lláh." Every believer can contribute to the Fund. Not all believers can give public talks, not all are called upon to serve on administrative institutions. But all can pray, fight their own spiritual battles, and contribute to the fund. If every believer will carry out these sacred duties, we shall be astonished at the accession of power which will result to the whole body, and which in its turn will give rise to further growth and the showering of greater blessings on all of us.

The real secret of universal participation lies in the Master's oft expressed wish that the friends should love each other, constantly encourage each other, work together, be as one soul in one body, and in so doing become a true, organic, healthy body illumined by the spirit. In such a body all will receive spiritual health and vitality from the organism itself, and the most perfect flowers and fruits will be brought forth.

Our prayers for the happiness and success of the friends everywhere are constantly offered at the Holy Shrines.

Messages from the Universal House of Justice 1963-1986, paras 19.1, and 19.2-19.7, pp. 42-43.
(September 1964.)

Individual Enterprise

It is the duty and privilege of the National and Local Assemblies if they find that the pressing requirements of their local and national budgets have been adequately met, to encourage individuals and groups to initiate and conduct, with their knowledge and consent, any undertaking that would serve to enhance the work which they have set themselves to achieve. Not content with appeals addressed to each and every believer to offer any constructive suggestions or plan that would remedy an existing grievance, they should, by every means in their power, stimulate the spirit of enterprise among the believers in order to further the teaching as well as the administrative work of the Cause. They should endeavour by personal contact and written appeals, to imbue the body of the faithful with a deep sense of personal responsibility, and urge every believer, whether high or low, poor or wealthy, to conceive, formulate and execute such measures and projects as would redound, in the eyes of their representatives, to the power and the fair name of this sacred Cause.

Shoghi Effendi, *Bahá'í Administration*, p. 128.

Shoghi Effendi underscored the absolute necessity of individual initiative and action. He explained that without the support of the individual, "at once wholehearted, continuous and generous," every measure and plan of his National Spiritual Assembly is "foredoomed to failure," the purpose of the Master's Divine Plan is "impeded"; furthermore, the sustaining strength of Bahá'u'lláh Himself "will be withheld from every and each individual who fails in the long run to arise and play his part." Hence, at the very crux of any progress to be made is the individual believer, who possesses the power of execution which only he can release through his own initiative and sustained action. Regarding the sense of inadequacy that sometimes hampers individual initiative, a letter written on his behalf conveys the Guardian's advice: "Chief among these, you mention the lack of courage and of initiative on the part of the believers, and a feeling of inferiority which prevents them from addressing the public. It is precisely these weaknesses that he wishes the friends to overcome, for these do not only paralyse their efforts but actually serve to quench the flame of faith in their hearts. Not until all the friends come to realize that every one of them is able, in his own measure, to deliver the Message, can they ever hope to reach the goal that has been set before them by a loving and wise Master ... Everyone is a potential teacher. He has only to use what God has given him and thus prove that he is faithful to his trust."

The Universal House of Justice, *Riḍván Message to the Bahá'ís of the World*, BE 153/AD 1996, para. 22.

As to your worry about over-controlling the friends: by appreciating the nature of the power of action which they possess, you will be able to gauge how best to guide and direct them. A wide latitude for action must be allowed them, which means that a large margin for mistakes must also be allowed. Your National Spiritual Assembly and the Local Spiritual Assemblies must not react automatically to every mistake, but distinguish between those that are self-correcting with the passage of time and do no particular harm to the community and those which require Assembly intervention. Related to this is the tendency of the friends to criticize each other at the slightest provocation, whereas the teachings call upon them to encourage each other. Such tendencies are of course motivated by a deep love for the Faith, a desire to see it free of any flaw. But human beings are not perfect. The Local Assemblies and the friends must be helped through your example and through loving counsel to refrain from such a pattern of criticism, which stunts the growth and development of the community. You should also be fearful of laying down too many rules and regulations. The Cause is not so fragile that a degree of mistakes cannot be tolerated. When you feel that certain actions may become trends with harmful consequences, you may, instead of making a new rule, discuss the matter with the Counsellors, enlisting their support in educating the friends in a manner that will improve their understanding and conduct.

A new burst of energy would accrue to the operation of the Three year Plan if the friends, both individually and collectively, could feel a greater sense of freedom to engage in a wide range of activities originating with themselves. Even if you are doing nothing deliberately to discourage such freedom, their accumulated impression of institutional disapproval, however derived, and their fear of criticism are, to a considerable extent, inhibiting their exercise of initiative. At this exact time in history when the peoples of the world are weighed down with soul-crushing difficulties and the shadow of despair threatens to eclipse the light of hope, there must be revived among the individual believers a sense of mission, a feeling of empowerment to minister to the urgent need of humanity for guidance and thus to win victories for the Faith in their own sphere of life. The community as a whole should be involved in efforts to resolve such issues. A single answer would, of course, be inadequate, there being so many diverse elements and interests in the community. These matters require not only your own independent consultation but consultation with the Counsellors as well. Although Spiritual Assemblies are good at specifying goals, they have not yet mastered the art of making use of the talents of individuals and rousing the mass of friends to action in fulfilment of such goals. Removing this deficiency would be a mark of the maturation of these institutions. May your assembly lead the way.

The Universal House of Justice, *Rights and Responsibilities*, pp. 45-47. (19 May 1994.)

Recognizing the Capacity of Women

*I*n this day the duty of everyone, whether man or woman, is to teach the Cause. In America, the women have outdone the men in this regard and have taken the lead in this field. They strive harder in guiding the peoples of the world, and their endeavours are greater. They are confirmed by divine bestowals and blessings. It is my hope that in the East the handmaids of the Merciful will also exert such effort, reveal their powers, and manifest their capacities ....

'Abdu'l-Bahá, *The Compilation of Compilations*, Vol. II (Women), no. 2191, p. 398.

*W*oman must endeavour then to attain greater perfection, to be man's equal in every respect, to make progress in all in which she has been backward, so that man will be compelled to acknowledge her equality of capacity and attainment.

In Europe women have made greater progress than in the East, but there is still much to be done! When students have arrived at the end of their school term an examination takes place, and the result thereof determines the knowledge and capacity of each student. So will it be with woman; her actions will show her power, there will no longer be any need to proclaim it by words.

It is my hope that women of the East, as well as their Western sisters, will progress rapidly until humanity shall reach perfection.

God's Bounty is for all and gives power for all progress. When men own the equality of women there will be no need for them to struggle for their rights! One of the principles then of Bahá'u'lláh is the equality of sex.

Women must make the greatest effort to acquire spiritual power and to increase in the virtue of wisdom and holiness until their enlightenment and striving succeeds in bringing about the unity of mankind. They must work with a burning enthusiasm to spread the Teaching of Bahá'u'lláh among the peoples, so that the radiant light of the Divine Bounty may envelop the souls of all the nations of the world!

Public Talk of 'Abdu'l-Bahá, *Paris Talks*, pp. 171-172. (14 November 1912.)

*H*is Holiness Bahá'u'lláh has greatly strengthened the cause of women, and the rights and privileges of women is one of the greatest principles of 'Abdu'l-Bahá. Rest ye assured! Ere long the days shall come when the men addressing the women, shall say:

'Blessed are ye! Blessed are ye! Verily ye are worthy of every gift. Verily ye deserve to adorn your heads with the crown of everlasting glory, because in sciences and arts, in virtues and perfections ye shall become equal to man, and as regards tenderness of heart and the abundance of mercy and sympathy ye are superior'

Public Talk of 'Abdu'l-Bahá, *Paris Talks*, p. 197. (28 August 1913.)

*T*he youth have long been in the forefront of the teaching work, and now our hearts rejoice to see the women, in so many lands where previously their capacities were largely left unused, devoting their capable services to the life of the Bahá'í community.

The Universal House of Justice, *Messages from the Universal House of Justice 1963-1986*, para. 207.10, pp. 379-380. (Riḍván Message, BE 135/AD 1978, para. 10.)

Providing Spiritual Education for Children

*A*nd among the teachings of Bahá'u'lláh is the promotion of education. Every child must be instructed in sciences as much as is necessary. If the parents are able to provide the expenses of this education, it is well, otherwise the community must provide the means for the teaching of that child.

'Abdu'l-Bahá, *Selections from the Writings of 'Abdu'l-Bahá*, no. 227, p. 304.

*T*he root cause of wrongdoing is ignorance, and we must therefore hold fast to the tools of perception and knowledge. Good character must be taught. Light must be spread afar, so that, in the school of humanity, all may acquire the heavenly characteristics of the spirit, and see for themselves beyond any doubt that there is no fiercer hell, no more fiery abyss, than to possess a character that is evil and unsound; no more darksome pit nor loathsome torment than to show forth qualities which deserve to be condemned.

The individual must be educated to such a high degree that he would rather have his throat cut than tell a lie, and would think it easier to be slashed with a sword or pierced with a spear than to utter calumny or be carried away by wrath.

Thus will be kindled the sense of human dignity and pride, to burn away the reapings of lustful appetites. Then will each one of God's beloved shine out as a bright moon with qualities of the spirit, and the relationship of each to the Sacred Threshold of his Lord will be not illusory but sound and real, will be as the very foundation of the building, not some embellishment on its facade.

'Abdu'l-Bahá, *Selections from the Writings of 'Abdu'l-Bahá*, no. 111, pp. 136-137.

*E*ven though children's activities have been a part of past Plans, these have fallen short of the need. Spiritual education of children and junior youth are of paramount importance to the further progress of the community. It is therefore imperative that this deficiency be remedied. Institutes must be certain to include in their programmes the training of teachers of children's classes, who can make their services available to local communities. But although providing spiritual and academic education for children is essential, this represents only a part of what must go into developing their characters and shaping their personalities. The necessity exists, too, for individuals and the institutions at all levels, which is to say the community as a whole, to show a proper attitude towards children and to take a general interest in their welfare. Such an attitude should be far removed from that of a rapidly declining order.

Children are the most precious treasure a community can possess, for in them are the promise and guarantee of the future. They bear the seeds of the character of future society which is largely shaped by what the adults constituting the community do or fail to do with respect to children. They are a trust no community can neglect with impunity. An all-embracing love of children, the manner of treating them, the quality of the attention shown them, the spirit of adult behaviour toward them—these are all among the vital aspects of the requisite attitude. Love demands discipline, the courage to accustom children to hardship, not to indulge their whims or leave them entirely to their own devices. An atmosphere needs to be maintained in which children feel that they belong to the community and share in its purpose. They must lovingly but insistently be guided to live up to Bahá'í standards, to study and teach the Cause in ways that are suited to their circumstances.

Among the young ones in the community are those known as junior youth, who fall between the ages of, say, 12 and 15. They represent a special group with special needs as they are somewhat in between childhood and youth when many changes are occurring within them. Creative attention must be devoted to involving them in programmes of activity that will engage their interests, mould their capacities for teaching and service, and involve them in social interaction with older youth. The employment of the arts in various forms can be of great value in such activity.

And now we wish to address a few words to parents who bear the primary responsibility for the upbringing of their children. We appeal to them to give constant attention to the spiritual education of their children. Some parents appear to think that this is the exclusive responsibility of the community; others believe that in order to preserve the independence of children to investigate truth, the Faith should not be taught to them. Still others feel inadequate to take on such a task. None of this is correct. The beloved Master has said that "it is enjoined upon the father and mother, as a duty, to strive with all effort to train the daughter and the son," adding that, "should they neglect this matter, they shall be held responsible and worthy of reproach in the presence of the stern Lord." Independent of the level of their education, parents are in a critical position to shape the spiritual development of their children. They should not ever underestimate their capacity to mould their children's moral character. For they exercise indispensable influence through the home environment they consciously create by their love of God, their striving to adhere to His laws, their spirit of service to His Cause, their lack of fanaticism, and their freedom from the corrosive effects of backbiting. Every parent who is a believer in the Blessed Beauty has the responsibility to conduct herself or himself in such a way as to elicit the spontaneous obedience to parents to which the Teachings attach so high a value. Of course, in addition to the efforts made at home, the parents should support Bahá'í children's classes provided by the community. It must be borne in mind, too, that children live in a world that informs them of harsh realities through direct experience with the horrors already described or through the unavoidable outpourings of the mass media. Many of them are thereby forced to mature prematurely, and among these are those who look for standards and discipline by which to guide their lives. Against this gloomy backdrop of a decadent society, Bahá'í children should shine as the emblems of a better future.

The Universal House of Justice, Riḍván Message to the Bahá'ís of the World, BE 157/AD 2000, paras 25-28.

Drawing upon the Vitality of the Youth

*B*lessed is he who in the prime of his youth and the heyday of his life will arise to serve the Cause of the Lord of the beginning and of the end, and adorn his heart with His love. The manifestation of such a grace is greater than the creation of the heavens and of the earth. Blessed are the steadfast and well is it with those who are firm.

Bahá'u'lláh, cited in Messages from the Universal House of Justice 1963-1986, para. 321.5a, p. 538. (Riḍván 1982.)[99]

*N*o greater demonstration can be given to the peoples of both continents of the youthful vitality and the vibrant power animating the life, and the institutions of the nascent Faith of Bahá'u'lláh than an intelligent, persistent, and effective participation of the Bahá'í youth, of every race, nationality, and class, in both the teaching and administrative spheres of Bahá'í activity. Through such a participation the critics and enemies of the Faith, watching with varying degrees of scepticism and resentment, the evolutionary processes of the Cause of God and its institutions, can best be convinced of the indubitable truth that such a Cause is intensely alive, is sound to its very core, and its destinies in safe keeping.

Shoghi Effendi, The Advent of Divine Justice, pp. 69-70.

*T*he Bahá'í youth must be taught how to teach the Cause of God. Their knowledge of the fundamentals of the Faith must be deepened and the standard of their education in science and literature enhanced. They must become thoroughly familiar with the language used and the example set by 'Abdu'l-Bahá in His public addresses throughout the West. They must also be acquainted with those essential prerequisites of teaching as recorded in the Holy Books and Tablets.

Shoghi Effendi, Youth, The Compilation of Compilations, Vol. I (The Importance of Deepening), no. 431, p. 206; and Vol. II, no. 2237, p. 416. (9 June 1925.)

I need not tell you what great hopes he cherishes for the future role which young Bahá'ís will be inevitably called upon to play in the teaching as well as in the administra-

---

[99] Also *The Compilation of Compilations*, Vol. II (Youth), no. 2232, p. 415.

tive fields of Bahá'í activity. It is on them that he centres his essential and vital hopes for the effective and wide spread of the Message, and for the strengthening of the basis of the nascent Bahá'í administrative institutions which are gradually taking shape amidst storms of an unprecedented severity, and under extremely tragic circumstances.

His brotherly advice to you, and to all loyal and ardent young believers like you, is that you should deepen your knowledge of the history and of the tenets of the Faith, not merely by means of careful and thorough study, but also through active, whole-hearted and continued participation in all the activities, whether administrative or otherwise, of your community. The Bahá'í community life provides you with an indispensable laboratory, where you can translate into living and constructive action the principles which you imbibe from the Teachings. By becoming a real part of that living organism you can catch the real spirit which runs throughout the Bahá'í Teachings. To study the principles, and to try to live according to them, are, therefore, the two essential mediums through which you can ensure the development and progress of your inner spiritual life and of your outer existence as well. May Bahá'u'lláh enable you to attain this high station, and may He keep the torch of faith for ever burning in your heart!

Shoghi Effendi, *The Compilation of Compilations*, Vol. II (Youth), no. 2259, pp. 424-425.
(2 November 1933.)

*W*hat impressed him most in the account of your services was the statement that the old and the young Bahá'ís are firmly united and co-operating in bearing the burdens of the Faith in that locality. Nothing will attract God's blessings and grace more than the unity of the friends, and nothing is more destructive of their highest purpose than divisions and misunderstandings. Cling therefore to unity if you desire to succeed and abide by the will of your Lord Bahá'u'lláh; for that is the true objective of His Mission in this world.

Letter dated 11 October 1932 written on behalf of Shoghi Effendi, *The Compilation of Compilations*, Vol. II (Youth), no. 2252, p. 421.

*T*hree great fields of service lie open before young Bahá'ís, in which they will simultaneously be remaking the character of human society and preparing themselves for the work that they can undertake in their later lives.

First, the foundation of all their other accomplishments is their study of the teachings, the spiritualization of their lives and the forming of their characters in accordance with the standards of Bahá'u'lláh. As the moral standards of the people around us collapse and decay, whether of the centuries-old civilizations of the East, the more recent cultures of Christendom and Islám; or of the rapidly changing tribal societies of the world, the Bahá'ís must increasingly stand out as pillars of righteousness and forbearance. The life of a Bahá'í will be characterized by truthfulness and decency; he will walk uprightly among his fellowmen, dependent upon none save God, yet linked by bonds of love and brotherhood with all mankind; he will be entirely detached from the loose standards, the decadent theories, the frenetic experimentation, the desperation of present-day society, will look upon his neighbours with a bright and friendly face and be a beacon of light and a haven for all those who would emulate his strength of character and assurance of soul.

The second field of service, which is linked intimately with the first, is teaching the Faith, particularly to their fellow-youth, among whom are some of the most open and seeking minds in the world. Not yet having acquired all the responsibilities of a family or a long-established home and job, youth can more easily choose where they will live and study or work. In the world at large young people travel hither and thither seeking amusements, education and experiences. Bahá'í youth, bearing the incomparable treasure of the Word of God for this Day, can harness this mobility into service for mankind and can choose their places of residence, their areas of travel and their types of work with the goal in mind of how they can best serve the Faith.

The third field of service is the preparation of the youth for their later years. It is the obligation of a Bahá'í to educate his children; likewise it is the duty of the children to acquire knowledge of the arts and sciences and to learn a trade or profession whereby they, in turn, can earn a living and support their families. This, for a Bahá'í youth, is in itself a service to God, a service, moreover, which can be combined with teaching the Faith and often with pioneering. The Bahá'í community will need men and women of many skills and qualifications; for, as it grows in size the sphere of its activities in the life of society will increase and diversify. Let Bahá'í youth, therefore, consider the best ways in which they can use and develop their creative abilities for the service of mankind and the Cause of God, whether this be as farmers, teachers, doctors, artisans, musicians or any one of the multitude of livelihoods that are open to them.

Messages from the Universal House of Justice 1963-1986, no. 37.4-37.7, pp. 93-94. (10 June 1966.)

Youth Year of Service

Further to these aspirations is the need for a mighty mobilization of teaching activities reflecting regularity in the patterns of service rendered by young Bahá'ís. ... One pattern of this mobilization could be short-term projects, carried out at home or in other lands, dedicated to both teaching the Faith and improving the living conditions of people. Another could be that, while still young and unburdened by family responsibilities, you give attention to the idea of volunteering a set period, say, one or two years, to some Bahá'í service, on the home front or abroad, in the teaching or development field. It would accrue to the strength and stability of the community if such patterns could be followed by succeeding generations of youth. Regardless of the modes of service, however, youth must be understood to be fully engaged, at all times, in all climes and under all conditions. In your varied pursuits you may rest assured of the loving support and guidance of the Bahá'í institutions operating at every level.

The Universal House of Justice, *Messages from the Universal House of Justice 1963-1986*, para. 386.8, pp. 616-617. (3 January 1984.)[100]

---

100   Also *Unrestrained as the Wind*, pp. 185-186.

Encouraging Minorities

*H*e urges you all to devote particular attention to the contact with racial minorities. In a country which has such a large element of prejudice against its coloured citizens as the United States, it is of the greatest importance that the Bahá'ís—and more especially the youth—should demonstrate actively our complete lack of prejudice and, indeed, our prejudice in favour of minorities.

We cannot very well prosecute a teaching campaign successfully in Africa if we do not in our home communities demonstrate to the fullest extent our love for the people who spring from the African population!

Letter dated 11 November 1951 written on behalf of Shoghi Effendi, *The Compilation of Compilations*, Vol. II (Youth), no. 2295, p. 437.

*S*hoghi Effendi is also most anxious for the Message to reach the aboriginal inhabitants of the Americas. These people, for the most part downtrodden and ignorant, should receive from the Bahá'ís a special measure of love, and every effort be made to teach them. Their enrolment in the Faith will enrich them and us and demonstrate our principle of the Oneness of Man far better than words or the wide conversion of the ruling races ever can.

Letter dated 11 July 1951 written on behalf of Shoghi Effendi, *Lights of Guidance*, no. 1775, p. 524.

*T*he beloved Guardian feels that sufficient attention is not being paid to the matter of contacting minorities in the United States. A great impetus could be lent to the work in the European countries, in certain far-eastern areas, and in Latin America if the Bahá'ís residing in the big cities and university towns would make a determined and sufficient effort to extend friendship and hospitality to students and nationals from countries where the Bahá'ís are struggling so hard to establish the Faith. They would not only have the possibility of making more local believers, but they might also increase the membership of communities abroad, by sending back Bahá'ís from the United States. This has happened already a number of times with Chinese and Japanese friends, etc., to the great advantage of the Cause.

Letter dated 19 July 1956 written on behalf of Shoghi Effendi, *The Compilation of Compilations*, Vol. II (Youth), no. 2300, p. 438.

Protection of Minorities

*U*nlike the nations and peoples of the earth, be they of the East or of the West, democratic or authoritarian, communist or capitalist, whether belonging to the Old World or the New, who either ignore, trample upon, or extirpate, the racial, religious, or political minorities within the sphere of their jurisdiction, every organized community enlisted under the banner of Bahá'u'lláh should feel it to be its first and inescapable obligation to nurture, encourage, and safeguard every minority belonging to any faith, race, class, or nation within it. So great and vital is this principle that in such circumstances, as when an equal number of ballots have been cast in an election, or where the qualifications for any office are balanced as between the various races, faiths or nationalities within the community, priority should unhesitatingly be accorded the party representing the minority, and this for no other reason except to stimulate and encourage it, and afford it an opportunity to further the interests of the community. In the light of this principle, and bearing in mind the extreme desirability of having the minority elements participate and share responsibility in the conduct of Bahá'í activity, it should be the duty of every Bahá'í community so to arrange its affairs that in cases where individuals belonging to the divers minority elements within it are already qualified and fulfil the necessary requirements, Bahá'í representative institutions, be they Assemblies, conventions, conferences, or committees, may have represented on them as many of these divers elements, racial or otherwise, as possible. The adoption of such a course, and faithful adherence to it, would not only be a source of inspiration and encouragement to those elements that are numerically small and inadequately represented, but would demonstrate to the world at large the universality and representative character of the Faith of Bahá'u'lláh, and the freedom of His followers from the taint of those prejudices which have already wrought such havoc in the domestic affairs, as well as the foreign relationships, of the nations.

Shoghi Effendi, *Advent of Divine Justice*, pp. 35-36.

To discriminate against any tribe because they are in a minority is a violation of the spirit that animates the Faith of Bahá'u'lláh. As followers of God's Holy Faith it is our obligation to protect the just interests of any minority element within the Bahá'í Community. In fact in the administration of our Bahá'í affairs, representatives of minority groups are not only enabled to enjoy equal rights and privileges, but they are even favoured and accorded priority. Bahá'ís should be careful never to deviate from this noble standard even if the course of events of public opinion should bring pressure to bear upon them.

The principles in the Writings are clear, but usually it is when these principles are applied that questions arise.

The Universal House of Justice, *Messages from the Universal House of Justice 1963-1986*, paras 77.11-77.12, p. 166. (8 February 1970.)[101]

Valuing Indigenous Believers

Your Assembly should bear in mind ... the importance of increasing the representation of minority races, such as the Aborigines and Maoris, within the Bahá'í Community. Special effort should be made to contact these people and to teach them; and the Bahá'ís in Australia and New Zealand should consider that every one of them that can be won to the Faith is a precious acquisition.

Shoghi Effendi, *Letters from the Guardian to Australia and New Zealand: 1923-1957*, p. 124. (24 July 1955.)[102]

---

101 Also *Lights of Guidance*, no. 1797, pp. 528-529.
102 Also *Messages to the Antipodes*, p. 389.

Preserving Spiritual Relationships

*M*ost important of all is that love and unity should prevail in the Bahá'í Community, as this is what people are most longing for in the present dark state of the world. Words without the living example will never be sufficient to breathe hope into the hearts of a disillusioned and often cynical generation.

> Letter dated 20 October 1945 written on behalf of Shoghi Effendi, *The Compilation of Compilations*, Vol. II (Living the Life), no. 1307, p. 15.

*H*e was very pleased to hear that the Convention was so well attended, and the believers enthusiastic and united. One of the most paramount needs of the Cause in ... is that the friends should unite, should become really keenly conscious of the fact that they are one spiritual family, held together by bonds more sacred and eternal than those physical ties which make people of the same family. If the friends will forget all personal differences and open their hearts to a great love for each other for the sake of Bahá'u'lláh, they will find that their powers are vastly increased; they will attract the heart of the public, and will witness a rapid growth of the Holy Faith in ... The National Spiritual Assembly should do all in its power to foster unity among the believers, and to educate them in the Administration as this is the channel through which their community life must flow, and which, when properly understood and practiced, will enable the work of the Cause to go ahead by leaps and bounds.

> Letter dated 26 October 1943 written on behalf of Shoghi Effendi, *Dawn of a New Day*, p. 106.[103]

*I*f we Bahá'ís cannot attain to cordial unity among ourselves, then we fail to realize the main purpose for which the Báb, Bahá'u'lláh and the Beloved Master lived and suffered.

In order to achieve this cordial unity one of the first essentials insisted on by Bahá'u'lláh and 'Abdu'l-Bahá is that we resist the natural tendency to let our attention dwell on the faults and failings of others rather than on our own. Each of us is responsible for one life only, and that is our own. Each of us is immeasurably far from being "perfect as our heavenly father is perfect" and the task of perfecting our own life and character is one that requires all our attention, our will-power and energy. If we allow our attention and energy to be taken up in efforts to keep others right and remedy their faults, we are wasting precious time. We are like ploughmen each of whom has his team to manage and his plough to direct, and in order to keep his furrow straight he must keep his eye on his goal and concentrate on his own task. If he looks to this side and that to see how Tom and Harry are getting on and to criticize their ploughing, then his own furrow will assuredly become crooked.

On no subject are the Bahá'í teachings more emphatic than on the necessity to abstain from faultfinding and backbiting while being ever eager to discover and root out our own faults and overcome our own failings.

---

103   Also *The Compilation of Compilations*, Vol. II (Living the Life), no. 1296, pp. 11–12.

If we profess loyalty to Bahá'u'lláh, to our Beloved Master and our dear Guardian, then we must show our love by obedience to these explicit teachings. Deeds not words are what they demand, and no amount of fervour in the use of expressions of loyalty and adulation will compensate for failure to live in the spirit of the teachings.

Letter dated 12 May 1925 written on behalf of Shoghi Effendi, The Compilation of Compilations, Vol. II (Living the Life), no. 1272, pp. 3-4.

*H*owever, he feels very strongly that if ... is in the state your letter would seem to indicate it is certainly conducting its affairs in the wrong way. This does not mean the Assembly, it means everyone. For where is Bahá'í love? Where is putting unity and harmony first? Where is the willingness to sacrifice one's personal feelings and opinions to achieve love and harmony? What makes the Bahá'ís think that when they sacrifice the spiritual laws the administrative laws are going to work?

...

He urges you to exert your utmost to get the ... Bahá'ís to put aside such obnoxious terms as "radical", "conservative", "progressive", "enemies of the Cause", "squelching the teachings", etc. If they paused for one moment to think for what purpose the Báb and the Martyrs gave their lives, and Bahá'u'lláh and the Master accepted so much suffering, they would never let such definitions and accusations cross their lips when speaking of each other. As long as the friends quarrel amongst themselves their efforts will not be blessed for they are disobeying God.

Letter dated 24 February 1950 written on behalf of Shoghi Effendi, The Compilation of Compilations, Vol. II (Living the Life), no. 1325, p. 21.

When Differences Arise

*Y*e have been forbidden in the Book of God to engage in contention and conflict, to strike another, or to commit similar acts whereby hearts and souls may be saddened. ... Wish not for others what ye wish not for yourselves; fear God and be not of the prideful. Ye are all created out of water, and unto dust shall ye return.

Bahá'u'lláh, The Kitáb-i-Aqdas (The Most Holy Book), para. 148, pp. 72-73.

*I*t is Our wish and desire that every one of you may become a source of all goodness unto men, and an example of uprightness to mankind. Beware lest ye prefer yourselves above your neighbours. Fix your gaze upon Him Who is the Temple of God amongst men. He, in truth, hath offered up His life as a ransom for the redemption of the world. He, verily, is the All-Bountiful, the Gracious, the Most High. If any differences arise amongst you, behold Me standing before your face, and overlook the faults of one another for My name's sake and as a token of your love for My manifest and resplendent Cause. We love to see you at all times consorting in amity and concord within the paradise of My good-pleasure, and to inhale from your acts the fragrance of friendliness and unity, of loving-kindness and fellowship. Thus counselleth you the All-Knowing, the

Faithful. We shall always be with you; if We inhale the perfume of your fellowship, Our heart will assuredly rejoice, for naught else can satisfy Us. To this beareth witness every man of true understanding.

> Bahá'u'lláh, *Gleanings from the Writings of Bahá'u'lláh*, section CXLVI, pp. 315-316.

Since you have turned to him for guidance, he will very frankly give you his opinion.

He feels that the present inharmony prevailing amongst you ... is very detrimental to the advancement of the Cause, and can only lead to disruption and the chilling of the interest of new believers. You ... should forget about your personal grievances, and unite for the protection of the Faith which he well knows you are all loyally devoted to and ready to sacrifice for.

Perhaps the greatest test Bahá'ís are ever subjected to is from each other; but for the sake of the Master they should be ever ready to overlook each other's mistakes, apologize for harsh words they have uttered, forgive and forget. He strongly recommends to you this course of action.

Also he feels that you and ... should not remain away from the meetings and Feasts in ...; you have now got an enthusiastic group of young Bahá'ís in ..., and you should show them a strong example of Bahá'í discipline and the unity which can and must prevail amongst the Community of the Most Great Name.

> Letter dated 18 December 1945 written on behalf of Shoghi Effendi, *The Compilation of Compilations*, Vol. II (Living the Life), no. 1308, p. 15.

The Bahá'ís are fully entitled to address criticisms to their Assemblies; they can freely air their views about policies or individual members of elected bodies to the Assembly, Local or National, but then they must whole-heartedly accept the advice or decision of the Assembly, according to the principles already laid down for such matters in Bahá'í administration.

> Letter dated 13 May 1945 written on behalf of Shoghi Effendi, *Letters from the Guardian to Australia and New Zealand: 1923-1957*, p. 55.[104]

The Bahá'í Calendar

The Bahá'í year consists of 19 months of 19 days each (i.e., 361 days), with the addition of certain "intercalary days" (four in ordinary and five in leap years) between the eighteenth and nineteenth months in order to adjust the calendar to the solar year. The Báb named the months after the attributes of God. The Bahá'í New Year, like the ancient Persian New Year, is astronomically fixed, commencing at the March equinox (21 March), and the Bahá'í era commences with the year of the Báb's declaration (i.e., AD 1844–AH 1260).

---

[104] Also *The Compilation of Compilations*, Vol. II (The National Spiritual Assembly), no. 1470, pp. 112-113; and *Lights of Guidance*, no. 285, p. 81.

In the not far distant future it will be necessary that all peoples in the world agree on a common calendar.

It seems, therefore, fitting that the new age of unity should have a new calendar free from the objections and associations which make each of the older calendars unacceptable to large sections of the world's population, and it is difficult to see how any other arrangement could exceed in simplicity and convenience that proposed by the Báb.

J. E. Esselmont, *Bahá'u'lláh and the New Era*, The Bahá'í Calendar section, pp. 166-167.[105]

*T*he Bahá'í day starts and ends at sunset, and consequently the date of the celebration of Bahá'í feasts should be adjusted to conform to the Bahá'í calendar time.

Letter dated 27 November 1938 written on behalf of Shoghi Effendi, *Directives from the Guardian*, no. 79, p. 31. (revised.)

Bahá'í Holy Days

The Bahá'í Feasts, Anniversaries and Days of Fasting

- The fasting season lasts 19 days beginning with the first day of the month of 'Alá, 2 March—the Feast of Naw-Rúz follows immediately afterwards.
- Feast of Naw-Rúz (Bahá'í New Year), 21 March, commemorating the Declaration of the Báb, 22 May 1844 (2 hours and 11 minutes after sunset).
- Feast of Riḍván (Declaration of Bahá'u'lláh), 21 April–2 May 1863.
- Declaration of the Báb, 22 May 1844 (2 hours and 11 minutes after sunset).
- Birth of 'Abdu'l-Bahá, 23 May 1844.
- Ascension of Bahá'u'lláh, 29 May 1892 (3 am).
- Martyrdom of the Báb, 9 July 1850 (noon).
- Birth of the Báb, 20 October 1819.
- Birth of Bahá'u'lláh, 12 November 1817.
- The Day of the Covenant, 26 November.
- Ascension of 'Abdu'l-Bahá, 28 November 1921 (1 am).

Bahá'í Holy Days on which Work should be Suspended

- The Feast of Naw-Rúz (Bahá'í New Year), 21 March
- First day of Riḍván, 21 April (Declaration of Bahá'u'lláh)
- Ninth day of Riḍván, 29 April
- Twelfth day of Riḍván, 2 May

---

105 Also *The Bahá'í World*, Vol. X, 1944-1946, p. 425.

- The anniversary of the declaration of the Báb
- The anniversary of the ascension of Bahá'u'lláh, 29 May (3 a.m.)
- The anniversary of the martydom of the Báb, 9 July (noon)
- The anniversary of the birth of Báb, 20 October
- The anniversary of the birth of Bahá'u'lláh, 12 November

Suspension of Work

'Abdu'l-Bahá, in one of His Tablets addressed to a believer of Nayríz, Persia, has written the following: "Nine days in the year have been appointed on which work is forbidden. Some of these days have been specifically mentioned in the Book. The rest follows as corollaries to the Text. ... Work on the Day of the Covenant (Fête Day of 'Abdu'l-Bahá), however, is not prohibited. ... Its observance is not obligatory. The days pertaining to the Abhá Beauty (Bahá'u'lláh) and the Primal Point (the Báb), that is to say these nine days, are the only ones on which work connected with trade, commerce, industry and agriculture is not allowed. In like manner, work connected with any form of employment, whether governmental or otherwise, should be suspended."

As a corollary of this Tablet it follows that the anniversaries of the birth and ascension of 'Abdu'l-Bahá are not to be regarded as days on which work is prohibited. The celebration of these two days, however, is obligatory.

Bahá'ís in East and West, holding administrative positions, whether public or private, should exert the utmost effort to obtain special leave from their superiors to enable them to observe these nine holy days.

The Bahá'í World, Vol. XI (1946-1950), p. 346; and Vol. XV (1968-1973), p. 689.)

Remembrance

*F*orget not My bounties while I am absent. Remember My days during thy days, and My distress and banishment in this remote prison.

Bahá'u'lláh, Tablet of Aḥmad, *Bahá'í Prayers (US)*, p. 211.

*T*he praise which hath dawned from Thy most august Self, and the glory which hath shone forth from Thy most effulgent Beauty, rest upon Thee, O Thou Who art the Manifestation of Grandeur, and the King of Eternity, and the Lord of all who are in heaven and on earth! I testify that through Thee the sovereignty of God and His dominion, and the majesty of God and His grandeur, were revealed, and the Daystars of ancient splendour have shed their radiance in the heaven of Thine irrevocable decree, and the Beauty of the Unseen hath shone forth above the horizon of creation.

Bahá'u'lláh, Tablet of Visitation, *Bahá'í Prayers (US)*, p. 230.

The Nineteen-Day Feast

This festivity, which is held on a day of the nineteen-day month, was established by His Holiness the Bab, and the Blessed Beauty [Bahá'u'lláh] directed, confirmed and warmly encouraged the holding of it. It is, therefore, of the utmost importance. You should unquestionably see to it with the greatest care, and make its value known, so that it may become solidly established on a permanent basis. Let the beloved of God gather together and associate most lovingly and spiritually and happily with one another, conducting themselves with the greatest courtesy and self-restraint. Let them read the holy verses, as well as essays which are of benefit, and the letters of 'Abdu'l-Baha; encourage and inspire one another to love each and all; chant the prayers with serenity and joy; give eloquent talks, and praise the matchless Lord.

The host, with complete self-effacement, showing kindness to all, must be a comfort to each one, and serve the friends with his own hands.

If the Feast is befittingly held, in the manner described, then this supper will verily be the Lord's Supper, for its fruits will be the very fruits of that Supper, and its influence the same.

'Abdu'l-Bahá, Tablets of Abdul-Baha Abbas, Vol. II, p. 468-9. (revised.)

Concerning the nature of the Nineteen-Day Feast, in the *Aqdas*, Bahá'u'lláh clearly revealed the spiritual and social character of this Institution. Its administrative significance, however, has been stressed by the Guardian in direct response to the growing needs of the Bahá'í Community in this formative period of the Bahá'í era for better training in the principles and practice of Bahá'í administration.

Letter written on behalf of Shoghi Effendi, Directives from the Guardian, no. 74, p. 29.

... *We* feel that all friends, whatever their circumstances, should be encouraged to observe the Nineteen Day Feast. Obviously it can only be an official administrative occasion where there is a Local Spiritual Assembly to take charge of it, present reports to the friends, and receive recommendations. But groups, spontaneous gatherings of friends, and even isolated believers should certainly remember the day and say prayers together. In the case of a group it may well hold the Feast in the manner in which a Local Spiritual Assembly would do so, recognizing of course that it has no official administrative standing.

The Universal House of Justice, Lights of Guidance, no. 806, pp. 242-243. (1 December 1968.)

As to visitors to a Nineteen Day Feast, Bahá'ís from anywhere in the world should of course be warmly welcomed, and may take part in consultation. However, only members of the local community can vote on recommendations to the Local Spiritual Assembly.

The Universal House of Justice, Lights of Guidance, no. 801, p. 241. (1 December 1968.)

*D*uring the period of consultation the Bahá'ís should be able to enjoy perfect freedom to express their views on the work of the Cause, unembarrassed by the feeling that all they are saying is being heard by someone who has not accepted Bahá'u'lláh and who might, thereby, gain a very distorted picture of the Faith. It would also be very embarrassing for any sensitive non-Bahá'í to find himself plunged into the midst of a discussion of the detailed affairs of a Bahá'í Community of which he is not a part.

The Universal House of Justice, *Lights of Guidance*, no. 802, p. 241. (24 March 1970.)

*W*ith regard to the attendance of non-Bahá'ís at a Nineteen Day Feast, you can explain to ... the essentially domestic, administrative nature of the Nineteen Day Feast. ... The Guardian's secretary wrote on his behalf on 21 September 1946:

'As regards your question concerning Nineteen Day Feasts ... as to non-Bahá'ís attending, this should by all means be avoided, but if non-believers come to a Nineteen Day Feast, they should not be put out, as this might hurt their feelings.'

The Universal House of Justice, *Lights of Guidance*, no. 804, p. 242. (13 March 1967.)

Programme

*T*he Writings of the Báb and Bahá'u'lláh can certainly be read any time at any place; likewise the Writings of 'Abdu'l-Bahá are read freely during the spiritual part of the Feast. The Guardian has instructed that during the spiritual part of the Feast, his own writings should not be read. In other words, during the spiritual part of the Feast, readings should be confined to the Writings of the Báb, Bahá'u'lláh and, to a lesser extent, of the Master; but during that part of the Feast the Guardian's writings should not be read. During the period of administrative discussion of the Feast, then the Guardian's Writings may be read. Of course during the administrative part of the Feast there can be no objection to the reading of the Writings of the Báb, Bahá'u'lláh or 'Abdu'l-Bahá.

Letter dated 27 April 1956 written on behalf of Shoghi Effendi, *The Compilation of Compilations*, Vol. I (19 Day Feast), no. 989, p. 450.[106]

*W*ith regard to your question concerning the use of music in the Nineteen Day Feasts, he wishes you to assure all the friends that not only he approves of such a practice, but thinks it even advisable that the believers should make use in their meetings of hymns composed by Bahá'ís themselves, and also of such hymns, poems and chants as are based on the Holy Words.

Letter dated 7 April 1935 written on behalf of Shoghi Effendi, *The Compilation of Compilations*, Vol. I (19 Day Feast), no. 982, p. 448; and Vol. II (Music), no. 1427, p. 81.[107]

---

106   Also *Lights of Guidance*, no. 819, p. 246.
107   Also *Lights of Guidance*, no. 823, p. 247.

... *A*lthough one of the principal functions of the Nineteen Day Feast is to provide a forum for "open and constructive criticism and deliberation regarding the state of affairs within the local Bahá'í community", complaints about the actions of an individual member of an Assembly should be made directly and confidentially to the Assembly itself, not made to other individuals or even raised at a Nineteen Day Feast.

Letter dated 2 July 1996 written on behalf of the Universal House of Justice,
Rights and Responsibilities, p. 54.

Attaining the Spiritual Reality of the Bahá'í Feast

... *W*hen the friends have the intention of entering in these meetings and assemblies, they must first make the purpose pure, disengage the heart from all other reflections, ask the inexhaustible divine confirmation and with the utmost devotion and humility set their feet in the gathering-place.

'Abdu'l-Bahá, *Bahá'í World Faith*, p. 407.

*M*ake ye an effort in every meeting that the Lord's Supper may become realized and the heavenly food descend. This heavenly food is knowledge, understanding, faith, assurance, love, affinity, kindness, purity of purpose, attraction of hearts and the union of souls. It was this manner of the Lord's Supper which descended from the heavenly kingdom in the day of Christ. When the meeting is conducted after this manner, then 'Abdu'l-Bahá also is present in heart and soul, though His body may not be with you.

'Abdu'l-Bahá, *Bahá'í World Faith*, pp. 407-8.

The Nineteen-Day Feast Calendar

Bahá'í month		First day of month starts at sunset on
Bahá	Splendour	20 March
Jalál	Glory	8 April
Jamal	Beauty	27 April
'Aẓamat	Grandeur	16 May
Núr	Light	4 June
Raḥmat	Mercy	23 June
Kalimát	Words	12 July
Kamál	Perfection	31 July
Asmá'	Names	19 August
'Izzat	Might	7 September
Mashíyyat	Will	26 September
'Ilm	Knowledge	15 October
Qudrat	Power	3 November
Qawl	Speech	22 November
Masá'il	Questions	11 December
Sharaf	Honour	30 December
Sulṭán	Sovereignty	18 January
Mulk	Dominion	6 February
'Alá'	Loftiness	1 March*

* Ayyám-i-Há (Intercalary Days)—26 February to 1 March inclusive—four in ordinary years and five in leap years.

*N*aw-Rúz is the first day of the new year. It coincides with the spring equinox in the northern hemisphere, which usually occurs on 21 March. Bahá'u'lláh explains that this feast day is to be celebrated on whatever day the sun passes into the constellation of Aries (i.e. the vernal equinox), even should this occur one minute before sunset (Q & A 35). Hence Naw-Rúz could fall on 20, 21, or 22 March, depending on the time of the equinox.

Bahá'u'lláh has left the details of many laws to be filled in by the Universal House of Justice. Among these are a number of matters affecting the Bahá'í calendar. The Guardian has stated that the implementation, world-wide, of the law concerning the timing of Naw-Rúz will require the choice of a particular spot on earth which will serve as the standard for the fixing of the time of the spring equinox. He also indicated that the choice of this spot has been left to the decision of the Universal House of Justice.

The Universal House of Justice, *The Kitáb-i-Aqdas*, (The Most Holy Book), Notes no. 26, pp. 177-178.

Devotional Meetings and the Institution of the Mashriqu'l-Adhkár

*B*lessed is he who, at the hour of dawn, centring his thoughts on God, occupied with His remembrance, and supplicating His forgiveness, directeth his steps to the Mashriqu'l-Adhkár and, entering therein, seateth himself in silence to listen to the verses of God, the Sovereign, the Mighty, the All-Praised. Say: The Mashriqu'l-Adhkár is each and every building which hath been erected in cities and villages for the celebration of My praise. Such is the name by which it hath been designated before the throne of glory, were ye of those who understand.

They who recite the verses of the All-Merciful in the most melodious of tones will perceive in them that with which the sovereignty of earth and heaven can never be compared. From them they will inhale the divine fragrance of My worlds—worlds which today none can discern save those who have been endowed with vision through this sublime, this beauteous Revelation. Say: These verses draw hearts that are pure unto those spiritual worlds that can neither be expressed in words nor intimated by allusion. Blessed be those who hearken.

Bahá'u'lláh, *The Kitáb-i-Aqdas* (The Most Holy Book), paras 115–116, p. 61.

*T*each your children the verses revealed from the heaven of majesty and power, so that, in most melodious tones, they may recite the Tablets of the All-Merciful in the alcoves within the Mashriqu'l-Adhkárs. Whoever hath been transported by the rapture born of adoration for My Name, the Most Compassionate, will recite the verses of God in such wise as to captivate the hearts of those yet wrapped in slumber. Well is it with him who hath quaffed the Mystic Wine of everlasting life from the utterance of his merciful Lord in My Name—a Name through which every lofty and majestic mountain hath been reduced to dust.

Bahá'u'lláh, *The Kitáb-i-Aqdas* (The Most Holy Book), para. 150, p. 74.

*Y*ou had asked about places of worship and the underlying reason therefor. The wisdom in raising up such building is that at a given hour, the people should know it is time to meet, and all should gather together, and, harmoniously attuned one to another, should engage in prayer; with the result that out of this coming together, unity and affection shall grow and flourish in the human heart.

'Abdu'l-Bahá, *Selections from the Writings of 'Abdu'l-Bahá*, no. 58, p. 94. (revised.)[108]

*P*raised be God, ye two have demonstrated the truth of your words by your deeds, and have won the confirmations of the Lord God. Every day at first light, ye gather the Bahá'í children together and teach them the communes and prayers. This is a most praiseworthy act, and bringeth joy to the children's hearts: that they should, at every morn, turn their faces toward the Kingdom and make mention of the Lord and praise His Name, and in the sweetest of voices, chant and recite.

---

108 Also *Lights of Guidance*, no. 2058, p. 607.

These children are even as young plants, and teaching them the prayers is as letting the rain pour down upon them, that they may wax tender and fresh, and the soft breezes of the love of God may blow over them, making them to tremble with joy.

'Abdu'l-Bahá, *Selections from the Writings of 'Abdu'l-Bahá*, no. 115, p. 139.

The Bahá'í House of Worship is dedicated to the praise of God. The House of Worship forms the central edifice of the Ma<u>sh</u>riqu'l-A<u>dh</u>kár (the Dawning-place of the Praise of God), a complex which, as it unfolds in the future, will comprise in addition to the House of Worship a number of dependencies dedicated to social, humanitarian, educational, and scientific pursuits. 'Abdu'l-Bahá describes the Ma<u>sh</u>riqu'l-A<u>dh</u>kár as *"one of the most vital institutions in the world"*, and Shoghi Effendi indicates that it exemplifies in tangible form the integration of "Bahá'í worship and service". Anticipating the future development of this institution, Shoghi Effendi envisages that the House of Worship and its dependencies "shall afford relief to the suffering, sustenance to the poor, shelter to the wayfarer, solace to the bereaved, and education to the ignorant". In the future, Bahá'í Houses of Worship will be constructed in every town and village.

The Universal House of Justice added to: Bahá'u'lláh, *The Kitáb-i-Aqdas* (The Most Holy Book), Notes no. 53, pp. 190-191.

As to the character of the meetings in the Auditorium of the Temple, he feels that they should be purely devotional in character; Bahá'í addresses and lectures should be strictly excluded. ... Shoghi Effendi would urge that choir singing by men, women and children be encouraged in the Auditorium and that rigidity in the Bahá'í service be scrupulously avoided. The more universal and informal the character of Bahá'í worship in the Temple the better. Images and pictures, with the exception of the Greatest Name, should be strictly excluded. Prayers revealed by Bahá'u'lláh and the Master as well as sacred Writings of the Prophets should be read or chanted as well as hymns based upon Bahá'í or non-Bahá'í sacred Writings."

Letter dated 2 April 1931 written on behalf of Shoghi Effendi, *Lights of Guidance*, no. 2059, p. 608.

Your Assembly is free to use its discretion in choosing excerpts from the generally recognized scriptures of the older religions.

...

Music in the House of Worship is to be vocal only, whether by singers or a singer. It does not matter if a guest a Capella choir or soloist is used, provided such use is not made the occasion to publicize services of Worship and the precautions you mention are taken. No doubt the excellent recordings available today would assure the highest quality of performance at low cost, but all references to vocal music in the central Edifice imply the physical presence of the singers.

Letter dated 13 March 1974 of the Universal House of Justice, *Lights of Guidance*, no. 2063, p. 609.

National and Local Bahá'í Centres: Ḥaẓíratu'l-Quds

Simultaneous with the establishment and incorporation of local and national Bahá'í Assemblies, with the formation of their respective committees, the formulation of national and local Bahá'í constitutions and the founding of Bahá'í endowments, undertakings of great institutional significance were initiated by these newly founded Assemblies, among which the institution of the Ḥaẓíratu'l-Quds—the seat of the Bahá'í National Spiritual Assembly and pivot of all Bahá'í administrative activity in future—must rank as one of the most important. ... Complementary in its functions to those of the Mashriqu'l-Adhkár—an edifice exclusively reserved for Bahá'í worship—this institution, whether local or national, will, as its component parts, such as the Secretariat, the Treasury, the Archives, the Library, the Publishing Office, the Assembly Hall, the Council Chamber, the Pilgrims' Hostel, are brought together and made jointly to operate in one spot, be increasingly regarded as the focus of all Bahá'í administrative activity, and symbolize, in a befitting manner, the ideal of service animating the Bahá'í community in its relation alike to the Faith and to mankind in general.

Shoghi Effendi, *God Passes By*, pp. 339-340.

When a Local Spiritual Assembly acquires a Bahá'í Centre, it should regard this meeting place as an embryonic Ḥaẓíratu'l-Quds and should do everything possible to foster in the community a proper attitude of respect for the Centre ...

When a community grows in size and in the resources at its disposal, the Assembly may well acquire a community centre for recreational and other uses, in addition to the Bahá'í Centre. However, if it is able to acquire only one centre, that meeting place should be designated as the Bahá'í Centre since it is the focus of Bahá'í community activity and the seat of the Spiritual Assembly, in addition to its being identified with the Bahá'í Faith in the eyes of the public.

Letter written on behalf of the Universal House of Justice, *Local Spiritual Assembly Handbook*, no. 19.1.3, p. 391.

As we have said in an earlier message, the flourishing of the community, especially at the local level, demands a significant enhancement in patterns of behaviour: those patterns by which the collective expression of the virtues of the individual members and the functioning of the Spiritual Assembly are manifest in the unity and fellowship of the community and the dynamism of its activity and growth. ... It involves the practice of collective worship of God. Hence, it is essential to the spiritual life of the community that the friends hold regular devotional meetings in local Bahá'í centres, where available, or elsewhere, including the homes of believers.

The Universal House of Justice, *Riḍván Message to the Bahá'ís of the World*, BE 153/AD 1996 para. 26.

Part four
The Advancement of Civilisation

Chapter Eleven

The Establishment and Maintenance of the Lesser Peace Requisites for World Peace

The Principle of Collective Security

We pray God—exalted be His glory—and cherish the hope that He may graciously assist the manifestations of affluence and power and the daysprings of sovereignty and glory, the kings of the earth—may God aid them through His strengthening grace—to establish the Lesser Peace. This, indeed, is the greatest means for ensuring the tranquillity of the nations. It is incumbent upon the Sovereigns of the world—may God assist them—unitedly to hold fast unto this Peace, which is the chief instrument for the protection of all mankind. It is Our hope that they will arise to achieve what will be conducive to the well-being of man. It is their duty to convene an all-inclusive assembly, which either they themselves or their ministers will attend, and to enforce whatever measures are required to establish unity and concord amongst men. They must put away the weapons of war, and turn to the instruments of universal reconstruction. Should one king rise up against another, all the other kings must arise to deter him. Arms and armaments will, then, be no more needed beyond that which is necessary to ensure the internal security of their respective countries. If they attain unto this all-surpassing blessing, the people of each nation will pursue, with tranquillity and contentment, their own occupations, and the groanings and lamentations of most men would be silenced. We beseech God to aid them to do His will and pleasure. He, verily, is the Lord of the throne on high and of earth below, and the Lord of this world and of the world to come. It would be preferable and more fitting that the highly-honoured kings themselves should attend such an assembly, and proclaim their edicts. Any king who will arise and carry out this task, he, verily will, in the sight of God, become the cynosure of all kings. Happy is he, and great is his blessedness!

Bahá'u'lláh, Epistle to the Son of the Wolf, pp. 30-31.

O ye rulers of the earth! Wherefore have ye clouded the radiance of the Sun, and caused it to cease from shining? Hearken unto the counsel given you by the Pen of the Most High, that haply both ye and the poor may attain unto tranquillity and peace. We beseech God to assist the kings of the earth to establish peace on earth. He, verily, doth what He willeth.

O kings of the earth! We see you increasing every year your expenditures, and laying the burden thereof on your subjects. This, verily, is wholly and grossly unjust. Fear the sighs and tears of this Wronged One, and lay not excessive burdens on your peoples. Do not rob them to rear palaces for yourselves; nay rather choose for them that which ye choose for yourselves. Thus We unfold to your eyes that which profiteth you, if ye but perceive. Your people are your treasures. Beware lest your rule violate the commandments of God, and ye deliver your wards to the hands of the robber. By them ye rule, by their means ye subsist, by their aid ye conquer. Yet, how disdainfully ye look upon them! How strange, how very strange!

Now that ye have refused the Most Great Peace, hold ye fast unto this, the Lesser Peace, that haply ye may in some degree better your own condition and that of your dependents.

O rulers of the earth! Be reconciled among yourselves, that ye may need no more armaments save in a measure to safeguard your territories and dominions. Beware lest ye disregard the counsel of the All-Knowing, the Faithful.

Be united, O kings of the earth, for thereby will the tempest of discord be stilled amongst you, and your peoples find rest, if ye be of them that comprehend. Should any one among you take up arms against another, rise ye all against him, for this is naught but manifest justice.

Bahá'u'lláh, *Gleanings from the Writings of Bahá'u'lláh*, section CXIX, pp. 253-254.

Global Reconstruction and Demilitarization

*T*rue civilization will unfurl its banner in the midmost heart of the world whenever a certain number of its distinguished and high-minded sovereigns—the shining exemplars of devotion and determination—shall, for the good and happiness of all mankind, arise, with firm resolve and clear vision, to establish the Cause of Universal Peace. They must make the Cause of Peace the object of general consultation, and seek by every means in their power to establish a Union of the nations of the world. They must conclude a binding treaty and establish a covenant, the provisions of which shall be sound, inviolable and definite. They must proclaim it to all the world and obtain for it the sanction of all the human race. This supreme and noble undertaking—the real source of the peace and well-being of all the world—should be regarded as sacred by all that dwell on earth. All the forces of humanity must be mobilized to ensure the stability and permanence of this Most Great Covenant. In this all-embracing Pact the limits and frontiers of each and every nation should be clearly fixed, the principles underlying the relations of governments towards one another definitely laid down, and all international agreements and obligations ascertained. In like manner, the size of the armaments of every government should be strictly limited, for if the preparations for war and the military forces of any nation should be allowed to increase, they will arouse the suspicion of others. The fundamental principle underlying this solemn Pact should be so fixed that if any government later violate any one of its provisions, all the governments on earth should arise to reduce it to utter submission, nay the human race as a whole should resolve, with every power at its disposal, to destroy that government. Should this greatest of all remedies be applied to the sick body of the world, it will assuredly recover from its ills and will remain eternally safe and secure.

Observe that if such a happy situation be forthcoming, no government would need continually to pile up the weapons of war, nor feel itself obliged to produce ever new military weapons with which to conquer the human race. A small force for the purposes of internal security, the correction of criminal and disorderly elements and the prevention of local disturbances, would be required—no more. In this way the entire population would, first of all, be relieved of the crushing burden of expenditure currently imposed for military purposes, and secondly, great numbers of people would cease to devote their time to the continual devising of new weapons of destruction—those testimonials of greed and bloodthirstiness, so inconsistent with the gift of life—and would instead bend their efforts to the production of whatever will foster human existence and peace and well-being, and would become the cause of universal development and prosperity. Then every nation on earth will reign in honour, and every people will be cradled in tranquillity and content.

A few, unaware of the power latent in human endeavour, consider this matter as highly impracticable, nay even beyond the scope of man's utmost efforts. Such is not the case, however. On the contrary, thanks to the unfailing grace of God, the loving-kindness of His favoured ones, the unrivalled endeavours of wise and capable souls, and the thoughts and ideas of the peerless leaders of this age, nothing whatsoever can be regarded as unattainable. Endeavour, ceaseless endeavour, is required. Nothing short of an indomitable determination can possibly achieve it. Many a cause which past ages have regarded as purely visionary, yet in this day has become most easy and practicable. Why should this most great and lofty Cause—the daystar of the firmament of true civilization and the cause of the glory, the advancement, the well-being and the success of all humanity—be regarded as impossible of achievement? Surely the day will come when its beauteous light shall shed illumination upon the assemblage of man.

The apparatus of conflict will, as preparations go on at their present rate, reach the point where war will become something intolerable to mankind.

'Abdu'l-Bahá, *The Secret of Divine Civilization*, pp. 64-67.

*T*here is not one soul whose conscience does not testify that in this day there is no more important matter in the world than that of universal peace. Every just one bears witness to this and adores that esteemed Assembly because its aim is that this darkness may be changed into light, this bloodthirstiness into kindness, this torment into bliss, this hardship into ease and this enmity and hatred into fellowship and love. Therefore, the effort of those esteemed souls is worthy of praise and commendation.

But the wise souls who are aware of the essential relationships emanating from the realities of things consider that one single matter cannot, by itself, influence the human reality as it ought and should, for until the minds of men become united, no important matter can be accomplished. At present universal peace is a matter of great importance, but unity of conscience is essential, so that the foundation of this matter may become secure, its establishment firm and its edifice strong.

'Abdu'l-Bahá, *Selections from the Writings of 'Abdu'l-Bahá*, no. 227, p. 297.

*I*n cycles gone by, though harmony was established, yet, owing to the absence of means, the unity of all mankind could not have been achieved. Continents remained widely divided, nay even among the peoples of one and the same continent association and interchange of thought were well nigh impossible. Consequently intercourse, understanding and unity amongst all the peoples and kindreds of the earth were unattainable. In this day, however, means of communication have multiplied, and the five continents of the earth have virtually merged into one. ... In like manner all the members of the human family, whether peoples or governments, cities or villages, have become increasingly interdependent. For none is self-sufficiency any longer possible, inasmuch as political ties unite all peoples and nations, and the bonds of trade and industry, of agriculture and education, are being strengthened every day. Hence the unity of all mankind can in this day be achieved. Verily this is none other but one of the wonders of this wondrous age, this glorious century. Of this past ages have been deprived, for this century—the century of light—has been endowed with unique and unprecedented glory, power and illumination. Hence the miraculous unfolding of a fresh marvel every day. Eventually it will be seen how bright its candles will burn in the assemblage of man.

Behold how its light is now dawning upon the world's darkened horizon. The first candle is unity in the political realm, the early glimmerings of which can now be discerned. The second candle is unity of thought in world undertakings, the consummation of which will ere long be witnessed. The third candle is unity in freedom which will surely come to pass. The fourth candle is unity in religion which is the cornerstone of the foundation itself, and which, by the power of God, will be revealed in all its splendour. The fifth candle is the unity of nations—a unity which in this century will be securely established, causing all the peoples of the world to regard themselves as citizens of one common fatherland. The sixth candle is unity of races, making of all that dwell on earth peoples and kindreds of one race. The seventh candle is unity of language, i.e., the choice of a universal tongue in which all peoples will be instructed and converse. Each and every one of these will inevitably come to pass, inasmuch as the power of the Kingdom of God will aid and assist in their realization.

'Abdu'l-Bahá, *Selections from the Writings of 'Abdu'l-Bahá*, no. 15, pp. 31-32.

*S*ome form of a world super-state must needs be evolved, in whose favour all the nations of the world will have willingly ceded every claim to make war, certain rights to impose taxation and all rights to maintain armaments, except for purposes of maintaining internal order within their respective dominions. Such a state will have to include within its orbit an international executive adequate to enforce supreme and unchallengeable authority on every recalcitrant member of the commonwealth; a world parliament whose members shall be elected by the people in their respective countries and whose election shall be confirmed by their respective governments; and a supreme tribunal whose judgement will have a binding effect even in such cases where the parties concerned did not voluntarily agree to submit their case to its consideration.

Shoghi Effendi, *The World Order of Bahá'u'lláh*, pp. 40-41.

*A*s regards your teaching work: the Guardian has already advised you to stress in your talks the idea of a world superstate, and the concept of the Oneness of Mankind underlying it. In addition, he wishes you also to emphasize the fact that humanity, taken as a whole, has entered the most critical and momentous stage of its evolution, the stage of maturity. This idea of the coming of age of mankind constitutes the central core of the Bahá'í Teachings, and is the most distinguishing feature of the Revelation of Bahá'u'lláh. A proper understanding of this concept gives the key to an adequate appreciation of the tremendous claim made by the Author of the Faith, both with regard to His own station, and to the incomparable greatness of His Dispensation.

> Letter dated 12 October 1936 written on behalf of Shoghi Effendi, *The Compilation of Compilations*, Vol. II (Peace), no. 1624, p. 194.

*T*he Great Peace towards which people of goodwill throughout the centuries have inclined their hearts, of which seers and poets for countless generations have expressed their vision, and for which from age to age the sacred scriptures of mankind have constantly held the promise, is now at long last within the reach of the nations. For the first time in history it is possible for everyone to view the entire planet, with all its myriad diversified peoples, in one perspective. World peace is not only possible but inevitable. It is the next stage in the evolution of this planet—in the words of one great thinker, "the planetization of mankind."

Whether peace is to be reached only after unimaginable horrors precipitated by humanity's stubborn clinging to old patterns of behaviour, or is to be embraced now by an act of consultative will, is the choice before all who inhabit the earth. At this critical juncture when the intractable problems confronting nations have been fused into one common concern for the whole world, failure to stem the tide of conflict and disorder would be unconscionably irresponsible.

> The Promise of World Peace, *Messages of the Universal House of Justice 1963-1986*, paras 438.1-438.2, p. 681. (October 1985.)

A candid acknowledgement that prejudice, war and exploitation have been the expression of immature stages in a vast historical process and that the human race is today experiencing the unavoidable tumult which marks its collective coming of age is not a reason for despair but a prerequisite to undertaking the stupendous enterprise of building a peaceful world. That such an enterprise is possible, that the necessary constructive forces do exist, that unifying social structures can be erected, is the theme we urge you to examine.

> The Promise of World Peace, *Messages of the Universal House of Justice 1963-1986*, para. 438.10, p. 683. (October 1985.)

*T*wo points bear emphasizing in all these issues. One is that the abolition of war is not simply a matter of signing treaties and protocols; it is a complex task requiring a new level of commitment to resolving issues not customarily associated with the pursuit of peace. Based on political agreements alone, the idea of collective security is a chimera. The other point is that the primary challenge in dealing with issues of peace is to raise the context to the level of principle, as distinct from pure pragmatism. For, in essence, peace stems from an inner state supported by a spiritual or moral attitude, and it is chiefly in evoking this attitude that the possibility of enduring solutions can be found.

There are spiritual principles, or what some call human values, by which solutions can be found for every social problem. Any well-intentioned group can in a general sense devise practical solutions to its problems, but good intentions and practical knowledge are usually not enough. The essential merit of spiritual principle is that it not only presents a perspective which harmonizes with that which is immanent in human nature, it also induces an attitude, a dynamic, a will, an aspiration, which facilitate the discovery and implementation of practical measures. Leaders of governments and all in authority would be well served in their efforts to solve problems if they would first seek to identify the principles involved and then be guided by them.

The Promise of World Peace, Messages of the Universal House of Justice 1963-1986, paras 438.36-438.37, pp. 689-690. (October 1985.)

Acceptance of the oneness of mankind is the first fundamental prerequisite for reorganization and administration of the world as one country, the home of humankind. Universal acceptance of this spiritual principle is essential to any successful attempt to establish world peace. It should therefore be universally proclaimed, taught in schools, and constantly asserted in every nation as preparation for the organic change in the structure of society which it implies.

In the Bahá'í view, recognition of the oneness of mankind "calls for no less than the reconstruction and the demilitarization of the whole civilized world—a world organically unified in all the essential aspects of its life, its political machinery, its spiritual aspiration, its trade and finance, its script and language, and yet infinite in the diversity of the national characteristics of its federated units."

The Promise of World Peace, Messages of the Universal House of Justice 1963-1986, paras 438.40-438.41, p. 690. (October 1985.)

The Collaborative Role of the Bahá'í Community

Bahá'u'lláh's principal mission in appearing at this time in human history is the realization of the oneness of mankind and the establishment of peace among the nations; therefore, all the forces which are focused on accomplishing these ends are influenced by His Revelation. We know, however, that peace will come in stages. First, there will come the Lesser Peace, when the unity of nations will be achieved, then gradually the Most Great Peace—the spiritual as well as social and political unity of mankind, when the Bahá'í World Commonwealth, operating in strict accordance with the laws and ordinances of the Most Holy Book of the Bahá'í Revelation, will have been established through the efforts of the Bahá'ís.

As to the Lesser Peace, Shoghi Effendi has explained that this will initially be a political unity arrived at by decision of the governments of various nations; it will not be established by direct action of the Bahá'í community. This does not mean, however, that the Bahá'ís are standing aside and waiting for the Lesser Peace to come before they do something about the peace of mankind. Indeed, by promoting the principles of the Faith, which are indispensable to the maintenance of peace, and by fashioning the instruments of the Bahá'í Administrative Order, which we are told by the beloved Guardian is the pattern for future society, the Bahá'ís are constantly engaged in laying the groundwork for a permanent peace, the Most Great Peace being their ultimate goal.

The Lesser Peace itself will pass through stages; at the initial stage the governments will act entirely on their own without the conscious involvement of the Faith; later on, in God's good time, the Faith will have a direct influence on it in ways indicated by Shoghi Effendi in his "The Goal of a New World Order". In connection with the steps that will lead to this latter stage, the Universal House of Justice will certainly determine what has to be done, in accordance with the guidance in the Writings, such as the passage you quoted from *Tablets of Bahá'u'lláh*, page 89. In the meantime, the Bahá'ís will undoubtedly continue to do all in their power to promote the establishment of peace.

Messages from the Universal House of Justice 1963-1986, paras 422.2-422.4, pp. 655-656. (31 January 1985.)[109]

Guided by the external affairs strategy communicated to National Spiritual Assemblies in 1994, the community's capacity in the fields of diplomatic and public information likewise expanded at an astonishing rate, placing the Bahá'í community in a dynamic relationship with the United Nations, governments, non-governmental organizations (NGOs) and the media. The strategy focused activities at international and national levels on two key objectives: to influence the processes towards world peace, and to defend the Faith. Through the measures adopted for the defence of our dearly loved co-religionists in Iran, the Bahá'í International Community won a new measure of respect and support that created opportunities for other aims of the strategy to be pursued ...

With regard to the other objectives of the external affairs strategy, the lines of action were guided by four themes: human rights, the status of women, global prosperity, and moral development. Our records show a huge step forward in the work on human rights and the status of women.

The Universal House of Justice, *Riḍván Message to the Bahá'ís of the World*, BE 157/AD 2000

---

109 Also *The Compilation of Compilations*, Vol. II (Peace), no. 1637, pp. 199-200; and *Lights of Guidance*, no. 1430, pp. 437-438.

Collaboration for Social and Economic Development

As the Movement extends the bounds of its influence and its opportunities for fuller recognition multiply, the twofold character of the obligations imposed on its National elected representatives should, I feel, be increasingly emphasized. Whilst chiefly engaged in the pursuit of their major task, consisting chiefly in the formation and the consolidation of Bahá'í administrative institutions, they should endeavour to participate, within recognized limits, in the work of institutions which though unaware of the claim of the Bahá'í Cause are prompted by a sincere desire to promote the spirit that animates the Faith. In the pursuit of their major task their function is to preserve the identity of the Cause and the purity of the mission of Bahá'u'lláh. In their minor undertaking their purpose should be to imbue with the spirit of power and strength such movements as in their restricted scope are endeavouring to achieve what is near and dear to the heart of every true Bahá'í.

Shoghi Effendi, *Bahá'í Administration*, p. 126.

The growing maturity of a world-wide religious community which all these processes indicate is further evidenced in the reaching out, by a number of national communities, to the social and economic life of their countries, exemplified by the founding of tutorial schools, the inception of radio stations, the pursuit of rural development programmes and the operation of medical and agricultural schemes. To these early beginnings must be added the undoubted skills acquired, as a result of the Iránian crisis, in dealing with international organizations, national governments and the mass media—the very elements of society with which it must increasingly collaborate toward the realization of peace on earth.

The Universal House of Justice, *Riḍván Message to the Bahá'ís of the World*, BE 140/AD 1983, para. 6.[110]

There can be no doubt that the progress of the Cause from this time onward will be characterized by an ever increasing relationship to the agencies, activities, institutions and leading individuals of the non-Bahá'í world. We shall acquire greater stature at the United Nations, become better known in the deliberations of governments, a familiar figure to the media, a subject of interest to academics, and inevitably the envy of failing establishments. Our preparation for the response to this situation must be a continual deepening of our faith, an unwavering adherence to its principles of abstention from partisan politics and freedom from prejudices, and above all an increasing understanding of its fundamental verities and relevance to the modern world.

The Universal House of Justice, *Riḍván Message to the Bahá'ís of the World*, BE 141/AD 1984, para. 9.[111]

---

110   Also *Messages from the Universal House of Justice 1963-1986*, para. 358.6, p. 576.
111   Also *Messages from the Universal House of Justice 1963-1986*, para. 394.9, p. 624.

From the beginning of His stupendous mission, Bahá'u'lláh urged upon the attention of nations the necessity of ordering human affairs in such a way as to bring into being a world unified in all the essential aspects of its life. In unnumbered verses and tablets He repeatedly and variously declared the "progress of the world" and the "development of nations" as being among the ordinances of God for this day. The oneness of mankind, which is at once the operating principle and ultimate goal of His Revelation, implies the achievement of a dynamic coherence between the spiritual and practical requirements of life on earth. The indispensability of this coherence is unmistakably illustrated in His ordination of the Mashriqu'l-Adhkár, the spiritual centre of every Bahá'í community round which must flourish dependencies dedicated to social, humanitarian, educational and scientific advancement of mankind. Thus, we can readily appreciate that although it has hitherto been impracticable for Bahá'í institutions generally to emphasize development activities, the concept of social and economic development is enshrined in the sacred Teachings of our Faith. The beloved Master, through His illuminating words and deeds, set the example for the application of this concept to the reconstruction of society. Witness, for instance, what social and economic progress the Iránian believers attained under His loving guidance, and, subsequently, with the unfailing encouragement of the Guardian of the Cause.

Messages from the Universal House of Justice 1963–1986, para. 379.2, p. 602. (20 October 1983.)

We now call upon National Spiritual Assemblies to consider the implications of this emerging trend for their respective communities, and to take well-conceived measures to involve the thought and actions of Local Spiritual Assemblies and individuals in the devising and implementing of plans within the constraints of existing circumstances and available resources. Progress in the development field will largely depend on natural stirrings at the grass roots, and it should receive its driving force from those sources rather than from an imposition of plans and programmes from the top. The major task of the National Assemblies, therefore, is to increase the local communities' awareness of needs and possibilities, and to guide and co-ordinate the efforts resulting from such awareness. Already in many areas the friends are witnessing the confirmations of their initiatives in such pursuits as the founding of tutorial and other schools, the promotion of literacy, the launching of rural development programmes, the inception of educational radio stations, and the operation of agricultural and medical projects. As they enlarge the scope of the endeavours other modes of development will undoubtedly emerge.

This challenge evokes the resourcefulness, flexibility and cohesiveness of the many communities composing the Bahá'í world. Different communities will, of course, perceive different approaches and different solutions to similar needs. Some can offer assistance abroad, while, at the outset, others must of necessity receive assistance; but all, irrespective of circumstances or resources, are endowed with the capacity to respond in some measure; all can share; all can participate in the joint enterprise of applying more systematically the principles of the Faith to upraising the quality of human life. The key to success is unity in spirit and in action ....

Messages from the Universal House of Justice 1963–1986, paras 379.6–379.7, p. 603. (20 October 1983.)

*U*ltimately, the call to action is addressed to the individual friends, whether they be adult or youth, veteran or newly enrolled. Let them step forth to take their places in the arena of service where their talents and skills, their specialized training, their material resources, their offers of time and energy and, above all, their dedication to Bahá'í principles, can be put to work in improving the lot of man.

May all derive enduring inspiration from the following statement written in 1933 by the hand of our beloved Guardian:

'The problems which confront the believers at the present time, whether social, spiritual, economic or administrative will gradually be solved as the number and the resources of the friends multiply and their capacity for service and for the application of Bahá'í principles develops. They should be patient, confident and active in utilizing every possible opportunity that presents itself within the limits now necessarily imposed upon them. May the Almighty aid them to fulfil their highest hopes ..."

Messages from the Universal House of Justice 1963-1986, paras 379.9-379.10a, p. 604. (20 October 1983.)

*I*n the light of experience, however, it is now clear that we should have no misgivings in encouraging young Bahá'ís to enrol in such voluntary service organization programmes as the United Nations Volunteers, United States Peace Corps, Canadian University Services Overseas (CUSO) and similar Canadian agencies, the British Volunteer Programme (BVP) of the United Kingdom, and other voluntary service organizations. Other countries such as Germany, the Netherlands, and the Scandinavian lands are understood to have similar service organizations which are compatible with Bahá'í development goals as now tentatively envisaged.

Messages from the Universal House of Justice 1963-1986, para. 384.3, p. 611. (13 December 1983.)

Areas of Collaboration

Human Rights

*T*he fourth Taráz concerneth trustworthiness. Verily it is the door of security for all that dwell on earth and a token of glory on the part of the All-Merciful. He who partaketh thereof hath indeed partaken of the treasures of wealth and prosperity. Trustworthiness is the greatest portal leading unto the tranquillity and security of the people. In truth the stability of every affair hath depended and doth depend upon it. All the domains of power, of grandeur and of wealth are illumined by its light.

Ṭarázát (Ornaments), Bahá'u'lláh, *Tablets of Bahá'u'lláh*, p. 37.

O oppressors of earth!

Withdraw your hands from tyranny, for I have pledged Myself not to forgive any man's injustice. This is My covenant which I have irrevocably decreed in the preserved tablet and sealed with My seal of glory.

Bahá'u'lláh, *The Hidden Words*, Persian No. 64.

... *B*ahá'u'lláh taught that an equal standard of human rights must be recognized and adopted. In the estimation of God all men are equal; there is no distinction or preferment for any soul in the dominion of His justice and equity.

'Abdu'l-Bahá, *The Promulgation of Universal Peace*, p. 182. (9 June 1912.)

*T*he increasing attention being focused on some of the most deep-rooted problems of the planet is yet another hopeful sign. Despite the obvious shortcomings of the United Nations, the more than two score declarations and conventions adopted by that organization, even where governments have not been enthusiastic in their commitment, have given ordinary people a sense of a new lease on life. The Universal Declaration of Human Rights, the Convention on the Prevention and Punishment of the Crime of Genocide, and the similar measures concerned with eliminating all forms of discrimination based on race, sex or religious belief; upholding the rights of the child; protecting all persons against being subjected to torture; eradicating hunger and malnutrition; using scientific and technological progress in the interest of peace and the benefit of mankind—all such measures, if courageously enforced and expanded, will advance the day when the spectre of war will have lost its power to dominate international relations. There is no need to stress the significance of the issues addressed by these declarations and conventions.

The Promise of World Peace, *Messages of the Universal House of Justice 1963-1986*, para. 438.28, pp. 687-688. (October 1985.)

Moral Education

*M*an is the supreme Talisman. Lack of a proper education hath, however, deprived him of that which he doth inherently possess. Through a word proceeding out of the mouth of God he was called into being; by one word more he was guided to recognize the Source of his education; by yet another word his station and destiny were safeguarded. The Great Being saith: Regard man as a mine rich in gems of inestimable value. Education can, alone, cause it to reveal its treasures, and enable mankind to benefit therefrom.

Bahá'u'lláh, *Gleanings from the Writings of Bahá'u'lláh*, section CXXII, pp. 259-260.

*B*end your minds and wills to the education of the peoples and kindreds of the earth, that haply the dissensions that divide it may, through the power of the Most Great Name, be blotted out from its face, and all mankind become the upholders of one Order, and the inhabitants of one City.

Bahá'u'lláh, *Gleanings from the Writings of Bahá'u'lláh*, section CLIV, pp. 333-334.0

*T*he education and training of children is among the most meritorious acts of humankind and draweth down the grace and favour of the All-Merciful, for education is the indispensable foundation of all human excellence and alloweth man to work his way to the heights of abiding glory. If a child be trained from his infancy, he will, through the loving care of the Holy Gardener, drink in the crystal waters of the spirit and of knowledge, like a young tree amid the rilling brooks. And certainly he will gather to himself the bright rays of the Sun of Truth, and through its light and heat will grow ever fresh and fair in the garden of life.

Therefore must the mentor be a doctor as well: that is, he must, in instructing the child, remedy its faults; must give him learning, and at the same time rear him to have a spiritual nature. Let the teacher be a doctor to the character of the child, thus will he heal the spiritual ailments of the children of men.

If, in this momentous task, a mighty effort be exerted, the world of humanity will shine out with other adornings, and shed the fairest light. Then will this darksome place grow luminous, and this abode of earth turn into Heaven.

'Abdu'l-Bahá, *Selections from the Writings of 'Abdu'l-Bahá*, no. 103, pp. 129-130.

*T*hey must promote by every means in their power the material as well as the spiritual enlightenment of youth, the means for the education of children, institute, whenever possible, Bahá'í educational institutions, organize and supervise their work and provide the best means for their progress and development.

Shoghi Effendi, *Bahá'í Administration*, p. 38.

Equality of Women and Men

*P*raised be God, the Pen of the Most High hath lifted distinctions from between His servants and handmaidens, and, through His consummate favours and all-encompassing mercy, hath conferred upon all a station and rank on the same plane.

Bahá'u'lláh, *The Compilation of Compilations*, Vol. II (Women), no. 2093, p. 357.

*U*ntil the reality of equality between man and woman is fully established and attained, the highest social development of mankind is not possible. Even granted that woman is inferior to man in some degree of capacity or accomplishment, this or any other distinction would continue to be productive of discord and trouble. The only remedy is education, opportunity; for equality means equal qualification. ...

... And let it be known once more that until woman and man recognize and realize equality, social and political progress here or anywhere will not be possible.

Words of 'Abdu'l-Bahá, *The Promulgation of Universal Peace*, pp. 76-77. (2 May 1912.)

*W*hen all mankind shall receive the same opportunity of education and the equality of men and women be realized, the foundations of war will be utterly destroyed. Without equality this will be impossible because all differences and distinction are conducive to discord and strife. Equality between men and women is conducive to the abolition of warfare for the reason that women will never be willing to sanction it.

Words of 'Abdu'l-Bahá, *The Promulgation of Universal Peace*, p. 175. (9 June 1912.)

*T*herefore, strive to show in the human world that women are most capable and efficient, that their hearts are more tender and susceptible than the hearts of men, that they are more philanthropic and responsive toward the needy and suffering, that they are inflexibly opposed to war and are lovers of peace. Strive that the ideal of international peace may become realized through the efforts of womankind, for man is more inclined to war than woman, and a real evidence of woman's superiority will be her service and efficiency in the establishment of universal peace.

Words of 'Abdu'l-Bahá, *The Promulgation of Universal Peace*, p. 284. (26 August 1912.)

*T*he emancipation of women, the achievement of full equality between the sexes, is one of the most important, though less acknowledged prerequisites of peace. The denial of such equality perpetrates an injustice against one half of the world's population and promotes in men harmful attitudes and habits that are carried from the family to the workplace, to political life, and ultimately to international relations. There are no grounds, moral, practical, or biological, upon which such denial can be justified. Only as women are welcomed into full partnership in all fields of human endeavour will the moral and psychological climate be created in which international peace can emerge.

The Promise of World Peace, *Messages of the Universal House of Justice 1963–1986*, para. 438.3, p. 689. (October 1985.)

Racial Unity

O children of men!

Know ye not why We created you all from the same dust? That no one should exalt himself over the other. Ponder at all times in your hearts how ye were created. Since We have created you all from one same substance it is incumbent on you to be even as one soul, to walk with the same feet, eat with the same mouth and dwell in the same land, that from your inmost being, by your deeds and actions, the signs of oneness and the essence of detachment may be made manifest. Such is My counsel to you, O concourse of light! Heed ye this counsel that ye may obtain the fruit of holiness from the tree of wondrous glory.

Bahá'u'lláh, *The Hidden Words*, Arabic No. 68.

*T*he diversity in the human family should be the cause of love and harmony, as it is in music where many different notes blend together in the making of a perfect chord. If you meet those of a different race and colour from yourself, do not mistrust them and withdraw yourself into your shell of conventionality, but rather be glad and show them kindness.

Public Talk of 'Abdu'l-Bahá, *Paris Talks*, p. 45. (28 October 1911.)

I had a servant who was black; his name was Isfandíyár. If a perfect man could be found in the world, that man was Isfandíyár. He was the essence of love, radiant with sanctity and perfection, luminous with light. Whenever I think of Isfandíyár, I am moved to tears, although he passed away fifty years ago...

Then it is evident that excellence does not depend on colour. Character is the true criterion of humanity. Anyone who possesses a good character, who has faith in God and is firm, whose actions are good, whose speech is good - that one is accepted at the threshold of God no matter what colour he may be... My hope is that the white and the black will be united in perfect love and fellowship, with complete unity and brotherhood...

I hope you will continue in unity and fellowship. How beautiful to see black and white together! I hope, God willing, the day may come when I shall see the red men, the Indians, with you, also Japanese and others. Then there will be white roses, yellow roses, red roses, and a very wonderful rose garden will appear in the world.

'Abdu'l-Bahá, *The Promulgation of Universal Peace*, pp. 427-428.

I hope that ye may cause that downtrodden race to become glorious, and to be joined with the white race, to serve the world of man with the utmost sincerity, faithfulness, love, and purity. This opposition, enmity, and prejudice among the white race and the coloured cannot be effaced except through faith, assurance, and the teachings of the Blessed Beauty. This question of the union of the white and the black is very important for if it is not realized, erelong great difficulties will arise, and harmful results will follow. If this matter remaineth without change, enmity will be increased day by day, and the final result will be hardship and may end in bloodshed.

'Abdu'l-Bahá, cited by Shoghi Effendi, *The Advent of Divine Justice*, p. 39.

*L*et the white make a supreme effort in their resolve to contribute their share to the solution of this problem, to abandon once for all their usually inherent and at times subconscious sense of superiority, to correct their tendency towards revealing a patronizing attitude towards the members of the other race, to persuade them through their intimate, spontaneous and informal association with them of the genuineness of their friendship and the sincerity of their intentions, and to master their impatience of any lack of responsiveness on the part of a people who have received, for so long a period, such grievous and slow-healing wounds. Let the Negroes, through a corresponding effort on their part, show by every means in their power the warmth of their response, their readiness to forget the past, and their ability to wipe out every trace of suspicion that may still linger in their hearts and minds. Let neither think that the solution of so vast a problem is a matter that exclusively concerns the other. Let neither think that such a problem can either easily or immediately be resolved. Let neither think that they can wait confidently for the solution of this problem until the initiative has been taken, and the favourable circumstances created, by agencies that stand outside the orbit of their Faith. Let neither think that anything short of genuine love, extreme patience, true humility, consummate tact, sound initiative, mature wisdom, and deliberate, persistent, and prayerful effort, can succeed in blotting out the stain which this patent evil has left on the fair name of their common country.

Shoghi Effendi, *The Advent of Divine Justice*, p. 40.

... *R*ECALL WITH PROFOUND EMOTION MESSAGE BELOVED GUARDIAN OCCASION 1953 CONFERENCE WHEREIN HE EXTOLLED PUREHEARTED SPIRITUALLY RECEPTIVE INDIGENOUS PEOPLE AFRICA WHOM BAHÁ'U'LLÁH COMPARED PUPIL EYE THROUGH WHICH LIGHT OF SPIRIT SHINETH FORTH AND FOR WHOSE CONVERSION BOTH GUARDIAN AND MASTER BEFORE HIM YEARNED AND LABOURED ...

The Universal House of Justice, cable to the International Conference, Kampala, Uganda, 6 October 1967. Cited in *Lights of Guidance*, no. 1783, p. 526.

*R*acism, one of the most baneful and persistent evils, is a major barrier to peace. Its practice perpetuates too outrageous a violation of the dignity of human beings to be countenanced under any pretext. Racism retards the unfoldment of the boundless potentialities of its victims, corrupts its perpetrators, and blights human progress. Recognition of the oneness of mankind, implemented by appropriate legal measures, must be universally upheld if this problem is to be overcome.

The Promise of World Peace, *Messages of the Universal House of Justice 1963–1986*, para. 438.29, p. 688. (October 1985.)

Harmony Between Religions

*T*here can be no doubt whatever that the peoples of the world, of whatever race or religion, derive their inspiration from one heavenly Source, and are the subjects of one God. The difference between the ordinances under which they abide should be attributed to the varying requirements and exigencies of the age in which they were revealed.

Bahá'u'lláh, *Gleanings from the Writings of Bahá'u'lláh*, section CXI, p. 217.

*G*ird up the loins of your endeavour, O people of Bahá, that haply the tumult of religious dissension and strife that agitateth the peoples of the earth may be stilled, that every trace of it may be completely obliterated.

Bahá'u'lláh, *Epistle to the Son of the Wolf*, pp. 13–14.[112]

*M*ost regrettable of all is the state of difference and divergence we have created between each other in the name of religion, imagining that a paramount duty in our religious belief is that of alienation and estrangement, that we should shun each other and consider each other contaminated with error and infidelity. In reality, the foundations of the divine religions are one and the same.

'Abdu'l-Bahá, *The Promulgation of Universal Peace*, p. 403. (8 November 1912.)

---

112   Also *Gleanings from the Writings of Bahá'u'lláh*, section CXXXII, p. 288.

*R*eligious strife, throughout history, has been the cause of innumerable wars and conflicts, a major blight to progress, and is increasingly abhorrent to the people of all faiths and no faith. Followers of all religions must be willing to face the basic questions which this strife raises, and to arrive at clear answers. How are the differences between them to be resolved, both in theory and in practice? The challenge facing the religious leaders of mankind is to contemplate, with hearts filled with the spirit of compassion and a desire for truth, the plight of humanity, and to ask themselves whether they cannot, in humility before their Almighty Creator, submerge their theological differences in a great spirit of mutual forbearance that will enable them to work together for the advancement of human understanding and peace.

The Promise of World Peace, *Messages of the Universal House of Justice 1963-1986*, para. 438.32, p. 689. (October 1985.)

*T*hose who have held blindly and selfishly to their particular orthodoxies, who have imposed on their votaries erroneous and conflicting interpretations of the pronouncements of the Prophets of God, bear heavy responsibility for this confusion—a confusion compounded by the artificial barriers erected between faith and reason, science and religion. For from a fair-minded examination of the actual utterances of the Founders of the great religions, and of the social milieus in which they were obliged to carry out their missions, there is nothing to support the contentions and prejudices deranging the religious communities of mankind and therefore all human affairs.

The teaching that we should treat others as we ourselves would wish to be treated, an ethic variously repeated in all the great religions, lends force to this latter observation in two particular respects: it sums up the moral attitude, the peace-inducing aspect, extending through these religions irrespective of their place or time of origin; it also signifies an aspect of unity which is their essential virtue, a virtue mankind in its disjointed view of history has failed to appreciate.

Had humanity seen the Educators of its collective childhood in their true character, as agents of one civilizing process, it would no doubt have reaped incalculably greater benefits from the cumulative effects of their successive missions. This, alas, it failed to do.

The Promise of World Peace, *Messages of the Universal House of Justice 1963-1986*, no. 438.15-438.17, pp. 684-685. (October 1985.)

Global Prosperity

*N*o deed of man is greater before God than helping the poor. Spiritual conditions are not dependent upon the possession of worldly treasures or the absence of them. When one is physically destitute, spiritual thoughts are more likely. Poverty is a stimulus toward God. Each one of you must have great consideration for the poor and render them assistance. Organize in an effort to help them and prevent increase of poverty. The greatest means for prevention is that whereby the laws of the community will be so framed and enacted that it will not be possible for a few to be millionaires and many destitute.

One of Bahá'u'lláh's teachings is the adjustment of means of livelihood in human society. Under this adjustment there can be no extremes in human conditions as regards wealth and sustenance. For the community needs financier, farmer, merchant and labourer just as an army must be composed of commander, officers and privates. All cannot be commanders; all cannot be officers or privates. Each in his station in the social fabric must be competent—each in his function according to ability but with justness of opportunity for all.

Words of 'Abdu'l-Bahá, *The Promulgation of Universal Peace*, p. 216. (1 July 1912.)

*A*ll too many of these ideologies, alas, instead of embracing the concept of the oneness of mankind and promoting the increase of concord among different peoples, have tended to deify the state, to subordinate the rest of mankind to one nation, race or class, to attempt to suppress all discussion and interchange of ideas, or to callously abandon starving millions to the operations of a market system that all too clearly is aggravating the plight of the majority of mankind, while enabling small sections to live in a condition of affluence scarcely dreamed of by our forebears.

How tragic is the record of the substitute faiths that the worldly-wise of our age have created. In the massive disillusionment of entire populations who have been taught to worship at their altars can be read history's irreversible verdict on their value. The fruits these doctrines have produced, after decades of an increasingly unrestrained exercise of power by those who owe their ascendancy in human affairs to them, are the social and economic ills that blight every region of our world in the closing years of the twentieth century. Underlying all these outward afflictions is the spiritual damage reflected in the apathy that has gripped the mass of the peoples of all nations and by the extinction of hope in the hearts of deprived and anguished millions.

The time has come when those who preach the dogmas of materialism, whether of the east or the west, whether of capitalism or socialism, must give account of the moral stewardship they have presumed to exercise. Where is the "new world" promised by these ideologies? Where is the international peace to whose ideals they proclaim their devotion? Where are the breakthroughs into new realms of cultural achievement produced by the aggrandizement of this race, of that nation or of a particular class? Why is the vast majority of the world's peoples sinking ever deeper into hunger and wretchedness when wealth on a scale undreamed of by the Pharaohs, the Caesars, or even the imperialist powers of the nineteenth century is at the disposal of the present arbiters of human affairs?

Most particularly, it is in the glorification of material pursuits, at once the progenitor and common feature of all such ideologies, that we find the roots which nourish the falsehood that human beings are incorrigibly selfish and aggressive. It is here that the ground must be cleared for the building of a new world fit for our descendants.

The Promise of World Peace, *Messages of the Universal House of Justice 1963-1986*, paras 438.19-438.22, pp. 685-686. (October 1985.)

*T*he inordinate disparity between rich and poor, a source of acute suffering, keeps the world in a state of instability, virtually on the brink of war. Few societies have dealt effectively with this situation. The solution calls for the combined application of spiritual, moral and practical approaches. A fresh look at the problem is required, entailing consultation with experts from a wide spectrum of disciplines, devoid of economic and ideological polemics, and involving the people directly affected in the decisions that must urgently be made. It is an issue that is bound up not only with the necessity for eliminating extremes of wealth and poverty but also with those spiritual verities the understanding of which can produce a new universal attitude. Fostering such an attitude is itself a major part of the solution.

The Promise of World Peace, Messages of the Universal House of Justice 1963-1986, para. 438.30, pp. 688. (October 1985.)

Protection of the Environment

Nature in its essence is the embodiment of My Name, the Maker, the Creator. Its manifestations are diversified by varying causes, and in this diversity there are signs for men of discernment. Nature is God's Will and is its expression in and through the contingent world. It is a dispensation of Providence ordained by the Ordainer, the All-Wise.

Lawḥ-i-Ḥikmat (Tablet of Wisdom), Bahá'u'lláh, Tablets of Bahá'u'lláh, p. 142.

Were one to observe with an eye that discovereth the realities of all things, it would become clear that the greatest relationship that bindeth the world of being together lieth in the range of created things themselves, and that co-operation, mutual aid and reciprocity are essential characteristics in the unified body of the world of being, inasmuch as all created things are closely related together and each is influenced by the other or deriveth benefit therefrom, either directly or indirectly.

'Abdu'l-Bahá, The Compilation of Compilations, Vol. I (Conservation of the Earth's Resources), no. 2.1.1, p. 71; Vol. I (Ḥuqúqu'lláh), no. 1159, p. 509. (October 1989.)

... When thou lookest at the orderly pattern of kingdoms, cities and villages, with the attractiveness of their adornments, the freshness of their natural resources, the refinement of their appliances, the ease of their means of travel, the extent of knowledge available about the world of nature, the great inventions, the colossal enterprises, the noble discoveries and scientific researches, thou wouldst conclude that civilization conduceth to the happiness and the progress of the human world. Yet shouldst thou turn thine eye to the discovery of destructive and infernal machines, to the development of forces of demolition and the invention of fiery implements, which uproot the tree of life, it would become evident and manifest unto thee that civilization is conjoined with barbarism. Progress and barbarism go hand in hand, unless material civilization be confirmed by Divine Guidance, by the revelations of the All-Merciful and by godly virtues, and be reinforced by spiritual conduct, by the ideals of the Kingdom and by the outpourings of the Realm of Might.

Consider now, that the most advanced and civilized countries of the world have been turned into arsenals of explosives, that the continents of the globe have been transformed into huge camps and battlefields, that the peoples of the world have formed themselves into armed nations, and that the governments of the world are vying with each other as to who will first step into the field of carnage and bloodshed, thus subjecting mankind to the utmost degree of affliction.

Therefore, this civilization and material progress should be combined with the Most Great Guidance so that this nether world may become the scene of the appearance of the bestowals of the Kingdom, and physical achievements may be conjoined with the effulgences of the Merciful. This in order that the beauty and perfection of the world of man may be unveiled and be manifested before all in the utmost grace and splendour. Thus everlasting glory and happiness shall be revealed.

'Abdu'l-Bahá, Selections from the Writings of 'Abdu'l-Bahá, no. 225, pp. 284-285.

Shoghi Effendi links the preservation and reclamation of the earth's resources with both the "protection [of the] physical world and [the] heritage [of] future generations". He affirms that the work of such groups as the Men of the Trees and the World Forestry Charter is "essentially humanitarian", and he applauds their "noble objective" of reclaiming the "desert areas [of] Africa".

Letter written on behalf of Shoghi Effendi, The Compilation of Compilations, Vol. I (Conservation of the Earth's Resources), no. 3.1, p. 83. (October 1989.)

We cannot segregate the human heart from the environment outside us and say that once one of these is reformed everything will be improved. Man is organic with the world. His inner life moulds the environment and is itself also deeply affected by it. The one acts upon the other and every abiding change in the life of man is the result of these mutual reactions.

No movement in the world directs its attention upon both these aspects of human life and has full measures for their improvement, save the teachings of Bahá'u'lláh. And this is its distinctive feature. If we desire therefore the good of the world we should strive to spread those teachings and also practice them in our own life. Through them will the human heart be changed, and also our social environment provides the atmosphere in which we can grow spiritually and reflect in full the light of God shining through the revelation of Bahá'u'lláh.

Letter written on behalf of Shoghi Effendi,, The Compilation of Compilations, Vol. I (Conservation of the Earth's Resources), no. 3.3, p. 84-85. (October 1989.)

Until such time as the nations of the world understand and follow the admonitions of Bahá'u'lláh to whole-heartedly work together in looking after the best interests of all humankind, and unite in the search for ways and means to meet the many environmental problems besetting our planet, the House of Justice feels that little progress will be made towards their solution ....

The Universal House of Justice, Conservation of the Earth's Resources, The Compilation of Compilations, Vol. I, no. 3.3, p. 85. (October 1989.)

Global Governance

Loyalty and Obedience to Government

*T*he cardinal principle which we must follow, (in connection with your questions), is obedience to the Government prevailing in any land in which we reside. We cannot, because, say, we do not personally like a totalitarian form of government, refuse to obey it when it becomes the ruling power. Nor can we join underground Movements which are a minority agitating against the prevailing government.

If a state of Revolution and complete chaos exist in a Country, so that it is impossible to say there is one government in power, then the friends must consult with their National or their Local Assembly, and be guided by what the Assembly considers the proper action to take; in other words which party might be best considered the legal governing authority.

We see, therefore, that we must do two things—shun politics like the plague, and be obedient to the Government in power in the place where we reside. We cannot start judging how a particular government came into power, and therefore whether we should obey it or not. This would immediately plunge us into politics. We must obey in all cases except where a spiritual principle is involved, such as denying our Faith. For these spiritual principles we must be willing to die. What we Bahá'ís must face is that fact that society is rapidly disintegrating—so rapidly that moral issues which were clear half a century ago are now hopelessly confused, and what is more, thoroughly mixed up with battling political interests. That is why the Bahá'ís must turn all their forces into the channel of building up the Bahá'í Cause and its administration. They can neither change nor help the world in any other way at present. If they become involved in the issues the Governments of the world are struggling over, they will be lost. But if they build up the Bahá'í pattern they can offer it as a remedy when all else has failed.

Letter dated 21 December 1948 written on behalf of Shoghi Effendi, *Lights of Guidance*, no. 1453, p. 446.

*F*or whereas the friends should obey the government under which they live, even at the risk of sacrificing all their administrative affairs and interests, they should under no circumstances suffer their inner religious beliefs and convictions to be violated and transgressed by any authority whatever. A distinction of a fundamental importance must, therefore, be made between spiritual and administrative matters. Whereas the former are sacred and inviolable, and hence cannot be subject to compromise, the latter are secondary and can consequently be given up and even sacrificed for the sake of obedience to the laws and regulations of the government. Obedience to the state is so vital a principle of the Cause that should authorities in ... decide today to prevent the Bahá'ís from holding any meeting or publishing any literature they should obey ... But, as already pointed out, such an allegiance is confined merely to administrative matters which if checked can only retard the progress of the Faith for some time. In matters of belief, however, no compromise whatever should be allowed, even though the outcome of it be death or expulsion.

Letter dated 11 February 1934 written on behalf of Shoghi Effendi, *Lights of Guidance*, no. 1455, p. 446.

Let them proclaim that in whatever country they reside, and however advanced their institutions, or profound their desire to enforce the laws, and apply the principles, enunciated by Bahá'u'lláh, they will, unhesitatingly, subordinate the operation of such laws and the application of such principles to the requirements and legal enactments of their respective governments. Theirs is not the purpose, while endeavouring to conduct and perfect the administrative affairs of their Faith, to violate, under any circumstances, the provisions of their country's constitution, much less to allow the machinery of their administration to supersede the government of their respective countries.

Shoghi Effendi, The Golden Age of the Cause of Bahá'u'lláh, *The World Order of Bahá'u'lláh*, pp. 65-66.

... Bahá'ís obey the laws, Federal or state, unless submission to these laws amounts to a denial of their Faith. We live the Bahá'í life, fully and continuously, unless prevented by the authorities. This implies, if it does not categorically state, that a Bahá'í is not required to make a judgement as to the precedence of Federal or state law—this is for the courts to decide.

The Universal House of Justice, *Lights of Guidance*, no. 1462, p. 450. (30 March 1965.)

Non-involvement in Politics

I feel it, therefore, incumbent upon me to stress, now that the time is ripe, the importance of an instruction which, at the present stage of the evolution of our Faith, should be increasingly emphasized, irrespective of its application to the East or to the West. And this principle is no other than that which involves the non-participation by the adherents of the Faith of Bahá'u'lláh, whether in their individual capacities or collectively as local or national Assemblies, in any form of activity that might be interpreted, either directly or indirectly, as an interference in the political affairs of any particular government. ...

Let them refrain from associating themselves, whether by word or by deed, with the political pursuits of their respective nations, with the policies of their governments and the schemes and programmes of parties and factions. In such controversies they should assign no blame, take no side, further no design, and identify themselves with no system prejudicial to the best interests of that world-wide Fellowship which it is their aim to guard and foster.

Shoghi Effendi, *The World Order of Bahá'u'lláh*, pp. 63-64.

As the number of the Bahá'í communities in various parts of the world multiplies and their power, as a social force, becomes increasingly apparent, they will no doubt find themselves increasingly subjected to the pressure which men of authority and influence, in the political domain, will exercise in the hope of obtaining the support they require for the advancement of their aims. These communities will, moreover, feel a growing need of the good-will and the assistance of their respective governments in their efforts to widen the scope, and to consolidate the foundations, of the institutions committed to their charge. Let them beware lest, in their eagerness to further the aims of their beloved

Cause, they should be led unwittingly to bargain with their Faith, to compromise with their essential principles, or to sacrifice, in return for any material advantage which their institutions may derive, the integrity of their spiritual ideals.

Shoghi Effendi, *The World Order of Bahá'u'lláh*, p. 65.

Such a rectitude of conduct must manifest itself, with ever-increasing potency, in every verdict which the elected representatives of the Bahá'í community, in whatever capacity they may find themselves, may be called upon to pronounce. ... It must characterize the attitude of every loyal believer towards non-acceptance of political posts, non-identification with political parties, non-participation in political controversies, and non-membership in political organizations and ecclesiastical institutions.

Shoghi Effendi, *The Advent of Divine Justice*, p. 26.

If a Bahá'í were to insist on his right to support a political party, he could not deny the same degree of freedom to other believers. This would mean that within the ranks of the Faith, whose primary mission is to unite all men as one great family under God, there would be Bahá'ís opposed to each other. Where, then, would be the example of unity and harmony which the world is seeking?

If the institutions of the Faith, God forbid, became involved in politics, the Bahá'ís would find themselves arousing antagonism instead of love. If they took one stand in one country, they would be bound to change the views of the people in another country about the aims and purposes of the Faith. By becoming involved in political disputes, the Bahá'ís instead of changing the world or helping it, would themselves be lost and destroyed. The world situation is so confused and moral issues which were once clear have become so mixed up with selfish and battling factions, that the best way Bahá'ís can serve the highest interests of their country and the cause of true salvation for the world, is to sacrifice their political pursuits and affiliations and whole-heartedly and fully support the divine system of Bahá'u'lláh.

The Faith is not opposed to the true interests of any nation, nor is it against any party or faction. It holds aloof from all controversies and transcends them all, while enjoining upon its followers loyalty to government and a sane patriotism. This love for their country the Bahá'ís show by serving its well-being in their daily activity, or by working in the administrative channels of the government instead of through party politics or in diplomatic or political posts. The Bahá'ís may, indeed are encouraged to, mix with all strata of society, with the highest authorities and with leading personalities as well as with the mass of the people, and should bring the knowledge of the Faith to them; but in so doing they should strictly avoid becoming identified, or identifying the Faith, with political pursuits and party programmes.

Messages of the Universal House of Justice 1963-1986, paras 77.4c-77.4e, p 164. (8 February 1970.)

The Guardian wishes me to draw the attention of the friends through you that they should be very careful in their public utterance not to mention any political figures ... either to side with them or denounce them. This is the first thing to bear in mind.

Otherwise they will involve the friends in political matters, which is infinitely dangerous for the Cause.

Letter dated 12 January 1933 written on behalf of Shoghi Effendi, *Directives from the Guardian*, no. 149, p. 55.[113]

*R*egarding your question: the Guardian does not see how Bahá'í participation, with other organizations and religious bodies in a non-political meeting to promote civic unity and welfare along some line can be considered political. Much as the friends must guard against in any way ever seeming to identify themselves or the Cause with any political party, they must also guard against the other extreme of never taking part with other progressive groups, in conferences or committees designed to promote some activity in entire accord with our teachings—such as, for instance, better race relations.

Letter dated 21 November 1948 written on behalf of Shoghi Effendi, *Lights of Guidance*, no. 1815, p. 5.

*F*ully aware of the repeated statements of 'Abdu'l-Bahá that universality is of God, Bahá'ís in every land are ready, nay anxious, to associate themselves by word and deed with any association of men which, after careful scrutiny, they feel satisfied is free from every tinge of partisanship and politics and is wholly devoted to the interests of all mankind. In their collaboration with such associations they would extend any moral and material assistance they can afford, after having fulfilled their share of support to those institutions that affect directly the interests of the Cause.

Shoghi Effendi, *Baha'i Administration*, pp. 125–126.

The United Nations and Global Institutions Necessary for the Lesser Peace

*A*s an international organization, the United Nations has demonstrated humanity's capacity for united action in health, agriculture, education, environmental protection, and the welfare of children. It has affirmed our collective moral will to build a better future, evinced in the widespread adoption of international human rights Covenants. It has revealed the human race's deep-seated compassion, evidenced by the devotion of financial and human resources to the assistance of people in distress. And in the all-important realms of peace-building, peace-making and peace-keeping, the United Nations has blazed a bold path toward a future without war.

Yet the overall goals set out in the Charter of the United Nations have proved elusive. Despite the high hopes of its founders, the establishment of the United Nations some fifty years ago did not usher in an era of peace and prosperity for all. Although the United Nations has surely played a role in preventing a third world war, the last half decade has nevertheless been marked by numerous local, national and regional conflicts

---

113 Also *Lights of Guidance*, no. 1440, p. 442; and *Principles of Bahá'í Administration*, p. 32.

costing millions of lives. No sooner had improved relations between the superpowers removed the ideological motivation for such conflicts, than long-smouldering ethnic and sectarian passions surfaced as a new source of conflagration. In addition, although the end of the Cold War has reduced the threat of a global, terminal war, there remain instruments and technologies—and to some extent the underlying passions—which could bring about planet-wide destruction.

> The Bahá'í International Community, *Turning Point For All Nations*, section I, paras 7-8, p. 2.

*E*xtraordinary care must be taken in designing the architecture of the international order so that it does not over time degenerate into any form of despotism, of oligarchy, or of demagogy corrupting the life and machinery of the constituent political institutions.

In 1955, during the first decade review of the UN charter, the Bahá'í International Community offered a statement to the United Nations, based on ideas articulated nearly a century before by Bahá'u'lláh. "The Bahá'í concept of world order is defined in these terms: A world Super-State in whose favour all the nations of the world will have ceded every claim to make war, certain rights to impose taxation and all rights to maintain armaments, except for the purposes of maintaining internal order within their respective dominions. This State will have to include an International Executive adequate to enforce supreme and unchallengeable authority on every recalcitrant member of the Commonwealth; a World Parliament whose members are elected by the peoples in their respective countries and whose election is confirmed by their respective governments; a Supreme Tribunal whose judgement has a binding effect even in cases where the parties concerned have not voluntarily agreed to submit their case to its consideration."

While we believe this formulation of a world government is at once the ultimate safeguard and the inevitable destiny of humankind, we do recognize that it represents a long-term picture of a global society. Given the pressing nature of the current state of affairs, the world requires bold, practical and actionable strategies that go beyond inspiring visions of the future. Nevertheless, by focusing on a compelling concept, a clear and consistent direction for evolutionary change emerges from the mire of contradictory views and doctrines.

> The Bahá'í International Community, *Turning Point For All Nations*, section II, paras 12-14, pp. 5-6.

*A*n evolutionary mindset implies the ability to envision an institution over a long time frame perceiving its inherent potential for development, identifying the fundamental principles governing its growth, formulating high-impact strategies for short-term implementation, and even anticipating radical discontinuities along its path.

Studying the United Nations from this perspective unveils significant opportunities to strengthen the current system without the wholesale restructuring of its principal institutions or the intensive re-engineering of its core processes. In fact, we submit that no proposal for UN reform can produce high impact unless its recommendations are internally consistent and direct the UN along a projected evolutionary path toward a distinctive and relevant role within the future international order.

We believe the combination of recommendations described herein meets these conditions and that their adoption would represent a measured but significant step toward building a more just world order.

The Bahá'í International Community, *Turning Point For All Nations*, section III, paras 6-8, p. 7.

Bahá'í Attitude to Military Service

*I*t is true that Bahá'ís are not pacifists since we uphold the use of force in the service of justice and upholding law. But we do not believe that war is ever necessary and its abolition is one of the essential purposes and brightest promises of Bahá'u'lláh's revelation. His specific command to the kings of the earth is: "Should any one among you take up arms against another, rise ye all against him, for this is naught but manifest justice." (Tablet to Queen Victoria, *The Proclamation of Bahá'u'lláh*, p. 13) The beloved Guardian has explained that the unity of mankind implies the establishment of a world commonwealth, a world federal system, "... liberated from the curse of war and its miseries in which Force is made the servant of Justice ..." whose world executive "backed by an international Force, ... will safeguard the organic unity of the whole commonwealth." This is obviously not war but the maintenance of law and order on a world scale. Warfare is the ultimate tragedy of disunity among nations where no international authority exists powerful enough to restrain them from pursuing their own limited interests. Bahá'ís therefore ask to serve their countries in non-combatant ways during such fighting; they will doubtless serve in such an international Force as Bahá'u'lláh envisions, whenever it comes into being.

Letter dated 11 September 1984 written on behalf of the Universal House of Justice, *The Compilation of Compilations*, Vol. II (Peace), no. 1636, p. 199.[114]

*I*t is still his firm conviction that the believers, while expressing their readiness to unreservedly obey any directions that the authorities may issue concerning national service in time of war, should also, and while there is yet no outbreak of hostilities, appeal to the government for exemption from active military service in a combatant capacity, stressing the fact that in doing so they are not prompted by any selfish considerations but by the sole and supreme motive of upholding the Teachings of their Faith, which make it a moral obligation for them to desist from any act that would involve them in direct warfare with their fellow-humans of any other race or nation.

Letter dated 4 June 1939 written on behalf of Shoghi Effendi, *Unfolding Destiny*, p. 128.

---

114   Also *Lights of Guidance*, no. 1440, p. 442; and *Principles of Bahá'í Administration*, p. 32.

Chapter Twelve
The Most Great Peace: Creating a Spiritual Civilisation

Spiritual Civilization

*A*ll men have been created to carry forward an ever-advancing civilization.
Bahá'u'lláh, *Gleanings from the Writings of Bahá'u'lláh*, section CIX, p. 215.

*A*ll the peoples of Europe, notwithstanding their vaunted civilization, sink and drown in this terrifying sea of passion and desire, and this is why all the phenomena of their culture come to nothing. Let no one wonder at this statement or deplore it. The primary purpose, the basic objective, in laying down powerful laws and setting up great principles and institutions dealing with every aspect of civilization, is human happiness; and human happiness consists only in drawing closer to the Threshold of Almighty God, and in securing the peace and well-being of every individual member, high and low alike, of the human race; and the supreme agencies for accomplishing these two objectives are the excellent qualities with which humanity has been endowed.

A superficial culture, unsupported by a cultivated morality, is as "a confused medley of dreams" and external lustre without inner perfection is "like a vapour in the desert which the thirsty dreameth to be water." For results which would win the good pleasure of God and secure the peace and well-being of man, could never be fully achieved in a merely external civilization.
'Abdu'l-Bahá, *The Secret of Divine Civilization*, pp. 60-61.

*U*niversal benefits derive from the grace of the Divine religions, for they lead their true followers to sincerity of intent, to high purpose, to purity and spotless honour, to surpassing kindness and compassion, to the keeping of their covenants when they have covenanted, to concern for the rights of others, to liberality, to justice in every aspect of life, to humanity and philanthropy, to valour and to unflagging efforts in the service of mankind. It is religion, to sum up, which produces all human virtues, and it is these virtues which are the bright candles of civilization. If a man is not characterized by these excellent qualities, it is certain that he has never attained to so much as a drop out of the fathomless river of the waters of life that flows through the teachings of the Holy Books, nor caught the faintest breath of the fragrant breezes that blow from the gardens of God; for nothing on earth can be demonstrated by words alone, and every level of existence is known by its signs and symbols, and every degree in man's development has its identifying mark.

The purpose of these statements is to make it abundantly clear that the Divine religions, the holy precepts, the heavenly teachings, are the unassailable basis of human happiness, and that the peoples of the world can hope for no real relief or deliverance without this one great remedy. This panacea must, however, be administered by a wise and skilled physician, for in the hands of an incompetent all the cures that the Lord of men has ever created to heal men's ills could produce no health, and would on the contrary only destroy the helpless and burden the hearts of the already afflicted.

'Abdu'l-Bahá, *The Secret of Divine Civilization*, pp. 98-99.

*T*he teachings of Bahá'u'lláh will establish a new way of life for humanity. Those who are Bahá'ís must endeavour to establish this way of life just as rapidly as possible. Now that the hour has arrived when the Bahá'í Faith is gaining prominence, and is being viewed and reviewed by so many peoples, it is necessary that the adherents of the Faith should live up to the high ideals of the Faith in every way. In this way they can demonstrate that the Bahá'í Faith does create a new way of life, which brings to the individual a complete association with the Will of God, and thus the establishment of a peaceful and universal society. Divisional attachments are of man, while universal service is of God.

The Guardian is now anxious that all the friends achieve a universal consciousness and a universal way of life.

Letter dated 20 November 1955 written on behalf of Shoghi Effendi, *Lights of Guidance*, no. 1424, p. 435.

*T*he unity of the human race, as envisaged by Bahá'u'lláh, implies the establishment of a world commonwealth in which all nations, races, creeds and classes are closely and permanently united, and in which the autonomy of its state members and the personal freedom and initiative of the individuals that compose them are definitely and completely safeguarded. This commonwealth must, as far as we can visualize it, consist of a world legislature, whose members will, as the trustees of the whole of mankind, ultimately control the entire resources of all the component nations, and will enact such laws as shall be required to regulate the life, satisfy the needs and adjust the relationships of all races and peoples. A world executive, backed by an international Force, will carry out the decisions arrived at, and apply the laws enacted by, this world legislature, and will safeguard the organic unity of the whole commonwealth. A world tribunal will adjudicate and deliver its compulsory and final verdict in all and any disputes that may arise between the various elements constituting this universal system. A mechanism of world inter-communication will be devised, embracing the whole planet, freed from national hindrances and restrictions, and functioning with marvellous swiftness and perfect regularity. A world metropolis will act as the nerve centre of a world civilization, the focus towards which the unifying forces of life will converge and from which its energizing influences will radiate. A world language will either be invented or chosen from among the existing languages and will be taught in the schools of all the federated nations as an auxiliary to their mother tongue. A world script, a world literature, a uniform and universal system of currency, of weights and measures, will simplify and facilitate intercourse and understanding among the nations and races of mankind. In such a world society, science and religion, the two most potent forces in human life, will be reconciled, will co-operate, and will harmoniously develop. The press will, under such a system, while giving full scope to the expression of the diversified views and convictions of mankind, cease to be mischievously manipulated by vested interests, whether private or public, and will be liberated from the influence of contending governments and peoples. The economic resources of the world will be organized, its sources of raw materials will be tapped and fully utilized, its markets will be co-ordinated and developed, and the distribution of its products will be equitably regulated.

National rivalries, hatreds, and intrigues will cease, and racial animosity and prejudice will be replaced by racial amity, understanding and co-operation. The causes of religious strife will be permanently removed, economic barriers and restrictions will be completely abolished, and the inordinate distinction between classes will be obliterated. Destitution on the one hand, and gross accumulation of ownership on the other, will disappear. The enormous energy dissipated and wasted on war, whether economic or political, will be consecrated to such ends as will extend the range of human inventions and technical development, to the increase of the productivity of mankind, to the extermination of disease, to the extension of scientific research, to the raising of the standard of physical health, to the sharpening and refinement of the human brain, to the exploitation of the unused and unsuspected resources of the planet, to the prolongation of human life, and to the furtherance of any other agency that can stimulate the intellectual, the moral, and spiritual life of the entire human race.

A world federal system, ruling the whole earth and exercising unchallengeable authority over its unimaginably vast resources, blending and embodying the ideals of both the East and the West, liberated from the curse of war and its miseries, and bent on the exploitation of all the available sources of energy on the surface of the planet, a system in which Force is made the servant of Justice, whose life is sustained by its universal recognition of one God and by its allegiance to one common Revelation—such is the goal towards which humanity, impelled by the unifying forces of life, is moving.

Shoghi Effendi, The Unfoldment of World Civilization, *The World Order of Bahá'u'lláh*, pp. 203-204.

Cultural Diversity

*B*ahá'ís should obviously be encouraged to preserve their inherited cultural identities, as long as the activities involved do not contravene the principles of the Faith. The perpetuation of such cultural characteristics is an expression of unity in diversity. Although most of these festive celebrations have no doubt stemmed from religious rituals in bygone ages, the believers should not be deterred from participating in those in which, over the course of time, the religious meaning has given way to purely culturally oriented practices. For example, Naw-Rúz itself was originally a Zoroastrian religious festival, but gradually its Zoroastrian connotation has almost been forgotten. Iránians, even after their conversion to Islám, have been observing it as a national festival. Now Naw-Rúz has become a Bahá'í Holy Day and is being observed throughout the world, but, in addition to the Bahá'í observance, many Iránian Bahá'ís continue to carry out their past cultural traditions in connection with this Feast. Similarly, there are a number of national customs in every part of the world which have cultural rather than religious connotations.

In deciding whether or not to participate in such traditional activities, the Bahá'ís must guard against two extremes. The one is to disassociate themselves needlessly from harmless cultural observances and thus alienate themselves from their non-Bahá'í families and friends; the other is to continue the practice of abrogated observances of previous dispensations and thus undermine the independence of the Bahá'í Faith and create undesirable distinctions between themselves and their fellow-Bahá'ís. In this connection there is a difference between what Bahá'ís do among themselves and what they do in companionship with their non-Bahá'í friends and relations. For example, in a letter written on behalf of the Guardian there appears the following guidance:

> As regards the celebration of the Christian Holidays by the believers: it is surely preferable and even highly advisable that the friends should in their relation to each other discontinue observing such holidays as Christmas and New Year, and to have their festal gatherings of this nature instead during the intercalary days and Naw-Rúz.
>
> Letter dated 26 May 1982 written on behalf of the Universal House of Justice to a National Spiritual Assembly.

*Y*our letter raises the issue of cultural diversity within the Bahá'í community. The Faith seeks to maintain cultural diversity while promoting the unity of all peoples. Indeed, such diversity will enrich the tapestry of human life in a peaceful world society. The House of Justice supports the view that in every country the cultural traditions of the people should be observed within the Bahá'í community as long as they are not contrary to the Teachings. The general attitude of the Faith towards the traditional practices of various peoples is expressed in the following statement of Shoghi Effendi's, published in *The World Order of Bahá'u'lláh*, US 1982 edition, pages 41–42.

> Let there be no misgivings as to the animating purpose of the world-wide Law of Bahá'u'lláh. ... It does not ignore, nor does it attempt to suppress, the diversity of ethnical origins, of climate, of history, of language and tradition, of thought and habit, that differentiate the peoples and nations of the world. ... Its watchword is unity in diversity such as 'Abdu'l-Bahá Himself has explained:
>
> > "Consider the flowers of a garden. ... Diversity of hues, form and shape enricheth and adorneth the garden, and heighteneth the effect thereof."

Of course, many cultural elements everywhere inevitably will disappear or be merged with related ones from their societies, yet the totality will achieve that promised diversity within world unity. We can expect much cultural diversity in the long period before the emergence of a world commonwealth of nations in the Golden Age of Bahá'u'lláh's new world order. Much wisdom and tolerance will be required, and much time must elapse until the advent of that great day ....

When a Spiritual Assembly is faced with questions of possible conflict between tribal practices and Bahá'í law, it should distinguish between aspects of tribal community life which are related to fundamental laws (such as monogamy) and matters of lesser importance, from which the friends can and should extricate themselves gradually. Furthermore, the House of Justice has offered the advice that the institutions of the Faith should be careful not to press the friends to arbitrarily discard those local traditions which are harmless and often colourful characteristics of particular peoples and tribes. Were a new Bahá'í suddenly to cease following the customs of his people, it is possible that they might misunderstand the true nature of the Bahá'í Faith, and the Bahá'ís could be regarded as having turned against the traditions of the land. However, Bahá'ís should exercise vigilance, with the aid of the institutions of the Faith, to avoid inadvertent involvement in events which appear at first sight to be purely cultural and traditional in nature, but which are, in fact, held as a cover for politically oriented gatherings.

Letter dated 25 July 1988 written on behalf of the Universal House of Justice to a National Spiritual Assembly.

The Special Contribution of Music

We have made it lawful for you to listen to music and singing. Take heed, however, lest listening thereto should cause you to overstep the bounds of propriety and dignity. Let your joy be the joy born of My Most Great Name, a Name that bringeth rapture to the heart, and filleth with ecstasy the minds of all who have drawn nigh unto God. We, verily, have made music as a ladder for your souls, a means whereby they may be lifted up unto the realm on high; make it not, therefore, as wings to self and passion. Truly, We are loath to see you numbered with the foolish.

Bahá'u'lláh, The Kitáb-i-Aqdas (The Most Holy Book), para. 51, p. 38.

O bird that singeth sweetly of the Abhá Beauty! In this new and wondrous dispensation the veils of superstition have been torn asunder and the prejudices of eastern peoples stand condemned. Among certain nations of the East, music was considered reprehensible, but in this new age the Manifest Light hath, in His holy Tablets, specifically proclaimed that music, sung or played, is spiritual food for soul and heart.

The musician's art is among those arts worthy of the highest praise, and it moveth the hearts of all who grieve. Wherefore, ... play and sing out the holy words of God with wondrous tones in the gatherings of the friends, that the listener may be freed from chains of care and sorrow, and his soul may leap for joy and humble itself in prayer to the realm of Glory.

'Abdu'l-Bahá, Selections from the Writings of 'Abdu'l-Bahá, no. 74, p. 112.

Thank thou God that thou art instructed in music and melody, singing with pleasant voice the glorification and praise of the Eternal, the Living. I pray to God that thou mayest employ this talent in prayer and supplication, in order that the souls may become quickened, the hearts may become attracted and all may become inflamed with the fire of the love of God!

'Abdu'l-Bahá, *The Compilation of Compilations*, Vol. II (Music), no. 1413, p. 74.[115]

O servant of Bahá! Music is regarded as a praiseworthy science at the Threshold of the Almighty, so that thou mayest chant verses at large gatherings and congregations in a most wondrous melody and raise such hymns of praise at the Ma<u>sh</u>riqu'l-A<u>dh</u>kár to enrapture the Concourse on High. By virtue of this, consider how much the art of music is admired and praised. Try, if thou canst, to use spiritual melodies, songs and tunes, and to bring the earthly music into harmony with the celestial melody. Then thou wilt notice what a great influence music hath and what heavenly joy and life it conferreth. Strike up such a melody and tune as to cause the nightingales of divine mysteries to be filled with joy and ecstasy.

'Abdu'l-Bahá, *The Compilation of Compilations*, Vol. II (Music), no. 1419, p. 76.

What a wonderful meeting this is! These are the children of the Kingdom. The song we have just listened to was very beautiful in melody and words. The art of music is divine and effective. It is the food of the soul and spirit. Through the power and charm of music the spirit of man is uplifted. It has wonderful sway and effect in the hearts of children, for their hearts are pure, and melodies have great influence in them. The latent talents with which the hearts of these children are endowed will find expression through the medium of music. Therefore, you must exert yourselves to make them proficient; teach them to sing with excellence and effect. It is incumbent upon each child to know something of music, for without knowledge of this art the melodies of instrument and voice cannot be rightly enjoyed. Likewise, it is necessary that the schools teach it in order that the souls and hearts of the pupils may become vivified and exhilarated and their lives be brightened with enjoyment.

Words of 'Abdu'l-Bahá, *The Promulgation of Universal Peace*, p. 52. (24 April 1912.)

Whatever is in the heart of man, melody moves and awakens. If a heart full of good feelings and a pure voice are joined together, a great effect is produced. For instance: if there be love in the heart, through melody, it will increase until its intensity can scarcely be borne; but if bad thoughts are in the heart, such as hatred, it will increase and multiply. For instance: the music used in war awakens the desire for bloodshed. The meaning is that melody causes whatever feeling is in the heart to increase.

Some feelings occur accidentally and some have a foundation. For example: some people are naturally kind, but they may be accidentally upset by a wave of anger. But if they hear music, the true nature will reassert itself. Music really awakens the real, natural nature, the individual essence.

'Abdu'l-Bahá, *The Compilation of Compilations*, Vol. II (Music), no. 1422, p. 79.

---

[115] Also *Tablets of Abdul-Baha Abbas,* Vol. III, p. 512.

The Development of Arts and Crafts

At the outset of every endeavour, it is incumbent to look to the end of it. Of all the arts and sciences, set the children to studying those which will result in advantage to man, will ensure his progress and elevate his rank.

> *Lawḥ-i-Maqṣúd* (Tablet of Maqṣúd), Bahá'u'lláh, *Tablets of Bahá'u'lláh*, p. 168.

The purpose of learning should be the promotion of the welfare of the people, and this can be achieved through crafts. It hath been revealed and is now repeated that the true worth of artists and craftsmen should be appreciated, for they advance the affairs of mankind. Just as the foundations of religion are made firm through the Law of God, the means of livelihood depend upon those who are engaged in arts and crafts. True learning is that which is conducive to the well-being of the world, not to pride and self-conceit, or to tyranny, violence and pillage.

> Bahá'u'lláh, *The Compilation of Compilations*, Vol. I (Arts and Crafts), no. 10, p. 3.

Through the mere revelation of the word "Fashioner," issuing forth from His lips and proclaiming His attribute to mankind, such power is released as can generate, through successive ages, all the manifold arts which the hands of man can produce. This, verily, is a certain truth. No sooner is this resplendent word uttered, than its animating energies, stirring within all created things, give birth to the means and instruments whereby such arts can be produced and perfected. All the wondrous achievements ye now witness are the direct consequences of the Revelation of this Name. In the days to come, ye will, verily, behold things of which ye have never heard before. Thus hath it been decreed in the Tablets of God, and none can comprehend it except them whose sight is sharp.

> Bahá'u'lláh, *Gleanings from the Writings of Bahá'u'lláh*, section LXXIV, pp. 141-142.

Make every effort to acquire the advanced knowledge of the day, and strain every nerve to carry forward the divine civilization. Establish schools that are well organized, and promote the fundamentals of instruction in the various branches of knowledge through teachers who are pure and sanctified, distinguished for their high standards of conduct and general excellence, and strong in faith; scholars and educators with a thorough knowledge of sciences and arts.

Included must be promotion of the arts, the discovery of new wonders, the expansion of trade, and the development of industry. The methods of civilization and the beautification of the country must also be encouraged ...

> 'Abdu'l-Bahá, *The Compilation of Compilations*, Vol. II (Arts and Crafts), no. 22, p. 6.

He sincerely hopes that as the Cause grows and talented persons come under its banner, they will begin to produce in art the divine spirit that animates their soul. Every religion has brought with it some form of art—let us see what wonders this Cause is going to bring along. Such a glorious spirit should also give vent to a glorious art. The Temple with all its beauty is only the first ray of an early dawn; even more wondrous things are to be achieved in the future.

> Letter dated 11 December 1931 written on behalf of Shoghi Effendi, *The Compilation of Compilations*, Vol. I (Arts and Crafts), no. 25, p. 7.

Shoghi Effendi was very much interested to learn of the success of the "Pageant of the Nations" you produced. He sincerely hopes that all those who attended it were inspired by the same spirit that animated you while arranging it.

It is through such presentations that we can arouse the interest of the greatest number of people in the spirit of the Cause. The day will come when the Cause will spread like wildfire when its spirit and teachings will be presented on the stage or in art and literature as a whole. Art can better awaken such noble sentiments than cold rationalizing, especially among the mass of the people.

We have to wait only a few years to see how the spirit breathed by Bahá'u'lláh will find expression in the work of the artists. What you and some other Bahá'ís are attempting are only faint rays that precede the effulgent light of a glorious morn. We cannot yet value the part the Cause is destined to play in the life of society. We have to give it time. The material this spirit has to mould is too crude and unworthy, but it will at last give way and the Cause of Bahá'u'lláh will reveal itself in its full splendour.

> Letter dated 10 October 1932 written on behalf of Shoghi Effendi, *The Compilation of Compilations*, Vol. I (Arts and Crafts), no. 26, pp. 7-8.

Although now is only the very beginning of Bahá'í art, yet the friends who feel they are gifted in such matters should endeavour to develop and cultivate their gifts and through their works to reflect, however inadequately, the Divine Spirit which Bahá'u'lláh has breathed into the world.

> Letter dated 4 November 1937 written on behalf of Shoghi Effendi, *The Compilation of Compilations*, Vol. I (Arts and Crafts), no. 27, p. 8.

The Advancement of Science

The third Tajallí is concerning arts, crafts and sciences. Knowledge is as wings to man's life, and a ladder for his ascent. Its acquisition is incumbent upon everyone. The knowledge of such sciences, however, should be acquired as can profit the peoples of the earth, and not those which begin with words and end with words. Great indeed is the claim of scientists and craftsmen on the peoples of the world. Unto this beareth witness the Mother Book on the day of His return.

> *Tajallíyát* (Effulgences), Bahá'u'lláh, *Tablets of Bahá'u'lláh*, pp. 51-52.

*A*mong the greatest of all great services is the education of children, and promotion of the various sciences, crafts and arts. Praised be God, ye are now exerting strenuous efforts toward this end. The more ye persevere in this most important task, the more will ye witness the confirmations of God, to such a degree that ye yourselves will be astonished.

'Abdu'l-Bahá, *The Compilation of Compilations*, Vol. I (Arts and Crafts), no. 18, pp. 4–5; and Vol. I (Education), no. 619, p. 276.

O ye recipients of the favours of God! In this new and wondrous Age, the unshakeable foundation is the teaching of sciences and arts. According to explicit Holy Texts, every child must be taught crafts and arts, to the degree that is needful. Wherefore, in every city and village, schools must be established and every child in that city or village is to engage in study to the necessary degree.

It followeth that whatever soul shall offer his aid to bring this about will assuredly be accepted at the heavenly Threshold, and extolled by the Company on high.

'Abdu'l Bahá, *Selections from the Writings of 'Abdu'l-Bahá*, no. 109, pp. 134–135.

*A*ll blessings are divine in origin, but none can be compared with this power of intellectual investigation and research, which is an eternal gift producing fruits of unending delight. Man is ever partaking of these fruits. All other blessings are temporary; this is an everlasting possession. Even sovereignty has its limitations and overthrow; this is a kingship and dominion which none may usurp or destroy. Briefly, it is an eternal blessing and divine bestowal, the supreme gift of God to man. Therefore, you should put forward your most earnest efforts toward the acquisition of science and arts. The greater your attainment, the higher your standard in the divine purpose. The man of science is perceiving and endowed with vision, whereas he who is ignorant and neglectful of this development is blind. The investigating mind is attentive, alive; the callous and indifferent mind is deaf and dead. A scientific man is a true index and representative of humanity, for through processes of inductive reasoning and research he is informed of all that appertains to humanity, its status, conditions and happenings. He studies the human body politic, understands social problems and weaves the web and texture of civilization. In fact, science may be likened to a mirror wherein the infinite forms and images of existing things are revealed and reflected. It is the very foundation of all individual and national development. Without this basis of investigation, development is impossible. Therefore, seek with diligent endeavour the knowledge and attainment of all that lies within the power of this wonderful bestowal.

'Abdu'l-Bahá, *The Promulgation of Universal Peace*, p. 50. (23 April 1912.)

The Development of Health and Healing

*R*esort ye, in times of sickness, to competent physicians; We have not set aside the use of material means, rather have We confirmed it through this Pen, which God hath made to be the Dawning-place of His shining and glorious Cause.

Bahá'u'lláh, *The Kitáb-i-Aqdas* (The Most Holy Book), para. 113, p. 60.

*W*hatever competent physicians or surgeons prescribe for a patient should be accepted and complied with, provided that they are adorned with the ornament of justice. If they were to be endued with divine understanding, that would certainly be preferable and more desirable.

Bahá'u'lláh, *The Compilation of Compilations,* Vol. I (Health and Healing), no. 1014, p. 459.

*W*ell is it with the physician who cureth ailments in My hallowed and dearly-cherished Name.

Bahá'u'lláh, *The Compilation of Compilations,* Vol. I (Health and Healing), no. 1015, p. 459.

*D*o not neglect medical treatment when it is necessary, but leave it off when health has been restored. ... Treat disease through diet, by preference, refraining from the use of drugs; and if you find what is required in a single herb, do not resort to a compounded medicament. Abstain from drugs when the health is good, but administer them when necessary.

Bahá'u'lláh, *The Compilation of Compilations,* Vol. I (Health and Healing), no. 1019, p. 460.

*T*he child must, from the day of his birth, be provided with whatever is conducive to his health; and know ye this: so far as possible, the mother's milk is best for, more agreeable and better suited to the child, unless she should fall ill or her milk should run entirely dry ....

"Abdu'l-Bahá, *The Compilation of Compilations,* Vol. I (Health and Healing), no. 1026, p. 461.

... *C*oming to man, we see he hath neither hooked teeth nor sharp nails or claws, nor teeth like iron sickles. From this it becometh evident and manifest that the food of man is cereals and fruit. Some of the teeth of man are like millstones to grind the grain, and some are sharp to cut the fruit. Therefore he is not in need of meat, nor is he obliged to eat it. Even without eating meat he would live with the utmost vigour and energy. For example, the community of the Brahmins in India do not eat meat; notwithstanding this they are not inferior to other nations in strength, power, vigour, outward senses or intellectual virtues. Truly, the killing of animals and the eating of their meat is somewhat contrary to pity and compassion, and if one can content oneself with cereals, fruit, oil and nuts, such as pistachios, almonds and so on, it would undoubtedly be better and more pleasing.

"Abdu'l-Bahá, *The Compilation of Compilations,* Vol. I (Health and Healing), no. 1028, p. 462.

There are two ways of healing sickness, material means and spiritual means. The first is by the treatment of physicians; the second consisteth in prayers offered by the spiritual ones to God and in turning to Him. Both means should be used and practiced.

Illnesses which occur by reason of physical causes should be treated by doctors with medical remedies; those which are due to spiritual causes disappear through spiritual means. Thus an illness caused by affliction, fear, nervous impressions, will be healed more effectively by spiritual rather than by physical treatment. Hence, both kinds of treatment should be followed; they are not contradictory. Therefore thou shouldst also accept physical remedies inasmuch as these too have come from the mercy and favour of God, Who hath revealed and made manifest medical science so that His servants may profit from this kind of treatment also. Thou shouldst give equal attention to spiritual treatments, for they produce marvellous effects.

Now, if thou wishest to know the true remedy which will heal man from all sickness and will give him the health of the divine kingdom, know that it is the precepts and teachings of God. Focus thine attention upon them.

'Abdu'l-Bahá, *Selections from the Writings of 'Abdu'l-Bahá*, no. 133, pp. 151-152.

The greatest form of healing which the Bahá'ís can practice is to heal the spiritually sick souls of men by giving this greatest of all Messages to them. We can also try to help them, both physically and spiritually, through prayer.

Shoghi Effendi, *The Compilation of Compilations*, Vol. I (Health and Healing), no. 1073, p. 481. (25 March 1926.)

... You should not neglect your health, but consider it the means which enables you to serve. It—the body—is like a horse which carries the personality and spirit, and as such should be well cared for so it can do its work! You should certainly safeguard your nerves, and force yourself to take time, and not only for prayer and meditation, but for real rest and relaxation ....

Shoghi Effendi, *The Compilation of Compilations*, Vol. I (Health and Healing), no. 1076, p. 482. (23 November 1947.)

The Role of Bahá'í Scholarship

The spiritually learned are lamps of guidance among the nations, and stars of good fortune shining from the horizons of humankind. ...

For every thing, however, God has created a sign and symbol, and established standards and tests by which it may be known. The spiritually learned must be characterized by both inward and outward perfections; they must possess a good character, an enlightened nature, a pure intent, as well as intellectual power, brilliance and discernment, intuition, discretion and foresight, temperance, reverence, and a heartfelt fear of God.

"Abdu'l-Bahá, *The Secret of Divine Civilization*, pp. 33-34.

*T*he Cause needs more Bahá'í scholars, people who not only are devoted to it and believe in it and are anxious to tell others about it, but also who have a deep grasp of the Teachings and their significance, and who can correlate its beliefs with the current thoughts and problems of the people of the world.

> Letter dated 21 October 1943 written on behalf of Shoghi Effendi, *The Compilation of Compilations*, Vol. I (The Importance of Deepening, no. 495, p.226; and Vol. II (Youth), no. 2273, pp. 430-431.[116]

*I*t seems what we need now is a more profound and co-ordinated Bahá'í scholarship in order to attract such men as you are contacting. The world has—at least the thinking world—caught up by now with all the great and universal principles enunciated by Bahá'u'lláh over 70 years ago, and so of course it does not sound "new" to them. But we know that the deeper teachings, the capacity of His projected World Order to re-create society, are new and dynamic. It is these we must learn to present intelligently and enticingly to such men!

> Letter 3 July 1949 written on behalf of Shoghi Effendi, *The Compilation of Compilations*, Vol. I (The Importance of Deepening, no. 510, p.230; and Vol. II (Prominent People), no. 1858, p. 272; Vol. II (Guidelines for Teaching), no. 1966, p. 314.[117]

*A*s the Bahá'í community grows it will acquire experts in numerous fields—both by Bahá'ís becoming experts and by experts becoming Bahá'ís. As these experts bring their knowledge and skill to the service of the community and, even more, as they transform their various disciplines by bringing to bear upon them the light of the Divine Teachings, problem after problem now disrupting society will be answered. In such developments they should strive to make the utmost use of non-Bahá'í resources and should collaborate fully with non-Bahá'ís who are working in the same fields. Such collaboration will, in the long run, be of far more benefit than any attempt now to treat such scientific endeavours as specifically Bahá'í projects operating under Bahá'í institutions and financed by investment of Bahá'í funds.

Paralleling this process, Bahá'í institutional life will also be developing, and as it does so the Assemblies will draw increasingly upon scientific and expert knowledge—whether of Bahá'ís or of non-Bahá'ís—to assist in solving the problems of their communities.

In time great Bahá'í institutions of learning, great international and national projects for the betterment of human life will be inaugurated and flourish.

> *Messages of the Universal House of Justice 1963-1986*, paras 195.6-195.8, pp. 369-370. (21 August 1977.)

*T*he House of Justice feels that Bahá'í scholars must beware of the temptations of intellectual pride. 'Abdu'l-Bahá has warned the friends in the West that they would be subjected to intellectual tests, and the Guardian reminded them of this warning. There are many aspects of western thinking which have been exalted to a status of unassailable

---

116   Also *Bahá'í Scholarship: A Compilation and Essays*, p. 5.
117   Also *Bahá'í Scholarship: A Compilation and Essays*, p. 6.

principle in the general mind, that time may well show to have been erroneous or, at least, only partially true. Any Bahá'í who rises to eminence in academic circles will be exposed to the powerful influence of such thinking. One of the problems of modern times is the degree to which the different disciplines have become specialized and isolated from one another. Thinkers are now faced with a challenge to achieve a synthesis, or at least a coherent correlation, of the vast amount of knowledge that has been acquired during the past century. The Bahá'ís must be aware of this factor and of the moderation and all-embracing nature of this Revelation. In a letter written on 5 July 1947 to an individual believer the Guardian's secretary wrote on his behalf:

"One might liken Bahá'u'lláh's teachings to a sphere; there are points poles apart, and in between the thoughts and doctrines that unite them. We believe in balance in all things; we believe in moderation in all things—we must not be too emotional, nor cut and dried and lacking in feeling, we must not be so liberal as to cease to preserve the character and unity of our Bahá'í system, nor fanatical and dogmatic."

In the application of the social laws of the Faith, most of the difficulties can be seen to arise not only from outright disobedience, but also from the actions of those who, while careful to observe the letter of the law, try to go as far as it will permit them away from the spirit which lies at its heart. A similar tendency can be noted among some Bahá'í scholars.

The great advances in knowledge and understanding in the vital field of Bahá'í scholarship will be made by those who, while well versed in their subjects and adhering to the principles of research, are also thoroughly imbued with love for the Faith and the determination to grow in the comprehension of its teachings.

Letter dated 23 March 1983 written on behalf of the Universal House of Justice, *Bahá'í Scholarship: A Compilation and Essays*, pp. 17-18.

The House of Justice advises you not to attempt to define too narrowly the form that Bahá'í scholarship should take, or the approach that scholars should adopt. Rather should you strive to develop within your Association respect for a wide range of approaches and endeavours. No doubt there will be some Bahá'ís who will wish to work in isolation, while others will desire consultation and collaboration with those having similar interests. Your aim should be to promote an atmosphere of mutual respect and tolerance within which will be included scholars whose principal interest is in theological issues as well as those scholars whose interests lie in relating the insights provided by the Bahá'í teachings to contemporary thought in the arts and sciences.

A similar diversity should characterize the endeavours pursued by Bahá'í scholars, accommodating their interests and skills as well as the needs of the Faith. The course of world events, the development of new trends of thought and the extension of the teaching work all tend to highlight attractive and beneficial areas to which Bahá'í scholars might well direct their attention. Likewise, the expansion of the activities of the Bahá'í International Community in its relationship with United Nations agencies and other international bodies creates attractive opportunities for scholars to make a direct and highly valued contribution to the enhancement of the prestige of the Faith and to its proclamation within an influential and receptive stratum of society. As the Bahá'í community continues to emerge inexorably from obscurity, it will be confronted by enemies, from both within and without, whose aim will be to malign and misrepresent its principles, so that its admirers might be disillusioned and the faith of its adherents might be shaken; Bahá'í scholars have a vital role to play in the defence of the Faith through their contribution to anticipatory measures and their response to defamatory accusations levelled against the Faith.

> Letter dated 23 January 1991 written on behalf of the Universal House of Justice, *Bahá'í Scholarship: A Compilation and Essays*, pp. 23-24.

... *I*ndividual interpretation is considered the fruit of man's rational power and conducive to a better understanding of the teachings, provided that no disputes or arguments arise among the friends and the individual himself understands and makes it clear that his views are merely his own. Individual interpretations continually change as one grows in comprehension of the teachings. ... although individual insights can be enlightening and helpful, they can also be misleading. The friends must therefore learn to listen to the views of others without being overawed or allowing their faith to be shaken, and to express their own views without pressing them on their fellow Bahá'ís.

> The Universal House of Justice, *Messages from the Universal House of Justice 1963-1986*, para. 35.13, p. 88. (27 May 1966.)[118]

*T*he combination of absolute loyalty to the Manifestation of God and His Teachings, with the searching and intelligent study of the Teachings and history of the Faith which those Teachings themselves enjoin, is a particular strength of this Dispensation. In past Dispensations the believers have tended to divide into two mutually antagonistic groups: those who held blindly to the letter of the Revelation, and those who questioned and doubted everything. Like all extremes, both [of] these can lead into error. The beloved Guardian has written that "The Bahá'í Faith ... enjoins upon its followers the primary duty of an unfettered search after truth ...." Bahá'ís are called upon to follow the Faith with intelligence and understanding. Inevitably believers will commit errors as they strive to rise to this degree of maturity, and this calls for forbearance and humility on the part of all concerned, so that such matters do not cause disunity or discord among the friends.

> Letter dated 7 October 1980 written on behalf of the Universal House of Justice, *Bahá'í Scholarship: A Compilation and Essays*, p. 34.

*F*rom the passage of the Guardian's writings dealing with the attributes to which a Bahá'í scholar should aspire, it is evident that Bahá'í scholarship is an endeavour accessible to all members of the Bahá'í community, without exception. All believers can aspire to the attributes described by the Guardian, and can strive to relate the Bahá'í teachings to the thinking and concerns of the non-Bahá'í population around them. You can perform a

---

118 Also *Bahá'í Scholarship: A Compilation and Essays*, p. 37.

valuable service in bringing this potential role to the attention of all the believers—including those who may lack formal education, and those who dwell in remote areas, villages and islands—and to discourage any thought that Bahá'í scholarship is an activity open only to those who are highly educated or who are pursuing an academic career.

International Teaching Centre, *Bahá'í Scholarship: A Compilation and Essays*, pp. 31-32. (5 July 1949.)

The Process of Bahá'í Review

The House of Justice suggests that you consider the following steps through which the scholars of the Faith can overcome the problems which some of them perceive as presented by review of their publications.

- Let them accept unreservedly that 'Abdu'l-Bahá was right in instituting the temporary system of review, and that the decisions of the Guardian and the Universal House of Justice to not yet eliminate the system are in accordance with the Divine will.
- Let them recognize the fundamental difference between errors propagated by Bahá'ís from those issuing from non-Bahá'í sources. The review system is not an attempt to prevent errors or attacks on the Faith from being published; it is an attempt to prevent Bahá'ís from promulgating them in their published writings.
- Let them strive to understand the wisdom of this policy and its true nature, and to present it in its proper light to their fellow-academics ....
- Let Bahá'í scholars look upon their fellow Bahá'ís with trust and affection, not with disdain as to their qualifications and suspicion as to their motives. Let them regard them as devoted Bahá'ís striving to perform a service which the policies of the Faith require of them. And let them not hesitate to discuss openly with such reviewers the points which they raise. If it appears that a National Spiritual Assembly does not permit such open discussion, let them appeal to the Universal House of Justice for clarification of the situation. It is well understood by the Universal House of Justice that in some cases the process of review works inefficiently and with problems. These deficiencies could be overcome if the scholars themselves would collaborate with the process and openly raise questions about its functioning, rather than fostering an atmosphere of antagonism and mutual distrust.
- If the question of review is raised by non-Bahá'í academics, let the Bahá'í academics say that in this early stage in the development of the Faith this is a species of peer review which they welcome, since it is primarily among their fellow-Bahá'ís that they would find at this time those who would have sufficiently wide and deep understanding of the Faith and its Teachings to raise issues of importance which they would want to consider before publication. Of course, to be able to say this with sincerity, the scholars must have been able to accept the other steps mentioned above.

Letter dated 10 December 1992 written on behalf of the Universal House of Justice, *Issues Related to the Study of the Bahá'í Faith*, pp. 7-8.

The Internet

The opportunity which electronic communication technology provides for more speedy and thorough consultation among the friends is highly significant. Without doubt, it represents another manifestation of a development eagerly anticipated by the Guardian when he foresaw the creation of "a mechanism of world intercommunication ... embracing the whole planet, freed from national hindrances and restrictions, and functioning with marvellous swiftness and perfect regularity".

As you well appreciate, the extent to which such technology advances the work of the Faith depends, of course, on the manner in which it is used. As a medium for Bahá'ís to exchange views, it imposes on participants the same requirements of moderation, candour, and courtesy as would be the case in any other discussion ....

The ease and relative impersonality of the electronic medium require in some ways an even higher level of self-discipline than is the case in situations where a spirit of unity is reinforced by the opportunity for direct personal contact and social interaction. In the pursuit of such a spirit of unity, Bahá'ís will, without doubt, wish to assist the consultative processes by sharing and discussing relevant Bahá'í texts. This will itself have the further effect of drawing attention back to the framework of Bahá'í belief.

Letter dated 19 May 1995 written on behalf of the Universal House of Justice to an individual believer.

The House of Justice notes that you have been disturbed by some of the postings made to the email discussion group of which you have recently been a member. Email discussion groups are a new phenomenon; they can provide immense benefits for communication between people and for the teaching of the Faith, but, as you have seen, they can also give rise to far-reaching problems. The use of email requires an adjustment of perception. In the past, discussions among Bahá'ís would take place orally among groups of friends in private, or at summer schools and other Bahá'í events, or in letters between individuals. Inevitably, many erroneous statements were made; not all comments were as temperate as they should have been; many statements were misunderstood by those who heard them. After all, not all Bahá'ís have a profound knowledge of the teachings, and it is clear that even academic eminence is no guarantee of a correct understanding of the Revelation of God. Before email such extravagances had a limited range and were of an ephemeral nature. Now, the same kind of discussion is spread among a hundred or more people, who often do not know one another, is in a form more durable than speech, and can be disseminated to a vast readership at the touch of a button. A new level of self-discipline, therefore, is needed by those who take part. Such discussions among Bahá'ís call for self-restraint and purity of motive as well as cordiality, frankness and openness ....

Thus, if any participant in an email discussion feels that a view put forward appears to contradict or undermine the provisions of the Covenant, he should be free to say so, explaining candidly and courteously why he feels as he does. The person who made the initial statement will then be able to re-evaluate his opinion and, if he still believes it to be valid, he should be able to explain why it is not contrary to either the letter or the spirit of the Covenant. The participants in such a discussion should avoid disputation and, if they are unable to resolve an issue, they should refer the point to the Universal House of Justice since, in accordance with the Will and Testament of 'Abdu'l-Bahá, "By this body all the difficult problems are to be resolved ..." and it has the authority to decide upon "all problems which have caused difference, questions that are obscure, and matters that are not expressly recorded in the Book." In this way the Covenant can illuminate and temper the discourse and make it fruitful.

Letter dated 16 February 1996 written on behalf of the Universal House of Justice to an individual believer.

The Special Role of the Bahá'í Faith

O Ye the elected representatives of the people in every land! Take ye counsel together, and let your concern be only for that which profiteth mankind, and bettereth the condition thereof, if ye be of them that scan heedfully. Regard the world as the human body which, though at its creation whole and perfect, hath been afflicted, through various causes, with grave disorders and maladies. Not for one day did it gain ease, nay its sickness waxed more severe, as it fell under the treatment of ignorant physicians, who gave full reign to their personal desires, and have erred grievously. ...

We behold it, in this day, at the mercy of rulers so drunk with pride that they cannot discern clearly their own best advantage, much less recognize a Revelation so bewildering and challenging as this. ...

That which the Lord hath ordained as the sovereign remedy and mightiest instrument for the healing of all the world is the union of all its peoples in one universal Cause, one common Faith. This can in no wise be achieved except through the power of a skilled, an all-powerful and inspired Physician. This, verily, is the truth ....

Bahá'u'lláh, *Gleanings from the Writings of Bahá'u'lláh*, section CXX, pp. 254-255.[119]

*W*hen Bahá'u'lláh proclaimed His message to the world in the nineteenth century He made it abundantly clear that the first step essential for the peace and progress of mankind was its unification. As He says, "The well-being of mankind, its peace and security are unattainable unless and until its unity is firmly established." (*The World Order of Bahá'u'lláh*, p. 203) To this day, however, you will find most people take the opposite point of view: they look upon unity as an ultimate almost unattainable goal and concentrate first on remedying all the other ills of mankind. If they did but know it, these other ills are but various symptoms and side effects of the basic disease—disunity.

Bahá'u'lláh has, furthermore, stated that the revivification of mankind and the curing of all its ills can be achieved only through the instrumentality of His Faith. "The vitality of men's belief in God is dying out in every land; nothing short of His wholesome

---

[119] Also The Proclamation of Bahá'u'lláh, p. 67.

medicine can ever restore it. ... (*Gleanings*, XCIX) ... In a similar vein the Guardian wrote:

"Humanity, whether viewed in the light of man's individual conduct or in the existing relationships between organized communities and nations, has, alas, strayed too far and suffered too great a decline to be redeemed through the unaided efforts of the best among its recognized rulers and statesmen—however disinterested their motives, however concerted their their action, however unsparing their zeal and devotion to its cause. ...(*The World Order of Bahá'u'lláh*, pp. 33-34).

We are told by Shoghi Effendi that two great processes are at work in the world: the great Plan of God, tumultuous in its progress, working through mankind as a whole, tearing down the barriers to world unity and forging humankind into a unified body in the fires of suffering and experience. This process will produce in God's due time, the Lesser Peace, the political unification of the world. Mankind at that time can be likened to a body that is unified but without life. The second process, the task of breathing life into this unified body—of creating true unity and spirituality culminating in the Most Great Peace—is that of the Bahá'ís, who are labouring consciously, with detailed instructions and continuing divine guidance, to erect the fabric of the Kingdom of God on earth, into which they call their fellowmen, thus conferring upon them eternal life.

The working out of God's Major Plan proceeds mysteriously in ways directed by Him alone, but the Minor Plan that He has given us to execute, as our part in His grand design for the redemption of mankind, is clearly delineated. It is to this work that we must devote all our energies, for there is no one else to do it. So vital is this function of the Bahá'ís that Bahá'u'lláh has written: "O friends! Be not careless of the virtues with which ye have been endowed, neither be neglectful of your high destiny. Suffer not your labours to be wasted through the vain imaginations which certain hearts have devised. Ye are the stars of the heaven of understanding, the breeze that stirreth at the break of day, the soft-flowing waters upon which must depend the very life of all men, the letters inscribed upon His sacred scroll. With the utmost unity and in a spirit of perfect fellowship, exert yourselves, that ye may be enabled to achieve that which beseemeth this Day of God." (*Gleanings*, XCVI).

Messages of the Universal House of Justice 1963-1986, paras 55.3-55.6, pp. 125-127. (8 December 1967).

*T*he amelioration of the conditions of the world requires the reconstruction of human society and efforts to improve the material well-being of humanity. The Bahá'í approach to this task is evolutionary and multifaceted, involving not only the spiritual transformation of individuals but the establishment of an administrative system based on the application of justice, a system which is at once the "nucleus" and the "pattern" of the future World Order, together with the implementation of programmes of social and economic development that derive their impetus from the grass roots of the community. Such an integrated approach will inevitably create a new world, a world where human dignity is restored and the burden of inequity is lifted from the shoulders of humanity.

Then will the generations look back with heartfelt appreciation, for the sacrifices made by Bahá'ís and non-Bahá'ís alike, during this most turbulent period in human history.
> Messages of the Universal House of Justice 1963-1986, para. 425.8, p. 663. (14 March 1985.)

Into the Future

*N*o man that seeketh Us will We ever disappoint, neither shall he that hath set his face towards Us be denied access unto Our court ....
> Bahá'u'lláh, *Gleanings from the Writings of Bahá'u'lláh*, section CXXVI, pp. 271-272.

*H*e Who is the Eternal Truth hath, from the Day Spring of Glory, directed His eyes towards the people of Bahá, and is addressing them these words: "Address yourselves to the promotion of the well-being and tranquillity of the children of men. Bend your minds and wills to the education of the peoples and kindreds of the earth, that haply the dissensions that divide it may, through the power of the Most Great Name, be blotted out from its face, and all mankind become the upholders of one Order, and the inhabitants of one City. Illumine and hallow your hearts; let them not be profaned by the thorns of hate or the thistles of malice. Ye dwell in one world, and have been created through the operation of one Will. Blessed is he who mingleth with all men in a spirit of utmost kindliness and love."
> Bahá'u'lláh, *Gleanings from the Writings of Bahá'u'lláh*, section CLVI, pp. 333-334.

O My Letters! Verily I say, immensely exalted is this Day above the days of the Apostles of old. Nay, immeasurable is the difference! You are the witnesses of the Dawn of the promised Day of God. You are the partakers of the mystic chalice of His Revelation. Gird up the loins of endeavour, and be mindful of the words of God as revealed in His Book: "Lo, the Lord thy God is come, and with Him is the company of His angels arrayed before Him!"
> Words of the Báb to the Letters of the Living, Nabíl-i-A'ẓam, *The Dawn-Breakers*, p. 93.

*H*ow great, how very great is the Cause! How very fierce the onslaught of all the peoples and kindreds of the earth. Ere long shall the clamour of the multitude throughout Africa, throughout America, the cry of the European and of the Turk, the groaning of India and China, be heard from far and near. One and all, they shall arise with all their power to resist His Cause. Then shall the knights of the Lord, assisted by His grace from on high, strengthened by faith, aided by the power of understanding, and reinforced by the legions of the Covenant, arise and make manifest the truth of the verse: "Behold the confusion that hath befallen the tribes of the defeated!"
> 'Abdu'l-Bahá, cited by Shoghi Effendi, The Onslaught of all Peoples and Kindreds, *The World Order of Bahá'u'lláh*, p. 17.

*I*n the *Bayán* the Báb says that every religion of the past was fit to become universal. The only reason why they failed to attain that mark was the incompetence of their followers. He then proceeds to give a definite promise that this would not be the fate of the Revelation of "Him Whom God would make manifest", that it will become universal and include all the people of the world. This shows that we will ultimately succeed. But could we not through our shortcomings, failures to sacrifice and reluctance to concentrate our efforts in spreading the Cause, retard the realization of that ideal? And what would that mean? It shall mean that we will be held responsible before God, that the race will remain longer in its state of waywardness, that wars would not be so soon averted, that human suffering will last longer.

Letter dated 20 February 1932 written on behalf of Shoghi Effendi, *The Compilation of Compilations*, Vol. II (Living the Life), no. 1275, pp. 4–5.

*T*he permanence and stability achieved by any association, group or nation is a result of—and dependent upon—the soundness and worth of the principles upon which it bases the running of its affairs and the direction of its activities. The guiding principles of the Bahá'ís are: honesty, love, charity and trustworthiness; the setting of the common good above private interest; and the practice of godliness, virtue and moderation. Ultimately, then, their preservation and happiness are assured. Whatever misfortunes they may encounter, wrought by the wiles of the schemer and ill-wisher, shall all pass away like waves, and hardship shall be succeeded by joy. The friends are under the protection of the resistless power and inscrutable providence of God. There is no doubt that every blessed soul who brings his life into harmony with this all-swaying power shall give lustre to his works and win an ample recompense. The actions of those who choose to set themselves against it should provoke not antipathy on our part, but prayers for their guidance. Such was the way of the Bahá'ís in days gone by, and so must it be, now and for always.

Shoghi Effendi, *The Compilation of Compilations*, Vol. I (Crisis and Victory), no. 342, p. 174; and Vol. II (Trustworthiness), no. 2084, p.350. (18 December 1928.)

*T*o the general character, the implications and features of this world commonwealth, destined to emerge, sooner or later, out of the carnage, agony, and havoc of this great world convulsion, I have already referred in my previous communications. Suffice it to say that this consummation will, by its very nature, be a gradual process, and must, as Bahá'u'lláh has Himself anticipated, lead at first to the establishment of that Lesser Peace which the nations of the earth, as yet unconscious of His Revelation and yet unwittingly enforcing the general principles which He has enunciated, will themselves establish. This momentous and historic step, involving the reconstruction of mankind, as the result of the universal recognition of its oneness and wholeness, will bring in its wake the spiritualization of the masses, consequent to the recognition of the character, and the acknowledgement of the claims, of the Faith of Bahá'u'lláh—the essential condition to that ultimate fusion of all races, creeds, classes, and nations which must signalize the emergence of His New World Order.

Then will the coming of age of the entire human race be proclaimed and celebrated by all the peoples and nations of the earth. Then will the banner of the Most Great Peace be hoisted. Then will the world-wide sovereignty of Bahá'u'lláh—the Establisher of the Kingdom of the Father foretold by the Son, and anticipated by the Prophets of God before Him and after Him—be recognized, acclaimed, and firmly established. Then will a world civilization be born, flourish, and perpetuate itself, a civilization with a fullness of life such as the world has never seen nor can as yet conceive. Then will the Everlasting Covenant be fulfilled in its completeness. Then will the promise enshrined in all the Books of God be redeemed, and all the prophecies uttered by the Prophets of old come to pass, and the vision of seers and poets be realized. Then will the planet, galvanized through the universal belief of its dwellers in one God, and their allegiance to one common Revelation, mirror, within the limitations imposed upon it, the effulgent glories of the sovereignty of Bahá'u'lláh, shining in the plenitude of its splendour in the Abhá Paradise, and be made the footstool of His Throne on high, and acclaimed as the earthly heaven, capable of fulfilling that ineffable destiny fixed for it, from time immemorial, by the love and wisdom of its Creator.

Not ours, puny mortals that we are, to attempt, at so critical a stage in the long and checkered history of mankind, to arrive at a precise and satisfactory understanding of the steps which must successively lead a bleeding humanity, wretchedly oblivious of its God, and careless of Bahá'u'lláh, from its Calvary to its ultimate resurrection. Not ours, the living witnesses of the all-subduing potency of His Faith, to question, for a moment, and however dark the misery that enshrouds the world, the ability of Bahá'u'lláh to forge, with the hammer of His Will, and through the fire of tribulation, upon the anvil of this travailing age, and in the particular shape His mind has envisioned, these scattered and mutually destructive fragments into which a perverse world has fallen, into one single unit, solid and indivisible, able to execute His design for the children of men.

Ours rather the duty, however confused the scene, however dismal the present outlook, however circumscribed the resources we dispose of, to labour serenely, confidently, and unremittingly to lend our share of assistance, in whichever way circumstances may enable us, to the operation of the forces which, as marshalled and directed by Bahá'u'lláh, are leading humanity out of the valley of misery and shame to the loftiest summits of power and glory.

Shoghi Effendi, *The Promised Day is Come*, pp. 123-124.

Bibliography
Authoritative Bahá'í Sources

Writings of Bahá'u'lláh

Epistle to the Son of the Wolf. Wilmette, Illinois: Bahá'í Publishing Trust, 1962.

Gleanings from the Writings of Bahá'u'lláh. Translated by Shoghi Effendi. Wilmette, Illinois: Bahá'í Publishing Trust, 1963.

The Hidden Words of Bahá'u'lláh. Wilmette, Illinois: Bahá'í Publishing Committee, 1954.

The Kitáb-i-Aqdas: The Most Holy Book. Haifa: Bahá'í World Centre, 1992.

The Kitáb-i-Íqán: The Book of Certitude. Wilmette, Illinois: Bahá'í Publishing Trust, 1960.

Prayers and Meditations. Wilmette, Illinois: Bahá'í Publishing Trust, 1979.

The Proclamation of Bahá'u'lláh to the Kings and Leaders of the World. Haifa: Bahá'í World Centre, 1967.

The Seven Valleys and the Four Valleys. Translated by Marzieh Gail (with 'Alí-Kuli Khán). Wilmette, Illinois: Bahá'í Publishing Trust, rev. ed. 1978.

Tablets of Bahá'u'lláh revealed after the Kitáb-i-Aqdas. Compiled by the Research Department of the Universal House of Justice and translated by Habib Taherzadeh with the assistance of a Committee at the Bahá'í World Centre. Haifa: Bahá'í World Centre, 1978.

Writings of the Báb

Selections from the Writings of the Báb. Haifa: Bahá'í World Centre, 1976.

Writings and Talks of 'Abdu'l-Bahá

Paris Talks. London: Bahá'í Publishing Trust, 12th ed., 1995.

The Promulgation of Universal Peace. Compiled by Howard MacNutt. Wilmette, Illinois: Bahá'í Publishing Trust, 2nd ed., 1982.

The Secret of Divine Civilization. Translated by Marzieh Gail. Wilmette, Illinois: Bahá'í Publishing Trust, 1957.

Selections from the Writings of 'Abdu'l-Bahá.
Compiled by the Research Department of the Universal House of Justice.
Translated by a Committee at the Bahá'í World Centre and by Marzieh Gail.
Haifa: Bahá'í World Centre, 1978.

Some Answered Questions. Collected and Translated from the Persian by Laura Clifford Barney. Wilmette, Illinois: Bahá'í Publishing Trust, 1964.

Tablets of Abdul-Baha Abbas. Vol. I (1909), II (1915, 2nd ed. 1919), III (1916), Chicago: Bahá'í Publishing Society.

Tablets of the Divine Plan. Wilmette, Illinois: Bahá'í Publishing Trust, rev. ed., 1977.

Will and Testament of 'Abdu'l-Bahá. Wilmette, Illinois: Bahá'í Publishing Committee, 1944.

Writings of or on behalf of Shoghi Effendi

Arohanui: Letters from Shoghi Effendi to New Zealand.
Suva, Fiji Islands: Bahá'í Publishing Trust, 1982.

The Advent of Divine Justice. Wilmette, Illinois:
Bahá'í Publishing Trust, rev. ed., 1963.

Bahá'í Administration: Selected Messages 1922-1932. Wilmette, Illinois:
Bahá'í Publishing Trust, 1974.

Citadel of Faith: Messages to America 1947-1957. Wilmette, Illinois:
Bahá'í Publishing Trust, 1965.

Dawn of a New Day: Messages to India 1923-1957. New Delhi:
Bahá'í Publishing Trust, 1970.

Directives from the Guardian. Compiled by G. Garrida. New Delhi:
Bahá'í Publishing Trust, 1973.

God Passes By. Wilmette, Illinois: Bahá'í Publishing Trust, rev. ed., 1974.

High Endeavours: Messages to Alaska.
Compiled by the National Spiritual Assembly of the Bahá'ís of Alaska. [N.p.]:
National Spiritual Assembly of the Bahá'ís of Alaska, 1976.

Japan Will Turn Ablaze. Japan, Bahá'í Publishing Trust, 1974.
Letters from the Guardian to Australia and New Zealand: 1923-1957. Sydney:
National Spiritual Assembly of the Bahá'ís of Australia, 1970.

Messages to America: Selected Letters and Cablegrams Addressed to the Bahá'ís of North America 1932-1946. Wilmette: Bahá'í Publishing Committee, 1947.

Messages to the Antipodes: Communications from Shoghi Effendi to the Bahá'í Communities of Australasia. Edited by G. Hassall. Mona Vale, New South Wales: Bahá'í Publications Australia, 1997.

Messages to the Bahá'í World 1950-1957. Wilmette, Illinois: Bahá'í Publishing Trust, 1958.

Messages to Canada. N.p.: National Spiritual Assembly of the Bahá'ís of Canada, 1965.

The Promised Day is Come. Wilmette, Illinois: Bahá'í Publishing Trust, 1967.

The Unfolding Destiny of the British Bahá'í Community: The Messages from the Guardian of the Bahá'í Faith to the Bahá'ís of the British Isles. London: Bahá'í Publishing Trust, 1981.

The World Order of Bahá'u'lláh. Wilmette, Illinois: Bahá'í Publishing Trust, 1955.

Writings of or on behalf of the Universal House of Justice

The Constitution of the Universal House of Justice. Haifa: Bahá'í World Centre, 1972.
Issues Relating to the Study of the Bahá'í Faith. Wilmette, Illinois: Bahá'í Publishing Trust, 1999.
Messages from the Universal House of Justice: 1963-1986 The Third Epoch of the Formative Age. Wilmette, Illinois: Bahá'í Publishing Trust, 1996.
Rights and Responsibilities: The Complementary Roles of the Individual and Institutions. Thornhill, Ontario: Bahá'í Canada Publications, 1997.

Compilations

A Selection of Bahá'í Prayers and Holy Writings. Kuala Lumpur: Bahá'í Publishing Trust of the Spiritual Assembly of the Bahá'ís of Malaysia, 1996.

Bahá'í Prayers. Wilmette, Illinois: Bahá'í Publishing Trust, 1982.

Bahá'í Scholarship: A Compilation and Essays. Parkville, Victoria: Association for Bahá'í Studies Australia, 1993.

Bahá'í World Faith. Wilmette, Illinois: Bahá'í Publishing Trust, rev. ed., 1976.

Bahíyyih Khánum, The Greatest Holy Leaf. A compilation from Bahá'í sacred texts and writings of the Guardian of the Faith and Bahíyyih Khánum's own letters made by the Research Department at the Bahá'í World Centre. Haifa: Bahá'í World Centre, 1982.
The Compilation of Compilations. Vol. I. Ingleside, New South Wales: Bahá'í Publications Australia, 1991.

The Compilation of Compilations. Vol II. Ingleside, New South Wales: Bahá'í Publications Australia, 1991.

The Compilation of Compilations. Vol III. Ingleside, New South Wales: Bahá'í Publications Australia, 2000.

The Importance of Obligatory Prayer and Fasting. Mona Vale, New South Wales: Bahá'í Publications Australia, 2000.

Lights of Guidance. Compiled by Helen Hornby. New Delhi: Bahá'í Publishing Trust, 1983.

Local Spiritual Assembly Handbook. Mona Vale, New South Wales: Bahá'í Publications Australia, 3rd rev. ed., 1996.

Principles of Bahá'í Administration. London: Bahá'í Publishing Trust, 1969.

Promoting Entry by Troops. Reprinted. Mona Vale, New South Wales: Bahá'í Publications Australia, 1994.

Unrestrained as the Wind. Wilmette, Illinois: Bahá'í Publishing Trust, 1985.

Journals, Newsletters and Yearbooks

The American Bahá'í. Evanston, Illinois: National Spiritual Assembly of the Bahá'ís of the United States.

Australian Bahá'í Bulletin. Ingleside, New South Wales: National Spiritual Assembly of the Bahá'ís of Australia.

The Bahá'í World. Reprinted. Wilmette, Illinois: Bahá'í Publishing Trust, 1980.

Star of the West. Reprinted. Oxford: George Ronald, 1984.

Sacred Writings of Other Faiths

The Holy Bible: Containing the Old and New Testaments. Revised Standard Version. London: Thomas Nelson and Sons Ltd, 1958.

The Holy Qur-an. Translation and Commentary by Abdullah Yusuf Ali. Lahore, Pakistan: Sh. Muhammad Ashraf, 1938; repr. 1969.

Other Sources

The Bahá'í International Community, *Turning Point for All Nations: A Statement by the Bahá'í International Community on the Occasion of the 50th Anniversary of the United Nations.* New York: Bahá'í International Community, 1995.

Balyuzi, H. M., *Bahá'u'lláh, King of Glory.* Oxford: George Ronald, 1980.

Lady Blomfield (Sitárih Khánum), The Chosen Highway. Reprinted. Wilmette, Illinois: Bahá'í Publishing Trust, 1975.

Einstein, A, *Ideas and Opinions*. New York: Crown, 1954.

Esslemont, J. E., *Bahá'u'lláh and the New Era*. Wilmette, Illinois: Bahá'í Publishing Trust, 4th rev. ed., 1976.

Honnold, A. (Ed.), *Vignettes from the Life of 'Abdu'l-Bahá*. Oxford: George Ronald, 1982.

Ives, H. C., *Portals to Freedom*. Reprinted. Oxford: George Ronald, 1990.

Khan, J. A., & Khan, P. J., *Advancement of Women*. Wilmette, Illinois: Bahá'í Publishing Trust, 1998.

Nabíl-i-A'ẓam, *The Dawn-Breakers: Nabíl's Narrative of the Early Days of the Bahá'í Revelation*. Wilmette, Illinois: Bahá'í Publishing Trust, 1962.

Declaration of Trust and By-Laws of a National Spiritual Assembly, By-Laws of a Local Spiritual Assembly: As Authorized by the Guardian and Amended by the Universal House of Justice. National Spiritual Assembly of the Bahá'ís of Australia, 1975.

The Ministry of the Custodians 1957-1963: An Account of the Stewardship of the Hands of the Cause. Introduction by Amatu'l-Bahá Rúhíyyih Khánum. Haifa: Bahá'í World Centre, 1992.

Momen, W. (Ed.), *A Basic Bahá'í Dictionary*. Reprinted. Oxford: George Ronald, 1991.

Rabbani, R., *Poems of the Passing*. Oxford: George Ronald, 1996.

The Secret of the Golden Flower: A Chinese Book of Life. Translated and explained by Richard Wilhelm with a Foreword and Commentary by C. G. Jung. London: Routledge & Kegan Paul, 1962.

Samimi, C., *Firesides*. Oxford: George Ronald, 1999.

Tarnas, R., *The Passion of the Western Mind: Understanding the Ideas That Have Shaped Our World View*. New York: Ballantine, 1991.

Thompson, J., *The Diary of Juliet Thompson*. Los Angeles: Kalimát Press, 1983.

Ward, A., *239 Days: 'Abdu'l-Bahá's Journey in America*. Wilmette, Illinois: Bahá'í Publishing Trust, 1979.

Index

A

'Abdu'l-Bahá
    duties of, 67, 71
    life of, 31, 44, 60-71
    station of, 82, 86, 83-87
    Tablets of the Divine Plan, 171, 202
    Will and Testament, 31, 72-73, 74, 87, 88, 168, 202, 203, 205, 214, 311
Aborigines, 255, 256. See also Indigenous People.
Ádhirbáyján, 35, 39
Administrative Order
    Auxiliary Boards, 75, 76, 213, 211-13
    Continental Board of Counsellors, 76, 209-13, 223, 225, 228, 240, 248, 249
    evolution of, 74-76, 199
    Guardianship, 80, 203-6, 309
    Hands of the Cause of God, 72, 75, 87, 91, 205, 209-10, 204-5. See also learned.
    International Teaching Centre, 76, 210, 211
    Local Spiritual Assembly, 167, 191, 197, 213, 222-28, 262, 268.
        See also Houses of Justice.
    National and Unit Conventions, 221
    National Committees and Institutions, 223
    National Spiritual Assembly, 76, 167, 198, 202, 213, 214, 213-28, 225, 247, 248, 257, 268
    nature of, 199-203, 243, 244
    Regional Bahá'í Councils, 224-25
    Universal House of Justice, 72-76, 87, 91, 195, 199-212, 208, 240, 265, 309, 311
Adrianople, 54-57
adultery, 194, 196. See also chastity.
Africa, 27, 78, 255, 288, 313
Africans, 27, 70, 255, 284
agriculture, 28, 261, 273, 277, 278, 292
'Akká, 24, 57-60, 64-72, 133, 166
alcohol, 142. See also drugs.
Aleppo, 62
'Alí Khán, 36
America
    'Abdu'l-Bahá's journeys, 63-70
    challenges facing, 149, 158, 171, 194, 229, 241, 249
    destiny of, 171
    members of a global community, 27, 63, 78, 313
Ancient Beauty, 81, 168, 226 . See also *Bahá'u'lláh*.

animal world, 130
animals, 41, 90, 146, 304
antipathy, 192, 193, 314. See also divorce.
appeals, 37, 215, 216, 233, 238, 239, 247
Áqá Ján-i-Khamsih, 41
Áqáy-i-Kalím, 47, 55, 56
armaments, 29, 270, 271, 272, 273, 287, 293
Armenian, 40
arms, 29, 51, 148, 199, 271, 294. See also armaments.
arson, 148
arts. See also crafts.
    developing skills in, 187, 250, 254, 299-303, 307
    importance of, 30, 122, 251
asceticism, 148
Asia, 27, 78
Ásíyih Khánum, 44, 47
assistants, 212, 213, 225. See also Administrative Order: Auxiliary Boards.
Australia, 157, 173, 256
Auxiliary Boards. See Administrative Order:Auxiliary Boards.
auxiliary langauge. See langauge:auxiliary.
Ayyám-i-Há (Intercalary Days), 259, 265
Azíz Khán-i-Sardár, 42

B

Báb
    Bayán, 26, 35, 37, 48, 50, 120, 132, 314
    life of, 31-43, 80
    prophecies of, 50, 53
    station of, 72, 81, 82, 168
    Súrih of Mulk, 33. See Báb:Súrih of Mulk.
Bábí Dispensation, 33, 35, 37, 38, 39, 57, 63, 82, 120, 121. See also Revelation: of the Báb.
Bábís, 42, 45, 50, 55
backbiting, 148, 149, 239, 251, 257
Badasht, 38, 39, 45
Baghdád, 24, 47-53, 132
Bahá'í community, 235-68
Bahá'í Faith
    Administrative Order. See Administrative Order
    beliefs, 25, 96, 108, 144, 150, 178, 194, 196, 197, 274, 276, 278, 283, 294, 297, 298
    community life, 245-68
    history, 31-79
    protection of, 150
    teaching. See teaching.
    tributes, 133
Bahá'ís
    challenges and tests
        achieving confidence, 87
    chastity, 181

PATHWAYS TO TRANSFORMATION   ***321***

freedom from addictions, 142
materialism, 77
mistrust of institutions, 244, 309
opposition, 78, 79
overcoming apathy, 77, 286
prejudices of all kinds, 137, 158, 175, 196, 234, 255
self-interest, 67, 100, 301
unity, 127, 308
fields of service
advancing the equality of women and men, 282
Bahá'í scholarship, 305-9
developing the Administrative Order, 199-244
fostering Bahá'í community life, 245-68
protection of the environment, 287
rearing and educating children, 185-88
supporting human rights, 190, 192, 200
teaching the Faith, 152-75
working in a chosen profession, 128
hopes and aims, 24-30
not perfect, 100
qualities they must acquire
consultative skills, 236-41
faith and steadfastness, 102
happiness, 137
knowledge and insight, 105-7
love and sacrifice, 105
prayerfulness, 114
purity, 140
station to which they are called, 91
Bahá'u'lláh
aims and purposes, 24-30
covenant of, 62-63, 83-87
life of, 43-62
revelation of, 82
station of, 80-81
writings of
Book of Certitude (Kitáb-i-Íqán), 50
Book of My Covenant (Kitáb-i-'Ahd), 37, 62, 85, 209
Epistle to the Son of the Wolf, 45, 62
Hidden Words, 50, 132, 149
Most Holy Book (Kitáb-i-Aqdas), 50, 58, 87, 151, 168, 179, 206, 275
Seven Valleys, 50
Súrih of Kings (Súriy-i-Múlúk), 57
Súrih of the Temple (Súratu'l-Haykal), 46
Tablet of Aḥmad, 117
bastinado, 45
Bayán. See Báb:Bayán.
Baytu'l-'Adl-i-A'zam. See Administrative Order: Universal House of Justice.

Beirut, 62, 64
bestowals, 109, 110, 138, 185, 186, 249, 288
Blessed Perfection, 24, 104, 166, 262. See also Bahá'u'lláh.
bloodshed, 28, 283, 288, 300
Book of Certitude (Kitáb-i-íqán). See Bahá'u'lláh:writings of.
Bowery, 69
brevity, 25
bride, 42, 180. See also marriage.
British Army, 71
British Government, 71
brotherhood, 29, 51, 253
burial, 196, 198. See also death, wills.
Búshihr, 32

C

Cairo, 62
calamities, 24. See also crises, tests.
calendar, 259, 260, 265
Caliphate, 54, 55, 201
calumny, 148, 250
century of light, 28, 273
certitude, 105, 106, 138, 139, 181
character
development of, 135, 139, 158, 184, 187, 189, 194, 210, 239, 246-52, 253, 257, 281
of desired spouse, 178, 179
upright, 34, 51, 86, 108, 127, 179, 238, 254, 305
charity, 32, 314
chastity, 140, 141, 158, 181, 182. See also marriage.
Chester I. Thacher, 65
Chihríq, 35, 36, 37, 38, 45
children
and family planning, 144, 178-85, 192, 195
integration into the Bahá'í community, 227, 245, 250, 251, 267
rearing and educating, 145, 146, 185-88, 246, 250-52, 254, 266, 281, 301, 303
children of God, 27, 153, 241, 300
children of men, 86, 126, 159, 171, 281, 313, 315
chocolate, 70
Christ. See Jesus Christ
Christianity, 46, 50, 170, 173, 200, 201, 298
Christians, 40, 62, 68
citizens, 28, 29, 89, 112, 129, 255, 273
civilization
advancing, 30, 244, 288, 295, 301
breakdown of, 73, 142, 200, 295
divine, 103, 170, 228, 241, 271, 272, 295, 301
world. See world civilization.

cleanliness, 140
clergy, 200
collaboration, 90, 202, 223, 306, 307
commandments, 78, 83, 101, 179, 231, 271. See also Divine Law, laws.
commentaries, 33, 37, 167
committees, 175, 233, 256, 268, 292. See also Administrative Order:National Committees and Institutes, Local Spiritual Assembly.
communion, 115-19
community, 245
community building, 245
concord
   in the wider community, 25, 86, 143, 270, 286
   within a marriage, 188
   within the Bahá'í community, 131, 227, 258
confidence
   in God, 108, 117, 119, 186
   of others, 214, 220, 222, 244
   to serve, 113, 240
   to teach, 113, 129, 154
confirmations, 86, 138
   as an outcome of unity, 214
   faith and steadfastness, 79, 102
   firmness in the Covenant, 88
   from service, 154, 266, 278, 303
   from teaching, 128, 161
   seeking, 246, 264
conflict
   amongst men, 86, 106, 148, 241, 258, 272, 274
   avoidance in consultation, 190
conscience, 90, 238, 272
   freedom of. See freedom:of conscience.
   when making decisions, 89, 141, 142, 201, 233
consciousness, 77, 90, 129, 139, 244, 296
consolidation
   of Bahá'í property, 133
   of the Bahá'í community, 129
Constantinople, 24, 52, 53-54, 57, 66
consultation, 157, 173, 226, 249, 262, 263, 271, 287, 307, 310
   in Administrative Institutions, 76, 175, 227, 238
   true characteristics, 219, 220, 236-41
   within the family, 181, 191
contention, 86, 90, 148, 241, 258
Continental Board of Counsellors. See Administrative Order:Continental Boards of Counsellors.
conventions. See National Convention, Unit Convention.
co-operation, 130, 131, 287
counsel
   and consultation, 29, 189, 191, 196, 206, 214, 228, 235, 248, 311

   from God, 107, 125, 136, 270, 282
   from parents to children, 186, 187
Counsellors. See Administrative Order:Continental Boards of Counsellors.
Countenance of God, 33, 82. See also the Báb.
courtesy, 33, 90, 146, 147, 190, 236, 310
Covenant, 85
   Breaking, 91
   concerning Bahá'u'lláh as the Supreme Manifestation of God (Everlasting Covenant), 315
   concerning Bahá'u'lláh's successor (Lesser Covenant), 47, 62-63, 62, 63, 65, 82, 85-91, 206, 207, 260, 261. See also 'Abdu'l-Bahá.
   concerning the next Manifestation (Greater Covenant), 85, 84-85
   faithfulness and obedience towards, 25, 83, 226
   of marriage. See marriage.
crafts, 30, 108, 128, 301, 302, 303. See also arts.
craftsmen, 30, 301, 302
creation
   and God's Revelation, 46, 53, 83, 151, 252
   and its relationship with love, 103, 252
   of world intercommunication, 310
   perfection of. See perfection:of creation.
   worlds of, 130, 131, 167
Crimson Book, 62. See also Bahá'u'lláh:writings of:Book of My Covenant (Kitáb-i-'Ahd).
crises, 48, 78, 277
criticism, 237, 238, 239, 240, 248, 264
cruelty to animals, 148. See also animals.
cultural diversity, 297, 298
Cyprus, 56, 57
Czar of Russia, 42

D

daily prayer, 24. See also prayer.
Damascus, 62
Day of God, 34, 312, 313
death, 126, 137, 152, 180. See also martyrdom. See also burial, inheritance, will.
   and the next life, 95-96
   of Mírzá Midhí, 59, 133
   spiritual. See spiritual:blindness and death.
decisions
   by Administrative Institutions, 158, 208, 217-21, 237-44, 309
   made through consultation, 237
declaration
   new believers'. See Bahá'ís:declaration and enrolment.

Declaration
    Bab's, 31, 36-37, 39, 259
    Baha'u'llah's, 52, 53, 54, 61, 260
deepen, 24, 90, 108, 121, 155, 159, 172, 175, 213, 253, 277
deepening. See deepen.
demilitarization, 29, 270, 271, 275. See also armaments.
destiny
    of humanity, 92, 107, 280, 293, 312, 315
    of the Bahá'í community, 219, 224, 252
detachment, 27, 40, 78, 92, 103, 108, 115, 116, 139, 154, 189, 197, 210, 234, 235, 253, 282
devotion, 33, 34, 77, 108, 114, 126, 161, 190, 214, 215, 217, 220, 226, 234, 236, 264, 271, 286, 312
    between Bahá'u'lláh and the Báb, 38
    of Navváb to Bahá'u'lláh, 47
    to 'Abdu'l-Bahá, 60, 72
    to Bahá'u'lláh, 54, 61
    to humanity, 292
devotional meetings, 245, 266, 268
differences
    in the wider community, 88, 106, 137, 285
    within the Bahá'í community, 190, 192, 217, 218, 234, 236, 257, 258, 281
difficulties, 47, 100, 112, 172, 189, 191, 230, 235, 239, 248, 283, 307. See also tests, crises.
disciples, 35, 38, 39, 40, 44, 54
Dispensation
    of Báb, 38
    of Bahá'u'lláh, 37, 38, 47, 50, 54, 58, 62, 63, 71, 74, 76, 80, 83, 93, 120, 159, 200, 201, 203, 246, 274, 299, 308.
        See also Revelation:of Bahá'u'lláh.
    of past Prophets, 88, 308
    of the Báb. See Bábí Dispensation.
disputes, 28, 291, 296, 308
dissension, 86, 217, 284
dissertations, 37, 49, 105, 167
Divine Law, 90, 196
divorce, 192, 193. See also marriage, year of patience.
doctor, 281. See also physician.
dominion, 95, 98, 110, 130, 261, 280, 303
dreams, 43, 44, 46, 66, 295
drugs, 142, 196, 304
Druzes, 62
duties
    of 'Abdu'l-Bahá. See 'Abdu'l-Bahá:duties of.
    of Administrative Institutions. See Administrative Order, Institutions.
    of Bahá'ís, 80, 83, 126
    of everyone, 69
    of family members, 187, 188, 251, 254

of individual believers, 244, 247, 308
of world leaders, 270
to recognize God and His Manifestations, 83, 88, 101, 167, 168
duty
    to teach. See teaching:obligation to.

E

earth
    and heaven, 27, 46, 93, 123, 127, 230, 252, 261, 266, 281
    and its citizens, 25, 26, 28, 29, 30, 44, 56, 59, 73, 86, 93, 94, 129, 130, 143, 151, 155, 156, 163, 192, 214, 225, 231, 255, 272, 273, 274, 277, 279, 280, 284, 302, 313, 315
    and its nations, 314
    and its treasures, 46, 110, 130, 152, 231
    leaders and rulers of. See leaders.
ecclesiastics, 32, 43, 51, 54, 57, 151. See also clergy.
education. See also children:rearing and educating.
    importance of, 99, 109, 250, 280, 281, 303
    of Bahá'ís, 222, 245
    of children. See children:rearing and educating.
    of humanity by His Prophets, 86, 90
    universal, 28, 110, 267, 273, 280, 281, 292, 309, 313
Egypt, 43
Egyptians, 70
elections, 174, 233, 234, 245
email, 90, 310
emancipation of women, 42, 282. See also women.
England, 68. See also United Kingdom.
English, 70
environment, 141, 195, 238, 287, 288
Epistle to the Son of the Wolf. See Bahá'u'lláh:writings of.
epochs, 74, 75, 76
equality
    of races, 283
    of women and men, 181, 207, 246, 249, 250, 276, 281, 282
eternity, 119, 125
    of God, 83, 93, 95, 98, 107, 127, 152, 241
    of marriage, 178
Europe, 35, 42, 63, 68, 75, 90, 249, 255, 313
Europeans, 27, 36, 60, 90, 295
ever-advancing
    Bahá'í community, 228
    civilization. See civilization:advancing.
Everlasting Covenant. See Covenant:Everlasting.
Everlasting Mirror, 48. See also Mírzá Yaḥyá.
excitement, 36, 39

expansion, 174, 229, 307
and consolidation. See teaching:expansion and consolidation.
of the Bahá'í community, 73, 86, 175, 214, 222, 224, 228, 245, 246
eyes, 33, 61, 65, 69, 110, 126, 284

F

fairness, 90, 150
faith, 24, 34, 40, 77, 95, 101, 103, 105, 115, 117, 118, 119, 120, 154, 155, 158, 168, 169, 172, 179, 240, 248, 253, 264, 283, 285, 301, 308, 313. See Bahá'í Faith.
faiths, 151, 255, 285
Famagusta, 57
family, 178-98, 246, 254, 282
    Holy Family, 35, 47, 50, 54, 56, 58, 61, 62, 64, 72
    human, 257, 273, 282, 291. See also oneness of humanity.
fanaticism, 26, 137, 251
farrásh-báshí, 40, 41
farráshes, 42
Fárs, 32
fasting, 57, 117, 118, 124, 125, 174, 260
Fáṭimih, 35, 39, 42, 133
Feasts. See Nineteen Day Feast, Naw-Rúz.
federation, 29, 275, 296
felicity, 27, 53, 103, 131, 149
fellowship
    between Bahá'ís and the Administrative Institutions, 220
    with people of other faiths, 26, 143
    with the peoples of the world, 27, 164, 272, 312
    within marriage, 188
    within the Bahá'í community, 131, 169, 237, 245, 258, 268
fidelity, 53, 181, 182
Fiedler, 43
finance, 29, 275
firesides, 164, 165
firing squad, 40
firmness, 79, 215
flexibility, 160, 195, 198, 204, 206, 278
food, 124, 137, 161, 304
    spiritual, 122, 188, 264, 299, 300
forgiveness, 53, 57, 96, 146, 184, 266
Formative Age, 72, 74, 75, 76
frailty, 34
free will, 88, 240
freedom, 320

from negative qualities, 66, 67, 116, 158, 251, 256, 277
of choice, 56, 90, 291, 296
of conscience, 89
of thought and expression, 89, 90, 190, 220, 236, 263, 296
friendliness, 26, 27, 143, 164, 258
friendship, 144, 145, 158, 178, 188, 255, 283
fulfilment of past religions, 26
fund, 174, 211, 227-30, 233, 246, 247
fundamental Bahá'í Beliefs, 80
Futúḥát-i-Makkíyyih, 49

G

gambling, 148
Garden of Riḍván, 52, 53, 54
Gate of God, 33. See also the Báb.
global community, 27, 153
global governance, 289
glory
    attained by the martyrs, 45
    God's. See God:His glory.
    heaven of celestial, 125
    of a teacher, 152
    of Bahá'u'lláh, 44
    of Bahá'u'lláh's Revelation, 79
    of Glories. See Greatest Name
    of man, 109, 170, 178, 272, 281, 315
    of the twentieth century, 28, 273
    of women, 250
Glory
    of Glories. See Greatest Name.
    Pen of. See Pen of Glory.
God
    fear of, 86, 210
    His Glory, 25, 27, 28, 34, 43, 47, 53, 58, 93, 98, 123, 178, 179, 261, 280
    His love, 93, 98, 102, 103, 104, 241, 252, 267, 315
    His Revelation with humanity, 84, 243. See also covenant:great.
    His Wisdom, 115, 118, 120, 232, 315
    knowledge of. See knowledge:of God.
    love for. See love:for God.
    love from, 103
    love of. See love:for God.
    names and attributes, 92, 110, 134, 151, 259
    oneness of, 25, 58, 81, 84, 105, 110, 111, 115, 116, 117, 131, 168, 182, 183, 185, 186, 187, 236, 297
    Right of. See Ḥuqúqu'lláh.
    signs of, 116, 305

PATHWAYS TO TRANSFORMATION   *325*

trust in, 105, 157
    Word of. See Word of God.
Gospels, 43
government, 89, 122, 150, 173, 271, 272, 273, 275, 276, 277, 280, 288, 290, 293, 294, 297
    British, 71
    compared to the Administrative Order, 201, 241
    obedience towards. See obedience:towards governments.
    Persian, 50, 51, 55, 56, 62
    Turkish, 65, 66
    world. See world federal system.
grandeur, 146, 261, 279
gratitude, 137, 138, 180
Greater Covenant. See Covenant:concerning the next Manifestation (Greater Covenant).
Greatest Name, 84, 123, 267
Guardian, 87, 152, 168, 195, 202, 210, 211, 216, 220, 224, 239, 258, 263, 265, 310. See Shoghi Effendi, Administrative Order
Guardianship. See Administrative Order:Guardianship.
guidance
    from God, 84, 87, 92, 94, 103, 112, 113, 118, 119, 134, 137, 142, 152, 156, 163, 200, 202, 206, 208, 210, 234, 235, 236, 276, 278, 287, 288
    from the Assemblies, 191, 202, 217, 228, 246, 254, 312
    from the Guardian, 87, 195, 205, 217, 259, 298
    from the Universal House of Justice, 190, 199, 208, 240
    from the wider community, 191
    to humanity, 87, 107, 125, 152, 169, 183, 248, 305

H

Ḥájí Mírzá Áqásí, 36, 53
Ḥájí Mírzá Ḥasan-ʿAlí, 50
Ḥájí Mírzá Siyyid Muḥammad, 50
Ḥájí Mullá Ḥasan-i-ʾAmmú, 52
Ḥájí Sulaymán Khán, 41
happiness, 27, 66, 69, 86, 90, 136, 141, 146, 181, 188, 247, 271, 287, 288, 295, 296, 314
harm
    to animals. See cruelty to animals.
    to other people, 90, 147
    to the Faith, 230, 248
harmony, 135, 188, 216, 273, 282, 300, 314
    in the world, 26, 27, 108, 127, 284, 291
    within a family, 179, 185, 188, 190, 191, 192, 193
    within in an Assembly, 236, 238, 242, 258

hatred, 26, 36, 46, 143, 190, 272, 300
Ḥaẓíratuʾl-Quds, 268
health, 46, 68, 124, 247, 292, 296, 297, 304, 305
Heaven, 84, 111, 112, 136, 281
heavens, 83, 91, 99, 109, 110, 188, 230, 252
heedlessness, 83, 99, 129
Heroic Age, 39, 54, 71, 74. See also Apostolic Age.
heroism, 35, 39, 80
Hidden Imám, 33
Hidden Words. See Baháʾuʾlláh:writings of.
Ḥijáz, 34
Him Whom God shall make manifest, 26, 123, 314. See also Baháʾuʾlláh.
holiness, 27, 43, 53, 99, 104, 105, 110, 116, 136, 138, 140, 164, 226, 249, 282
Holy Land, 41
Holy Books, 95, 120, 252, 295.
    See also Word of God.
Holy Days, 260
Holy Land, 63, 64, 133, 205, 214
Holy Scriptures. See Scriptures.
home, 27, 29, 139, 145, 164, 180, 188, 192, 251, 254, 255
    of Baháʾuʾlláh, 56
    of ʿAbduʾl-Bahá, 70
homosexuality, 148, 194, 195, 196
honesty, 149, 150, 232, 314
honour, 66, 93, 137, 165, 186, 231, 272, 295
    in attaining His Presence, 61, 65, 134
    of teaching. See teaching:honour of.
    of the Faith, 131, 231
hope
    and joy, 45, 137, 169, 170
    to those in despair, 118, 174, 175, 215, 241, 248, 257, 283, 286, 296
    to understand, 95, 105, 115
Houses of Justice, 183, 202, 225. See also Administrative Order:Local Spiritual Assembly, National Spiritual Assembly, Universal House of Justice.
Houses of Worship. See Mashriquʾl-Adhkár.
Ḥujjat, 44
human race
    global security. See security.
    maturation, 24, 27, 274, 315.
        See also oneness of humanity.
    unity of. See oneness of humanity.
human rights, 276, 280, 292
humiliation, 88
humility, 110, 189, 235, 262, 264, 283, 285, 308
    of Assembly members, 215, 217, 220
    of teachers, 159
Ḥuqúquʾlláh (Right of God), 130, 131, 130-32, 230, 231, 232, 233

326   PATHWAYS TO TRANSFORMATION

I

ignorance, 27, 106, 113, 250
ignorant, 29, 33, 106, 145, 159, 171, 255, 267, 303, 311
Ílkhání garden, 42
image, 137
image of God, 24, 93, 98, 103
Imám, 33, 35, 41, 59
Imám Ḥusayn, 35, 59
Imám-Zádih-Ḥasan, 41
immortality, 95, 105
impostor, 84
incarnation, 39, 82
India, 43, 304, 313
Indians, 70
Indigenous People, 70, 171, 284
indignities, 24
individual
    Assembly members, 234, 239, 240, 268
    initiative and action, 77, 100, 158, 159, 213, 244, 247, 248, 279, 312
    interaction with Assemblies, 196, 220, 227, 228, 229, 240, 245, 264
    opinons and thoughts, 89, 90, 308
    rights and freedoms, 122, 142, 184, 195, 220, 229, 232, 233, 236, 259
    roles and responsiblities, 108, 158, 172, 196, 204, 214
    study, 215
    trials and errors, 195, 196, 217
industry, 28, 261, 273, 301
inheritance, 197. See also will, death.
initiative. See individual:initiative and action.
inner peace, 118
insight, 24, 49, 83, 86, 90, 122, 128, 146, 191, 243, 307, 308
insistence, 90
institutes, 221, 222, 223, 245
institutions. See also Administrative Order.
    attacks on, 239
    attitude to children and youth, 251
    attitudes towards, 242
    ecclesiastical, 151
    educational, 229, 281, 306
    evolution of, 74, 75, 173, 202, 203, 216, 224, 228, 229, 249, 253, 277
    functioning of, 174, 215
    Fund. See Fund.
    Mashriqu'l-Adhkár. See Mashriqu'l-Adhkár
    members of, 200
    membership of, 256
    nature of, 201, 203
    performance of, 238
    purpose of, 200, 228
    relationship with believers, 244
    relationship with individuals, 299
    relationship with the wider community, 277
    service on, 247
    stimulate individual initiative, 244
    the learned arm, 209
integrity, 32, 33, 34, 52, 80, 86, 91, 108, 155, 184, 200, 201, 204, 215, 226, 238
intellect, 31, 42, 89, 238, 246, 297, 303, 304, 305, 306
Intercalary Days. See Ayyám-i-Há.
International Bahá'í Council, 75. See also Administrative Order.
International House of Justice. See Administrative Order:Universal House of Justice.
International Teaching Centre. See Administrative Order:International Teaching Centre.
interpretation
    authorised, 24, 195, 204, 207
    individual, 308
interpreter, 38, 72, 168, 195, 202, 204. See also interpretation.
inventions, 122, 287, 297
investigation, 121, 303
'Iráq, 43, 47, 48, 51
Iron Age, 31. See also Formative Age.
Isfandíyár, 283
irreconcilable, 193. See also divorce.
Islám, 35, 43, 46, 49, 54, 121, 155, 201, 253
Israel, 208. See also Holy Land.

J

Jabal-i-Báṣit, 35
Jerusalem, 60, 71
Jesus Christ, 59, 69. See also Christianity.
Jews, 50, 62
journeys, 57, 68
joy, 27, 30, 45, 65, 71, 108, 111, 112, 120, 123, 127, 129, 131, 136, 137, 139, 143, 155, 188, 192, 231, 232, 244, 262, 266, 299, 300, 314
Judaism. See Mosaic Dispensation.
justice, 51, 54, 84, 96, 106, 109, 142, 147, 150, 162, 181, 230, 236, 238, 271, 280, 294, 295, 297, 304
    duty of Bahá'í institutions, 215, 217, 220, 226, 227, 236, 238, 240, 312

K

Kaaba, 35
Kalantar, 42
Karbilá, 50
Kárbilá, 47, 51
Kárkúk, 49
Káshánih, 57
Káẓimayn, 51
kindness, 51, 145–46, 149, 158, 160, 181, 262, 264, 272, 282, 295
Kingdom of God
  on earth, 312
kings, 29, 43, 57, 61, 71, 88, 270, 294
Kitáb-i-Aqdas (Most Holy Book). See Baha'u'lláh:writings of.
Kitáb-i-Íqán (Book of Certitude). See Bahá'u'lláh:writings of.
knowledge. See also children:rearing and educating
  of arts, crafts and sciences, 30, 187, 254, 300, 302
  of God, 83, 92, 93, 94, 101, 104, 105, 113, 116, 120, 127, 128, 134, 139, 143, 182, 195, 297. See also Manifestations of God.
  of self, 99, 178
  of spiritual truths, 32, 96, 105, 106, 109, 110, 113, 139, 146, 159, 185, 201, 250, 264, 305
  of the Manifestations of God, 83, 93
  of the Teachings, 194
  of the Teachings, 108, 113, 120, 121, 139, 154, 161, 168, 171, 174, 175, 252, 291, 306, 310
  through study, 215, 227, 253
Kurdistán, 48, 50
Kurds, 36, 50

L

lamp, 35, 67, 98, 154
language
  Auxiliary, 28, 29, 273
  of individual Bahá'ís, 142, 164, 175, 252
  of Scripture, 27, 37, 39, 72, 149
  unity of, 29, 273, 275, 296, 298. See also language:auxiliary.
laws. See also Divine Law.
  and freedom, 24, 90
  civil, 289, 290, 296
  codification, 74
  divine origin, 25, 83, 153, 167, 168
  enactment of supplementary, 201, 204, 206, 265
  enforcement, 169, 216, 290, 299
  knowledge of, 121, 168

obedience towards, 77, 90, 100, 151, 153, 159, 168, 180, 217, 251, 258, 275, 307
promulgation of, 74, 118
purpose of, 68, 179, 285, 295
leaders, 29, 43, 52, 58, 61, 86, 270, 294, 311, 312. See also kings.
learned, 48, 49, 51, 52, 70, 95, 142, 159, 200, 209, 238, 239, 305.
  See also Administrative Order.
learning, 32, 48, 156, 187, 201, 210, 222, 223, 234, 281, 301, 306
Lesser Covenant. See Covenant:concerning the Báb's successor (Lesser Covenant).
Lesser Peace, 58, 74, 199, 270, 271, 275, 276, 292, 312, 314. See also Most Great Peace.
Letters of the Living, 133
liberal, 33, 295, 307
Light of God, 33, 82, 181, 288
Light of Guidance, 152, 210
Lights of Unity. See Seven Lights of Unity.
likeness of God, 24. See also image of God.
Local Bahá'í Centres, 268
loftiness, 34, 166, 178
love
  for God, 93, 98, 101, 102, 103, 104, 108, 111, 114, 115, 125, 127, 129, 137, 141, 143, 144, 154, 161, 166, 174, 181, 186, 245, 251, 300
  for humanity, 26, 27, 101, 103, 108, 137, 140, 143, 145, 146, 157, 158, 169, 199, 253, 258, 272, 282, 283, 313
  for indigenous peoples, 255
  for the Faith, 179
  God's. See God:His love.
  of children in the community, 251
  of humanity, 314
  of one's country, 291
  of the Central Figures, 36, 38, 51, 69, 71, 108, 127, 159, 167
  of the Faith and its Institutions, 126, 219, 248, 307
  purpose of religion, 86
  sexual, 194, 195
  within the Bahá'í community, 115, 143, 144, 169, 174, 217, 236, 238, 239, 240, 243, 244, 247, 257, 258, 262
  within the family, 110, 179–91, 192, 193
lowliness, 33, 159, 178, 189, 235
luminaries, 235

M

Máh-Ku, 35, 37
Maid of Heaven, 46
Maiden. See Maid of Heaven.
malice, 25, 313
Manifestations of God. See also Bahá'u'lláh, Báb, Muḥammad, Jesus Christ.
    mission of, 25, 93
    oneness of, 25, 93
    our relationship to them, 162
    qualities of, 80, 93, 100, 102, 116, 162, 204
    recognition and obedience towards them, 88, 100, 105, 113, 308
    relationship to God, 80, 93, 134
    relationship to man, 105
    succession, 84, 85
    Supreme, 123, 163
    their suffering, 43
Maoris, 171, 256. See also Indigenous People.
marriage, 44, 141, 144, 172, 178, 179, 180, 182, 183, 178-83, 191, 192, 193, 194, 195, 226, 283
martyrdom, 289
    of believers, 53
    of past Prophets, 43
    of Tahirih, 42
    of the Báb, 43
Mary, 42, 133
Mashriqu'l-Adhkár, 70, 229, 230, 266, 267, 268, 278, 300, 302
    American, 157, 207
maturation
    of a child into adulthood, 124, 145, 169, 197
    of every believer, 77, 174, 215, 308
    of the Bahá'í Faith, 172, 227, 228, 247, 277
    of the world, 27, 74, 274. See oneness of humanity, Most Great Peace.
mausoleum, 42, 67
Mázindarán, 39, 40, 44
meditation, 83, 99, 113–25, 139, 155, 156, 235, 305
memorizing, 155
mendicancy, 148
merchants, 32, 68
mercy
    of God, 28, 84, 92, 101, 106, 110, 111, 112, 113, 118, 127, 132, 145, 146, 152, 162, 183, 184, 232, 281, 305
    towards others, 143, 146, 184, 220, 236, 250
Message
    of Bahá'u'lláh, 25, 38, 52, 69, 82, 93, 128, 135, 153, 154, 156, 158, 160, 163, 167, 172, 200, 227, 240, 248, 253, 255, 311.
    See also teaching.
    of the Báb, 36

Messengers. See Manifestations of God.
mineral kingdom, 94, 130
ministers, 32, 52, 53, 57, 58, 270
minorities, 255, 283
miracles, 24, 52
Mírzá Áqá Jan, 56
Mírzá Buzurg, 44, 52
Mírzá Buzurg Khán, 52
Mírzá Ḥusayn-'Alí, 44
Mírzá Ismá'íl-i-Vazír of Yálrúd, 44
Mírzá Mahmúd, 44
Mírzá Mihdí, 57, 59
Mírzá Muḥammad-'Alí, 64, 65, 88
Mírzá Muḥammad-Qulí, 47
Mírzá Músá, 47, 50
Mírzá Sa'íd Khán, 52
Mírzá Siyyid Ḥasan, 33
Mírzá Yaḥyá, 38, 48, 55, 56, 57, 64, 91
mischief, 25, 65
moderation, 90, 130, 142, 190, 236, 307, 310, 314
modesty, 36, 142, 220
moral education.
    See education:rearing and educating.
Mosaic Dispensation, 46. See also Moses.
Moses, 84
Most Great Covenant. See Lesser Peace.
Most Great House, 50
Most Great Peace, 24, 51, 58, 61, 69, 76, 199, 214, 271, 275, 295, 312, 315. See also Lesser Peace.
Most Great Prison, 30. See also 'Akká.
Most Great Tablet. See also Bahá'u'lláh:writings of:Book of My Covenant (Kitáb-i-'Ahd).
Most Holy Book (Kitáb-i-Aqdas). See Bahá'u'lláh:writings of.
Most Mighty Branch, 64, 87. See also 'Abdu'l-Bahá.
Mount Carmel, 70, 211
Muḥammad, 32, 35, 48
Muḥammad Sháh, 36
Muḥammad-'Alí, 48, 55
Mullá Ḥusayn, 34, 35, 40, 44, 133.
    See also Letters of the Living.
mullás, 41, 51
murder, 148
Muslim, 50, 57
Mystic way, 71
mystics, 49, 68

N

Najaf, 51
Najíbíyyih Garden, 52
names and attributes of God, 109, 110, 123, 134, 162, 182
Napoleon III, 57
national committees, 221
National Conventions, 218
national institutions, 75, 213
National Teaching Committee, 221, 222, 223
Navváb, 47, 133
Naw-Rúz, 40, 67, 124, 260, 265, 297, 298
Nayríz, 39, 40
Negroes, 283. See also Indigenous People.
next world, 34, 45, 93, 95, 96, 103, 104, 112, 144, 178, 180, 231
Nineteen Day Feast, 174, 213, 240, 262, 263, 264
Nineteen-Day Feast, 262
Níyálá, 45
nobility, 32, 47, 51, 126, 159
Núr, 45
nurturing new believers, 169. See also teaching:expansion and consolidation.

O

obedience
    to Bahá'í institutions, 204, 213
    to God and His Laws, 90, 185, 258
    to government, 289, 291
    to parents, 183, 186, 251
obligations, 29, 132, 167, 187, 232, 261
obligatory prayer. See prayer:obligatory.
Occident, 27
occupation. See profession.
Old Testament, 70
Oneness of God. See God, unity of.
oneness of humanity, 29, 88, 89, 129, 241, 242, 246, 255, 262, 274, 275, 278, 282, 284, 286, 296, 314
oneness of religion, 25, 26, 31, 59, 82, 83, 93, 273, 284, 285, 297, 311, 314, 315
opinions. See individual:opinions and thoughts.
opposition, 43, 48, 79, 154, 283
ordeals, 24, 27, 47. See also tests, difficulties, crises.
ordinances, 37, 58, 68, 83, 90, 101, 109, 126, 132, 151, 168, 199, 203, 204, 207, 232, 275, 278, 284
Orient, 133, 202
Ottoman, 35, 54
over-administration, 218. See also Administrative Order.

P

paradise, 27, 53, 105, 107, 114, 115, 164, 258
Paris, 43
patience, 90, 101, 106, 159, 160, 169, 174, 189, 215, 235, 239, 283
peace, 29, 51, 64, 69, 70, 86, 95, 102, 118, 128, 135, 138, 139, 170, 180, 188, 199, 241, 315. See also Lesser Peace, Most Great Peace.
Pen of Glory, 108, 126, 192, 200, 231. See also Bahá'u'lláh.
people of Bahá', 83. See also Bahá'ís.
perfection
    of God and His creation, 106, 130, 146, 170, 288, 295, 311
    striving, 94, 100, 111, 140, 227, 249
Persia
    Bahá'u'lláh in, 24, 51, 56
    the Báb in, 31, 35, 42
Persians, 50, 57, 70, 145
personality, 63, 69, 74, 80, 160, 194, 244, 305
philosophic, 43
physician, 59, 296, 304, 311
piety, 32, 47, 51, 149
pilgrimage, 35, 132, 134
pioneering, 165, 213, 254
politics, 172, 201, 241, 255, 273, 275, 281, 289, 293
    international, 28, 29, 78, 79, 90, 275, 282, 297, 312. See also government.
    non-interference, 151, 173, 291, 292
poor, 51, 62, 68, 69, 70, 71, 102, 129, 171, 183, 185, 247, 267, 270, 285, 286
poverty, 90, 98, 116, 130, 178, 230, 285, 287
prayer, 24, 59, 94, 99, 100, 111, 113, 114, 115, 116, 117, 118, 119, 124, 125, 129, 156, 157, 159, 173, 174, 181, 184, 195, 197, 198, 233, 237, 240, 266, 299, 305. See also meditation.
    obligatory, 116, 117, 124, 198
precepts, 49, 83, 112, 117, 130, 203, 296, 305. See also laws, ordinances.
prejudice, 33, 137, 158, 175, 196, 234, 255, 274, 283, 284, 297
pride, 29, 129, 145, 159, 250, 301, 306, 311
priests, 81. See also ecclesiastics.
Primal Point, 33, 82, 261. See also Báb.
principles
    administrative, 203, 217, 224, 259, 262
    and cultural practices, 297
    and the conscience of the individual, 238
    applying and exemplifying, 89, 151, 169, 215, 253, 256, 277, 278, 279, 289, 290, 297
    contrasting demands of, 220
    importance of, 275, 276, 295, 314
    of consultation, 181, 228, 235

of intergovernmental relations, 271
of research, 307, 308
of the Faith, 87, 135, 168, 173, 181, 236, 249, 289, 314
related to contemporary issues, 173
religious, 25, 83
problems and challenges. See Bahá'ís:challenges,world:problems and challenges.
proclamation
of Bahá'u'lláh, 43, 52, 54, 58
teaching, 154, 172, 308
professions, 57, 108, 128
progressive revelation, 82, 92.
See also oneness of religion.
prohibitions
in the Bahá'í Faith, 109, 148, 238
in the past, 163
promise
of assistance to those who teach.
See teaching:promise of Divine assistance.
of continual Guidance, 134
of the Most Great Peace, 26, 79, 274, 314, 315
Promise of All Ages, 26, 82, 163. See also Bahá'u'lláh.
proofs, 48, 81, 86, 168
Prophet. See Muhammad.
See also Manifestations of God.
prophetic cycle, 82
prosperity
of individuals, 123, 163, 231
of the world, 78, 131, 151, 272, 276, 279, 285, 292
protection
of the environment. See environment.
protection of minorities, 255
punishments, 95
Purest Branch, 59, 133.
See also Mírzá Mihdí.
purity of character, 33, 108, 127, 139, 140, 141, 295, 301
of motives and deeds, 107, 112, 125, 136, 140, 142, 189, 235, 238, 264, 305, 310
of the heart and spirit, 106, 112, 114, 136, 139, 140, 154, 186, 226, 234, 235, 283
of the Word of God, 121, 206, 277
purpose
of Bahá'í institutions. See Administrative Order.
of Bahá'u'lláh's suffering, 27
of creation, 25, 93, 94, 101, 102, 105, 110, 134
of education, 301
of justice, 147
of life, 94
of marriage, 182, 195
of prayer and fasting, 125

of religion, 86, 115, 143, 295, 297
of the Revelation of Bahá'u'lláh, 27, 28, 90, 127, 135, 199, 200, 295, 296, 298
of the Revelation of the Báb, 37

Q

Qájár, 31, 55
Qará-Guhar, 46
Qiblih, 133, 198
Quddús, 39, 40, 44, 133.
See also Letters of the Living.
questions
addressed to Bahá'u'lláh, 49, 50, 52
of seekers and believers, 165, 172, 309, 311
to God whilst in prayer, 121

R

race
discrimination, 150, 158, 280, 282, 283, 286
unity, 28, 151, 153, 252, 255, 273, 282, 283, 284, 292, 294. See also oneness of humanity.
radiance, 33, 43, 70, 82, 92, 98, 106, 108, 115, 120, 127, 131, 143, 151, 181, 188, 189, 192, 231, 232, 235, 261, 270
Rahím, 32
Rahmán, 32
rank and station
of 'Abdu'l-Bahá, 82, 85
of Bahá'u'lláh, 80, 81
of Counsellors, 212
of humanity, 301
of Mírzá Mihdí, 59
of Muhammad-'Alí, 48
of professions, 128
of Tahirih, 42
of the Báb, 80
of the Greatest Holy Leaf, 133
of the Hands of the Cause of God, 209, 210
of trustworthiness, 151
of women and men, 281
reading the Writings, 24, 84, 114, 119, 159, 183, 263
realm of glory, 25, 98
realm of spirit, 25
reconciliation, 50, 193, 236
reconstruction of society, 29, 270, 275, 278, 312, 314
redemption, 258, 312
reflection, 24, 27, 99, 103, 121, 233, 235
Regional Bahá'í Councils. See Administrative Order.
relationships

between institutions, 224, 225, 244
between nations, 79, 256, 312
between people, 158, 241
family, 180, 183, 189, 190
in a marriage, 141
sexual, 194, 195
spiritual. See spiritual relationships.
religion
leaders of, 78
previous, 83, 200, 209
previous, 267
purpose of. See purpose:of religion.
religions, 27, 50, 95, 135, 137, 143, 162, 285, 295, 296
unity of. See oneness of religion.
religious belief, 25, 280, 284, 289
remembrance, 40, 46, 53, 78, 185, 261, 266
representatives, 29, 59, 150, 203, 206, 208, 216, 218, 219, 220, 221, 247, 256, 277, 311
Revelation
adaption to circumstances, 25
of Bahá'u'lláh, 45-47, 50, 57-59, 241, 274, 294, 314. See also Bahá'u'lláh, Bahá'í Faith.
of the Báb, 33-35. See also Báb, Bábí Dispensation.
power of, 30, 155, 301
pre-eminence of the Bahá'í, 25, 26, 38, 76, 160, 163
purpose of, 24, 83, 103, 163, 199
study of, 120, 246, 310
revolution, 95
Russian, 43
Turkish, 66
rewards, 95, 109, 147, 164
Right of God. See Ḥuqúqu'lláh.
righteousness, 25, 34, 83, 86, 113, 120, 144, 167, 194, 253
rights
human. See human rights.
individual. See individual:rights and freedoms.
Rose Garden, 53
Roumelia, 24
rulers. See leaders.
and the learned, 209.
See also Administrative Order.
Russia, 35, 41, 42, 43, 47, 145

S

sacrifice, 59, 102-5, 191, 205, 229, 239, 258, 259
Sam Khán, 40, 41
Sámsún, 54
Sardár, 42

Sárih Khánum, 44
schism, 65, 86, 203, 204.
See also Lesser Covenant, unity.
scholarship, 305, 306, 307, 308
sciences, 30, 122, 187, 204, 250, 252, 254, 285, 297-307
scientists, 30, 302
Scriptures, 26, 32, 37, 59, 62, 94, 109, 114, 119, 120, 130, 134, 155, 163, 168
Secondary House of Justice. See also Administrative Order:National Spiritual Assembly.
security, 29, 83, 270, 271, 272, 275, 297, 311.
See security.
Self of God, 93, 94, 103, 131, 134, 162. See also Manifestations of God.
self-effacement, 33
selfless service. See service:selfless.
selflessness, 24, 234
serenity, 79
service
available to the youth, 251, 253, 254, 279
Bahá'í funeral, 198. See also burial, will.
in teaching the Faith, 152, 165, 169, 254
Mashriqu'l-Adhkár, 267, 268
military, 294
on Bahá'í institutions, 212
selfless, 24, 71, 114, 241
to humanity, 24, 66, 128, 145, 150, 174, 185, 241, 282, 295
to the Faith, 65, 88, 99, 100, 107, 113, 129, 183, 184, 185, 189, 241, 243, 254, 279, 309
servitude, 88, 184, 189, 235, 243
Seven Lights of Unity, 28
Seven Valleys. See Bahá'u'lláh:writings of.
Sháh of Persia, 43. See Náṣiri'd-Dín Sháh, Muḥammad Sháh.
Shaykh Aḥmad, 32
Shaykh Ismá'íl, 49
Shaykh Muḥyi'd-Dín-i-'Arabí, 49
Shaykh Murtaḍáy-i-Anṣárí, 51
Shaykh Ṭabarsí, 40
Shaykhuná, 32
Shoghi Effendi, 202. See also Guardian, Guardianship.
life of, 73-76
signature of the Universal House of Justice, 208
sin, 96, 149
sincerity, 57, 118, 140, 143, 183, 283, 295, 309
Síyáh-Chál, 38, 43
Siyyid Ḥusayn, 35, 40, 41, 133
Siyyid Káẓim, 32
Siyyid Muḥammad, 32
Siyyid Muḥammad-Riḍá, 32
slander, 86

social and economic development, 76, 277, 278, 312
soul
    after death, 95-96
    development of, 50, 65, 88, 90, 91, 99, 101, 102, 103, 120, 124, 125, 126, 137, 140, 148, 152, 159, 195, 231, 232, 299, 300, 301
    nature of, 95, 104, 143, 144, 162, 178, 280
speech, 110, 125, 155, 157, 159, 185, 187, 310
spirit, 126, 135, 140, 156, 166, 181, 218, 220, 228, 231, 243, 244, 247, 251, 278, 281
    animal, 146
    Holy, 116, 152, 161, 234, 250, 302
    human, 27, 94, 95, 99, 100, 102, 103, 116, 121, 122, 139, 140, 178, 186, 226, 300, 301
    of love, unity and friendship, 77, 154, 247, 285, 310, 311, 312, 313
    of the Faith, 60, 90, 150, 158, 160, 165, 166, 169, 174, 175, 196, 236, 242, 243, 253, 256, 258, 277, 302, 307
spiritual
    authority, 78, 170, 249
    blindness and death, 27, 77, 95. See spiritual:blindness and death.
    crusade, 75
    development, 88, 94, 98, 115, 140, 152, 238, 243, 250, 251, 295, 296, 300, 303. See spiritual growth:life of the individual.
    diseases, 91
    education. See children:rearing and educating.
    food. See food:spiritual.
    healing, 305
    life and activities of the community, 221, 228, 245, 246, 247, 268
    life of the individual, 77, 80, 89, 111, 114, 115, 122, 123, 125, 127, 141, 173, 179, 238, 247, 253, 275, 297, 312
    meanings in the Words of God, 120
    nature of the Faith and its Institutions, 115, 233, 242, 262
    relationships, 96, 131, 135, 144, 153, 169, 178, 182, 243, 257
    state of the world, 275, 286
    victories, 54
    virtues and qualities, 111, 137, 185, 187, 287
spiritual laws and principles, 100, 157, 217, 219, 233, 258, 275, 278, 287, 289
spirituality, 115, 136, 140, 185, 312
St. Petersburg, 43
Stapley, Richard, 69
steadfastness, 91, 101
strife, 25, 143, 206, 282, 284, 285, 297
striking, 148
study classes, 24, 222, 245. See also deepen, institutes.

Revelation, 167
success, 94, 112, 126, 131, 148, 153, 217, 223, 242, 247, 272, 278
    in teaching, 113, 153, 154, 156, 157, 158, 160
successor
    to Bahá'u'lláh. See Covenant:concerning Bahá'u'lláh's successor (Lesser Covenant).
    to Shoghi Effendi, 205, 207
    to the Báb, 38, 48
Sulaymán Khán, 41
Sulaymán-i-Ghannam, 50
Sulaymáníyyih, 48, 49, 50, 52, 59, 132
Sultán of Turkey, 43, 57
Sultánate, 55
Sunní, 43, 49, 51, 62
Supreme House of Justice. See Administrative Order:Universal House of Justice.
Supreme Manifestation of God, 81, 123, 163, 168. See also Bahá'u'lláh.
Súrih of Kings (Súriy-i-Múlúk). See Bahá'u'lláh:writings of.
Súriy-i-Amr, 56
Súriy-i-Múlúk. See Bahá'u'lláh:writings of.
suspension of work, 261. See also Holy Days.
Syria, 43
Syrians, 70
systematic study, 120
systems
    political, 79, 201, 202, 241, 245
    religious, 25, 63, 133, 201

T

Tablet of Aḥmad. See Bahá'u'llah:writings of.
Tabríz, 35, 36, 38, 41, 42, 45
Ṭáhirih, 39, 42, 44, 133
teachers
    of educational institutions, 250, 254, 301, 303
    of the Faith. See teaching.
teaching
    assurance of success, 158
    by the youth. See youth
    children. See children:rearing and educating
    expansion and consolidation, 172, 173-75, 173-75, 214, 222, 245, 277. See teaching:expansion and consolidation
    honour of, 128, 152
    importance of, 87
    Indigenous Peoples, 171
    methods of, 164-67
    need for perseverance, 153-55
    obligation to, 114, 152, 153, 158, 159, 249
    practice of, 157-64

preparation for, 155–57
promise of Divine assistance, 113, 128, 152, 154, 156, 159
responsibility of institutions towards, 211, 214, 221
supporting new believers, 167–69
the masses, 169–75
temple
human body, 24, 139
of God, 80, 258
Ten Year World Crusade, 75
tenderness, 80, 145, 250
tests, 57, 78, 100, 111, 112, 154, 305, 306. See also difficulties, crises.
Thacher, Chester I., 65
theft, 148
thoughts, 69, 89, 107, 131, 171, 188, 189, 236, 266, 272, 285, 306, 307
earthly, 116, 122, 300
Ṭihrán, 34, 36, 38, 41, 43, 44, 51, 59, 67
tolerance, 51, 90, 155, 299, 307
Tolstoy, 43
Tongue of Grandeur, 30
Tongue of the Ancient, 53, 83, 84
trade, 28, 29, 79, 114, 254, 261, 273, 275, 301
tranquillity, 29, 86, 90, 270, 272, 279, 313
transformation, 51, 89, 108, 127, 163, 173, 244, 312
travelling, 117, 165, 211, 221, 222
trials, 38, 54, 57, 78, 101, 111, 112, 153, 154, 195.
See also tests, difficulties, crises.
tribulations, 46, 59, 61, 78, 86.
See also tests, hardship, crises.
triumphs, 31, 54, 63, 64, 71, 79
trustworthiness, 151, 183, 279, 314
truthfulness, 126, 140, 148, 183, 253
truth-seeker, 27
Turks, 50, 56

U

Údí Khammár, 59, 61
understanding
and co-operation, 25, 157, 239, 241, 248, 273, 285, 287, 297, 315
divine, 27, 49, 92, 105, 106, 108, 126, 140, 150, 159, 164, 235, 259, 264, 304, 312, 313
of the Teachings, 108, 128, 154, 168, 172, 196, 200, 208, 213, 220, 239, 244, 274, 307, 308, 309, 310
unified, 29, 228, 246, 275, 278, 287, 312. See also unity.
union, 205
of humanity, 59, 311

of husband and wife, 33, 96, 178, 182, 192, 264.
See also marriage.
of races, 283
Unit Conventions, 218
united, 246, 253, 257, 271, 272, 283, 292, 296
United Kingdom, 279
unity
in action, 28, 172, 214, 238, 278
in marriage, 33, 179, 185, 188, 191
in the family, 184, 188, 189
in the political world, 28, 29, 241, 270, 273, 275, 294
of God, 81, 93
of language, 28
of religion, 28, 285
of the Bábí community, 38
of the Bahá'í community, 73, 77, 88, 103, 108, 127, 143, 169, 170, 196, 200, 204, 207, 227, 234, 236, 241, 242, 243, 245, 246, 253, 257, 258, 259, 266, 307
of the human race, 25, 27, 28, 29, 74, 86, 143, 145, 147, 192, 249, 260, 270, 273, 294, 296, 297, 298, 311, 312
within Bahá'í institutions, 236, 239, 242, 243, 244, 245, 258, 268
universal Manifestation. See Supreme Manifestation of God.
universal participation, 246, 247
universal religion. See Oneness of Religion. See also Most Great Peace.
universes, 83, 91
unlearned, 27
upheavals, 39, 40

V

Váhid, 35, 44
vegetable kingdom, 94, 130
verities, 80, 82, 160, 175, 201, 223, 245, 277, 287.
See also Bahá'í Faith:beliefs.
victory, 34, 78, 113, 129, 138, 153, 189
violence, 26, 40, 172, 301
virtues, 94, 104, 111, 122, 126, 127, 129, 147, 148, 150, 183, 245, 250, 268, 295, 304, 312
voluntary sharing of wealth, 129

W

war, 274, 282, 286, 294, 297, 300
abolition of, 28, 69, 272, 273, 274, 280, 281, 292, 293, 294, 297
weakness, 95, 139

wedlock, 33
welfare
  of children, 86, 227, 292
  of society, 155, 180, 220, 244, 245, 251, 292, 301
well-being
  of humanity, 29, 179, 270, 271, 272, 291, 295, 301, 311, 312
  of the individual, 179, 242, 295
Western Europe, 35, 42
wilderness, 47, 48, 142
Will and Testament, 205
  of 'Abdu'l-Bahá.
    See 'Abdu'l-Bahá:Will and Testament.
  of the Guardian, 205
Wine, 24, 84, 266
wisdom
  divine, 105, 106, 109, 110, 112, 118, 125, 128, 131, 138, 140, 164, 185, 191, 207, 208, 235, 249, 266, 283, 299, 309
  God's. See God:His Wisdom.
  of Administrative Institutions, 216
  required when teaching, 126, 159, 160, 174, 215
witnesses, 62, 180
women, 124, 172, 254, 267
  equality of men and.
    See equality:of women and men.
  exemptions, 132, 208
  qualities of, 208, 249, 282
Word of God, 24, 33, 81, 105, 107, 119, 120, 121, 154, 156, 158, 170, 171, 182, 200, 202, 205, 231, 254, 263, 266, 299, 313. See also Scriptures.
words, 109, 115, 120, 147, 259
  and deeds, 30, 34, 105, 107, 125, 139, 145, 210, 249, 257, 258, 266, 278, 295, 302
  when teaching, 120, 126, 157, 159, 164, 255
world
  and its affections, 154, 194
  and its environment. See environment.
  and the Administrative Order, 199, 228, 230, 267, 276, 277, 312
  Bahá'í, 78, 88, 170, 173, 214, 217, 242, 278
  guidance to the, 83, 86, 87, 147, 151, 159, 210, 249
  leaders, 54
  next. See next world.
  of existence, 130, 137, 231
  of God, 146
  peace, 170, 272, 282, 298. See also peace.
  problems and challenges, 29, 30, 51, 135, 149, 169, 172, 173, 174, 248, 257, 274, 275, 286, 288, 306, 311
  purpose of its creation, 101

service towards, 185, 283
unity, 192, 239, 291. See Lesser Peace, Most Great Peace.
World Bahá'í Commonwealth, 76
World Centre, 133
world civilization, 76, 287, 296, 315
world commonwealth, 296. See world federal system.
world federal system, 274, 293, 294, 297, 298, 314
world government. See world federal system.
world plans, 76
Writings, 24, 119, 120, 121, 140, 155, 189, 198, 199, 232, 236, 256, 263, 267, 276.
  See also Scriptures.

Y

Yaḥyá Khán, 36
year of patience, 192, 193. See also divorce.
year of waiting, 193. See year of patience.
youth, 35, 41, 141, 172, 185, 194, 227, 245, 246, 250, 251, 252, 254, 255, 279, 281
youth year of service, 254

Z

Zanján, 39, 40
Zoroastrianism, 46, 297